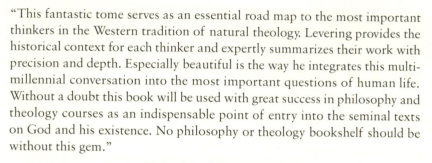
"This fantastic tome serves as an essential road map to the most important thinkers in the Western tradition of natural theology. Levering provides the historical context for each thinker and expertly summarizes their work with precision and depth. Especially beautiful is the way he integrates this multi-millennial conversation into the most important questions of human life. Without a doubt this book will be used with great success in philosophy and theology courses as an indispensable point of entry into the seminal texts on God and his existence. No philosophy or theology bookshelf should be without this gem."

—**Michael G. Sirilla**, Franciscan University of Steubenville

"Demonstrating a wide knowledge of the tradition and contemporary literature, Matthew Levering makes a significant contribution to the contemporary debate about atheism and the possibility of rationally demonstrating the existence of God. This fascinating account of the multiple attempts by brilliant thinkers over the centuries to show the rationality of belief in God is a uniquely original contribution that many will find of interest."

—**Ralph Martin**, STD, Sacred Heart Major Seminary, Archdiocese of Detroit

"In this extremely helpful book, Matthew Levering offers what is perhaps the best contemporary historical overview of the major positions on the subject of natural knowledge of God. His responsible and deeply insightful analysis of early Christians, great Scholastics, Enlightenment skeptics, and influential moderns produces an extremely varied tableau but also brings these diverse positions into effective conversation with one another. The book offers a strong defense of the contemporary importance of natural theology and its intellectual viability. This traditional position, largely eclipsed in modern Christian theology, is of vital significance to Christian intellectual life and Levering illustrates magnificently why and how this tradition can flourish today."

—**Fr. Thomas Joseph White**, OP, Thomistic Institute, Washington, DC

"*Proofs of God* is excellent. Matthew Levering has provided a much-needed resource that will greatly facilitate the rediscovery of neglected Christian thinkers in the history of natural theology."

—**Edward Feser**, Pasadena City College

PROOFS
of GOD

CLASSICAL ARGUMENTS FROM TERTULLIAN TO BARTH

MATTHEW LEVERING

Baker Academic
a division of Baker Publishing Group
Grand Rapids, Michigan

Published by Baker Academic
a division of Baker Publishing Group
P.O. Box 6287, Grand Rapids, MI 49516-6287
www.bakeracademic.com

Printed in the United States of America

Library of Congress Cataloging-in-Publication Data
Names: Levering, Matthew, 1971– author.
Title: Proofs of God : classical arguments from Tertullian to Barth / Matthew Levering.
Description: Grand Rapids, MI : Baker Academic, 2016. | Includes bibliographical references and
    index.
Identifiers: LCCN 2015043725 | ISBN 9780801097560 (pbk.)
Subjects: LCSH: God—Proof.
Classification: LCC BT103 .L48 2016 | DDC 212/.1—dc23 LC record available at http://lccn.loc
    .gov/2015043725

To Thomas Joseph White, OP

Contents

Acknowledgments

This book had its origins in a doctoral seminar on the proofs for God's existence that I "co-taught" with Steven A. Long at Ave Maria University some years ago. In that seminar, I spent most of my time taking careful notes! Steve has profound insight not only into Thomas Aquinas but also David Hume, Immanuel Kant, and Ludwig Wittgenstein, as all those privileged to take the seminar can attest.

My chapter drafts were greatly improved by generous scholars who read portions of the manuscript on which they have expertise: Don Briel, Thomas Hibbs, Andrew Hofer, OP, Robert Koerpel, John Michael McDermott, SJ, Sean McGrath, Benjamin Myers, Kenneth Oakes, Kevin O'Reilly, OP, and Andrew Rosato. Michael Sirilla and Thomas Joseph White, OP, read the whole manuscript and saved me from many omissions and mistakes. I have incorporated a number of suggestions from all of these friends and colleagues. Francesca Murphy, Matthew Ramage, Emery de Gaál, Michael Sirilla, and Chad Pecknold testified to the viability of the project as a Baker Academic textbook. Bishop Robert Barron enthusiastically encouraged the project and inspired me by his own expertise on the topic. At Baker Academic, Dave Nelson supported the project from the outset, guided the book to publication, and offered wise counsel for improvement. Baker Academic's Brian Bolger and the editorial staff did a superb job preparing the manuscript. My amazing research assistant, David Augustine, compiled the bibliography and indexes and provided numerous corrections and suggestions that I incorporated into the text.

I wrote this book for my children, in case it might ever be of use to them. May God, who in his infinite goodness is the meaning of life, give my beloved children eternal life in Christ Jesus. For my wife, Joy, my gratitude is so deep.

The simple words of Genesis 24:67 express what I wish Joy to know: "he loved her."

The book is dedicated to a master theologian and dear friend, born in the same year and month as myself: Fr. Thomas Joseph White, OP. Of him it may be said, "The crown of the wise is their wisdom" (Prov. 14:24). God's blessings be upon you, Fr. Thomas Joseph.

Introduction

In this textbook, I offer a concise survey of the major responses, pro and contra, in the Christian tradition to the question of whether the existence of God can be demonstrated by human reason. Readers and classroom teachers should feel free to use the book selectively, rather than studying all of the twenty-one figures I have chosen. My surveys of these twenty-one figures aim to be accurate, concise, and thorough. For readers who are interested, I give my assessment of these figures in the conclusions to the three chapters. In the surveys themselves, I try to be descriptive rather than evaluative.

In this introduction (as well as in the book's conclusion), I offer my view of where things stand in contemporary intellectual discourse and popular culture regarding the topic of whether God's existence can be demonstrated by human reason. In this introduction, I also give a rationale for choosing to study these twenty-one figures, and I examine the key biblical and Hellenistic ideas that set the terms for the demonstrations of God's existence in the Christian tradition.

To put my cards on the table, I think that the cosmos cannot be the source of its own existence. The cosmos is not a necessary being. In this regard, David Hart rightly remarks that "the contingent can only exist derivatively, receiving its existence from the Absolute."[1] When Stephen Hawking and Leonard Mlodinow claim that God's existence is no longer plausible because

---

1. David Bentley Hart, *The Experience of God: Being, Consciousness, Bliss* (New Haven: Yale University Press, 2013), 147. Hart helps to correct misperceptions of what Ilia Delio, OSF, critically calls "the Greek architecture of metaphysics" (Delio, *The Unbearable Wholeness of Being: God, Evolution, and the Power of Love* [Maryknoll, NY: Orbis, 2013], xx). The misperceptions are, unfortunately, apparent in Delio's book.

all things could have come forth from the quantum law of gravity, they fail to recognize, as Hart says, that the issue is "the very possibility of existence as such, not only of this universe but of all the laws and physical conditions that produced it."[2] It is not necessary that any finite thing, let alone a quantum law, exist. Finite things exist, but they are merely limited modes of being; they are not being as such. A quantum law, insofar as it *is*, must derive its being from a source.

Hawking and Mlodinow can be excused for their failure to grasp that the issue is "existence as such." Their misunderstanding is shared by many professional philosophers. Thus, in his *Arguing about Gods*, Graham Oppy supposes himself to be undermining Thomas Aquinas's five ways for demonstrating God's existence when he remarks that "it is hard to see that there is anything in Big Bang cosmology that rules out the existence of an infinite regress of changers, each changed by another."[3] Oppy's point would not have bothered Aquinas at all, of course, since Aquinas allows philosophically for an eternal universe. In fact, none of Aquinas's five ways depends on the universe having a temporal beginning. A similar mistake appears in Simon Blackburn's *Think: A Compelling Introduction to Philosophy*. Blackburn devotes a chapter to God where he purports to engage Aquinas's "cosmological argument." But for his description of Aquinas's argument, he rather oddly turns to Hume's *Dialogues concerning Natural Religion*. The

---

2. Hart, *Experience of God*, 40. See Stephen Hawking and Leonard Mlodinow, *The Grand Design* (New York: Bantam, 2010).

3. Graham Oppy, *Arguing about Gods* (Cambridge: Cambridge University Press, 1999), 103. For his part, Anthony Kenny directs a set of arguments against Aquinas's five ways, including the following claim: "If a thing cannot be moved by itself, it does not follow that it must be moved by something else. Why cannot it just be in motion, without *being moved* by anything, whether by itself or by anything else?" (Kenny, *The Five Ways: St. Thomas Aquinas' Proofs of God's Existence* [London: Routledge, 1969], 19). Seizing on Aquinas's example from the transmission of heat, Kenny suggests that Aquinas depends here on outdated Aristotelian physics. Edward Feser has responded to Kenny in his *Aquinas* (Oxford: Oneworld, 2009), 67–69. Feser points out that "Aquinas is not making the obviously false claim that only what is already on fire can cause fire; he is rather making the claim . . . that whatever causes fire must have an inherent power to cause it" (ibid., 68). In addition, Feser adds that Aquinas "is not saying that 'whatever causes something actually to be F must itself be F in some way,' but rather that 'whatever causes something must itself be actual,' that nothing merely potential can cause anything" (ibid.). See also the point made by Lawrence Dewan, OP, in commenting on Kenny's *Aquinas on Being* (Oxford: Oxford University Press, 2002), that "Kenny's word 'existence' really refers to the answer to the question: 'Does it exist?' rather than to the act of being (*actus essendi*). Thomas' word '*esse*,' though it does the work of signifying the answer to the question: 'does it exist?' (thus signifying the truth of propositions), also signifies the thing's own act which is 'to be,' as meaning the perfection which terminates a thing's generation" (Dewan, "On Anthony Kenny's *Aquinas on Being*," *Nova et Vetera* 3 [2005]: 335–400, at 340–41; cf. 400).

result is that Blackburn refutes an argument, supposedly Aquinas's own, that Aquinas himself would have immediately rejected.[4] Likewise, in his textbook *Philosophy of Religion: An Introduction*, William L. Rowe refutes the version of the "cosmological argument" put forward by William Clarke and Gottfried Leibniz in the early eighteenth century and thereby avoids having to address the problem of finite existence in terms of act and potency.[5] All too often, questions regarding "existence as such" are naively dismissed by supposing that "the physical universe is merely a brute fact."[6] Finite existence, far from being a self-sufficient "brute fact," requires explanation, since finite existence is not existence per se. This insight will be spelled out further as the chapters proceed.

I use the controversial term "proofs" in the title of the present book. When classical Christian thinkers such as Aquinas offered philosophical demonstrations of God's existence, did they think of them as proofs—that is, as rational arguments that strictly demonstrate that God exists? Rightly anxious to dissociate Aquinas from Cartesian or empiricist notions of "proof," some contemporary scholars deny that he intended his five ways to be rigorous demonstrations of God's existence. For example, in his generally excellent book responding to the new atheism, David Fergusson remarks that Aquinas's five ways "are less exercises in demonstration of God's existence than a directing of the human intellect towards a mysterious limit of thought that in

4. See Simon Blackburn, *Think: A Compelling Introduction to Philosophy* (Oxford: Oxford University Press, 1999), 159–62. Blackburn's presentation of the demonstrations of God's existence depends entirely on Hume, without exhibiting any knowledge of philosophical arguments prior to Hume's. For a similar caricature of arguments for God's existence (again, apparently without intention to caricature), see A. C. Grayling, *The God Argument: The Case against Religion and for Humanism* (London: Bloomsbury, 2013), chaps. 8–10. In discussing the argument from "design" or teleological order, for example, Grayling cites only Intelligent Design theorists, William Paley, and Hume; and Grayling states that the "cosmological argument" (for which his sole sources are Leibniz, Hume, and Kant) relies on "the facts that the world came into existence, that it could have been different (this is what is meant by the world being 'contingent'), and that everything is governed by causation" (ibid., 95)—thereby mischaracterizing these arguments in a number of major ways.

5. See William L. Rowe, *Philosophy of Religion: An Introduction*, 4th ed. (Belmont, CA: Wadsworth, 2007). For background, see *The Leibniz-Clarke Correspondence*, ed. H. G. Alexander (Manchester: Manchester University Press, 1956). See also Alexander R. Pruss, *The Principle of Sufficient Reason: A Reassessment* (Cambridge: Cambridge University Press, 2010).

6. David Fergusson, *Creation* (Grand Rapids: Eerdmans, 2014), 28. See also Grayling's response to his own caricatured version of the "cosmological" argument: "Why cannot the universe be its own reason for existing? Science has a very good account of how the universe we occupy—whether or not it is one of many, perhaps infinitely many—has evolved from a beginning whose nature can be carefully reconstructed, to within a minuscule fraction of time after the initial singularity (the 'Big Bang'), by tracing back the evolution of physical phenomena as they now are" (*God Argument*, 97).

the *Summa Theologiae* can only be further illumined by divine revelation."[7] Similarly, Stanley Hauerwas suggests that Aquinas's five ways merely seek to "'prove' that language/reason may find itself to be insufficient to testify to the God who is the beginning and end of all that is."[8] Hauerwas emphasizes that "the God we worship and the world God created cannot be truthfully known without the cross."[9]

Among philosophers and theologians who are not explicitly interpreting Aquinas, one finds the same concern regarding the use of the term "proof," which here means rational demonstration. Thus, Rémi Brague warns against using the term "proofs" with respect to the existence of God, noting that this is "a term that the best theologians avoid, or only employ with a thousand caveats."[10] From a quite different theological perspective, Hans Küng makes

7. David Fergusson, *Faith and Its Critics: A Conversation* (Oxford: Oxford University Press, 2009), 57. In the same vein, Alister McGrath supposes that "Aquinas does not actually claim that such considerations [the five ways] prove this existence [of God]; the argument is much more along the lines of 'providing support for' or 'resonating with' faith." See McGrath, *The Reenchantment of Nature: The Denial of Religion and the Ecological Crisis* (New York: Doubleday, 2002), 157. For this view see also Lubor Velecky, *Aquinas's Five Arguments in the Summa Theologiae Ia QQ. 2, 3* (Kampen: Kok Pharos, 1994). For the variety of interpretations of the five ways, and for their historical antecedents and the twentieth-century debates about them, see Fergus Kerr, OP, *After Aquinas: Versions of Thomism* (Oxford: Blackwell, 2002), 52–72. To his credit, in a more recent book, Fergusson grants that Aquinas's five ways do aim to demonstrate God's existence: "These arguments do not unfold the nature of God so much as show us that there must be something which owes its existence to nothing else and which is the cause of everything not itself" (Fergusson, *Creation*, 27). Even so, Fergusson still holds that the five ways are not "developed as watertight arguments intended to persuade skeptics who advance a different worldview" (ibid.). But Aquinas certainly considered them to be "watertight arguments" in the sense of demonstrative arguments, although Aquinas was not advancing these arguments against skeptics. For thoroughgoing skeptics such as Montaigne or Hume, who reject reasoning about being and causality, the five ways can of course only be conjecture. It is difficult to find fully consistent skeptics, since if we cannot reason about being and causality, there is nothing that reason can truly know. See Paul J. Griffiths, "On the Mistake of Thinking Reason's Products Transparent to Its Gaze: Denys Turner on Arguments for the Existence of God," *Pro Ecclesia* 15 (2006): 472–82.

8. Stanley Hauerwas, *With the Grain of the Universe: The Church's Witness and Natural Theology* (Grand Rapids: Brazos, 2001), 165n51. For Hauerwas, indebted to Karl Barth, "Aquinas understood that the existence of God does not depend on any proof because such a proof cannot help but submit God to human hands and, as a result, make God less than God" (ibid., 164). For a critique of this position of Barth's, see Denys Turner, *Faith, Reason and the Existence of God* (Cambridge: Cambridge University Press, 2004).

9. Hauerwas, *With the Grain of the Universe*, 17.

10. Rémi Brague, *On the God of Christians: (And on One or Two Others)*, trans. Paul Seaton (South Bend, IN: St. Augustine's Press, 2013), xvi. Similarly, in light of Kant, William Desmond observes that "almost always our search for 'proof' is tempted with falling under the bewitchment of univocity, and so with ending up as a rationalistic idol. . . . There is no apodeictic certainty" (Desmond, *God and the Between* [Oxford: Blackwell, 2008], 131, 140). Desmond prefers the term "probe." Although he defends the *Summa theologiae* as a theological text that "transforms Aristotelian metaphysics" in light of "the biblical picture," he worries

a similar point: "It must be admitted that, in so far as they seek to prove something, the proofs of God are meaningless. But in so far as they bring God into the discussion, they are very meaningful."[11]

However, this effort to avoid the term "proof" is mistaken, both as a reading of Aquinas and (in Brague and Küng) as a broader claim. Certainly, language and reason are radically insufficient when it comes to God, since God, who is transcendent and infinite, is in an obvious sense not comprehensible by finite minds. We cannot form a concept of *what God is* because God, to say the least, cannot be circumscribed by a finite concept.[12] Nor can the living God whom Christians worship be fully or adequately known without Jesus's cross or without the ecclesial communion established by Jesus. In this regard, Roger Scruton is surely right that the God of the proofs, if the proofs were all we had, would be too impersonal.[13] Yet, for good reason, Aquinas does not eschew the word "prove"—though his proofs are metaphysical, not empiricist or Cartesian. The word "prove" reminds us that we are not here dealing with an experiential intuition, a gesture toward infinite mystery, or an opinion based on personal sensibility. In the *Summa theologiae*, Aquinas states, "The existence of God can

"about how Aquinas's scholastic formulation displays a kind of forensic univocity in the mode of articulation. . . . His form of articulation seems sometimes more suitable to a legal disputation than a theme which calls also on meditative, even prayerful mindfulness" (ibid., 132–33). But Desmond ably sets forth and defends a version of Aquinas's *"third way,* called by him the proof from possibility and necessity" (ibid., 132).

11. Hans Küng, *Does God Exist? An Answer for Today*, trans. Edward Quinn (New York: Random House, 1981), 534. Küng rejects the demonstrability of God's existence on the Humean grounds that "the bridge supposed to be provided by the principle of causality, together with its supports, gets lost in the incomprehensible infinite, of which it is by no means certain whether it is fullness or emptiness" (ibid.). The proofs do not depend on navigating the "incomprehensible infinite."

12. John Haldane rightly points out, however, that not being able to know "what God is" does not mean that we know nothing of God other than that he is. See Haldane, *Reasonable Faith* (London: Routledge, 2010), 14. See also Brian Davies, OP, "Aquinas on What God Is Not," in *Thomas Aquinas: Contemporary Philosophical Perspectives*, ed. Brian Davies, OP (Oxford: Oxford University Press, 2002), 227–42; Gregory P. Rocca, *Speaking the Incomprehensible God: Thomas Aquinas on the Interplay of Positive and Negative Theology* (Washington, DC: Catholic University of America Press, 2004).

13. See Roger Scruton, *The Face of God* (London: Continuum, 2012), 10–21. Scruton presents Aquinas's third way, and he is tentatively willing to accept its validity so long as we do not imagine God as an empirical "cause" alongside the causes that we find in the world. But he insists that such Aristotelian demonstrations must be combined with a much more important appreciation of God's personal presence in the world; otherwise, the demonstrations end "by hiding God" (ibid., 15). God's personal presence in the world is experienced in the community of believers, and above all, for Scruton, in the Eucharist. He states, "The connection between belief in God and the community of believers is recognized in the Christian concept of communion. And this connection, far from casting doubt on the validity of transcendental theology, points the way to supplying what it lacks" (ibid., 20).

be proved [*probari*] in five ways."[14] After explaining what constitutes a rationally probative demonstration from effect to cause, he observes that "the existence of God . . . can be demonstrated [*demonstrari*] from those of his effects which are known to us" and adds that the existence of God "can be known by natural reason," even though "there is nothing to prevent a man, who cannot grasp a proof [*demonstrationem*], accepting, as a matter of faith, something which in itself is capable of being scientifically known and demonstrated."[15]

In making this claim about the ability of human reason to demonstrate conclusively that God exists, Aquinas is hardly alone. Rooted in such biblical passages as Wisdom 13 and Romans 1, his position is shared not only by his contemporaries and medieval predecessors but also (as we will see) by the leading Greek and Latin fathers of the church. Indeed, Ian Markham is quite right to insist, "From St. Paul in Romans 1, through to St. Augustine and St. Thomas, we find natural theology central. The Barthian and postmodern lack of interest in this way of thinking is a significant departure and, I would add, betrayal of the Christian tradition."[16] In the Christian tradition, the demonstration of God's existence by rational arguments has grounding in Hellenistic philosophy and in Scripture itself. Markham adds that "the tradition of natural theology should not be viewed as an exercise in seeking arguments to persuade the non-existent 'traditionless' person."[17] Even atheism is a "tradition," as is apparent in Julian Baggini's *Atheism: A Very Short Introduction*.[18] And far from being simply an apologetic or defensive ploy in the

14. Thomas Aquinas, *Summa theologiae* Ia.2.3. I employ the translation published in five volumes as *Summa Theologica*, trans. the Fathers of the English Dominican Province (Westminster, MD: Christian Classics, 1981).

15. Aquinas, *Summa theologiae* Ia.2.2, *respondeo* and ad 1. See also Steven A. Long, "Obediential Potency, Natural Knowledge, and the Natural Knowledge of God," *International Philosophical Quarterly* 37 (1997): 45–63.

16. Ian Markham, *Truth and the Reality of God: An Essay in Natural Theology* (Edinburgh: T&T Clark, 1998), 3. Drawing on Leibniz's principle of sufficient reason and Aquinas's third way (from contingency), Markham argues that there must be an explanation for the universe's existence and coherence. If so, then we cannot proceed to infinity in contingent explanations—that is, in explanations that require a further explanation. Without the existence of a self-explanatory, necessary being, the universe and rationality itself cannot be other than absurd. See ibid., 91.

17. Ibid., 83. The fact that human reason is always embedded in particular traditions does not mean that reasoners from distinct traditions lack the ability to reason together and to follow one another's logical arguments despite their diverse practices and stories. Thus I do not agree with Robert N. Bellah's denial that "one can give convincing reasons why one religious or philosophical position is better than all the others" (Bellah, *Religion in Human Evolution: From the Paleolithic to the Axial Age* [Cambridge, MA: Harvard University Press, 2011], 605). I share the view of human reason defended by Hart, *Experience of God*, 1–10, 15–19.

18. Julian Baggini, *Atheism: A Very Short Introduction* (Oxford: Oxford University Press, 2003). Baggini shows ignorance of the history of the demonstrations of God's existence. Thus

Christian tradition, the demonstrations are a mode of praising God as the "I am" (Exod. 3:14), a mode that Jewish and Muslim thinkers have also shared.[19]

It is urgent that Christians today reclaim the two-millennia-old Christian tradition of demonstrating God's existence without excluding the thinkers within this tradition who have attempted to *refute* the demonstrations. Thus, the main task of this textbook is to accurately set forth the ideas of twenty-one seminal thinkers about the possibility or impossibility of rationally demonstrating God's existence.[20] Each thinker is introduced by a brief biographical sketch. Although significant thinkers have unavoidably been left out, I hope to have provided a sufficiently representative sample of the major contributors and positions, so that the present widespread ignorance of this tradition will be overcome.[21]

The first time period spans the patristic and medieval eras. Importantly, the Greek and Latin fathers agree about the demonstrability of God's existence.

he states, "The cosmological argument is there whenever someone turns around and says to the naturalist, 'Ah, well the universe may have begun with the big bang, but what caused the big bang?'" (ibid., 94).

19. For the Christian tradition of philosophical reasoning, see Jacques Maritain, *An Essay on Christian Philosophy*, trans. Edward H. Flannery (New York: Philosophical Library, 1955). See also the texts compiled in *Reason Fulfilled by Revelation: The 1930s Christian Philosophy Debates in France*, ed. and trans. Gregory Sadler (Washington, DC: Catholic University of America Press, 2011). See also such works as Jaroslav Pelikan, *Christianity and Classical Culture: The Metamorphosis of Natural Theology in the Christian Encounter with Hellenism* (New Haven: Yale University Press, 1993); David B. Burrell, CSC, *Knowing the Unknowable God: Ibn-Sina, Maimonides, Aquinas* (Notre Dame: University of Notre Dame Press, 1986); Francisco Javier del Castillo Ornelas, *An Analysis of St. Thomas' Critiques of Maimonides' Doctrines on Divine Attributes* (Rome: Pontifical University of the Holy Cross, 2007); Lenn E. Goodman, *God of Abraham* (Oxford: Oxford University Press, 1996).

20. Anthony Kenny argues that "if we take natural theology to be the philosophical analysis of the concepts used in thinking and talking about God, then a disproof of God's existence, or a demonstration that the very notion of God was incoherent, would itself be a successful piece of natural theologizing" (Kenny, *The God of the Philosophers* [Oxford: Oxford University Press, 1979], 4). In agreement with Kenny's view here, I have included in this book the most eminent arguments for and against the demonstrability of God's existence. In his book, Kenny argues that the attribute of divine omniscience is opposed to the attribute of divine immutability, and so a demonstration of God's existence as pure act is rendered self-contradictory. This position depends, however, on the view that to know time one must be in time.

21. Among the figures whom unfortunately I could not treat is Friedrich Schleiermacher. His approach, based on religious intuition or the feeling of absolute dependence, has been recently adopted by Eric Reitan, *Is God a Delusion? A Reply to Religion's Cultured Despisers* (Oxford: Wiley-Blackwell, 2009). I do not treat thinkers such as Friedrich Nietzsche who simply assume, as an unargued given, that human reason cannot demonstrate God's existence. For a somewhat similar project to mine, see Aidan Nichols, OP's *A Grammar of Consent: The Existence of God in Christian Tradition* (Edinburgh: T&T Clark, 1991). Nichols treats the ways to God offered by John Henry Newman, Gregory of Nyssa, Augustine, Anselm, Thomas Aquinas, John of the Cross, Blaise Pascal, Immanuel Kant, Søren Kierkegaard, Gabriel Marcel, and G. K. Chesterton.

In Gregory of Nazianzus, we already find a deeply Aristotelian approach. This is even more the case with John of Damascus, though in both Gregory and John, Neoplatonic insights are also present. Tertullian draws on Stoic demonstrations of God's existence, and Augustine largely on Neoplatonic ones. Anselm develops Augustine's approach, while Aquinas adapts Aristotelian demonstrations and exhibits the influence of Augustine, Boethius, John of Damascus, Avicenna, and others. William of Ockham is known for his skepticism about standard ways of demonstrating God's existence and unity, in particular the argument from efficient causality.

The second period is the Baroque or modern period, inclusive here of the Reformers. John Calvin, known for his insistence on sin's profound impact on our minds and hearts, nevertheless holds that God can be known by demonstrative knowledge and that a sense of God's existence cannot be expunged from the human mind. Michel de Montaigne, educated in late-Renaissance humanism and possessed of a splendid grasp of classical Latin Stoic and Epicurean sources, offers a withering critique of the demonstrations of God's existence insofar as he knew them. Francisco Suárez develops a demonstration of God's existence that has roots both in Aquinas and in Ockham (and in John Duns Scotus as well); without agreeing with Suárez in certain important areas, I think that his arguments are successful in showing that God exists. René Descartes argues that skepticism can be answered by beginning with the thinking self's ability to conceive of perfections that we do not possess, perfections of which we therefore cannot be the source. Descartes also presents his own version of the Anselmian argument. Blaise Pascal's powerful reflections on demonstrating God's existence, including his brilliant wager, have Montaigne constantly in view. David Hume is in many respects a British Montaigne, and his critique of the cause-effect relation remains enormously influential in philosophical circles, despite its flaws. Immanuel Kant's argument that the cause-effect relation functions as a category of our mind, and thus can be used for certain purposes but certainly not for demonstration of an infinite cause, creatively recasts Hume. Kant's practical postulate of God's existence also merits attention, even though Kant does not consider it to be a basis of demonstrative speculative knowledge.

The third period comprises the nineteenth and twentieth centuries. Admittedly, these two centuries receive disproportionate treatment in the present book by comparison with the other eighteen centuries. I include both well-known and lesser-known figures who made particularly distinctive contributions. John Henry Newman's work is (among other things) a highly creative response to Hume just as Pascal had responded to Montaigne. Maurice Blondel argues that in the dynamism of action or volition, we experience ourselves to be always seeking more than contingent goods. Just as the universal Good is discernible at the root of our action, so also is the thought of God at the root of our thought. Pierre Rousselot argues that in knowing finite beings, we must affirm that "being exists," which implies the synthesis of essence and existence. This judgment is one that we cannot know intuitively but that is necessary for intelligence to proceed, and it implies God's existence. Rousselot also highlights the role of our loves, of our inclination toward being, within both natural and supernatural knowledge. Ludwig Wittgenstein develops a philosophy of language that builds on Kant's categories of the mind but does so, arguably, with greater room for mystery and for the values of particular cultures. In Wittgenstein's approaches to language, however, there is no room for a demonstration of God's existence. Réginald Garrigou-Lagrange provides a brilliant exposition of Aquinas's modes of demonstrating God's existence and in the process responds to a wide array of modern philosophical positions. Like Wittgenstein, but via a critique of any attempt to conceptualize being, Martin Heidegger rejects the demonstrations of God's existence as antiphilosophical and as an attempt to force the divine into an overarching human framework. Last, Karl Barth argues that the whole attempt of fallen humans to demonstrate that God exists leads only to the construction of an idol.

Wittgenstein, Heidegger, and Barth have the last word chronologically in this book. Along with Hume and Kant, their influence is felt deeply in the contemporary theological and philosophical academy, where there exists a "cultural presupposition" that "philosophical arguments for the existence of God as they existed in classical form are no longer intellectually tenable" and indeed may well be idolatrous.[22] But what S. L. Frank describes as "the inner psychical grave into which the question of the meaning of life is buried" is continually demanding to be explored.[23] Not surprisingly, therefore, a number of contemporary philosophers and theologians, such as David Braine, Pierre-Marie Emonet, Edward Feser, John Haldane, David Hart, Ian Markham, Christopher Martin, Barry Miller, Anna Moreland, Francesca Aran Murphy, Denys Turner, and Thomas Joseph White, have been rediscovering the classical demonstrations of God's existence.[24] Indeed, as D. Stephen Long remarks, "As

22. Thomas Joseph White, OP, "Toward a Post-Secular, Post-Conciliar Thomistic Philosophy: *Wisdom in the Face of Modernity* and the Challenge of Contemporary Natural Theology," *Nova et Vetera* 10 (2012): 521–30, at 522. For the same point, see also Turner, *Faith, Reason and the Existence of God*, 23.

23. S. L. Frank, *The Meaning of Life*, trans. Boris Jakim (Grand Rapids: Eerdmans, 2010), 3.

24. See David Braine, *The Reality of Time and the Existence of God: The Project of Proving God's Existence* (Oxford: Oxford University Press, 1988); Pierre-Marie Emonet, OP, *God Seen in the Mirror of the World: An Introduction to the Philosophy of God*, trans. Robert R. Barr

long as people continue to assume and act as if truth, goodness, and beauty matter (to do otherwise is impossible), and as long as some ask questions about God and being (to do otherwise is possible), metaphysics has not yet come to an end."[25]

The present textbook is a contribution to the metaphysical retrieval undertaken by these scholars. The demonstrations of God's existence have a necessary place within what the Episcopalian theologian Mark McIntosh describes as the "formation in holiness that liberates the mind, leaving it sensitive to the overwhelming reality of the divine mystery."[26] This is so not least because the demonstrations (and the attempts to refute them) help to purify what we mean by a "God" who is the Creator and sustainer of all finite things rather than a mere finite being among other finite beings. By so doing, the demonstrations nourish our encounter with the God who is "spirit" (John 4:24).[27]

(New York: Crossroad, 2000); Edward Feser, *The Last Superstition: A Refutation of the New Atheism* (South Bend, IN: St. Augustine's Press, 2008); Feser, *Aquinas*; Christopher Martin, *Thomas Aquinas: God and Explanations* (Edinburgh: Edinburgh University Press, 1997); J. J. C. Smart and John Haldane, *Atheism and Theism* (Oxford: Blackwell, 1996); Barry Miller, *A Most Unlikely God: A Philosophical Enquiry* (Notre Dame: University of Notre Dame Press, 1996); Miller, *From Existence to God: A Contemporary Philosophical Argument* (London: Routledge, 1992); Anna Bonta Moreland, *Known by Nature: Thomas Aquinas on Natural Knowledge of God* (New York: Crossroad, 2010); Francesca Aran Murphy, *God Is Not a Story: Realism Revisited* (Oxford: Oxford University Press, 2007); Turner, *Faith, Reason and the Existence of God*; Thomas Joseph White, OP, *Wisdom in the Face of Modernity: A Study in Thomistic Natural Theology* (Ave Maria, FL: Sapientia, 2009). See also Mats Wahlberg's *Reshaping Natural Theology: Seeing Nature as Creation* (New York: Palgrave Macmillan, 2012), which argues persuasively for the existence of a creator.

25. D. Stephen Long, *Speaking of God: Theology, Language, and Truth* (Grand Rapids: Eerdmans, 2009), 186. See also my *Scripture and Metaphysics: Aquinas and the Renewal of Trinitarian Theology* (Oxford: Blackwell, 2004) and Thomas G. Guarino's excellent "Philosophia Obscurans? Six Theses on the Proper Relationship between Theology and Philosophy," *Nova et Vetera* 12 (2014): 349–94. For further discussion see Guarino, *Foundations of Systematic Theology* (New York: T&T Clark, 2005); A. N. Williams, *The Architecture of Theology* (Oxford: Oxford University Press, 2011).

26. Mark A. McIntosh, *Discernment and Truth: The Spirituality and Theology of Knowledge* (New York: Crossroad, 2004), 174–75. For the point that "true knowledge of God is a fundamentally relational and transformative notion" and "full and authentic knowledge of God arises through divine self-disclosure," see Alister E. McGrath, *A Scientific Theology*, vol. 2, *Reality* (Grand Rapids: Eerdmans, 2002), 290–91. This does not undermine the fact that, as McGrath recognizes, "the Christian tradition holds that some knowledge of God may arise through nature" (ibid., 290).

27. Since this intellectual purification is always needed, it would be misleading to think of metaphysics as a mere foundation for revealed theology, to be set aside once we turn to revealed theology proper. See Wolfhart Pannenberg, *Metaphysics and the Idea of God*, trans. Philip Clayton (Grand Rapids: Eerdmans, 1990), chap. 1. In Pannenberg's view, however, "whenever philosophy claimed to be in the position to derive the true conception of the one God and to be able to prove his existence through the power of philosophical reflection alone, one finds, bound up unavoidably with that belief, the claim to stand in the place of the revelation-based knowledge of religion" (ibid., 19).

At the same time, as Aquinas observes, "human reason is very deficient in things concerning God" due to the effects of sin.[28] Joseph Ratzinger remarks that the history of religion shows on the one hand that "there has always been a kind of basic evidence for the reality of God," and on the other hand that there has also always been a "tremendous obscuring and twisting" of this reality.[29] It makes no sense, then, to hold that every "epistemically justified belief that God exists must be based on a sound *argument* for God's existence."[30] Furthermore, the demonstrations do not even touch, let alone sate, our desire for an interpersonal relationship with God, which can only be received through divine revelation; and neither do the demonstrations respond to the questions raised by our experience of evil. Thus, Fergus Kerr rightly insists that "even the theologically orientated metaphysics of antiquity (as Thomas supposed it to be), the best reasoned knowledge of the existence of the *arche kai telos*, could only leave one in a certain 'anguish.'"[31] Or, as Ratzinger puts it, "the basic certainty of the existence of God was and is always accompanied by a sense of its being an immense riddle."[32] The demonstrations do not resolve the "anguish" or answer the "immense riddle," but they encourage us to seek the resolution and the answer.[33] It is for this reason that I fully share Eric Mascall's

28. Aquinas, *Summa theologiae* IIa-IIae.2.4 See also my *Paul in the Summa Theologiae* (Washington, DC: Catholic University of America Press, 2014), chap. 7: "Romans 1:20 in the *Summa Theologiae*."

29. Joseph Ratzinger, *Behold the Pierced One: An Approach to a Spiritual Christology*, trans. Graham Harrison (San Francisco: Ignatius, 1986), 28.

30. Paul K. Moser, *The Evidence for God: Religious Knowledge Reexamined* (Cambridge: Cambridge University Press, 2010), 150. While correctly rejecting the view that such arguments are necessary for "epistemically justified belief," Moser goes astray in concluding that the living God wills to remain obscured and therefore entirely out of reach of rational demonstrations. Moser accepts Hume's view that even if we could reason to a first cause, the first cause would have to be *strictly* proportionate to "the observed causal chains in the sensory world" (ibid., 153). With regard to "epistemically justified belief" without arguments for God's existence, see also Martin Buber, *Eclipse of God: Studies in the Relation between Religion and Philosophy*, trans. Maurice S. Friedman (New York: Harper & Row, 1952), 28.

31. Kerr, *After Aquinas*, 66. As Henri de Lubac, SJ, rightly says, "The more we feel the proof as proof, the more conscious we become of the misery of the human condition which obliges us to resort to it, and which remains after it has been provided" (de Lubac, *The Discovery of God*, trans. Alexander Dru with Mark Sebanc and Cassian Fulsom, OSB [Grand Rapids: Eerdmans, 1996], 43).

32. Ratzinger, *Behold the Pierced One*, 28.

33. See also Alasdair MacIntyre, *God, Philosophy, Universities: A Selective History of the Catholic Philosophical Tradition* (Lanham, MD: Rowman & Littlefield, 2009); Robert J. Spitzer, SJ, *New Proofs for the Existence of God: Contributions of Contemporary Physics and Philosophy* (Grand Rapids: Eerdmans, 2010); Richard Swinburne, *The Existence of God*, 2nd ed. (Oxford: Oxford University Press, 2004); Keith Ward, *God and the Philosophers* (Minneapolis: Fortress, 2009); C. Stephen Evans, *Why Believe? Reason and Mystery as Pointers to God* (Grand Rapids: Eerdmans, 1996); Evans, *Natural Signs and Knowledge of God: A New Look at Theistic*

desire, in his Gifford Lectures of 1971, "to vindicate . . . a fundamentally and unashamedly metaphysical approach to theism."[34]

Biblical and Hellenistic Background

Since the present textbook does not include a chapter on the biblical and Hellenistic sources of the Christian tradition of demonstrating God's existence, let me briefly survey some of their most valuable contributions. The biblical books of Job and Wisdom of Solomon contain arguments for God's existence.[35] Job and his friends observe that the natural order testifies to the existence of God. Job states, for example, that God "stretches out the north over the void, and hangs the earth on nothing. He binds up the waters in his thick clouds, and the cloud is not rent under them. . . . Lo, these are but the outskirts of his ways; and how small a whisper do we hear of him!" (Job 26:7–8, 14). Similarly, Job's friend Elihu appeals to the ways in which this world bespeaks its own dependence: "Hear this, O Job; stop and consider the wondrous works of God. Do you know how God lays his command upon them, and causes the lightning of his cloud to shine? Do you know the balancings of the clouds, the wondrous works of him who is perfect in knowledge? . . . Can you, like him, spread out the skies, hard as a molten mirror?" (Job 37:14–16, 18). In the book of Job, it is the goodness of God, not his existence, that is contested.[36] For its part, the Wisdom of Solomon

Arguments (Oxford: Oxford University Press, 2010); Nathan Schneider, *God in Proof: The Story of a Search from the Ancients to the Internet* (Berkeley: University of California Press, 2013); W. Jay Wood, *God* (Montreal: McGill-Queen's University Press, 2011).

34. E. L. Mascall, *The Openness of Being: Natural Theology Today* (London: Darton, Longman & Todd, 1971), vii. For the opposite perspective, see Jeffrey W. Robbins's praise of the "radical death of God theology" as "a critical and prophetic voice" that criticized "the moral-metaphysical God of ontotheology" and established "the conditions for a recovery of a distinctly biblical faith that gives emphasis not to the power and glory of God but to God's suffering and love" (Robbins, introduction to John D. Caputo and Gianni Vattimo, *After the Death of God*, ed. Jeffrey W. Robbins [New York: Columbia University Press, 2007], 1–24, at 9–10). Robbins's seeming ignorance of the Christian tradition of demonstrating God's existence may be intentional, given his appreciation for John Caputo's classically liberal separation of faith from knowledge and of "religious tradition" from "actual historic faith communities" (ibid., 16). For a much richer (critical) engagement with the perspective of Gianni Vattimo, see Thomas G. Guarino's *Vattimo and Theology* (London: T&T Clark, 2009).

35. See my "The Book of Job and God's Existence," in *A Man of the Church: Honoring the Theology, Life, and Witness of Ralph del Colle*, ed. Michel René Barnes (Eugene, OR: Pickwick, 2012), 231–40. For psalms that are particularly instructive regarding "natural theology," see Psalms 19, 104, and 119.

36. In light of Job's protest against God, see Bernard Schweizer's literary study *Hating God: The Untold Story of Misotheism* (Oxford: Oxford University Press, 2011).

states that, "all men who were ignorant of God were foolish by nature; and they were unable from the good things that are seen to know him who exists, nor did they recognize the craftsman while paying heed to his works. . . . For from the greatness and beauty of created things comes a corresponding perception of their Creator" (Wis. 13:1, 5).[37]

In Romans 1:19–20, the apostle Paul testifies to the demonstrability of God's existence: "For what can be known about God is plain to them, because God has shown it to them. Ever since the creation of the world his invisible nature, namely, his eternal power and deity, has been clearly perceived in the things that have been made."[38] Philo of Alexandria also deserves mention here. Philo states that just as we know a well-built house (or city or ship) has a builder, so also the universe's order leads us to know that it has a maker, given that nonrational things could not otherwise arrange and coordinate themselves in an integrated whole. Philo concludes, "They, then, who draw their conclusions in this manner perceive God in his shadow, arriving at a due comprehension of the artist through his works."[39]

A few centuries earlier, Xenophon had attributed to Socrates the view that just as the mind governs the human body, so also "Thought indwelling in the

37. See my discussion of Wisdom of Solomon 13, Romans 1, and Acts 17 in chap. 8 of my *Engaging the Doctrine of Revelation: The Mediation of the Gospel through Church and Scripture* (Grand Rapids: Baker Academic, 2014). On the book of Wisdom (and the Psalms), see especially James Barr, *Biblical Faith and Natural Theology* (Oxford: Oxford University Press, 1993).

38. For the extent of Paul's debt to Wisdom of Solomon, see Douglas A. Campbell, *The Deliverance of God: An Apocalyptic Rereading of Justification in Paul* (Grand Rapids: Eerdmans, 2009), 360–62. Yet, for Campbell, Romans 1:18–32 recounts a position held by an anonymous opponent of Paul's, a position that Paul rejects. Campbell states that "the speaker [of Romans 1:18–32] is a recognizable 'Teacher' of some sort, whose influence at Rome Paul is seeking to neutralize throughout Romans. And Romans 1:18–32 is in fact the fullest presentation of the Teacher's position that we receive from the hand of Paul" (ibid., 542; cf. 162). For a rejoinder to Campbell, see N. T. Wright, *Paul and the Faithfulness of God* (Minneapolis: Fortress, 2013), 766–67; cf. 638–39. For the view that Paul does not intend Romans 1:20 to be taken as his own teaching, see also W. Schmithals, *Der Römerbrief* (Gütersloh: Gerd Mohn, 1988), 77, and, somewhat similarly, E. P. Sanders, *Paul, the Law, and the Jewish People* (Philadelphia: Fortress, 1983), 123. Barr responds to such approaches in his *Biblical Faith and Natural Theology*, 49–57. On Campbell's perspective in light of the work of other Pauline exegetes, see also Kerr, *After Aquinas*, 61–63.

39. Philo, *Allegorical Interpretation* 3.32.97, in *The Works of Philo: Complete and Unabridged*, trans. C. D. Yonge, rev. ed. (Peabody, MA: Hendrickson, 1993), 61. This proof appears in the midst of Philo's allegorical reading of the scriptural testimony to Joseph's sons (Ephraim and Manasseh) and to the temple craftsman Bezalel! See also Roberto Radice, "Philo's Theology and Theory of Creation," in *The Cambridge Companion to Philo*, ed. Adam Kamesar (Cambridge: Cambridge University Press, 2009), 124–45, esp. 126; Cristina Termini, "Philo's Thought within the Context of Middle Judaism," trans. Adam Kamesar, in *Cambridge Companion to Philo*, 95–123; Charles A. Anderson, *Philo of Alexandria's Views of the Physical World* (Tübingen: Mohr Siebeck, 2011).

Universal disposes all things according to its pleasure."[40] In arriving at this conclusion, Xenophon's Socrates argues on the basis of the wisdom present in created things. Thus, Socrates asks his interlocutor, Aristodemus, whether he admires any wise human beings. When Aristodemus names certain artists and poets, Socrates notes that these wise humans only created imaginary characters; by comparison, how wise must the "creators of living, intelligent, and active beings" be.[41] Aristodemus responds that living beings may have come to be by chance rather than by any wise design. In reply, Socrates urges Aristodemus to think about whether humans display the marks of chance or of design: "Suppose that it is impossible to guess the purpose of one creature's existence, and obvious that another's serves a useful end, which, in your judgment, is the work of chance, and which of design?"[42] The point is that if a creature serves a useful end, as the human body shows to be the case, then there appears to be design.

Nonetheless, Aristodemus confesses that he remains doubtful about the existence of a wise designer, because, as he says, "I don't see the master hand, whereas I see the makers of things in this world."[43] To this objection, Socrates points out that the soul or rational power in humans cannot be seen, and yet we willingly attribute design to it. Furthermore, the form of our body is so well suited to our soul, and our souls even have the dignity of being able to apprehend "the existence of gods who set in order the universe, greatest and fairest of things."[44] Aristodemus responds that he will believe in such things when the gods "send counsellors" to tell us what to do and what to

---

40. Xenophon, *Memorabilia* 1.4.17–18, trans. E. C. Marchant, in Xenophon, *Memorabilia, Oeconomicus, Symposium, Apology* (Cambridge, MA: Harvard University Press, 1923), 2–359, at 63. See also Mark L. McPherran, *The Religion of Socrates* (University Park, PA: Pennsylvania State University Press, 1996), 272–91. After a careful analysis of Xenophon's Socrates in light of the evidence of Plato's dialogues, McPherran concludes, "Socrates' endorsement of the *Memorabilia*'s teleological argument places him at the leading edge of fifth-century theological reform. Raised in a culture of passionate gods—gods hungry for honor, full of strife, morally distant, and confusedly and intermittently involved with the daily life of nature and humanity—Socrates managed to travel a very great conceptual distance indeed. For beginning there he appears to have arrived at an idea that was to dominate Western thought for many centuries to come: the existence of an immanent—albeit still anthropopsychic—cosmic intelligence and loving Maker" (*Religion of Socrates*, 290–91). See also the discussion of Xenophon's Socrates in David Sedley, *Creationism and Its Critics in Antiquity* (Berkeley: University of California Press, 2007), 78–86. Sedley argues, "Whatever Xenophon or his source may have done to shape or adapt the material, its originality and significance make it a natural assumption that its authorship really does in essence belong to Socrates. And it does contain . . . the first recorded antecedent of the Argument from Design" (ibid., 82).
41. Xenophon, *Memorabilia* 1.4.4, p. 55.
42. Xenophon, *Memorabilia* 1.4.4, p. 55.
43. Xenophon, *Memorabilia* 1.4.9, p. 59.
44. Xenophon, *Memorabilia* 1.4.13, p. 61.

avoid.[45] In Socrates's view, however, the gods are already doing this for the Athenians and other cities, and the key point is that if human wisdom is able to know many things, God's wisdom is so great that "he sees all things and hears all things alike, and is present in all places and heedful of all things."[46]

In the *Republic*, Plato presents Socrates as developing an account of the Good as the cause of all other things. In discussion with Glaucon, Socrates argues that we should "say that the objects of knowledge not only receive from the presence of the good their being known, but their very existence and essence is derived from it."[47] As is his wont, Socrates begins his discourse with Glaucon by noting that the greatest object of study is the Good, because the Good is what we all seek. He points out that most people consider the Good to be pleasure. Those who think more about it, however, recognize that this cannot be so, since there are bad pleasures; such persons posit that the Good is knowledge. In Socrates's view, however, it is the Idea of the Good that fixes our minds on the eternal forms; thus it is the Idea of the Good that "gives their truth to the objects of knowledge and the power of knowing to the knower."[48] He thereby arrives at the Good as the supreme principle, above being and truth, that in some way causes the being and truth of all things that can be objects of knowledge (i.e., the eternal forms).[49]

In the *Timaeus*, Plato (speaking through the figure of Timaeus) reflects on the origin of the cosmos by first distinguishing between being and becoming: "What is that which is Existent always and has no Becoming? And what is that which is Becoming always and never is Existent?"[50] Things that change

---

45. Xenophon, *Memorabilia* 1.4.15, p. 61.

46. Xenophon, *Memorabilia* 1.4.18, p. 63. Sedley connects Socrates's view here with Socrates's encounter, as a young man, with the philosophy of Anaxagoras, as recounted in Plato's *Phaedo* 96a–100d. In the *Phaedo*, Socrates criticizes Anaxagoras on the grounds that he "made no use of intelligence, and did not assign any real causes for the ordering of things, but mentioned as causes air and ether and water and many other absurdities. And it seemed to me it was very much as if one should say that Socrates does with intelligence whatever he does, and then, in trying to give the causes of the particular thing I do, should say first that I am now sitting here because my body is composed of bones and sinews" (*Phaedo* 98c, in Plato, *Euthyphro, Apology, Crito, Phaedo, Phaedrus*, trans. Harold North Fowler [Cambridge, MA: Harvard University Press, 1960], 339). Socrates goes on to argue that "if anything is beautiful besides absolute beauty it is beautiful for no other reason than because it partakes of absolute beauty" (Plato, *Phaedo* 100c, p. 345). On Anaxagoras, see L. P. Gerson, *God and Greek Philosophy: Studies in the Early History of Natural Theology* (London: Routledge, 1994), 28–32. See also R. K. Hack, *God in Greek Philosophy to the Time of Socrates* (Princeton: Princeton University Press, 1931).

47. Plato, *Republic* 509b, trans. Paul Shorey, in *The Collected Dialogues of Plato*, ed. Edith Hamilton and Huntington Cairns (Princeton: Princeton University Press, 1961), 744.

48. Plato, *Republic* 508d–e, p. 744.

49. See the succinct discussion in Gerd Van Riel, *Plato's Gods* (London: Ashgate, 2013), 105–6.

50. Plato, *Timaeus* 28a, in Plato, *Timaeus, Critias, Cleitophon, Menexenus, Epistles*, trans. R. G. Bury (Cambridge, MA: Harvard University Press, 1961), 49.

are "becoming." All changing things require something that causes them, "for without a cause it is impossible for anything to attain becoming."[51] Has the cosmos, then, come to be, or has it always existed? Plato answers, "It has come into existence; for it is visible and tangible and possessed of a body; and all such things are sensible, and things sensible . . . come into existence."[52] Given that the cosmos has come to be, it must have a transcendent cause—a cause that at least transcends the cosmos of changing things, even if Plato denies that one can say anything about this mysterious "Maker and Father of this Universe."[53] Emphasizing that "that which has come into existence must necessarily . . . have come into existence by reason of some Cause," Plato goes on to say that this cause is "good" and is "the supreme originating principle of Becoming and the Cosmos."[54] Plato calls this cause, who establishes the cosmos of changing things by fixing "his gaze on the Eternal" as on a model, "God" (ὁ θεὸς), "Father" (ὁ πατήρ), and the "Constructor" (ὁ δημιουργὸς, the "demiurge").[55]

Scholars debate how we should understand this argument for the existence of a creator God, since there are many other gods in the *Timaeus*, and since the status of the "demiurge" is not clear, other than that the demiurge is divine. Sarah Broadie comments that Plato's approach "resembles the Abrahamic schema in maintaining a sharp distinction between the cosmos and its divine maker," while at the same time allowing for "a plurality of gods and of divine cosmic principles."[56] This judgment seems correct to me.

51. Plato, *Timaeus* 28a, p. 49.
52. Plato, *Timaeus* 28b, p. 51.
53. Plato, *Timaeus* 28c, p. 51.
54. Plato, *Timaeus* 28c and 29e, pp. 51 and 53.
55. Plato, *Timaeus* 29a and 37c, pp. 29 and 37. For discussion of the *Timaeus* see Sedley, *Creationism and Its Critics in Antiquity*, 95–132. He notes that most readers, including himself, "take Timaeus to be insisting on the indispensability of divine causation as an explanatory principle" (ibid., 101). On the relationship between the *Timaeus*'s cosmology and its politics, see Catherine H. Zuckert, *Plato's Philosophers: The Coherence of the Dialogues* (Chicago: University of Chicago Press, 2009), chap. 6.
56. Sarah Broadie, *Nature and Divinity in Plato's* Timaeus (Cambridge: Cambridge University Press, 2012), 12, 22. L. P. Gerson argues that Plato implies "a similarity or even an identity between demiurge and Forms. But the demiurge is *nous* and Forms are *noēta*. It is difficult to resist the conclusion that at least in part the demiurge is hypothesized in order to provide the permanent intellectual activity required for Forms to do their work" (Gerson, *God and Greek Philosophy*, 69). On the grounds that Plato's ontology allows only for being and becoming, and the "demiurge" appears to fit neither, Gerd Van Riel suggests that for Plato the "demiurge" is not a self-standing divine principle, but rather "the gods enact cognitive intellect, and demiurgic intellect, in their souls" (*Plato's Gods*, 95). For Van Riel, "in the *Timaeus*, the intellect (the Demiurge) is not treated as a particular god, but rather as 'intellect (νοῦς) in general,' bringing all the operations of Platonic intellect under a single heading" (ibid., 107). By comparison, see John Peter Kenney's insistence that "the *Timaeus* does not support the claim

In his *Physics* and *Metaphysics*, Aristotle helps us to see why the cosmos's existence requires a self-sufficient source of all finite being. Since matter decays and changes without utterly going out of being, it may seem that we do not need to explain the existence of the cosmos, especially if with Aristotle we suppose the cosmos to have existed everlastingly. Perhaps the cosmos simply *is*.[57] Aristotle observes that the being of particular things is subject to change. Such things therefore have potency; they are not pure actuality. Insofar as a thing has potency, it cannot be the only source of its actuality and must depend on others ontologically. Aristotle argues, therefore, that although the cosmos has no beginning, it cannot account for its own limited actuality. Instead, its finite actuality must be grounded in a first mover, Pure Act, that does not depend on anything else for actuality and that has no potency. Pure Act causes "the simple locomotion of the universe" but does not itself "move" or change, since Pure Act cannot "be otherwise than as it is" (not because it is statically immobile, but because it is fully actual).[58] Aristotle also demonstrates that Pure Act must be one; there cannot be two or more pure actualities.[59]

How, according to Aristotle, does Pure Act cause the everlasting circular motion of the first moved mover? In book 12 of the *Metaphysics*, Aristotle states

that the forms are the derivative thoughts of a divine mind" (Kenney, *Mystical Monotheism: A Study in Ancient Platonic Theology* [Hanover, NH: Brown University Press, 1991], 16). For the argument that the "demiurge" is temporal, see Thomas K. Johansen, "The *Timaeus* on the Principles of Cosmology," in *The Oxford Handbook of Plato*, ed. Gail Fine (Oxford: Oxford University Press, 2008), 463–83.

57. For a response to such a view, drawing on Thomas Aquinas, see Patrick Masterson, *Approaching God: Between Phenomenology and Theology* (London: Bloomsbury, 2013), 46–53.

58. Aristotle, *Metaphysics* 1072b and 1073a, trans. Hippocrates G. Apostle (Grinnell, IA: The Peripatetic Press, 1979), 205–6; cf. book 9 on actuality and potency. See also the arguments for the unmoved mover found in Aristotle's *Physics*, trans. and ed. Glen Coughlin (South Bend, IN: St. Augustine's Press, 2005), esp. books 7–8. For discussion of Aristotle, see Gerson, *God and Greek Philosophy*, chap. 3; Sedley, *Creationism and Its Critics in Antiquity*, chap. 6; Joseph Owens, CSsR, "Pure Actuality and Primacy in Being," in Owens, *Aristotle's Gradations of Being in Metaphysics E–Z*, ed. Lloyd P. Gerson (South Bend, IN: St. Augustine's Press, 2007), 20–38; Christopher Shields, *Aristotle* (London: Routledge, 2007), 220–29. Owens shows that in important respects "Aristotelian separate substance" does not "coincide with a Judeo-Christian conception of God" ("Pure Actuality and Primacy in Being," 38).

59. Aristotle, *Metaphysics* 1074a, p. 208; 1073a–b, pp. 206–8. Since Aristotle suggests earlier that there might be fifty-five unmoved movers, Gerson proposes that "the fifty-five unmoved movers of *Lambda* chapter eight are the inseparable causes of self-moving spheres, arrived at by reasoning along the line of efficient causality" (*God and Greek Philosophy*, 133). These unmoved movers differ from "an unqualifiedly unmoved mover" because the latter "must be unique perfect actuality" (ibid.). Gerson explains why there can only be one Pure Act: "Let there be two gods or unmoved movers. Then being in the primary sense will be identified with them. But it cannot literally be identified with both of them; if one is being in the primary sense, then the other is not, or if it is, how does it differ from the first? Presumably, only by being something less than perfect actuality" (ibid., 130).

that Pure Act moves all things solely as their final cause—that is, by attraction. By contrast, in book 8 of the *Physics* he holds that the unmoved mover is the efficient cause of the everlasting motion of the first moved mover.[60] Either way, for Aristotle, God's existence consists simply in the perfect eternal contemplation of himself: "Thinking is the thinking of Himself through all eternity."[61] Over the centuries, interpreters have been divided about whether, in God's thinking of himself, all that is intelligible is included. In the *Nicomachean Ethics*, Aristotle teaches that the best human life is devoted to contemplating (and thereby imitating) God, but he does not say that God has knowledge, let alone love, of creatures.[62]

Aristotle's argument that the cosmos is not founded on sheer chance is also worth presenting here. With the philosophy of Empedocles in view, Aristotle remarks that some consider that "chance is the cause of this heaven and of everything in the cosmos. For they say that the vortex and the motion which distinguished and arranged the all into this order comes to be from chance."[63] As Aristotle points out, such thinkers accept that particular plants and animals (for example) come to be from recognizable causes rather than from chance. How, then, can such thinkers suppose that the whole cosmos, far more extraordinary than particular plants or animals, comes to be by chance? Aristotle goes on to argue that even when things come to be by chance, chance functions as an "accidental" cause rather than as a "per se" cause: in every case, "chance and luck are posterior to mind and nature."[64] Thus, the cosmos—keeping in mind that the cosmos (in Aristotle's view) is everlasting—cannot ultimately be traced to mere chance: "it is necessary that mind and nature is the prior cause both of many other things and of the all."[65]

---

60. For discussion see Gerson, *God and Greek Philosophy*, 119–28, 134–41; Gerson, *Aristotle and Other Platonists* (Ithaca, NY: Cornell University Press, 2005), 200–204. For the view that Aristotle considers the unmoved mover to be both a final and efficient cause, see for example Ernesto Berti, "Metaphysics Lambda 6," in *Aristotle's Metaphysics Lambda: Symposium Aristotelicum*, ed. Michael Frede and David Charles (Oxford: Oxford University Press, 2000), 181–206. For the contrast between Aristotle's account of the unmoved mover (God) and the Neoplatonic account of God, see Gerson's *Aristotle and Other Platonists*, chap. 6.

61. Aristotle, *Metaphysics* 1075a, p. 210. For discussion see Gerson, *Aristotle and Other Platonists*, 195–200; Sedley, *Creationism and Its Critics in Antiquity*, 170. See also Myles F. Burnyeat, *Aristotle's Divine Intellect* (Milwaukee: Marquette University Press, 2008).

62. See Aristotle, *Nicomachean Ethics*, trans. H. Rackham (Cambridge, MA: Harvard University Press, 1934).

63. Aristotle, *Physics* 196a, p. 32.

64. Aristotle, *Physics* 198a, p. 36.

65. Aristotle, *Physics* 198a, p. 36. For discussion, see Sedley, *Creationism and Its Critics in Antiquity*, 186–94. Sedley concludes that for Aristotle "the priority must be causal or explanatory, rather than temporal. The world is an eternal purposive structure, causally dependent on intelligence and nature. The 'intelligence' (*nous*) he intends cannot be a Platonic Demiurge: instead,

A generation after Aristotle's death, Zeno of Citium undertook a response to Epicurus as well as an updating of Socratic (as distinct from Platonic) philosophy. In Stoic philosophy, founded by Zeno and carried forward by numerous prominent figures, the argument from design takes on a particular prominence. Thus, in Cicero's *On the Nature of the Gods*, Balbus—representing Stoic views—argues that "the parts of the world are in such a condition that they could not possibly have cohered together if they were not controlled by intelligence and by divine providence."[66] The regularities of the cosmos, says Balbus, require philosophers "to infer the presence not merely of an inhabitant of this celestial and divine abode, but also of a ruler and governor, the architect as it were of this mighty and monumental structure."[67] The biblical scholar Luke Timothy Johnson observes that Stoic philosophers equate God "with the immanent principle of reason governing the world" and conclude that "since the world is itself in some sense divine, it is providentially guided: all that is and that happens bears the signs of rational design."[68] Denying the existence of immaterial substances, and associating the cosmos's divine rational principle (*logos*) with the fire-air composite (*pneuma*) constitutive of the cosmos, Stoic philosophers suggest that God repeatedly re-creates the cosmos anew out of himself.[69] One can see, then, how Stoics such as Chrysippus and Plutarch can say that "God" is creative, immortal, and invisible

he can only be referring to that detached divine intellect, the Prime Mover, which as the ultimate source of all change he does indeed consider causally prior to the world, and, as the ultimate model for emulation, the *per se* cause of all the changes lower down the scale" (ibid., 194). See also Monte Ransome Johnson's emphasis that Aristotle offers a proof for the necessity of a first (unmoved) mover, but not a "'teleological' proof for god's existence" (Johnson, *Aristotle on Teleology* [Oxford: Oxford University Press, 2005], 258). Another student of Plato, Xenocrates, influenced by the Pythagoreans, appears to have held that the divine intellect, comprising all number, makes the world. See John Dillon's reconstruction of Xenocrates's position in Dillon, *The Heirs of Plato: A Study of the Old Academy (347–274 BC)* (Oxford: Oxford University Press, 2003), 98–107; cf. however the critical engagement with Dillon's reconstruction by John Peter Kenney, *Mystical Monotheism*, 26–27.

66. Cicero, *De natura deorum* 2.34, in Cicero, *De natura deorum and Academica*, trans. H. Rackham (Cambridge, MA: Harvard University Press, 1951), 207.

67. Cicero, *De natura deorum* 2.35, p. 211. For discussion of the various arguments advanced by Cicero's Balbus, see Gerson, *God and Greek Philosophy*, 154–66. Gerson links the Stoic argument from design with that of William Paley.

68. Luke Timothy Johnson, *Among the Gentiles: Greco-Roman Religion and Christianity* (New Haven: Yale University Press, 2009), 69. For discussion, including the relationship of Stoic thought to the *Timaeus* and Xenophon's Socrates, see Sedley, *Creationism and Its Critics in Antiquity*, chap. 7. See also chap. 4 (on Stoicism) in Gerson's *God and Greek Philosophy*.

69. See Michael Frede, "The Case for Pagan Monotheism in Greek and Graeco-Roman Antiquity," in *One God: Pagan Monotheism in the Roman Empire*, ed. Stephen Mitchell and Peter Van Nuffelen (Cambridge: Cambridge University Press, 2010), 53–81, at 71–72; Gerson, *God and Greek Philosophy*, 148–49, 173.

without implying a transcendent or immaterial God.[70] One can also see how Stoicism provoked the response of Academic Skepticism (or Pyrrhonism), well represented in the work of Sextus Empiricus, who rejects all Stoic attempts to demonstrate the existence of a divine source.[71]

Among first-century BC thinkers, the Neo-Pythagorean Eudorus of Alexander deserves mention for his theory that there is a supreme One beyond either the monad or the dyad. The One is the supreme principle or origin of all things, whereas the monad and the dyad are causal principles within the universe. Eudorus was indebted to Plato's *Parmenides* for his speculations. Similarly, the first-century AD Neo-Pythagorean Moderatus of Gades appears to have taught that the One is beyond being and intellect, which come forth from the One as the second principle. This second principle is termed the Logos and is connected with the Demiurge of the *Timaeus*. I mention these thinkers largely because of their influence on Plotinus, the final thinker that I treat in this section.[72]

Plotinus wrote in the third century AD and was aware of Christianity; his first biographer, Porphyry, records a respectful encounter between Plotinus and Origen of Alexandria. In book 6 of the *Enneads*, indebted especially to Plato's *Parmenides* and in critical dialogue with Aristotle and the Stoics (via Neo-Pythagorean and Neoplatonic thought), Plotinus states of the One, "It is in virtue of unity that beings are beings. This is equally true of things whose existence is primal and of all that are in any degree to be numbered among beings."[73] Everything that is not Absolute Unity must receive its unity, even if it also imparts unity. For example, the soul gives unity to the body, but the soul has various powers. The soul differs from other souls and even is distinct from its own unity. Unity is not the same thing as the soul; therefore the soul,

70. Robert Sokolowski argues that "human reason left to itself will always tend to see the divine as the ultimate principle in the world. . . . The biblical word of God, the biblical and Christian understanding of God, always has to resist the natural impulse to see the divine as the best part of the world" (Robert Sokolowski, *The God of Faith and Reason: Foundations of Christian Theology*, 2nd ed. [Washington, DC: Catholic University of America Press, 1995], xi).

71. See Gerson, *God and Greek Philosophy*, 174–84; Gerson replies to Sextus Empiricus at 179.

72. For Eudorus and Moderatus, see Kenney, *Mystical Monotheism*, 36–43. I skip over another important influence on Plotinus, Numenius of Apamea, discussed by Kenney at 59–74. On Plotinus, see Kenney's *Mystical Monotheism*, 91–156.

73. Plotinus, *The Enneads* 6.9.1, trans. Stephen MacKenna (Burdett, NY: Larson, 1992), 698. This edition of the *Enneads* also contains Porphyry's short biography of Plotinus. For Plotinus, the One is above both being and thinking (by contrast to Aristotle's view). As Gerson observes, "In saying that the One is beyond being he is actually saying that being as understood by Aristotle (and many others) is not the *archē*" (*God and Greek Philosophy*, 201). Gerson suggests that Plotinus, in locating the One above being, is speaking about finite, composite being; cf. Gerson's *Aristotle and Other Platonists*, 207. For Plotinus's critique of Aristotle on God, see especially *Aristotle and Other Platonists*, 205–8.

like the body, must participate in unity. Indeed, everything other than Absolute Unity (including thinking and being) participates in unity. Absolute Unity is "the principle of all, the Good and the First."[74] Without participation in Absolute Unity, there could be no unity, and things would break apart.

Christian Faith and Metaphysical Reason

Biblical scholar N. T. Wright observes with regard to Romans 1:19–20, "Paul clearly does believe that when humans look at creation they are aware, at some level, of the power and divinity of the creator," so that there is a "divine self-revelation in creation."[75] Yet, can it really be said that pagans arrived at some knowledge of the living God? Certainly, Plato's "Maker," Aristotle's Pure Act, and Plotinus's One are not the Christian God. There are simply too many differences. But when these thinkers argue for the existence of a Maker, for the existence of Pure Act as the first principle, or for the existence of the supreme One, they do in fact touch the living God. I disagree, therefore, with the position—well described by Bruce Marshall—that "while anyone can make a valid argument for an unmoved mover or first cause, only under the conditions of Christian faith can we recognize that this mover or cause is the God Christians are talking about."[76] There cannot be a God who creates and transcends everything but is not Pure Act. If there is Pure Act but the Christian

74. Plotinus, *Enneads* 6.9.3, p. 700. Gerson notes that according to Plotinus's demonstration, the One is "that without which any composite would not exist" (*God and Greek Philosophy*, 186). See also John Bussanich, "Plotinus's Metaphysics of the One," in *The Cambridge Companion to Plotinus*, ed. Lloyd P. Gerson (Cambridge: Cambridge University Press, 1996), 38–65. For Plotinus's view of divine causality, see Bussanich, "Plotinus's Metaphysics of the One," 46–57; Cristina D'Ancona Costa, "Plotinus and Later Platonic Philosophers on the Causality of the First Principle," in *Cambridge Companion to Plotinus*, 356–85; Gerson, *Aristotle and Other Platonists*, 202. For further discussion of Plotinus, see Gerson, *Plotinus* (London: Routledge, 1994); John M. Rist, *Plotinus: The Road to Reality* (Cambridge: Cambridge University Press, 1967); Rist, "The One of Plotinus and the God of Aristotle," *Review of Metaphysics* 27 (1974): 74–87. See also William F. Lynch, SJ's *An Approach to the Metaphysics of Plato through the Parmenides* (Washington, DC: Georgetown University Press, 1959).

75. N. T. Wright, *The Letter to the Romans: Introduction, Commentary, and Reflections*, in *The New Interpreter's Bible*, vol. 10, *Acts, Romans, 1 Corinthians* (Nashville: Abingdon, 2002), 395–770, at 432. Even so, Wright regrets that Romans 1:19–20 has "had to bear the weight of debates about 'natural theology'" (ibid.).

76. Bruce D. Marshall, introduction to George A. Lindbeck, *The Nature of Doctrine: Religion and Theology in a Postliberal Age*, 2nd ed. (Louisville: Westminster John Knox, 2009), vii–xxvii, at xx. Marshall inclines toward this view but makes clear that his thought remains in development on this point, noting that "there is surely more work to be done on this question" (ibid., xxvii n35). See also his "*Quod Scit Una Uetula*: Aquinas on the Nature of Theology," in *The Theology of Thomas Aquinas*, ed. Rik Van Nieuwenhove and Joseph P. Wawrykow (Notre Dame: University of Notre Dame Press, 2005), 1–35, at 17–20.

God is lesser, then the Christian God is not God at all. The demonstration of Pure Act is the demonstration of God, though it is not all that needs to be said about the living God, the God of Christians.[77]

David Hart states matters with his customary forcefulness. Remarking that "there are many persons who object in principle to any fraternization between different religious vocabularies," he argues that it would be churlish to suppose that knowledge of the true God's existence is only possible for those whose minds have been healed and elevated by faith in God's revelation of himself in Jesus Christ and the Holy Spirit.[78] This seems right to me, not least as an interpretation of Wisdom 13, Romans 1, and other New Testament texts such as Acts 17 and 19. Indeed, Hart goes so far as to assert that "all the major theistic traditions claim that humanity as a whole has a knowledge of God, in some form or another, and that a perfect ignorance of God is impossible for any people."[79]

Whether or not this can be substantiated for each of the major theistic traditions, it is surely what the Catholic Church teaches. After criticizing "rationalism or naturalism," the First Vatican Council's dogmatic constitution *Dei Filius* proclaims that "God, the source and end of all things, can be known with certainty from the consideration of created things, by the natural power of human reason."[80] Along broadly similar lines, the Second Vatican Council's declaration *Nostra Aetate* states, "From ancient until modern time there is found among various peoples a certain perception of that unseen force which is present in the course of things and in events in human life, and sometimes even an acknowledgement of a supreme deity or even of a Father."[81] The arguments for

77. Richard B. Hays rightly says that the Gospels,
> precisely through their reading of the OT to identify Jesus, force us to rethink what we mean when we say the word "God.". . . The Gospels narrate the story of how the God of Israel was embodied in Jesus. This means, *inter alia*, that we should stop using the terms "high" Christology and "low" Christology to characterize the four canonical Gospels. These very categories presuppose an a priori philosophical account of 'God' that the Gospel narratives contradict. (Hays, *Reading Backwards: Figural Christology and the Fourfold Gospel Witness* [Waco: Baylor University Press, 2014], 108)

Here it is necessary to add, however, that the Gospel narratives contradict the "philosophical account of 'God'" in some ways but not in all ways, particularly once one recognizes that "transcendence" does not mean "aloofness" (though it often does in Greek philosophy) but rather simply means that God is not ontologically on the same level as creatures. Indeed, precisely to be incarnate in Jesus (and to be Creator), Israel's God must be transcendent, Pure Act: see Thomas G. Weinandy, OFM Cap, *Does God Suffer?* (Notre Dame: University of Notre Dame Press, 2000), 55–57; cf. 108–12, 120–27.

78. Hart, *Experience of God*, 3.

79. Ibid.

80. See Vatican I, *Dei Filius*, prol. and chap. 2, in *Decrees of the Ecumenical Councils*, vol. 2, *Trent to Vatican II*, ed. Norman P. Tanner, SJ (Washington, DC: Georgetown University Press, 1990), 804, 806.

81. Vatican II, *Nostra Aetate* 2, in *Decrees of the Ecumenical Councils*, 2:969.

God's existence arrive at self-subsistent Act, the source of all things, the cause of order in the universe, the infinitely perfect source of all finite perfections. It is in this sense that, as Hart comments, "the God of faith and the God of the philosophers are in many crucial respects recognizably one and the same."[82]

Even so, Rémi Brague voices a common opinion when he states that the personal and living God "is only accessible to faith."[83] Indebted to Pascal, Brague holds that God reveals himself only to those who seek knowledge of him as one would seek to know a transcendent *person* rather than as one would seek to know an empirical *fact*. This is no doubt true regarding intimate knowledge of God. But God also wills that the truth of his existence be knowable by human reason. There need be no competition between revelation and reason.[84] God created our minds to stretch toward God and to know him. Of course, it is personal intimacy with God—the saving God who loves us, heals us, and draws us to union with him forever—that we most desire rather than simply demonstrative knowledge that God exists. As Albert Dondeyne observes, "The believer is not content with thinking of the world as created by a transcendent first cause; in the act of faith he cleaves to God himself, he addresses him directly, opens his heart to him as to an absolute Thou, in the hope that God will be his light, his truth and his life."[85] But the demonstration of a transcendent first cause is good too.

82. Hart, *Experience of God*, 9. As Hart states, "God is Spirit, incorporeal, not an object located somewhere in space, not subject to the limitations of time, not a product of cosmic nature, not simply some craftsman who creates by manipulating materials external to himself, not composed of parts, but rather residing in all things while remaining perfectly one, present to us in the depths of our own beings" (ibid.).

83. Brague, *On the God of Christians*, 40.

84. Denys Turner refers in this regard to the "ancient scholastic distinction between the 'material' and the 'formal' objects of knowledge" as a "way of construing the relationship between the God of the philosophers and the God of faith—the same God can be known under different descriptions . . . and within different relations of knowing" (Turner, *Faith, Reason and the Existence of God*, 17–18). Turner notes that Giles of Rome

> explained that the God of the philosophers is known as it were "by sight," and the God of the theologians by "touch" and "taste"; for the philosophers know God "at a distance" and intellectually across a gap crossed not by means of direct experience but by means of evidence and inference, and so through a medium, as sight sees; whereas, through grace and revelation, the theologian is in an immediate and direct experiential contact with God, as touch and taste are with their objects. (ibid., 18)

But Turner considers that Aquinas provides "us with a probably more helpful, because less polarized, account of sameness and difference of 'object.' What I see at a distance is a dark patch I can distinguish as a human being moving towards me. When it is close enough to me, I can see that it is Peter. When the object was at a distance what I saw *was* Peter, but it was not *as* Peter that I saw him. Thus the God of reason in relation to the God of faith" (ibid., 18–19).

85. Albert Dondeyne, "The Existence of God and Contemporary Materialism," in *God, Man and the Universe: A Christian Answer to Modern Materialism*, ed. Jacques de Bivort de La Saudée (London: Burns & Oates, 1954), 3–32, at 9.

It may seem, however, that by this emphasis on the demonstrations of God's existence I am falling into the error that Michael Buckley attributes to his fellow Jesuit Leonard Lessius (1554–1623). Lessius's *De providentia numinis* sought to counter Enlightenment atheism by critiquing skeptical ancient philosophers rather than by critiquing the Enlightenment denial of the divinity of Jesus Christ. Buckley observes that "atheism in the sixteenth and seventeenth centuries is treated as if it were a philosophic issue, rather than a religious one; this shift characterizes Catholic apologetics for the succeeding four hundred years."[86] Christology became "irrelevant in establishing the reality of god"; Christ's revelation of God was displaced in the quest for certitude about God.[87] According to Buckley, Lessius's approach lasted so long because theologians forgot that the defense of God's existence primarily requires attention to Christ and the Holy Spirit.

I agree with Buckley that metaphysical reasoning on its own, without the God who reveals himself, cannot nourish the real relationship with the living God that is the true purpose of knowing that God exists. Buckley, however, undermines the significant, though secondary, value of the demonstrations of God's existence for the Christian tradition by his claim that "if one abrogates this [Christological and Pneumatological] evidence, one abrogates this god."[88] This would be so only if the God whose existence is demonstrable by reason were necessarily a distortion of the biblical God. In fact, as Denys Turner observes, "the proofs of God prove very little indeed, but just enough: as 'proofs' they fall into that class of 'demonstrations' which merely show *that* something exists by way of explanation (*demonstratio quia*), from which, no doubt some properties are derivable which must hold true."[89] What the proofs show is that a transcendent, infinite source of all finite things exists.

To demonstrate God's existence, then, is not to encapsulate God in a concept—which of course cannot be done—but rather to exercise what Thomas Joseph White terms "the deep human tendency toward God enrooted in the spiritual faculties of intellect and will."[90] Since our created reason is ordered

86. Michael J. Buckley, SJ, *At the Origins of Modern Atheism* (New Haven: Yale University Press, 1987), 47.

87. Ibid.

88. Ibid., 361. Buckley's full sentence reads, "Within the context of a Christology and a Pneumatology of both communal and personal religious experience, one can locate and give its own philosophical integrity to metaphysics, but Christology and Pneumatology are fundamental. If one abrogates this evidence, one abrogates this god."

89. Turner, *Faith, Reason and the Existence of God*, 19.

90. White, *Wisdom in the Face of Modernity*, 252. White underscores that "there are capacities proper to human nature that do not need grace in order to exist, and . . . the capacity to know God and even to desire God as one's true final end is one of these. However, in the

to God in this way, and since we can know through reason that God exists and possesses "eternal power and deity" (Rom. 1:20), divine revelation does not introduce us to an alien God—even as it reveals to us the wondrous "depth of the riches and wisdom and knowledge of God" (Rom. 11:33), clarifies the meaning of "eternal power and deity," and frees the nations from "the times of ignorance" (Acts 17:30). As White points out, philosophical wisdom "intensifies our recognition of the transcendence of God, and correspondingly makes us acutely aware of the limitations of our human knowledge."[91] Far from threatening to make divine revelation redundant, the demonstrability of God's existence makes revelation all the more desirable and urgent. In the words of Ronald Knox, "If you once prove that he [God] exists, you will find that he fills the whole stage."[92]

With the ancient Israelites, then, let us seek the God who gives to rational creatures, whose days "are like a passing shadow" (Ps. 144:4) and who are "like the beasts that perish" (Ps. 49:20), the ability to perceive the One whose "glory is above earth and heaven" (Ps. 148:13). "The heavens are telling the glory of God; and the firmament proclaims his handiwork. Day to day pours forth speech, and night to night declares knowledge" (Ps. 19:1–2).

concrete historical state of fallen and redeemed humanity, such capacities *in order to be exercised properly, or perhaps at all*, may well stand in need of the healing and corrective effects of grace and revelation" (ibid., 283n103). He adds that

in the concrete historical order, in order to recognize God as one's true final end, *even naturally*, some kind of *supernatural grace* of God (that itself implies—but is not limited to—the gift of supernatural faith) is necessary. Last, it should go without saying that the natural knowledge of and desire for God are in no way a substitute (according to Aquinas or Catholic doctrine) for the activity of justifying faith, informed by charity, and the revealed knowledge of God that accompanies this faith (*ST* I–II, q. 109, aa. 5–10). The latter alone leads to salvation. Our wounded natural capacity for God, therefore, can *in no way* procure for us the gift of justification or salvation. (ibid.)

91. Ibid., 290. See also White's "Engaging the Thomistic Tradition and Contemporary Culture Simultaneously: A Response to Burrell, Healy, and Schindler," *Nova et Vetera* 10 (2012): 605–23. D. C. Schindler argues for a specifically Christian metaphysics in his "Discovering the Given: On Reason and God," *Nova et Vetera* 10 (2012): 563–604. He holds that "our most basic philosophical concepts have been colored in profound and subtle ways by revelation" (ibid., 601). The example that Schindler gives is that of the divine goodness, which he interprets on the basis of divine revelation as pure self-donation. He argues that goodness and being are revealed to be love, so that kenotic love (gift) is the fundamental ontological reality. I agree that Pure Act is infinite love/gift (and infinite wisdom). But I think that the transcendentals cannot be conflated in our mode of thinking without causing problems (in this case, an incipient voluntarism, and difficulties in conceiving divine unity). When we think of existence, the categories of actuality (act of being) and potency, fully knowable to non-Christians, remain the definitive ones. Schindler cites Stefan Oster, "Thinking Love at the Heart of Things: The Metaphysics of Being as Love in the Work of Ferdinand Ulrich," *Communio* 37 (2010): 660–700.

92. Ronald A. Knox, *In Soft Garments: A Collection of Oxford Conferences*, 2nd ed. (New York: Sheed & Ward, 1953), 25.

1

Patristic and Medieval Arguments
for God's Existence

In her *The Divine Sense: The Intellect in Patristic Theology*, A. N. Williams points out that for fathers of the church, humans after the fall continued to possess the light of reason. The fathers ruled out any "pessimistic apophaticism" or any effort "to impugn our capacity to know God, at least dimly," because such views "would amount to claiming God had deliberately left us bereft of the only means to good, happy and purposeful lives, and would deny, therefore, any conceivable telos to creation."[1] In this chapter, I show that the fathers of the church, along with almost all medieval theologians, held that humans can rationally demonstrate the existence of God.

1. A. N. Williams, *The Divine Sense: The Intellect in Patristic Theology* (Cambridge: Cambridge University Press, 2007), 4. Williams focuses in particular on five authors: Clement of Alexandria, Origen, Gregory of Nazianzus, Gregory of Nyssa, and Augustine. The whole purpose of the mind, for these fathers, is to contemplate divine things. The fall did not take away the mind's ability to achieve this purpose, although the fall did focus the will (and the passions) on created things, making it easier for the mind to ignore God. See also Jaroslav Pelikan, *Christianity and Classical Culture: The Metamorphosis of Natural Theology in the Christian Encounter with Hellenism* (New Haven: Yale University Press, 1993), 57–73, 185–99. Pelikan attends especially to Gregory of Nyssa, whose assurance regarding the easy knowability of the first cause seems similar to John Calvin's. Athanasius shares the patristic confidence about the demonstrability of God's existence: see Athanasius, *On the Incarnation* 12, trans. and ed. a Religious of CSMV (Crestwood, NY: St. Vladimir's Seminary Press, 1993), 39.

I focus on four fathers and three medievals. In Tertullian, we find the same proof that Xenophon attributed to Socrates: the ordered cosmos could not have made and governed itself. Tertullian insists that Christianity does not introduce a new God: despite the fall, the majority of humans already knew God, even though they also worshiped other gods. There is a human yearning for God that also testifies to God's existence. Gregory of Nazianzus demonstrates God's existence in three ways: through the order of the universe, through the fact that every finite thing is dependent and cannot move the whole, and from finite perfections to infinite perfection. He compares the universe to a beautiful lyre and to such things as birds' nests and bees' honeycombs. The universe cannot account for its order, movement, existence, and perfections, as Gregory also shows in his poetry. Augustine makes much of human desire for God, as well as the contingency of all things. His favorite demonstration of God's existence has its starting point in the soul's intellectual light, which discerns (as the measure of all truth) an immutable, eternal Light—eternal truth, goodness, and beauty. Like Tertullian, Augustine argues that almost all humans prior to Christ knew of the existence of a supreme Creator God, despite their idolatry. Augustine grants, however, that even when humans are aware that God is that than which there is nothing better, humans can falsely imagine that finite things are the highest, despite the fact that nothing merely living can be as good as infinite Life. John of Damascus offers various demonstrations of God's existence, including from the fact that changeable things require a source, from the order of creation whose disparate elements could not otherwise hold together, and from the fact that things cannot spontaneously come to be and preserve themselves in being.

Turning to the medieval period, I first discuss Anselm of Canterbury. In his *Monologion*, Anselm demonstrates God's existence from our desire for good, from the fact that existing things require a self-subsistent source of existence, and from degrees of perfection. But Anselm is most famous for the demonstration that he offers in his *Proslogion*, which begins with Augustine's definition of God as that than which nothing better exists. Anselm argues that once we understand the terms of this definition, we can show that God must indeed exist. Gaunilo responds to Anselm, arguing that Anselm has conflated the order of knowing with the order of being; in turn, Anselm responds to certain errors that Gaunilo makes in his presentation of Anselm's ideas. Thomas Aquinas is best known for his adaptation of the Aristotelian proofs from motion (or change), from efficient causality, and from contingency. He also sets forth demonstrations based on the degrees of perfection and the order of the universe. Although we find similar proofs in the fathers, Aquinas gives a more metaphysically detailed exposition of each proof. He adds an explanation of why Anselm's proof in the *Proslogion* does not work. The last figure treated in this chapter, William of Ockham, does not think that the demonstrations from motion or efficient causality work, but he does argue that human reason can demonstrate God's existence on the basis of the universe's conservation in being. Ockham denies, however, that human reason can demonstrate the unity of God, thereby throwing into doubt whether human reason can demonstrate *God*'s existence even from the universe's conservation in being.

It should be clear that this chapter covers a wide terrain. Most of the fundamental kinds of demonstrations of God's existence appear in this chapter, and also, in Ockham, the first significant doubts about their efficacy. Let us now turn to the writings of these seven seminal contributors to the Christian tradition of demonstrating the existence of God.

Tertullian (ca. 150–ca. 220)

A native of Carthage and a married layman, Tertullian was a lawyer who was well educated in philosophy and rhetoric. An author of numerous seminal theological and ascetical works, he is known for developing much of the Latin terminology for the theology of the Trinity. Tertullian is sometimes thought to have separated from the church toward the end of his life. Although he adhered to the prophecy of Montanus and admired its moral rigor, Tertullian at least technically remained within the church, because during his lifetime the church in North Africa had not yet expelled the followers of Montanus's prophecy. Later North African bishop-theologians, notably Cyprian of Carthage and Optatus of Milevis, held Tertullian in high regard. Augustine read Tertullian carefully and was deeply influenced by him, although he criticized him for teaching that second marriage was forbidden and for founding separatist congregations.[2]

In his *Apology*, after describing the persecution of Christians in the Roman Empire and criticizing at length the worship of the gods, Tertullian begins his defense of Christianity by proclaiming the one God: "The object of our worship is the One God, He who by His commanding word, His arranging wisdom, His mighty power, brought forth from nothing this entire mass of our world, with all its array of elements, bodies, spirits, for the glory of His

2. See David Rankin, *Tertullian and the Church* (Cambridge: Cambridge University Press, 1995); Alistair Stewart-Sykes, Introduction to Tertullian, Origen, and Cyprian, *On the Lord's Prayer*, trans. Alistair Stewart-Sykes (Crestwood, NY: St. Vladimir's Seminary Press, 2004), 13–39, at 13–17.

majesty."[3] Tertullian describes this God as invisible, incomprehensible, and infinite. Even when we know him, he remains unknown. Humans, however, can and should know him, and humans who fail to know and worship him are culpable.

In this light, Tertullian goes on to offer two ways of demonstrating the existence of God.[4] First, we can demonstrate that God exists on the basis of the existence and order of the cosmos. Tertullian appeals to the fact that such a vast, well-ordered cosmos cannot have made and governed itself. He terms this "the proof from the works of His hands, so numerous and so great, which both contain you and sustain you, which minister at once to your enjoyment, and strike you with awe."[5] The second proof comes from the soul and is based on human experience. Although we are often enslaved to our bodily desires, when our soul wakes up from this enslavement we find ourselves yearning for God. As evidence of this yearning and of our knowledge of the One for whom we yearn, Tertullian points to the frequency of reference to "God" (*deus*) in common pagan speech. Looking toward the heavens, humans often praise God or appeal to God for help and for justice. The soul looks up to God and knows God must exist.

At this juncture, Tertullian turns to revelation. The transcendent, invisible God whom the things of this world and our own experience teach us must exist has indeed revealed himself so that we can "attain an ampler and more authoritative knowledge" of God.[6] This ampler knowledge was first communicated to the prophets of Israel, who taught that there is one Creator God who communicated his law and his plan for eternal judgment. Of the ancient and majestic Scriptures of Israel, Tertullian states, "Whoever gives ear will find God in them; whoever takes pains to understand, will be compelled to believe."[7] He proceeds to set forth how the Scriptures of Israel promised the coming of the Messiah, so that "in the last days of the world, God would, out of every nation, and people, and country, choose for Himself more faithful worshippers, upon whom He would bestow His grace, and that indeed in ampler measure, in keeping with the enlarged capacities of a nobler dispensation."[8] Although

---

3. Tertullian, *Apology* 17, trans. S. Thelwall, in *Latin Christianity: Its Founder, Tertullian*, in *Ante-Nicene Fathers* 3, ed. Alexander Roberts and James Donaldson, rev. A. Cleveland Coxe (Peabody, MA: Hendrickson, 1994), 31. Subsequent references to Tertullian's works are from this edition.

4. For discussion, see Eric Osborn, *Tertullian: First Theologian of the West* (Cambridge: Cambridge University Press, 1997), 77–79.

5. Tertullian, *Apology* 17, p. 32.

6. Tertullian, *Apology* 17, p. 33.

7. Tertullian, *Apology* 17, p. 33.

8. Tertullian, *Apology* 21, p. 34.

some consider Jesus to be merely human, Tertullian emphasizes that he is divine, the Son and Word of God. Tertullian remarks that Christ, in his divinity, "is called God from unity of substance with God," so that "Christ is Spirit of Spirit, and God of God, as light of light is kindled."[9] He fully shares the divine nature, although he comes forth from the Father. He took flesh in the womb of the Virgin Mary. Misunderstood by his people, he died for our sins, rose from the dead, and will come again in glory to judge the whole world.

Thus, Tertullian's *Apology* starts from the one God and from two ways of proving God's existence, and then shows that Jesus Christ reveals God (and God's providence) in a much fuller manner. But Tertullian's view that human reason can attain to the knowledge that God exists does not imply that he has a general admiration for the Greco-Roman philosophers. On the contrary, in his *To the Nations*, he argues that the philosophers managed to obscure human wisdom about God by their variety of opinions. Whereas the Platonists considered God to be within the world and to care about worldly matters, the Epicureans thought of God as nonexistent, and the Stoics thought of the world as God. The result was that "among the philosophers there was not only an ignorance, but actual doubt, about the divinity."[10] Tertullian goes on especially to criticize the Stoic view that the elements are divine. Elsewhere, in his *The Prescription against Heretics*, he warns against the way in which too strong a devotion to pagan philosophy can lead to heresies, and he observes, "What indeed has Athens to do with Jerusalem? . . . Away with all attempts to produce a mottled Christianity of Stoic, Platonic, and dialectical composition!"[11] His affinity for the ability of human reasoning to prove the existence of God, and his placement of these proofs at the outset of his discussion of the Christian God, do not lead him to an uncritical acceptance of ancient philosophical theories. This is so even though he accepts the Stoic view that God is in some sense material, because substantial. In his *Against Praxeas*, he argues that "Spirit has a bodily substance, of its own kind, in its own form."[12]

Tertullian's *Against Marcion* also provides testimony in affirmation of the demonstrations of God's existence. Here Tertullian wishes both to defend Moses against Marcion and to hold that Moses was not the first human to know of God. After all, it would hardly make sense that God would create rational creatures and leave them incapable of knowing him. Tertullian observes that Moses himself, in writing the Torah, makes clear that the knowledge of

9. Tertullian, *Apology* 21, p. 34.
10. Tertullian, *Ad Nationes* 2, p. 130.
11. Tertullian, *The Prescription against Heretics* 7, p. 246.
12. Tertullian, *Against Praxeas* 7, p. 602.

God does not begin with God's revelation to Moses (or to Abraham). Rather, true knowledge of God "is to be traced from Paradise and Adam, not from Egypt and Moses."[13] By contrast, Marcion claims to know a newly revealed God who is not the Creator, a God unknown and concealed prior to the coming of Christ. The Marcionites, says Tertullian, bring "forward a new god, as if we were ashamed of the old one!"[14] Tertullian emphasizes that there can only be one God: either the God of Israel is the one eternal God, or the god of Marcion is, but there cannot be two. The Marcionites, however, accept that the Creator exists, even though they disparage him. Tertullian points out that if the known Creator exists, we should not believe in an unknown new God of Marcion. He underscores that the true eternal Creator God has made himself known from the beginning through the things that he created. According to Tertullian, these things manifest the existence of their transcendent Creator: "For indeed, as the Creator of all things, He was from the beginning discovered equally with them, they having been themselves manifested that He might become known as God."[15]

In Tertullian's view, this knowledge of the true God never disappeared, even during the long period of idolatry. He claims that the majority of the human race, despite not knowing anything about Moses, still knew "the God of Moses" and "still spoke of Him separately by His own name as God, and the God of gods."[16] Insisting again that "God has for His witnesses this whole being of ours, and this universe wherein we dwell," Tertullian refutes the Marcionite idea that the true God would ever conceal himself: "Never shall God be hidden, never shall God be wanting."[17] The Marcionites respond that on this view the Creator is known by things foreign to him, whereas the true God should be known by things inherent to him. Tertullian replies that "no one is proved to exist to whom nothing is proved to belong. For as the Creator is shown to be God, God without any doubt, from the fact that all things are His, and nothing is strange to Him; so the rival god is seen to be no god, from the circumstance that nothing is his, and all things are therefore strange to him."[18] The fact that things manifest their eternal Creator is central to Tertullian's argument against Marcion on behalf of the God of Israel.

As a final point, I should note that Tertullian, like Paul at the Areopagus, defends Christianity against its pagan persecutors by arguing that Christianity

13. Tertullian, *Against Marcion* 1.10, p. 278.
14. Tertullian, *Against Marcion* 8, p. 276.
15. Tertullian, *Against Marcion* 10, p. 278.
16. Tertullian, *Against Marcion* 10, p. 278.
17. Tertullian, *Against Marcion* 10, p. 278.
18. Tertullian, *Against Marcion* 11, pp. 278–79.

proclaims the one God who was already known, even if not properly worshiped, by the pagans. In his *The Soul's Testimony*, Tertullian emphasizes that a careful reading of Greco-Roman poets and philosophers will show that Christians "have embraced nothing new or monstrous."[19] He goes on to complain, "We give offence by proclaiming that there is one God, to whom the name of God alone belongs, from whom all things come, and who is the Lord of the universe."[20] In his view, as we have seen, the human soul itself testifies to this living God by inevitably praising and praying to God. Tertullian does not thereby abandon the proclamation of Jesus Christ or the reality that God is Father, Son, and Holy Spirit. On the contrary, he is well known for developing the Latin trinitarian vocabulary of the church in his *Against Praxeas*. He states there that "this is the rule of faith which I profess; by it I testify that the Father, and the Son, and the Spirit are inseparable from each other. . . . The Father is one, and the Son one, and the Spirit one, and . . . they are distinct from each other."[21] As he goes on to make explicit, the Father, Son, and Holy Spirit are one God, distinct from each other by order of origin but not separate from each other.

Gregory of Nazianzus (ca. 329–ca. 390)

A theologian, poet, and pastor, Gregory of Nazianzus was born on an estate near Nazianzus in the region of Cappadocia (in modern-day Turkey). Gregory's father, a convert from a Jewish-Christian sect called the Hypsistarii, served for almost a half century as bishop of Nazianzus. As a young man, Gregory studied grammar and rhetoric both in Caesarea and in Athens. His friend Basil was among his fellow students. Gregory also traveled to Caesarea in Palestine, where Origen's library was preserved, and he spent a year in Alexandria. In 362, his father ordained him a priest. He subsequently became bishop of Sasima before becoming bishop of Nazianzus, and then, in 379 (though without full canonical status), archbishop of Constantinople, where he presided for a brief and turbulent period over the Council of Constantinople. Gregory is best known for his articulation and defense of the divinity of the Son and Holy Spirit in the unity of the Trinity.[22]

19. Tertullian, *The Soul's Testimony* 1, p. 175.
20. Tertullian, *The Soul's Testimony* 2, p. 176.
21. Tertullian, *Against Praxeas* 9, p. 603.
22. See Christopher A. Beeley, *Gregory of Nazianzus on the Trinity and the Knowledge of God: In Your Light We Shall See Light* (Oxford: Oxford University Press, 2008), 3–62; John A. McGuckin, *Saint Gregory of Nazianzus: An Intellectual Biography* (Crestwood, NY: St. Vladimir's Seminary Press, 2001); Frederick Norris, *Faith Gives Fullness to Reasoning: The*

In his *Second Theological Oration*, Gregory of Nazianzus demonstrates that God exists. The context of this demonstration is provided by the *First Theological Oration*. There Gregory inquires into what is required to discuss theology. Theology, he argues, is properly a subject only for those who are humbly undergoing purification of body and soul, who have taken the time to study, and who are filled with faith and recollected in spirit rather than curious or contentious. The theologian cannot hope to gain more than a small knowledge of the incomprehensible God, and so the theologian's inquiry should proceed in a modest and careful manner.

Gregory begins his *Second Oration* by recalling these strictures, and by "dedicating our sermon to our sermon's subjects, the Father, the Son, and the Holy Spirit, that the Father may approve, the Son aid, and the Holy Spirit inspire it—or rather that the single Godhead's single radiance, by mysterious paradox one in its distinctions and distinct in its connectedness, may enlighten it."[23] Gregory presents himself as a pastor able to communicate the fruits of his contemplation to his flock. Comparing himself to Moses and Elijah who ascended Mount Sinai, he states that he takes shelter in the "rock" who is the incarnate Word. From within faith in Christ, he sees the divine grandeur "inherent in the created things he has brought forth and governs."[24] God is so glorious that we can only see God through signs; even the angels cannot gaze on him directly. We can understand that God exists, but we cannot grasp the infinite in our finite minds. Thus the contemplative pastor occupies essentially the same humble position as the flock to which he preaches.

At this juncture, Gregory offers his brief demonstration that God exists. He sums up his case as follows: "That God, the creative and sustaining cause of all, exists, sight and instinctive law inform us—sight, which lights upon things seen as nobly fixed in their courses, borne along in, so to say, motionless movement; instinctive law, which infers their author through the things seen in their orderliness."[25] Rationality itself, in other words, requires that the universe must have received order and being from a transcendent cause. Gregory compares the universe to a "beautifully elaborated lyre."[26] A lyre cannot simply spring into being. It must have a craftsman who made it. Likewise, a lyre cannot make harmonious music on its own; it must have someone who

Five Theological Orations of Gregory Nazianzen (Leiden: Brill, 1997); Pelikan, *Christianity and Classical Culture*.

23. St. Gregory of Nazianzus, *On God and Christ: The Five Theological Orations and Two Letters to Cledonius*, trans. Frederick Williams and Lionel Wickham (Crestwood, NY: St. Vladimir's Seminary Press, 2002), *Second Oration* 28.1, p. 37.

24. Gregory of Nazianzus, *Second Oration* 28.3, p. 39.

25. Gregory of Nazianzus, *Second Oration* 28.6, pp. 40–41.

26. Gregory of Nazianzus, *Second Oration* 28.6, p. 41.

plays it. A lyre's existence and order are obvious to all, but equally obvious is the fact that of itself it cannot account for its existence and order. Just as a lyre receives existence and order from a craftsman, so too does the universe. That God exists is clear, therefore, but we should not on this basis imagine that we have formed an adequate concept of the infinite God. The Creator God infinitely surpasses every concept.

In the process of demonstrating that God fills all things without being bodily, Gregory adds another demonstration that God exists. He shows that God is not in the order of moving or moved things, since each of them depends on another, and none of them can say that they move the whole. The key question has to do with where the whole cosmos gets its being, movement, and order from. This question can only be answered by positing a transcendent mover who is not finite or dependent and who gives the whole cosmos its being and movement.

As we have seen, Gregory introduces his demonstration that God exists with a prayer to the Father, Son, and Holy Spirit. His arguments are philosophical rather than theological in the sense of requiring faith or revelation for their cogency. He contextualizes his arguments, however, fully within the life of Christian faith, and he includes in his arguments veiled references to the Psalms, 1 Corinthians, Jeremiah, and other scriptural texts. Are his arguments therefore not really rational demonstrations at all? Gregory considers that they certainly are rational demonstrations, accessible to those who think clearly about the matter. As he says after giving his comparison of the universe to a lyre that is making harmonious music, "Anyone who refuses to progress this far in following instinctive proofs must be very wanting in judgment."[27]

In the same *Oration*, Gregory goes on to consider metaphorical and proper names of God, such as spirit, fire, light, love, wisdom, justice, mind, and so forth. He urges his listeners to think of the perfection identified by each word, and then to realize that God is infinitely greater. Those who fail to do the latter, he explains, end up worshiping creatures such as the sun, the moon, the elements, the cosmos, or notable men and women. Enslaved by their passions, many humans have even worshiped gods who share their degraded passions. Here Gregory provides one more demonstration of the existence of God. Namely, when we recognize the finite perfection in the created thing and ascend from this finite perfection to the infinite perfection of God, we discover "God through the beauty and order of things seen, using sight as a guide to what transcends sight."[28] Gregory explains that this is the proper

27. Gregory of Nazianzus, *Second Oration* 28.6, p. 41.
28. Gregory of Nazianzus, *Second Oration* 28.13, p. 47.

work of our reason, which desires to find the maker of the sensible things we see around us. In reflecting on visible things, reason "leads us on through them to what transcends them, the very means of their continued existence."[29]

Gregory emphasizes that it is utterly unreasonable to suppose that the four elements, or any of the earthly or heavenly things that we can perceive, gave themselves being and ordered themselves. Speaking of a now-forgotten philosopher, Gregory states, "I commend the man, non-Christian though he was, who asked: 'What set these elements in motion and leads their cease-less, unimpeded flow?'"[30] The proofs from motion, from efficient causality, from degrees of perfection, and from the teleological order of things are here in view. As Gregory asks, "Supposing chance created them, what gave them order?"[31] What sustains them in being? Gregory answers that "it was surely their designer, who implants in all things reason whereby the universe is conducted and carried along."[32] He concludes that human reason, precisely because it was created by God, has the capacity to know God by reflecting on the things that we perceive by our senses. It is reason that leads "us up from things of sight to God."[33]

Gregory then considers the great men of Scripture—Jacob, Elijah, Manoah, Isaiah, Ezekiel, Paul, and so forth—who are depicted as in some way "seeing" God. None of them, he emphasizes, can thereby be said to have seen God's essence despite their enhanced knowledge of God. He ponders on the nature of human rationality and bodily inclinations, and on the natures of the land animals and of fish and birds. How is it, he asks, that birds come to be able to sing so beautifully? How can birds, who lack rationality, construct such efficient nests, and bees such elaborate honeycombs? How can packs of cranes execute such complicated in-flight patterns? From whence comes the beauty of the various plants, and the scents, tastes, and medicinal qualities of their fruits, leaves, and roots? If we ponder on these things, we will be able to see how bountiful the Creator is. Similarly, he invites us to ponder how it is that the Earth is supported in the heavens, how the oceans were formed, how the weather is regulated, how the stars were made and put in order, and how the sun and moon observe their constant course. His point here is not yet another proof that God exists but rather proof of what he calls "the richness of God" in creating and sustaining the good things of life.[34] But his reflections support

29. Gregory of Nazianzus, *Second Oration* 28.16, p. 49.
30. Gregory of Nazianzus, *Second Oration* 28.16, p. 49.
31. Gregory of Nazianzus, *Second Oration* 28.16, p. 49.
32. Gregory of Nazianzus, *Second Oration* 28.16, p. 49.
33. Gregory of Nazianzus, *Second Oration* 28.16, p. 49.
34. Gregory of Nazianzus, *Second Oration* 28.27, p. 59.

his earlier proofs, since we are reminded how extraordinary the existence and order of finite things are.

He concludes the *Second Oration* where he began: with the holy Trinity. After a brief consideration of the nature of the angels, who sing God's praise, he states, "If our hymn [the *Second Oration*] has been worthy of its theme, it is the grace of the Trinity, of the Godhead one and three; if desire remains incompletely satisfied, that way too my argument can claim success."[35] Reason can demonstrate that neither we ourselves nor anything that we see around us can be accounted for without appeal to the transcendent God. But in so doing, reason has to admit its own limitations as well, and thus the very success of our reasoning leads us to worship and praise the inexhaustible mystery of the Father, Son, and Holy Spirit—one God, who has revealed himself to us in Jesus Christ. Reason's limitations do not prevent it from demonstrating that God exists, but the inexhaustibly wonderful depths of God go far beyond what reason apprehends.

Gregory's poetry also sheds light on the paths that he finds fruitful for demonstrating God's existence, although the genre of poetry does not allow for fully spelled-out demonstrations. For example, in his poem "Concerning the World," he asks with respect to the combinations of things in the world (such as matter and form), "If things were commingled, how did they get to be mingled? Who mingled them if not God?"[36] If God is the "mingler," then surely, says Gregory, God is the Creator. He goes on to argue this more determinatively by employing the analogy of human craftsmanship. Since we can see that the universe shows clear signs of being ordered like a craft, we should accept that there must be a craftsman. Gregory states, "A potter . . . puts form to his clay when he turns the wheel, a goldsmith gives it to gold, and a sculptor to stones. Credit God with more than you do our mind, O lover of no origins."[37] The fact that Gregory is addressing a "lover of no origins" indicates the difficulty that some of his educated contemporaries had in accepting the idea of a Creator God.

Similarly, he makes use of the evidences of a craftsman's work in his poem "On Providence." As he points out, there is too much evidence of the work of a governing Mind to suppose that the universe had no Creator. Against those who appeal simply to chance to explain order in the universe, he responds forcefully, "For it's not by chance, the nature of such and so great a world, wherewith nothing comparable can be thought—do not credit so much to

35. Gregory of Nazianzus, *Second Oration* 28.31, p. 63.

36. Gregory of Nazianzus, *On God and Man: The Theological Poetry of St. Gregory Nazianzus*, trans. Peter Gilbert (Crestwood, NY: St. Vladimir's Seminary Press, 2001), 1.1.4, p. 48.

37. Gregory of Nazianzus, *On God and Man* 1.1.4, p. 49.

chancy reasons. Who ever saw a house not built by hands? Who's seen a self-built ship, or a fleet chariot? a shield and a helmet?"[38] He adds that it is not only the order of nonrational things that bears witness to a Creator God. The same witness is borne by the preservation of this order over time. The vast universe could hardly have retained its order were there no provident God. As Gregory puts it, "Nor would so much have lasted through time, minus a ruler; and the choir would have stopped, I'd say, without its conductor."[39] He is aware that these are not formal demonstrations of the existence of God, but they show how strong he thinks the evidence is, given the existence, order, and preservation of the vast universe of nonrational things.

Again, in another poem also titled "On Providence," Gregory responds to atheists—those who deny a creative cause of the universe—as well as to polytheists. Against atheists, Gregory states, "Away with them, those who deny what is divine, and ascribe no cause to the good, ineffable composition of the universe, whether in creation or in the upkeep of all things."[40] The goodness, composition, and preservation of the universe require a transcendent cause. Gregory goes on to say that "the deniers of Providence," seemingly out of fear of being redeemed by God, "either assign the universe to an erratic 'swoosh!' or else credit it to the movement of the stars."[41] The second option particularly interests him. Could it be that a part of the universe is the source of the movement of the whole? In answer, Gregory suggests that stars cannot be unmoved movers in the strict sense, and so they too require a source of motion as well as a source of order and preservation. He inquires in this regard, "And how, and whence, and by whom are these [stars] moved? If it's by God, how can that be first, which God turns round? . . . But, if it's not from God, how is it to stand up out of anarchy, or again, from battling with one stronger?"[42] Poetically, then, Gregory repeatedly calls attention to the fact that contingent things cannot be the fundamental source of their movement, order, and preservation.

Although it is not a demonstration of God's existence, it should also be mentioned that Gregory has a keen existential sense of the contingency and obscurity of our lives. Many of the problems that lead us today to ask urgently whether God exists were well known to Gregory. For instance, in a poem titled "Conversation with the World," he probes into the mystery of the earth's motion, in light of which humans seem mere insects: "I've an issue, world, to

38. Gregory of Nazianzus, *On God and Man* 1.1.5, p. 53.
39. Gregory of Nazianzus, *On God and Man* 1.1.5, p. 53.
40. Gregory of Nazianzus, *On God and Man* 1.1.6, p. 76.
41. Gregory of Nazianzus, *On God and Man* 1.1.6, p. 76.
42. Gregory of Nazianzus, *On God and Man* 1.1.6, p. 76.

bring up with you. Who are you, and whence, teach first, and whither do you roll? And how do you revolve me, like a wheel that carries an ant?"[43] The same comparison of the human being to an insignificant ant comes in his poem "On the Precariousness of Human Nature," where he speaks plaintively to the world, "Dear world, though not so very dear, why do you bear down on me, who trudge wheezing like a tiny ant distressed at his sore burden?"[44] In this poem, he confesses that God formed the world and that the world itself proclaims its Creator, and yet he remains existentially distressed. Likewise, in his poem "On Human Nature," he meditates closely on the fast-moving passage of time and on his ever-changing life, in which he can find no security. Describing himself as sitting in a beautiful shady grove on a sunny day, with a cool brook and the happy sound of birds and locusts, he nonetheless expresses discontent: "Who was I? Who am I? What shall I be? I don't know clearly. Nor can I find one better stocked with wisdom. But, as through thick fog, I wander every which way, with nothing, not a dream, of the things I long for."[45] This existential lack and longing prepares the way, as it does for many people, for reflection on God, especially since Gregory is not expressing agnostic doubt but rather misery at his as-yet unclear and always changing existential and spiritual condition.[46]

Augustine (354–430)

Augustine, born in Thagaste in North Africa to a pagan father and Christian mother, studied and taught rhetoric at Carthage before pursuing a career as a professional rhetorician in Rome and Milan. During his twenties, he was a Manichean, holding that earthly life was part of a cosmic drama between spirit (good) and matter (evil). His views on evil were changed by his reading of Neoplatonic philosophy, and his views on Christianity were altered by Ambrose's allegorical interpretation of the Old Testament. After converting to Christianity at age thirty-three, Augustine soon became bishop of Hippo and spent the rest of his life preaching and writing in an effort to understand more deeply the realities of faith. In addition to his polemical works against the Manicheans, Donatists, and Pelagians, he preached on the Psalms, the

43. Gregory of Nazianzus, *On God and Man* 1.2.11, p. 129.
44. Gregory of Nazianzus, *On God and Man* 1.2.12, p. 130.
45. Gregory of Nazianzus, *On God and Man* 1.2.14, p. 132.
46. For discussion of Gregory's poetry, see Brian E. Daley, SJ, "Systematic Theology in Homeric Dress: *Poemata Arcana*," in *Re-Reading Gregory of Nazianzus: Essays on History, Theology, and Culture*, ed. Christopher A. Beeley (Washington, DC: Catholic University of America Press, 2012), 3–12.

Gospel of John, and other biblical texts, and he wrote an account of his own life (*Confessions*), of human history (*City of God*), and of contemplative ascent to the Trinity (*De Trinitate*).[47]

In Augustine's *Confessions*, he is concerned with the question that preoccupied him for the first fifteen years of his adult life and indeed, in another way, for the remainder of his life: How can we come to know the true God? He begins the book with a famous description of human desire for God as constitutive of our nature. Even if we do not yet know God, we desire him: "You stir man to take pleasure in praising you, because you have made us for yourself, and our heart is restless until it rests in you."[48] By seeking God, we come to find him and praise him. Indeed, God himself causes us to know him by giving us the gift of faith in Christ Jesus, through the mediation of human preachers. Augustine here undertakes a biblically rooted discussion of the divine attributes, drawing on Genesis, the Psalms, Romans, and Jeremiah.

In these opening pages of the *Confessions*, Augustine is primarily interested in how our wills come to seek God and cling to him. As he says, "Who will enable me to find rest in you? Who will grant me that you come to my heart and intoxicate it, so that I forget my evils and embrace my one and only good, yourself?"[49] We have turned away from God by sin—both our own and that of our first parents. We need God to restore us by awakening us to his saving love in Christ and by enabling us to embrace Christ's love. Augustine frequently interjects comments to God such as, "In you are the constant causes of inconstant things. All mutable things have in you their immutable origins. In you all irrational and temporal things have the everlasting causes of their life."[50] These comments illustrate the contingency and dependence of creatures, and creatures' inability to be their own cause.

When Augustine tells the story of his youth, we learn how he became entranced by Cicero's *Hortensius*, with its advice to pursue wisdom; how

47. See Serge Lancel, *Saint Augustine*, trans. Antonia Nevill (London: SCM Press, 2002); Peter Brown, *Augustine of Hippo: A Biography*, 2nd ed. (Berkeley: University of California Press, 2000); John M. Rist, *Augustine: Ancient Thought Baptized* (Cambridge: Cambridge University Press, 1994); Matthew Levering, *The Theology of Augustine: An Introductory Guide to His Most Important Works* (Grand Rapids: Baker Academic, 2013).

48. Augustine, *Confessions* 1.1.1, trans. Henry Chadwick (Oxford: Oxford University Press, 1991), 3. For development of this theme in contemporary philosophy, see John Haldane, *Reasonable Faith* (London: Routledge, 2010), chap. 5: "The Restless Heart: Philosophy and the Meaning of Theism." See also C. S. Lewis, *Mere Christianity* (New York: Macmillan, 1952), 119–21; Lewis, "The Weight of Glory," in Lewis, *The Weight of Glory and Other Addresses*, ed. Walter Hooper (New York: Macmillan, 1980), 3–19; S. L. Frank, *The Meaning of Life*, trans. Boris Jakim (Grand Rapids: Eerdmans, 2010), chap. 5.

49. Augustine, *Confessions* 1.5.5, p. 5.

50. Augustine, *Confessions* 1.6.9, p. 7.

the Scriptures seemed insipid in comparison with Cicero; and how he joined the Manichees due to his inability otherwise to account for evil in the world. During this period, he believed in an ethereal but nonetheless bodily God. He also dabbled in astrology. In these chapters, Augustine intersperses very brief fragments of demonstrations of God's existence. For example, he states, "For wherever the human soul turns itself, other than to you, it is fixed in sorrows, even if it is fixed upon beautiful things external to you and external to itself, which would nevertheless be nothing if they did not have their being from you. . . . Let these transient things be the ground on which my soul praises you (Ps. 145:2), 'God creator of all.'"[51]

The demonstration of God's existence that Augustine eventually gives does not come from reflection on sensible things, although as we have seen from his fragmentary remarks, he is well aware of such demonstrations and values them. When he gives his full-fledged demonstration, he takes it from the Neoplatonists, since it was by reading their books that he finally overcame his erroneous idea that God possesses magnitude. As he says, "By the Platonic books I was admonished to return into myself."[52] They directed him to reflect on his soul and its acts. When he did so, he recognized that his soul's intellectual light was guided by an immutable, eternal light. When we make judgments of truth, we are perceiving the presence of eternal and unchanging Being, Truth, and Goodness. An example of this is mathematical truth: no matter whether there were human minds to know it, the three angles of a triangle would always equal 180 degrees. Our minds here encounter eternal Truth, unchanging and without magnitude, that does not depend in any way on the existence of finite, changing things. Augustine states, "The person who knows the truth knows it [Truth], and he who knows it knows eternity."[53] The eternal light of Truth exists in an infinite mode, unrestricted by any limitation, and it is Good. When with awe and love we encounter the eternal light, we encounter the source of everything changing and finite. Augustine therefore proclaims, "Eternal truth and true love and beloved eternity: you are my God. . . . When I first came to know you, you raised me up to make me see that what I saw is Being, and that I who saw am not yet Being. And you gave a shock to the weakness of my sight by the strong radiance of your rays, and I trembled with love and awe."[54] Since we are finite and changing, we are radically different from what we here encounter, and yet by entering

51. Augustine, *Confessions* 4.10.15, p. 62. The interior quotation is of Ambrose's hymn "Deus creator omnium."

52. Augustine, *Confessions* 7.10.16, p. 123.

53. Augustine, *Confessions* 7.10.16, p. 123.

54. Augustine, *Confessions* 7.10.16, p. 123.

into our souls we can ascend upward and touch the eternal source of all that is. By contemplating the Eternal, furthermore, our souls become likened to the Eternal.

Has Augustine thereby left behind Paul's claim that God "has been clearly perceived in the things that have been made" (Rom. 1:20)? On the contrary, the soul itself, with its ability to recognize the eternal source in which it participates, is one of "the things that have been made." Starting with the soul and its ascent to the eternal source of its intellectual light, he arrives at the fact that God exists (and is eternal, infinite, immaterial, and so forth). This procedure then enables him, in a downward movement, to reflect on finite, contingent things. He states, "I considered the other things below you, and I saw that neither can they be said absolutely to be or absolutely not to be. They are because they come from you. But they are not because they are not what you are."[55] In other words, they have finite, contingent, participated existence. They are good insofar as they exist, but they are not the infinite good. This insight that insofar as something exists, it is good, enables Augustine to account for evil as a corruption, a lack or privation in the being of a finite thing (including in the being of the human will). Despite the presence of such corruption in the cosmos, nonetheless Augustine can see that corrupt parts do not destroy the goodness of the whole.

In Neoplatonic fashion, Augustine also asks himself why he considers some bodies to be beautiful and others not. He recognizes that in making judgments about beauty, he makes judgments of truth and thereby encounters the light of eternal Truth transcending his mutable mind. His mind rises from the perception of external bodies, to the internal reception of sense impressions, to the power of reasoning based on sense impressions, to the power of reasoning simply in itself, to the unchangeable light of Truth that governs the power of reasoning, to the knowledge and love of the unchangeable and Eternal. Here Augustine encounters God: "So in the flash of a trembling glance it attained to that which is. At that moment I saw your 'invisible nature understood through the things which are made' (Rom. 1:20)."[56]

55. Augustine, *Confessions* 7.10.16, p. 124.

56. Augustine, *Confessions* 7.17.23, p. 127. For discussion of book 7, see Phillip Cary's "Book Seven: Inner Vision as the Goal of Augustine's Life," in *A Reader's Companion to Augustine's Confessions*, ed. Kim Paffenroth and Robert P. Kennedy (Louisville: Westminster John Knox, 2003), 107–26. Cary exaggerates, however, when he concludes, "Augustine clearly prays and worships and sings to the god of the Platonists, believing that this is no different from the Truth signified by Holy Scripture, to which Jesus Christ is the way. *Our* problem with Book Seven of the *Confessions*, I suggest, is what to make of this. Augustine wants us to worship and pray to the god of philosophy in the name of Jesus Christ. Shall we follow him in this?" Rather than praying, worshiping, and singing to the god of philosophy, Augustine is arguing that the Platonists

According to Augustine, a central problem with this intellectual demonstration is that our minds cannot focus for long on God without his help. Not only are our minds weak, but also, and more important, so are our wills. We need healing from our preference for sensible things over God. We need to learn Christ's humility and charity in order to be cured from our absurd pride and recognize our utter dependence on the Triune God. Yet the rational demonstration of God's existence remains an important stage in Augustine's path to faith in God.

Elsewhere, in numerous places in his vast corpus, Augustine makes reference to ways in which we can come to know that God exists. In "Tractate 106 on the Gospel of John," for instance, Augustine observes that God was in some way known throughout the world even before the spread of faith in Christ. This was so not only because God created humans to know him but also because God is so wondrously knowable. Augustine comments, "For such is the energy of the true Godhead, that it cannot be altogether and utterly hidden from any rational creature, so long as it makes use of its reason."[57] He thinks that despite the prevalence of sin, almost all humans prior to Christ recognized a supreme God who is the maker of the world, even though these same humans worshiped gods along with this God.

In *On Christian Doctrine*, Augustine remarks that "when the one God of gods is thought of, even by those who recognize, invoke, and worship other gods either in Heaven or on earth, He is thought of in such a way that the thought seeks to attain something than which there is nothing better or more sublime."[58] God is known as that "than which there is nothing better." Admittedly, this leads some people to worship the sky, the world, some luminous or infinite mass, or anthropomorphic gods. When we reflect rationally on God, however, we are able to perceive that God is elevated "above all things mutable, either visible and corporal or intelligible and spiritual," because all people recognize that there cannot be anything greater than God.[59] Augustine points out that "since all those who think of God think of something living, only they can think of Him without absurdity who think of Him as life itself."[60] Furthermore, since a foolish life is of less value than a wise life, it is necessary

were able to know truths about the living God—though it would not be appropriate to pray, worship, and sing to the "god of the Platonists" because they also had a number of false ideas.

57. Augustine, *Lectures or Tractates on the Gospel according to St. John*, trans. John Gibb and James Innes, in *Augustine: Homilies on the Gospel of John, Homilies on the First Epistle of John, Soliloquies*, ed. Philip Schaff (Peabody, MA: Hendrickson, 1995), 400.

58. Augustine, *On Christian Doctrine* 1.7, trans. D. W. Robertson Jr. (New York: Macmillan, 1958), 11.

59. Augustine, *On Christian Doctrine* 1.7, p. 11.

60. Augustine, *On Christian Doctrine* 1.8, p. 12.

to conceive of God as not only infinite life but infinite wisdom. Indeed, this conception itself constitutes a demonstration of God, since the truth that we perceive is immutable and compels assent. To cling steadfastly to this truth, however, requires faith in Christ.

In *City of God*, Augustine has high praise for the Platonists' knowledge of God. Augustine considers that either Plato's travels enabled him to come into contact with the books of Genesis and Exodus, or else Plato's superb insights simply confirm Paul's statement in Romans 1:20 that "ever since the creation of the world his invisible nature, namely, his eternal power and deity, has been clearly perceived in the things that have been made."[61] Augustine describes the Platonists as "philosophers who have conceived of God, the supreme and true God, as the author of all created things, the light of knowledge, the Final Good of all activity, and who have recognized him as being for us the origin of existence, the truth of doctrine and the blessedness of life."[62] Yet Plato and his successors still worshiped multiple gods.[63]

In his *First Catechetical Instruction* (*De catechizandis rudibus*), written to explain the steps of Christian catechesis, Augustine refers to the demonstration of God's existence from the order of the universe. He states that catechumens should be led away from focus on earthly things and toward "the contemplation of the skill or design of the contriver," so that they might "soar upward to the admiration and praise of the all-creating God."[64] The demonstration of God's existence played an important role in his own coming to faith, and so it is not surprising that it has a place in his catechetical handbook.[65]

John of Damascus (ca. 676–ca. 749)

Born into a prominent Christian family in Damascus under the Umayyad caliphate less than a half century after Muhammad died (632), John of Damascus, whose given name was Mansur ibn Sarjun, received a classical Hellenistic education. Like his father and grandfather, John served for a time in the fiscal administration of Damascus. Upon becoming a monk in Jerusalem, he took

61. See Augustine, *City of God* 8.12, trans. Henry Bettenson (New York: Penguin, 1984), 315.
62. Augustine, *City of God* 3.9, p. 311.
63. Augustine, *City of God* 1.8, p. 311.
64. Augustine, *The First Catechetical Instruction* 12, trans. Joseph P. Christopher (Westminster, MD: Newman, 1946), 41–42.
65. John Rist highlights Augustine's argument for the existence of God in book 2 of *On Human Responsibility*, which I have not treated here. See Rist, *Augustine*, 67–71. See also L. P. Gerson, "Saint Augustine's Neoplatonic Argument for the Existence of God," *The Thomist* 45 (1981): 571–84.

the name John. He seems to have been ordained a priest, perhaps serving the Church of the Anastasis, and to have been close to the patriarch of Jerusalem, John V, and to the metropolitan of Damascus, Peter II. In addition to liturgical poetry and homilies, John wrote against iconoclasm and monothelitism. He is best known for his three-part work *The Fount of Knowledge*, which helped to refine and define the content of Christian faith.[66]

The first part of *The Fount of Knowledge*, titled "The Philosophical Chapters," is devoted entirely to the study of philosophy, which he defines in various ways: "a knowledge of the nature of things which have being"; "knowledge of both divine and human things"; a knowledge of death; "the making of one's self like God" through wisdom; and "the love of God."[67] This first part largely consists in a summary of Aristotelian philosophical terms. The second part examines a large number of faulty philosophical schools, Jewish sects, and Christian heresies (among which he numbers Islam). The third part bears the title "An Exact Exposition of the Orthodox Faith," often published on its own as *The Orthodox Faith*. In this part, he attempts to summarize the whole of what Christians believe.

In his preface to *The Fount of Knowledge*, John first speaks of the purification that is necessary for the theologian who dares to speak of the highest realities. He identifies Moses as the model of the theologian. Moses received a divine theophany at the burning bush, and Moses was the first to learn the divine name "He who is." Yet even Moses was hesitant to speak publicly and asked that Aaron be appointed in his stead. John would have done the same, but his bishop had commanded him to write *The Fount of Knowledge*.

John then turns to the structure of his book. He explains his lengthy first part on philosophy as follows: "First of all I shall set forth the best contributions of the philosophers of the Greeks, because whatever there is of good has been given to men from above by God, since 'every best gift and every perfect gift is from above, coming down from the Father of lights' [James 1:17]."[68] Like a bee, he will gather what is good from the Greek philosophers, who as pagans are "our enemies," but who nonetheless teach much truth, intermixed though it is with error.[69] He notes that after treating Greek philosophy and the history of heresy, he will exposit in his third part "that truth which . . .

66. See Andrew Louth, *St. John Damascene: Tradition and Originality in Byzantine Theology* (Oxford: Oxford University Press, 2002), 3–14.
67. John of Damascus, *The Philosophical Chapters*, in *Writings*, trans. Frederick H. Chase (Washington, DC: Catholic University of America Press, 1958), chap. 3.
68. John of Damascus, *The Fount of Knowledge*, in *Writings*, trans. Frederick H. Chase (Washington, DC: Catholic University of America Press, 1958), pref., p. 5.
69. John of Damascus, *The Fount of Knowledge* pref., p. 5.

has been embellished and adorned by the sayings of the divinely inspired prophets, the divinely taught fishermen, and the God-bearing shepherds and teachers—that truth, the glory of which flashes out from within to brighten with its radiance, when they encounter it, them that are duly purified and rid of speculations."[70]

John's philosophical exposition in the first part of *The Fount of Knowledge* does not contain a demonstration of the existence of God. Instead, he devotes his labor to defining key philosophical terms, such as species, genus, substance, accident, predication, form, and habit, as well as to delineating the methods of dialectic and logic and to describing certain aspects of natural philosophy, such as what thunder and lightning are. In his third part, *The Orthodox Faith*, one might not expect to find a philosophical demonstration of God's existence, because this third part is supposed to be devoted to the teachings of the prophets, apostles, and bishops. Yet it is here that we find demonstrations of God's existence.

John begins this third part by noting that after the fall, not only humans but even angels need revelation in order to know God intimately. Nonetheless, God has given all humans a way to know him: "through nature the knowledge of the existence of God has been revealed by Him to all men."[71] Thus we do not depend solely on revelation for all our knowledge of God; human reason can know that God exists. In a brief description of the ways that God has made himself known, John first states that the harmony and order of the creation show God's majesty. He then discusses the Mosaic law and the prophets and the revelation given through Jesus Christ. Citing Psalm 14:1, "The fool says in his heart, 'There is no God,'" John comments that because some people deny that God exists, when the gospel was first announced the apostles did many miraculous signs and taught powerfully about God so as to "draw up those people alive in the net of their miracles from the depths of the ignorance of God to the light of his knowledge."[72] Now that miracles are no longer as frequent and the light of teaching no longer so pure, John invokes the aid of the Father, Son, and Holy Spirit with the goal of repeating the apostles' teaching about God. He does so first by means of rational demonstrations of God's existence.

The first demonstration is from movement and contingency. John begins by observing that "all things are either created or uncreated."[73] The created

70. John of Damascus, *The Fount of Knowledge* pref., pp. 5–6.
71. John of Damascus, *The Orthodox Faith* 1.1, in *Writings*, trans. Frederick H. Chase (Washington, DC: Catholic University of America Press, 1958), 166.
72. John of Damascus, *The Orthodox Faith* 1.3, p. 168.
73. John of Damascus, *The Orthodox Faith* 1.3, p. 169.

things are by definition changeable, having originated through a change. He notes that "all beings that fall within our experience, including even the angels, are subject to change and alteration and to being moved in various ways."[74] Material beings change by generation and corruption, or with respect to quantity, quality, or place. Immaterial beings such as angels (or demons) or our souls change "by free choice, progressing in good or receding, exerting themselves or slackening."[75] Things that change, John asserts, must have been created or caused by something else. Were there no uncreated Creator, then there would be an infinite explanatory regress with regard to the being of these changeable things. There must, then, be an uncreated and utterly unchangeable source of all things.

The second demonstration is from "the very harmony of creation, its preservation and governing."[76] If there were no God to put the universe together and to preserve it, then the universe would be unable to hold together or to continue in such an orderly fashion. The four elements are too contrary to combine together and to remain combined on their own. As the "architect," the one who combined, arranged, set in motion, and governs the elements must be the all-powerful Creator, the one who brings all things "into being."[77] The only other possible supposition would be that the elements arose from spontaneous generation. Even if one were to grant that spontaneous generation brought things into existence and gave things their arrangement—which John grants only by way of supposition—one would still have to account for the preservation of this order rather than its dissolution. If only spontaneous chance were involved, then dissolution would quickly follow. Therefore, chance cannot explain the existence of the universe. What explains the existence of the universe is none other than the existence of God. John makes clear that we can know that God exists but not what God's nature is. We cannot form an adequate concept of divine existence.

74. John of Damascus, *The Orthodox Faith* 1.3, p. 169.

75. John of Damascus, *The Orthodox Faith* 1.3, p. 169.

76. In *The Consolation of Philosophy*, similarly, Boethius argues that if there were no transcendent God, three kinds of order that we see in the universe could not be sustained. First, the universe's diverse parts would never have come together into a unified whole. Second, even if they had come together, they would break apart rather than remaining a unified whole. Third, the orderly movements of the cosmos would not remain orderly. Boethius concludes that "whatever this is by which created things continue in being and move, I call by the name used by all, God." See Boethius, *The Consolation of Philosophy* 3.12, trans. S. J. Tester, in Boethius, *The Theological Tractates and The Consolation of Philosophy* (Cambridge, MA: Harvard University Press, 1973), 299.

77. John of Damascus, *The Orthodox Faith* 1.3, p. 170.

It is worth noting that in the course of his ensuing discussion of the divine attributes, John critiques the Stoic view that there are immaterial bodies. John observes that even if there were such a thing as immaterial bodies, an immaterial body would be movable, since bodies are subject to motion. If so, then such a body could not be unmoved but would require a mover or efficient cause. To avoid infinite explanatory regress, and thereby to account for the existence of immaterial bodies, we would have to arrive at an unmoved mover. An unmoved mover would not be subject to motion, and thus would not be spatially contained as bodies inevitably are. John draws the conclusion that this unmoved mover, pure spirit, is God, "and by His immovability He moves all things."[78]

At the end of his section on the divine existence and attributes, John states, "It has been sufficiently demonstrated that God exists and that His essence is incomprehensible. Furthermore, those who believe in sacred Scripture have no doubt that He is one and not several."[79] He proceeds to identify biblical texts that support God's unity and to argue for it philosophically as well. The key point for our purposes is that God's revelation in the Law and the Prophets and in Jesus Christ does not change what we can and should learn from God's revelation in creation. For John, the rational demonstrations of God's existence continue to be helpful and instructive for believers.

Anselm of Canterbury (1033–1109)

Born in Aosta in the western Alps, southernmost outpost of the kingdom of Burgundy, Anselm became a clerk at the church in Aosta before quarreling with his father and crossing the Alps into Burgundy in his early twenties. He arrived at the Benedictine Abbey of Bec in western Normandy around 1059. Under the tutelage of Lanfranc, he acquired a superb education. When Lanfranc left to become archbishop of Canterbury, Anselm became abbot of Bec. In 1093 he succeeded Lanfranc as archbishop of Canterbury. For the remainder of his life, he struggled with King William II and King Henry I over investiture. In addition to his prayers and meditations, he authored numerous works on such subjects as God, original sin, predestination and free will, the virgin birth, and why God became human.[80]

---

78. John of Damascus, *The Orthodox Faith* 1.4, p. 171.
79. John of Damascus, *The Orthodox Faith* 1.5, p. 172.
80. See R. W. Southern, *Saint Anselm: A Portrait in a Landscape* (Cambridge: Cambridge University Press, 1990); G. R. Evans, "Anselm's Life, Works, and Immediate Influence," in *The Cambridge Companion to Anselm*, ed. Brian Davies and Brian Leftow (Cambridge: Cambridge University Press, 2004), 5–31.

Anselm begins his *Monologion* by explaining that his fellow Benedictine monks have requested him to write down his view of "how one ought to meditate on the divine essence, and about certain other things related to such a meditation."[81] One might imagine that such a meditation would be, for monks, a spiritual experience involving prayer, *lectio divina*, and ascetic mortification. But in fact Anselm observes that his fellow monks "prescribed the following form for me in writing this meditation: absolutely nothing in it would be established by the authority of Scripture; rather, whatever the conclusion of each individual investigation might assert, the necessity of reason would concisely prove, and the clarity of truth would manifestly show, that it is the case."[82] At first glance, given our modern idea of what medieval Benedictine monks should be, this seems quite surprising. Why did they bracket the authority of Scripture and instead seek proofs that bear "the necessity of reason"?

It should be kept in mind that the monastery at Bec was no rustic retreat center for those who wished to abandon the use of reason and enter into a purely ascetical-mystical life. By the time that Anselm arrived, the monastery at Bec had become a major center of learning, with its own school that drew students from across Europe. The monastery's abbot, Lanfranc, was "famous as a teacher of the liberal arts" (grammar, logic, dialectic, and rhetoric) and a brilliant theologian. He was the author of a *Commentary on the Epistles of St. Paul* as well as a major work that challenged Berengar's theory of the Eucharist and instead advocated an "account of the Eucharistic change" rooted in the "Aristotelian doctrine of substance."[83]

Even so, when Anselm speaks of a "meditation," he does not have in mind the work of a modern professor or teacher, whose research can be and often is abstracted from the spiritual life. Richard Southern notes that for Anselm, "*Cogitatio* can be, and often is, concerned with worldly things and even with corrupt aims, whereas *meditatio* is solely concerned with pure reflection on the essences of things, whether knowable from the empirical data of the senses or from the intuitive knowledge of the mind."[84] In the *Monologion*, Anselm is engaged in *meditatio*, and this task belongs to the virtuous movement of the mind to God. Southern comments, "Meditation may be described as embryonic contemplation, preparatory to the perfect contemplation of Heaven."[85]

---

81. Anselm, *Monologion* prol., in Anselm, *Monologion and Proslogion, with the Replies of Gaunilo and Anselm*, trans. Thomas Williams (Indianapolis: Hackett, 1995), 3. Subsequent references to Anselm's writings are found in this edition.
82. Anselm, *Monologion* prol.
83. Southern, *Saint Anselm*, 39, 49.
84. Ibid., 79.
85. Ibid., 78.

Minds that are purified can prepare themselves for heavenly contemplation, in eternal life, by means of meditation. This was Anselm's purpose.

Why, then, do Anselm's fellow monks, and clearly also Anselm himself, desire that this meditation proceed "by means of a plain style, unsophisticated arguments, and straightforward disputation"?[86] Why do they insist on demonstrative knowledge about God obtained solely on the basis of reason and without the aid of revelation in any way? The answer, I think, consists in their high view of human reason. Created by God as a finite participation in the infinite divine light (the infinite divine wisdom), human reason surely cannot have been left without a way to know God.

In the *Monologion*, Anselm argues that human reason receives from God the power to know him. Thus, Anselm's first chapter begins with the claim that if anyone does not already know the one, supreme, self-sufficient, happy, omnipotent, good Creator God, then "I think that he could at least convince himself of most of these things by reason alone, if he is even moderately intelligent."[87] Anselm thinks that many demonstrative paths to knowledge of the one God are available, but he settles on the one that starts from the fact that we desire good things rather than bad things for ourselves. We know a number of good things that we desire. But when many things, otherwise widely diverse, share "goodness," what is it that they are sharing? This is an especially pressing question when we recognize that things possess differing degrees of goodness. If it is possible to have more or less goodness, but if "goodness" itself is the same, then "goodness" can be distinguished from particular good things. Anselm concludes that all good things are good by sharing in goodness. On this basis, he seeks to identify what goodness is. It must be, as he says, a great good. It must also be good of itself, rather than being good by sharing in the goodness of another. In short, it must be self-subsistent goodness, having its goodness through itself rather than requiring an external source of goodness. Such a thing must be "supremely good and supremely great—in other words, supreme among all existing things."[88]

Anselm then points out that existence is like goodness. We know of many things that share in existence. None of these things is the source of its own existence. Yet they definitely share in existence as something common among them. Existence can therefore be distinguished from particular existents. Indeed, for particular existents to exist, they must receive or share in existence from an external source, since none of them is existence itself. As Anselm

---

86. Anselm, *Monologion* prol., p. 3.
87. Anselm, *Monologion* 1, p. 10.
88. Anselm, *Monologion* 1, p. 12.

puts it, "whatever exists, exists through something": existing things require a source of existence.[89] Since existence is the same in all things that exist, they must share in one common source. This common source cannot itself depend on another thing for existence, since in that case it would be simply one more thing among all the things that share in existence. Instead, it must exist of itself; it must be self-subsistent existence. As such, it must exist in a supreme fashion, and therefore must be the greatest of all things (the supreme good). In this way, Anselm thinks that he has proven the existence of God, the transcendent source of the existence and goodness of all things.

Anselm also provides a short proof based on degrees of perfection. Some things are better than others. Anselm envisions a set of natures—wood, horse, human, and so forth—of which we can rightly say that there are degrees of perfection. Wood cannot move on its own; a horse can. The question is whether this chain of ascending natures stretches infinitely upward, so that there is an infinite array of ever-greater natures in existence. This strikes Anselm as an absurd claim; it is not possible that the chain of ever-greater existing natures goes on infinitely. Therefore, some nature (or natures) must be supreme, so as to be inferior to no other nature. Anselm raises the possibility that there might be more than one nature that is inferior to no other nature. This would entail that the supreme natures be equals. But, as Anselm says, being equals means possessing something that is the same. If this same thing is their nature, then they are in fact the same nature. If the same thing that they share and that makes them inferior to no other nature is something less than their nature, then they are not supreme; they would be great through something else and therefore that something else would in fact be greater than they. It follows that there is one superior nature that is inferior to none. This superior nature must exist in the greatest way and be the greatest good. This can only be the case if the superior nature is self-subsistent existence, and all other things exist by sharing in it; such self-subsistent existence must be the supreme good. Again, Anselm concludes that he has demonstrated the existence of the transcendent God.

Anselm goes on to show that this supreme nature "is not included in any common classification of substances, since every other nature is excluded from having an essence in common with him."[90] Further, God exists "in an unqualified sense"; he is sheer, perfect existence, transcending any limitations such as temporality or change.[91] Anselm recognizes, therefore, that his demonstration

89. Anselm, *Monologion* 3, p. 12.
90. Anselm, *Monologion* 27, p. 46.
91. Anselm, *Monologion* 28, p. 47.

of the existence of the supreme nature, of self-subsistent existence and goodness, does not mean that we can understand or categorize this supreme nature
as though it were one nature among other natures. God is utterly ineffable.

Anselm draws out various other divine attributes on the basis of God's
self-subsistent existence. In the *Monologion*, he also has much to say about
the Trinity via the notion of God's Word or utterance.[92] He also treats the
human soul, which he takes to be the image of the Triune God (following
Augustine's triad of remembering, understanding, and loving). He concludes
that we are made to know and love God and, indeed, that "it is he alone
whom all other natures should lovingly worship and worshipfully love with
all their power, from whom alone they ought to hope for good things, to
whom alone they ought to flee from troubles, to whom alone they ought to
pray for anything at all."[93]

In the prologue of his *Proslogion*, Anselm tells us that after publishing the
Monologion, he began to wonder whether there is a simpler demonstration of
God's existence, one that would comprise not a set of arguments but a single
argument. As he recalls, he was looking for "a single argument that needed
nothing but itself alone for proof, that would by itself be enough to show
that God really exists; that he is the supreme good, who depends on nothing
else, but on whom all things depend for their being and for their well-being;
and whatever we believe about the divine nature."[94] Eventually, he recalls, he
gave up searching for such a proof. But then, all of a sudden, an idea came to
him regarding how this simple proof might be constructed. For Anselm, the
mind is made for knowing God, and so it should be no surprise that such a
proof might be possible.

Before presenting his simple proof in the *Proslogion*, Anselm begins with
the aspirations of prayer: "Come now, O Lord my God. Teach my heart where
and how to seek you, where and how to find you."[95] He depicts the existential
position of humans who wish to know God more directly and concretely.
We cannot perceive God by our senses in the way that we perceive creatures,
because God is ineffable. Here Anselm speaks as someone who, despite having been "remade" in Christ, is in many ways still a "distant exile" from
God.[96] Comparing himself to Adam before the fall, Anselm states, "He was
satisfied to the full; we sigh with hunger. He had everything he needed; we go

92. Anselm, *Monologion* 29, pp. 48–49.
93. Anselm, *Monologion* 80, p. 90.
94. Anselm, *Proslogion* prol., p. 93.
95. Anselm, *Proslogion* 1, p. 97.
96. Anselm, *Proslogion* 1, p. 97.

begging."[97] From this perspective, Anselm pleads with God to provide a path of intellectual knowledge of God. As he says, "Lord, if you are not here, where shall I seek you, since you are absent? But if you are everywhere, why do I not see you, since you are present?"[98] He bewails his fallen condition: "From our homeland into exile; from the vision of God into our blindness; from the joy of immortality into the bitterness and terror of death."[99]

In describing his neediness, Anselm cites eleven psalms, as well as Jeremiah and Job. His position is one of lamentation; to amplify this stance, he never explicitly refers to Christ or salvation but instead speaks of himself as "wretched," "woeful," lacking joy, "bitter" in heart, and "bent double" so as to be unable to raise his eyes to God.[100] In praising God, he begs to be renewed: "I acknowledge, Lord, and I thank you, that you have created in me this image of you so that I may remember you, think of you, and love you. Yet this image is so eroded by my vices, so clouded by the smoke of my sins, that it cannot do what it was created to do unless you renew and refashion it."[101] Since he goes on to describe himself as a believer, his complaints about his fallen condition may simply be depicting the renewal and refashioning that we all still need, even when Christ has revealed God to us. But it is clear that he leaves Christ out of this section on purpose so as to maximize the sense of neediness and of the real difficulty we have in knowing God. He explains that he is a believer in God's existence and that he is seeking understanding of what he believes about God.

He then proceeds to his proof. First, he states that he believes not only that God exists but also that God is "something than which nothing greater can be thought."[102] The question, then, is whether it is possible for "something than which nothing greater can be thought" *not* to exist. Certainly the fool can say, "There is no God" (Pss. 14:1; 53:1). But can even a fool say that "something than which nothing greater can be thought" does not exist? In answering this question, Anselm first notes the distinction between existing

97. Anselm, *Proslogion* 1, p. 98.
98. Anselm, *Proslogion* 1, p. 97.
99. Anselm, *Proslogion* 1, p. 98.
100. Anselm, *Proslogion* 1, pp. 98–99.
101. Anselm, *Proslogion* 1, p. 90.
102. Anselm, *Proslogion* 2, p. 99. For this description of God, see Augustine, *On Christian Doctrine* 1.7. See also Boethius, *The Consolation of Philosophy* 3.10: "Since nothing better than God can be conceived of, who can doubt that that, than which nothing is better, is good?" (ibid., 277). For discussion of the *Proslogion*'s demonstration of God, see Brian Davies, OP, "Anselm and the Ontological Argument," in *Cambridge Companion to Anselm*, 157–78. See also, from a critical perspective, Graham Oppy's *Ontological Arguments and Belief in God* (Cambridge: Cambridge University Press, 1995).

in one's understanding and existing in reality. Certainly, even the fool would grant that "something than which nothing greater can be thought" exists in the fool's understanding, insofar as the fool can understand what is meant by this phrase. But many things exist in one's understanding that do not exist in reality. Anselm gives the example of a painter's idea for a new painting. Before the painter has completed his painting, his painting exists in his mind but not in reality. When the painter completes his painting, then and only then does the painting also exist in reality.

Does this situation hold also for "something than which nothing greater can be thought"? The content of this phrase (like the idea for a painting) can certainly exist in our mind, since we can understand what it means. But when we do understand what the phrase means, we realize a strange paradox: if the content of this phrase only exists in our mind, then it is in fact not yet "something than which nothing greater can exist." This is so because it is greater to exist both in the mind and in reality than to exist solely in the mind. In a nutshell, "If that than which a greater cannot be thought exists only in the understanding, then that than which a greater *cannot* be thought is that than which a greater *can* be thought"—an obvious contradiction in terms.[103] Once we apprehend "something than which nothing greater can exist," therefore, we have necessarily apprehended something that exists both in the mind and in reality. When we have truly understood it and it exists in our mind, we realize that it must exist in reality too. God literally "cannot be thought not to exist," as the fool should be able to see once he understands the term "God" (and thereby ceases to be a fool).[104]

Having completed his proof, Anselm gives thanks to God for the illumination that God has made possible for him through the light of reason. Reason's ability to know God's existence ensures, Anselm says, "that even if I did not want to *believe* that you exist, I could not fail to *understand* that you exist."[105] God made our minds to know him; inscribed in our very rationality is the reality that even to think that God does not exist is a contradiction in terms, a sheer absurdity, once one realizes what "God" means. On this basis, Anselm in the *Proslogion* proceeds to spell out the attributes of God, which follow from the fact that God is "that than which nothing greater can exist." These attributes include intelligence, omnipotence, mercy, justice, and impassibility. Anselm shows that God is "life itself, light, wisdom, goodness, eternal happiness and happy eternity" and that God "exists always and everywhere."[106]

103. Anselm, *Proslogion* 2, p. 100.
104. Anselm, *Proslogion* 3, p. 101.
105. Anselm, *Proslogion* 4, p. 101.
106. Anselm, *Proslogion* 14, p. 108.

At the same time, Anselm expresses his longing to see more, to know more of God. Beyond what he has seen, he sees "darkness"—not because God is dark but because Anselm's mind "is both darkened in itself and dazzled by you [God]. Indeed it is both obscured by its own littleness and overwhelmed by your vastness."[107] Anselm proclaims, "How great is that light, for from it flashes every truth that enlightens the rational mind! . . . What purity, what simplicity, what certainty and splendor are there. Truly it is more than any creature can understand."[108] It is because God's "unapproachable light" (1 Tim. 6:16) is so dazzling that we cannot see God, even though God is perfectly present everywhere.[109]

Given God's dazzling light, Anselm returns to his original complaints about his inability to see God and finds that his proof only serves to make him more desirous of seeing God. His proof does not fill or satisfy his need for knowledge of God even though it is true knowledge of God. As Anselm puts it, "My soul hoped for satisfaction, and once again it is overwhelmed by need. I tried to eat my fill, but I hunger all the more."[110] He begs God for further strength so that he might strive again to know God more. Continuing his inquiry into God's attributes, he discerns God's simplicity, eternity, self-subsistent and unqualified existence, and goodness—the ineffable, glorious goodness of which we are promised a share as "heirs of God and fellow heirs with Christ" (Rom. 8:17). Anselm shows that God is so unimaginably good, and the communion of saints will be so joy-filled in rejoicing at God's sharing of his goodness, that indeed the saints' "whole heart, mind, and soul will be too small for the fullness of their joy."[111] After citing various biblical passages about the joy that is promised us (John 16:24; Matt. 25:21; 1 Cor. 2:9), Anselm concludes with a final prayer: "O Lord, I pray that I will know and love you that I might rejoice in you. And if I cannot do so fully in this life, I pray that I might grow day by day until my joy comes to fullness. Let the knowledge of you grow in me here, and there let it be full. Let your love grow in me here, and there let it be full."[112]

Anselm quickly received a reply "on behalf of the fool" from Gaunilo, a Benedictine monk of Marmoutiers. Gaunilo notes that he can think of numerous things that have no existence in reality. How can we be sure that what Anselm is describing exists in reality? How is it, asks Gaunilo, that "this

107. Anselm, *Proslogion* 14, p. 109.
108. Anselm, *Proslogion* 14, p. 109.
109. See Anselm, *Proslogion* 16, p. 109.
110. Anselm, *Proslogion* 18, p. 111.
111. Anselm, *Proslogion* 25, p. 116.
112. Anselm, *Proslogion* 26, p. 117.

being merely needs to be thought in order for the understanding to perceive with complete certainty that it undoubtedly exists?"[113] Especially given that God is beyond our understanding, as opposed to something that we can perceive directly, it seems possible to conceive of God and yet to suppose that God does not exist. Gaunilo sums up Anselm's argument as being about "that which is greater than everything else that can be thought" or about "something greater than everything else."[114] He grants that this idea "exists in my understanding," but he does not grant that it necessarily follows that "this thing also exists in reality."[115] We must first establish that God actually exists, before we can know that our concept of God describes a truly existing reality. Here Gaunilo provides an example of what he means: he pictures himself learning of the greatest possible island and then, since such an island now exists in his mind, being compelled to suppose that the island thereby must also exist in reality, since otherwise it would not be the greatest possible island. His point is that the fool would still need to be shown that "the island truly exists."[116] Thus, according to Gaunilo, the fool's position is a perfectly tenable and consistent one.

Anselm replies by pointing out that "that than which a greater cannot be thought cannot be thought of as beginning to exist."[117] If one is thinking of something for which there is even a *possibility* that it does not exist in reality, then one is quite simply not thinking of that than which nothing greater can be thought. The real question, then, is whether "that than which a greater cannot be thought can be thought at all."[118] Anything that can be conceived of as even possibly not existing in reality could be conceived of as existing in a greater way. Anselm repeats his point that "if that than which a greater *cannot* be thought exists only in the understanding, it is that than which a greater *can* be thought."[119] Therefore, something "than which a greater cannot be thought" is something that literally must exist, since its existence is necessary to its definition.

Anselm easily deals with Gaunilo's example of the greatest possible island. This example does not capture the paradox that applies only to that than which a greater cannot be thought, namely, that it either exists in reality or else it does not meet the definition. We can conceive of an island (even the

113. "Gaunilo's Reply on Behalf of the Fool," 122.
114. "Gaunilo's Reply on Behalf of the Fool," 123.
115. "Gaunilo's Reply on Behalf of the Fool," 124.
116. "Gaunilo's Reply on Behalf of the Fool," 125.
117. "Anselm's Reply to Gaunilo," 129.
118. "Anselm's Reply to Gaunilo," 130.
119. "Anselm's Reply to Gaunilo," 132.

greatest possible one), and have it possibly not exist. But if we are attempting to conceive of that than which nothing greater can exist, even the mere *possibility* of it not existing in reality would already mean that it is not what we are looking for, that it does not fit the definition of absolute existence. If we think that it is possible that "that than which nothing greater can be thought" does *not* exist in reality, then we have not yet in fact been able to conceive what is requisite for "that than which nothing greater can be thought." Existing in reality is implied necessarily in the very idea, in the very phrase. God is such that to conceive of him as possibly not existing is to fail to conceive of him properly. By contrast, every creature can be thought of as possibly not existing.

Anselm also points out that Gaunilo errs by describing Anselm's argument as involving "that which is greater than everything else," since Anselm in fact does not use this phrase. It is solely with regard to "that than which a greater cannot be thought" that Anselm denies that it can be thought possibly not to exist.[120] Since its existence is absolute, it is not simply greater than everything else, but rather it has existence in such a way that even the possibility of actual nonexistence would mean that one would be thinking of something lesser. Anselm observes, "For whatever does not exist is capable of not existing, and whatever is capable of not existing can be thought not to exist. Now whatever can be thought not to exist, if it does exist, is not that than which a greater cannot be thought."[121] By contrast, something that is "greater than everything else" need not (theoretically speaking) have necessary existence in its very definition.[122] Again, Anselm believes himself to have phrased the matter in such a way that the thing understood cannot even have a *possibility* of not existing in reality. We can conceive of "that than which a greater cannot be thought" via inference from "the things that have been made" (Rom. 1:20). When we conceive of this, we are conceiving of something that cannot even have a potency for nonexistence—that cannot even be *thought* as not existing in reality.

Thomas Aquinas (ca. 1225–74)

Born into a noble family at Roccasecca, near Aquino in southern Italy, Thomas Aquinas was sent at age five to be educated at the Benedictine Abbey of Monte Cassino. While studying at the University of Naples, Aquinas joined the relatively new Order of the Friars Preachers, despite the opposition of his family.

120. "Anselm's Reply to Gaunilo," 134.
121. "Anselm's Reply to Gaunilo," 134.
122. "Anselm's Reply to Gaunilo," 134–35.

He studied philosophy and theology under Albert the Great at Cologne, and he later taught at the University of Paris and helped to found a Dominican studium in Naples. Like Albert, Aquinas is well known for integrating Aristotle's philosophy into the exposition of Christian theology, although both Albert and Aquinas were deeply influenced as well by the late-Platonic reception of Aristotle and also by Boethius and Avicenna, among others. Aquinas wrote or dictated numerous commentaries on books of Scripture and on the works of Aristotle, and he also commented on Peter Lombard's *Sentences*, the Apostles' Creed, the *Divine Names* of Pseudo-Dionysius, the *Liber de causis* (drawn from Proclus's *Elements of Theology*), and Boethius's *De Trinitate*. He compiled the *Catena Aurea*, which brings together the commentary of numerous Latin and Greek fathers on the four Gospels. In addition to his liturgical poetry and hymns, which are still in use, he is best known for his *Summa theologiae* and his *Summa contra gentiles*.[123]

In *On Being and Essence*, one of his earliest writings, Aquinas distinguishes essence (beings) from *esse* (being). There are many kinds of beings, such as "man" or "a phoenix."[124] In the definition of these beings or essences, however, an actual act of being is not included. Aquinas observes in this regard that "every essence or quiddity [nature] can be understood without knowing anything about its being [*esse*, act of being]. I can know, for instance, what a man or a phoenix is and still be ignorant whether it has being in reality."[125] The definition of what a phoenix is (or, to take a contemporary example, what a passenger pigeon is) can be known even if there is no phoenix (or passenger pigeon) in existence. The nature of a thing thus differs from its act of being. Furthermore, a thing's nature cannot cause its act of being. If it could, then "that thing would then be its own cause and it would bring itself into being,

123. See Jean-Pierre Torrell, OP, *Saint Thomas Aquinas*, vol. 1, *The Person and His Work*, trans. Robert Royal (Washington, DC: Catholic University of America Press, 1996); M.-D. Chenu, OP, *Toward Understanding St. Thomas*, trans. A.-M. Landry, OP, and D. Hughes, OP (Chicago: Henry Regnery, 1964); Denys Turner, *Thomas Aquinas: A Portrait* (New Haven: Yale University Press, 2013). For detailed discussions of Aquinas's demonstrations of God's existence, see especially Edward Feser, *Aquinas* (Oxford: Oneworld, 2009); Thomas Joseph White, OP, *Wisdom in the Face of Modernity: A Study in Thomistic Natural Theology* (Ave Maria, FL: Sapientia, 2009); John F. Wippel, *The Metaphysical Thought of Thomas Aquinas: From Finite Being to Uncreated Being* (Washington, DC: Catholic University of America Press, 2000); Gregory Rocca, *Speaking the Incomprehensible God: Thomas Aquinas on the Interplay of Positive and Negative Theology* (Washington, DC: Catholic University of America Press, 2004); Rudi A. te Velde, *Aquinas on God: The "Divine Science" of the* Summa Theologiae (London: Ashgate, 2006); Pierre-Marie Emonet, OP, *God Seen in the Mirror of the World: An Introduction to the Philosophy of God*, trans. Robert R. Barr (New York: Crossroad, 2000).

124. Thomas Aquinas, *On Being and Essence* 4, trans. Armand Maurer, 2nd rev. ed. (Toronto: Pontifical Institute of Mediaeval Studies, 1968), 55.

125. Aquinas, *On Being and Essence* 4, p. 55.

which is impossible."[126] The fact that something has the nature of a "man" does not mean that a man could give himself his act of being. We can think of a man without thinking of him actually existing, and so the act of being does not come from the nature. Aquinas states, "It follows that everything whose being is distinct from its nature must have being from another."[127]

On this basis, Aquinas shows that there must be a reality whose nature is its act of being (Pure Act), and there can only be one such reality. If there were more than one Pure Act, more than one reality whose nature is subsistent act-of-being, then we could differentiate one instance of this nature from another. But such differentiation is not possible for Pure Act, because the differentiation could only consist in the addition of a specific difference (as, for example, the genus "animal" is found in various species) or in the addition of matter (as, for example, the species "man" is found in different individual humans). In both of these cases, Pure Act would no longer be Pure Act: in the first case, "it would not be being alone but being with the addition of a form [the specific difference]," and in the second case, "it would not be subsistent, but material, being."[128]

Given that there could only be one Pure Act, does Pure Act really exist? Aquinas argues that it does, because everything whose nature is not "to be" must receive its act of being from another. An essentially ordered series of beings is one in which the beings exist at the same time, each causing the act of being in the next in the series. Although Aquinas does not explain it here, he states that going "on to infinity" in essentially ordered dependent causes is impossible—since all the causes would be intermediate, dependent ones, and so the causal series could never get started.[129] As Aquinas says, "Because everything that exists through another is reduced to that which exists through itself as to its first cause, there must be a reality that is the cause of being for all other things, because it is pure being."[130] Fundamentally, Aquinas is arguing that no natural reality we experience is the cause of its own existence. Nothing that we see around us exists necessarily by reason of the kind of thing it is or the essence or nature it has. This invites us to probe further to find the cause of why things exist until we come to something that exists by its own nature or in which there is no real distinction of nature and existence.

Book 3 of the *Summa contra gentiles* contains an important brief reflection on human knowledge of God. In chapter 38, Aquinas denies that

126. Aquinas, *On Being and Essence* 4, p. 56.
127. Aquinas, *On Being and Essence* 4, p. 56.
128. Aquinas, *On Being and Essence* 4, p. 56.
129. Aquinas, *On Being and Essence* 4, p. 57.
130. Aquinas, *On Being and Essence* 4, pp. 56–57.

humans possess self-evident knowledge of God, but he affirms that "there is a common and confused knowledge of God which is found in practically all men."[131] What explains this "common and confused knowledge of God"? Aquinas reasons that "when men see that things in nature run according to a definite order, and that ordering does not occur without an orderer, they perceive in most cases that there is some orderer of the things that we see."[132] Aquinas grants that there is also a lot of disorder in the things of nature. His point is simply that the ordering toward a goal that we see in particular nonrational things is the kind of ordering that requires reason. (A modern thinker might appeal to the process of evolution, but this would not negate Aquinas's point, since even evolution presupposes underlying order.) Yet such knowledge of God, of the one who is the ultimate source of order in nonrational things, is "confused" because, as Aquinas says, "who or what kind of being, or whether there is but one orderer of nature, is not yet grasped immediately in this general condition."[133] For this reason, people who have a confused knowledge of God drawn from the order that they find in nonrational things can end up worshiping a finite thing as God or worshiping multiple gods.

In book 1 of the *Summa contra gentiles*, Aquinas speaks of a "twofold truth of divine things," namely, truth about God that can be known by the human mind's own powers and truth about God that requires divine revelation in order to be known.[134] With regard to truth about God that can be known by the mind's powers, Aquinas seeks "demonstrative arguments."[135] He notes that as far as human reason is concerned, knowledge of God first requires the demonstration that God exists "as the necessary foundation of the whole work. For, if we do not demonstrate that God exists, all consideration of divine things is necessarily suppressed."[136]

Before turning to the arguments for the existence of God that he considers to be demonstrative, Aquinas reflects on Anselm's *Proslogion*. Anselm's argument begins, as Aquinas says, with the fact that "by the name *God* we understand something than which a greater cannot be thought."[137] Since it

131. Thomas Aquinas, *Summa contra gentiles* 3.38, in Thomas Aquinas, *Summa contra gentiles, Book Three: Providence, Part One*, trans. Vernon J. Bourke (Notre Dame: University of Notre Dame Press, 1975), 125.

132. Aquinas, *Summa contra gentiles* 3.38, p. 125.

133. Aquinas, *Summa contra gentiles* 3.38, p. 125.

134. Aquinas, *Summa contra gentiles* 1.9, in Thomas Aquinas, *Summa contra gentiles, Book One: God*, trans. Anton C. Pegis, FRSC (Notre Dame: University of Notre Dame Press, 1975), 77.

135. Aquinas, *Summa contra gentiles* 1.9, p. 77.

136. Aquinas, *Summa contra gentiles* 1.9, p. 78.

137. Aquinas, *Summa contra gentiles* 1.10, p. 79.

is greater to exist in reality than not to do so, "God" cannot exist solely in the intellect. Indeed, for Alselm, God is such that his nonexistence literally cannot be conceived, once one recognizes that God must be absolute existence, without any potency (by contrast to all creatures). To Anselm's position, Aquinas adds two arguments that proceed in a similarly *a priori* fashion. The first is that we naturally desire God as our ultimate end, and so the existence of God is self-evident to us. The second is that we know truth through knowing God. God is at the root of all our knowledge because "the divine light is the principle of all intelligible knowledge; since the divine light is that in which intelligible illumination is found first and in its highest degree."[138] Here Aquinas compares the divine light with the light of the sun; our knowledge requires God just as much as our perception of things requires the sun. God grounds all truth, and so God's existence must be self-evident to the reflective mind.

In response to these arguments for the self-evidence of the existence of God, Aquinas states that they exhibit "a failure to distinguish between that which is self-evident in an absolute sense and that which is self-evident in relation to us."[139] Absolutely speaking, God's existence is self-evident because he is supremely intelligible. But in relation to our weak minds, God's existence is not self-evident. Even among those who profess to worship "God," there exists confusion about what this name entails. Furthermore, *pace* Anselm, even "granted that everyone should understand by the name *God* something than which a greater cannot be thought, it will still not be necessary that there exist in reality something than which a greater cannot be thought."[140] A conception in the mind exists in the mind, and one cannot thereby conclude that it exists in reality, no matter how compelling the logic is. Simply on the basis of a definition of God that shows that it would be a contradiction in terms for God not to exist, our weak minds cannot rule out the possibility that in reality God does not exist. Furthermore, although we have a natural desire for God because we desire happiness, in order for this natural desire to proceed, we need only know finite likenesses of God's goodness. Likewise, we need not know God before we can know truth about things, even though it is certainly the case that "all our knowledge is caused in us through His influence."[141]

After dismantling these arguments for God's existence, in chapter 13 of book 1 of the *Summa contra gentiles* Aquinas seeks to demonstrate God's

138. Aquinas, *Summa contra gentiles* 1.10, p. 80.
139. Aquinas, *Summa contra gentiles* 1.11, p. 81.
140. Aquinas, *Summa contra gentiles* 1.11, p. 82.
141. Aquinas, *Summa contra gentiles* 1.11, p. 83.

existence along broadly Aristotelian lines.[142] Before proceeding, he raises two problems: first, Aristotle considered that in order to demonstrate whether a thing exists, we must begin with a definition of what the thing is, which is impossible in the case of God; second, Aristotle also held that we rely on our senses for our knowledge of the principles of demonstration, whereas God utterly transcends sensible things. Appealing to Romans 1:20, Aquinas explains that the demonstration of God's existence works by moving from effects to cause. Admittedly, we do not know what God is, and we cannot define his "essence" in a concept. But since we are not seeking to demonstrate *what* God is, we do not need to employ a definition of God in our demonstration. Instead, we can use God's sensible effects (finite things) as the middle term of a demonstration *that* God exists.

Aquinas then follows this path of demonstration. The first argument for God's existence that he describes is from "motion" (or change), which is a movement from potency to actuality. The proof goes as follows: Since everything that is moved is moved by another, and we see that the sun (for example) is in motion, we must inquire into its mover(s). There are two options: either it has an infinite number of moved movers, or there is an unmoved mover. An infinite number of moved movers is impossible, and so an unmoved mover exists.

This proof, Aquinas observes, depends on two theses: "everything that is moved is moved by another," and "in movers and things moved one cannot proceed to infinity."[143] With respect to the first thesis, however, why could not things simply move themselves? Aquinas explains that Aristotle answers this question in three ways, which we find in books 7–8 of Aristotle's *Physics*. The first way begins with the fact that a self-mover must "have within itself the principle of its own motion" and must be moved by itself rather than by a part of itself.[144] Yet a self-moving being must also have parts, or else it would not be movable. Aristotle then argues that such a being must be "primarily moved—that is, moved as a whole rather than having one part move while another part is at rest.[145] But if it is "primarily moved," then it depends on the motion of another and is not in fact a self-mover. Aquinas explains that "the force of Aristotle's argument lies in this: *if* something moves itself primarily and through itself, rather than through its parts, that it is moved cannot depend on another. But the moving of the divisible itself, like its being, depends on its

142. For discussion of Aquinas's reinterpretation of Aristotle's proofs, see White, *Wisdom in the Face of Modernity*, 76–96; Rocca, *Speaking the Unknowable God*, 200–220.
143. Aquinas, *Summa contra gentiles* 1.13, p. 86.
144. Aquinas, *Summa contra gentiles* 1.13, p. 86.
145. Aquinas, *Summa contra gentiles* 1.13, p. 86.

parts; it cannot therefore move itself primarily and through itself."[146] Thus, things that we might suppose to be self-movers, which are movable because they have parts, are actually moved by another.

The second way that Aristotle demonstrates the thesis "everything that is moved is moved by another" is by noting that all things that are moved either by accident, by external force, or by parts of themselves (such as the soul), are in fact not moved by themselves. Since "whatever is moved is moved through itself or by accident," everything that is moved is moved by another.[147]

The third and final way that Aristotle demonstrates this thesis is by arguing that "the same thing cannot be at once in act and in potency with respect to the same thing," and "everything that is moved is, as such, in potency."[148] Since the thing moved is in *potency* for this motion, the thing moved cannot itself be the mover, because the mover must be in *act* with respect to the motion. It follows that "with respect to the same motion, nothing is both mover and moved. Thus, nothing moves itself."[149]

Given these three ways of showing the validity of the first thesis on which the demonstration depends, Aquinas turns to the second thesis, namely, "there is no procession to infinity among movers and things moved."[150] Aristotle offers three ways of proving this second thesis. First, since whatever is moved must be divisible or composite, and since mover and the thing moved must exist at the same time, each mover would itself be being moved *at the same time as* it is moving something else. If this chain of movers went on infinitely, then an infinite chain of movers, all moving together, would move in a *finite* time—which is impossible.

The second and third ways of proving that "there is no procession to infinity among movers and things moved" address the requirements of "an ordered series of movers and things moved."[151] Aristotle explains that if one removes the first mover from an ordered series, no other mover in the series will either move or be moved.[152] If the ordered series extends in an infinite chain, then by definition there can be no first mover. In such a scenario, the motion could never have gotten started. An infinite series of intermediate or instrumental causes does not suffice for actual motion.

Having demonstrated both that "everything that is moved is moved by another" and that "there is no procession to infinity among movers and things

146. Aquinas, *Summa contra gentiles* 1.13, p. 87.
147. Aquinas, *Summa contra gentiles* 1.13, p. 88.
148. Aquinas, *Summa contra gentiles* 1.13, p. 88.
149. Aquinas, *Summa contra gentiles* 1.13, p. 88.
150. Aquinas, *Summa contra gentiles* 1.13, p. 89.
151. Aquinas, *Summa contra gentiles* 1.13, p. 89.
152. Aquinas, *Summa contra gentiles* 1.13, p. 89.

moved," Aristotle has demonstrated the validity of his first argument for the existence of a first unmoved mover: the argument from motion. Aquinas next summarizes Aristotle's second argument for the existence of a first unmoved mover. In this second argument, Aristotle asks whether, if every mover is moved, this is necessary or accidental. If it is not necessary, then it is possible that no mover is moved. If so, at some time there would be no motion. Since there cannot have been a time in which there was no motion, it must be necessary that every mover is moved by another. Further, if the mover and the thing moved were only accidentally related, then one could find a mover without a thing moved. But if every mover is moved then "the mover must be moved either by the *same* kind of motion as that by which he moves, or another."[153] In fact, the *same* kind of motion is not possible, since it would require, for example, that a healer must be being healed. The mover *could* be moved by a different kind of motion, but this could not proceed to infinity, since the kinds of motion are finite in number. It follows that there has to be a first mover. But might this first mover be self-moved rather than unmoved? In a self-mover, the whole is not moved by the whole; rather, "one part of the self-moved mover is solely moving, and the other part solely moved."[154] This shows that the first mover must be an unmoved mover.

Further, Aristotle holds that "some self-moved being must be everlasting," because motion is everlasting and the generation of self-moving beings (animals) has no temporal beginning or end.[155] But no corruptible self-moving being could be the cause of endless motion; neither could endless motion be caused by all the corruptible self-moving beings together, since they do not exist simultaneously. Therefore, there must "be some endlessly self-moving being."[156] This incorruptible, endlessly self-moving being, however, must itself have a mover that "is not moved, either through itself or by accident," because "no self-moved being is moved everlastingly whose mover is moved either by itself or by accident."[157]

This second argument of Aristotle's for the existence of the unmoved mover is found in book 8 of his *Physics*. For Aquinas, the question is whether Aristotle's demonstration has arrived simply at an unmoved mover who is merely the greatest part of the universe and so could not be God. In Aquinas's view, therefore, we find the completion of Aristotle's proof in book 12 of *Metaphysics*. Here Aristotle seeks an unmoved mover who is not merely "part

153. Aquinas, *Summa contra gentiles* 1.13, p. 91 (italics added).
154. Aquinas, *Summa contra gentiles* 1.13, p. 92.
155. Aquinas, *Summa contra gentiles* 1.13, p. 93.
156. Aquinas, *Summa contra gentiles* 1.13, p. 93.
157. Aquinas, *Summa contra gentiles* 1.13, pp. 93–94.

of the self-moved mover" but rather "is absolutely separate."[158] Everything that is part of the universe moves by appetitive desire and thus is a moved mover. The object that is desired, by contrast, does not itself desire anything and is thus utterly unmoved. Since without such an object there would be no motion, Aristotle concludes that there must "be an absolutely unmoved, separate first mover."[159]

Since Aristotle's two arguments for God's existence presuppose the eternity of the world (endless motion), Aquinas asks whether such arguments can be employed by a Christian who knows that the world had a beginning. He answers that the arguments would be even more potent "if the world and motion had a first beginning," since "that which comes to be anew must take its origin from some innovating cause; since nothing brings itself from potency to act, or from non-being to being."[160] Aristotle's arguments, however, also presuppose that the first-moved being is self-moved, that is to say that the highest celestial sphere is conscious and animate. Aquinas points out that if one rejected this claim about the highest celestial sphere, one would simply arrive more directly at the "unmoved separate first mover."[161]

From books 1 and 4 of Aristotle's *Metaphysics* Aquinas briefly draws two additional arguments for the existence of God. The first has its basis in efficient causality. In an ordered series of efficient causes, if we suppress the first efficient cause, there will be no effect. In such a case, the intermediate efficient causes could not be causes. An infinite chain of intermediate causes, absent a first cause, would mean that there could be no effect and thus no intermediate causes, which is contrary to what we see around us. The second additional argument for God's existence hinges on the consideration that "what is most true is also most a being."[162] Further, of two false things, one

158. Aquinas, *Summa contra gentiles* 1.13, p. 94.
159. Aquinas, *Summa contra gentiles* 1.13, p. 94. Commenting on "Thomas's long and laborious presentation in SCG I, c. 13 of two arguments from motion for God's existence," Wippel points out that

> to some extent each runs the risk of ending at best with a besouled self-mover of the outermost heavenly sphere rather than with God, at least when each is placed within its Aristotelian and medieval physical world-view. . . . If, as Thomas has indicated, Aristotle's argumentation in *Physics* VIII leads only to a besouled self-mover, by appealing to *Metaphysics* XII Thomas believes he can enable it to conclude to the existence of a perfectly immobile first mover which is separate and which is God. (Wippel, *Metaphysical Thought of Thomas Aquinas*, 431)

As Wippel says, "Thomas introduces a much simpler and more direct argument based on motion in ST I, q. 2, a. 3 as his first way" (ibid.). See also Norman Kretzmann, *The Metaphysics of Theism: Aquinas's Natural Theology in* Summa contra gentiles I (Oxford: Clarendon, 1997).
160. Aquinas, *Summa contra gentiles* 1.13, p. 95–96.
161. Aquinas, *Summa contra gentiles* 1.13, p. 95.
162. Aquinas, *Summa contra gentiles* 1.13, p. 95.

can be false than the other. This means that there is a measure of absolute truth, and this absolute truth is absolute being: God.

Last, in chapter 13 of the *Summa contra gentiles*, Aquinas offers a demonstration of God's existence drawn from John of Damascus. This argument comes from the government of the world, namely, the fact that the world comprises "contrary and discordant things" that are nonetheless part of one intelligible order. If there were no providential orderer of the world, then the contrary and discordant things would at best rarely, or only by chance, come together in an intelligible order. As it stands, there is one stable order that comprises a tremendous number of widely diverse things. There must, then, be an orderer, who is God.

In his *Summa theologiae*, Aquinas very briefly offers five ways of demonstrating God's existence. These are found in question 2, article 3 of the *Prima Pars*. The first way is the argument from motion or change. Aquinas states that "motion is nothing else than the reduction of something from potentiality to actuality," and he adds that "nothing can be reduced from potentiality to actuality, except by something in a state of actuality."[163] The same thing cannot be in potency and actuality in the same respect, and so a thing cannot be both mover and moved in the same respect. This shows that "whatever is in motion must be put in motion by another," but this cannot proceed to infinity, since if there is no first mover, there can be no intermediate movers either.[164] The first unmoved mover, who is pure actuality and the source of all act and potency composites, is God.

The second way is the argument from efficient causality, understood again in terms of act and potency. Nothing is the efficient cause of its own finite actuality (or act of existing), and it is not possible to proceed to infinity in essentially ordered efficient causes, since without a first cause—which itself needs no efficient cause of its act of existing and is therefore pure actuality—there can be no intermediate causes and no ultimate effect.[165] Since there obviously are intermediate causes and an ultimate effect, there must be a first cause, which is God.

The third way is from possibility (or contingency) and necessity: if everything were "possible to be and not to be" rather than existing absolutely and

163. Thomas Aquinas, *Summa theologiae* Ia.2.3, in Thomas Aquinas, *Summa Theologica*, trans. Fathers of the English Dominican Province (Westminster, MD: Christian Classics, 1981).

164. Aquinas, *Summa theologiae* Ia.2.3.

165. In an essentially ordered series of causes, all of the causes must act simultaneously in causing the effect. By contrast, an accidentally ordered series of causes does not depend on all the causes being simultaneously in act. An example of an accidentally ordered series of causes is grandfather-father-son, in which the grandfather may no longer be alive when the son is begotten. Aquinas grants that it is philosophically possible that one could have an infinite accidentally ordered series of causes.

necessarily, then at some time (given infinite time on an endless continuum) *everything* would have not existed, since "that which is possible to be at some time is not." If so, then there would now be nothing in existence, since nothing can come from nothing. The fact that something now exists, therefore, means that there must be some thing or things whose existence is necessary. As shown by the argument from efficient causality (the second way), it is impossible to proceed to infinity in necessary things that are caused by another. There must be one uncaused necessary being that causes all others, and this is God.

The fourth way is from the degrees of perfection found in finite things: "Among beings there are some more and some less good, true, noble, and the like."[166] The predication of "more" or "less" good or true requires that there be a measure of the degree to which something "resembles" goodness or truth. This measure must be maximal goodness or truth, for otherwise it would itself be measured rather than being the measure. For a maximum in perfection to exist, it must be maximal actuality, "for those things that are greatest in truth are greatest in being." This maximum, as perfect actuality, "is to all beings the cause of their being, goodness, and every other perfection."[167]

The fifth and final way comes from the governance of the world. Nonrational things cannot direct themselves to an end, and yet nonrational things in the universe generally repeat the same actions to achieve the same ends. This

166. Edward Feser clarifies that "Aquinas is not in fact trying to argue in the Fourth Way that *everything* that we observe to exist in degrees (including heat, smelliness, sweetness, etc.) must be traceable to some single maximum standard of perfection. Here (as elsewhere in the Five Ways) his archaic scientific examples have led modern readers to misread him" (Feser, *Aquinas*, 104). Aquinas instead has transcendental perfections in view, such as true, good, and noble.

167. Boethius presents a version of this proof, as does Augustine. Boethius argues that perfect goodness must exist because imperfect finite goods exist: "For everything which is called imperfect is held to be imperfect because of some diminution of what is perfect" (*Consolation of Philosophy* 3.10, p. 275). If the perfect does not exist, then to call something imperfect would not make sense. There could not be an imperfect good if there were no perfect good, because without a standard of perfection there cannot be degrees of perfection. He states, "Hence it happens that if in any class something seems to be imperfect, there must also be something perfect of that class; for if we take away perfection altogether, it cannot even be imagined how that which is held to be imperfect can exist" (*Consolation of Philosophy* 3.10, p. 275). Boethius explains that only perfect being could be the source of imperfect beings. This is so because any imperfect being is dependent on something prior for its being; an imperfect being is a mere mode of being rather than the source of being. If God were not the perfect good, then God "could not be the principle of all things; for there would be something possessing perfect good more excellent than he, which in this would seem to be prior and more excellent" (*Consolation of Philosophy* 3.10, p. 277). The cause of all that exists must also be the highest good, and so God's being is sheer goodness.

could not be the result of chance.[168] Thus nonrational things are ordered to
their ends by an intelligent orderer who, as the one who orders this-worldly
things to their end, transcends and governs this world.

It follows that the things we see all around us—movement, causality, contingency, degrees of perfection, and teleological order—are paths to God.
Nonetheless, Aquinas recognizes the difficulty of knowing God. He holds that
we all naturally desire happiness and therefore we all naturally desire God, but
we do not necessarily know that it is *God* for whom we are yearning.[169] Indeed,
Aquinas considers that "human reason is very deficient in things concerning
God."[170] Even the best philosophers have disagreed with each other and have
fallen into numerous errors about God. In his *Commentary on the Gospel
of John*, Aquinas says of the pagan philosophers that "if they did have some
speculative knowledge of God, this was mixed with many errors: some denied
his providence over all things; others said he was the soul of the world; still
others worshipped other gods along with him."[171] Such errors are grave, since
in a certain sense those who err "only slightly in their knowledge of God"
are "entirely ignorant of him."[172] In addition, since metaphysics is the last of
the sciences, it takes a long time to learn and bears fruit relatively late in life.
Aquinas comments in the *Summa theologiae* that "many are unable to make
progress in the study of *scientia*, either through dullness of mind, or through
having a number of occupations and temporal needs, or even through laziness

168. Feser again makes a helpful clarification: Aquinas
    is not arguing (as advocates of the design argument might) that it is improbable that
    complex structures could arise by chance, which would invite the response that natu-
    ral selection shows how such structures might nevertheless arise by non-fortuitous but
    impersonal processes. For . . . he is not interested here in complexity per se in the first
    place; . . . even a simple physical phenomenon like the attraction between two particles
    would suffice for his purposes. What he is saying is rather that it is impossible that *every*
    apparent causal regularity can be attributed to chance, for chance itself presupposes
    causal regularity. (Feser, *Aquinas*, 113)
Feser goes on to point out that the countless nonintelligent causes, ordered to particular
ends, require not merely a cosmic designer in the past but an intelligent governer who sustains
the universe here and now.
    169. See Aquinas, *Summa theologiae* Ia.2.1, ad 1.
    170. Aquinas, *Summa theologiae* II-II.2.4.
    171. Thomas Aquinas, *Commentary on the Gospel of John: Chapters 13–21*, trans. Fabian
Larcher, OP, and James A. Weisheipl, OP, ed. Daniel A. Keating and Matthew Levering (Washington, DC: Catholic University of America Press, 2010), 195–96. Aquinas is commenting on
John 17:25, where Jesus says, "O righteous Father, the world has not known thee."
    172. Aquinas, *Commentary on the Gospel of John*, 196. For discussion see Thomas Joseph
White, OP, "'Through Him All Things Were Made' (John 1:3): The Analogy of the Word Incar-
nate according to St. Thomas Aquinas and Its Ontological Presuppositions," in *The Analogy
of Being: Invention of the Antichrist or the Wisdom of God?*, ed. Thomas Joseph White, OP
(Grand Rapids: Eerdmans, 2011), 246–79, esp. 247n3, 249–51, and 276–78.

in learning, all of whom would be altogether deprived of the knowledge of God, unless divine things were brought to their knowledge under the guise of faith."[173]

The difficulty of metaphysical reasoning helps to explain why Aquinas, in the *sed contra* immediately prior to his elucidation of the five ways, quotes God's words in Exodus 3:14, "I am who am." (or "I am who I am"). God names himself in this way to Moses in the course of commissioning Moses to lead the people of Israel out of slavery in Egypt. The God who can name himself in this way—and only God could name himself "I am," because only God is infinite existence rather than a finite mode of existence—is the same God who redeems and restores his idolatrous people. It is this redemption, and not philosophical knowledge of God, that grounds Christian faith.[174]

William of Ockham (ca. 1288–ca. 1349)

Born in Ockham, a village in Surrey not far from London, William of Ockham was either given to the Franciscan order to be educated or joined the order on his own volition at a young age. In 1306, he was ordained a subdeacon, having been a Franciscan since at least 1302. Ordained a priest, he studied philosophy and theology in London and Oxford, and he lectured on Peter Lombard's *Sentences* from 1317–19, largely in dialogue with the views of Henry of Ghent, Giles of Rome, John Duns Scotus, and Peter Aureoli. Between 1321 and 1324, he wrote commentaries on Aristotle's works on logic, a *Summa logicae*, a commentary on Aristotle's *Physics*, treatises on certain problems regarding predestination and the Eucharist, and quodlibetal disputations. Accused of heretical teaching, he spent four years at the papal court of John XXII in Avignon. In 1328 he fled Avignon along with the superior general of the Franciscan order, Michael of Cesena, first to Italy and then to Munich under the protection of the German emperor, Louis the Bavarian. Excommunicated by Pope John XXII, Ockham devoted the rest of his life to writing political treatises against Popes John XXII and Benedict XII on the grounds that the papacy had fallen into heresy with respect to apostolic poverty and the beatific vision.[175]

173. Aquinas, *Summa theologiae* II-II.2.4.

174. For further discussion of Aquinas's proofs see Lawrence Dewan, OP, "The Existence of God: Can It Be Demonstrated?," *Nova et Vetera* 10 (2012): 731–56; Antoine Guggenheim, "The 'Five Ways' and Aquinas's *De Deo Uno*," trans. Robert McKeon, *Analecta Hermeneutica* 2 (2010); Guggenheim, *Les preuves de l'existence de Dieu* (Paris: Parole et Silence, 2008); John F. X. Knasas, "The 'Suppositio' of Motion's Eternity and the Interpretation of Aquinas' Motion Proofs for God," in *God: Reason and Reality*, ed. Anselm Ramelow (Munich: Philosophia Verlag, 2014), 147–78.

175. See Philotheus Boehner, OFM, introduction to William of Ockham, *Philosophical Writings: A Selection*, trans. Philotheus Boehner, OFM, revised by Stephen F. Brown (Indianapolis:

For Ockham's views on whether God's existence can be demonstrated, I begin with his *Quaestiones in librum I physicorum*. Regarding the demonstration of a first (uncaused) efficient cause, Ockham responds to John Duns Scotus's position that "essentially ordered effects [i.e., effects that are simultaneous in time] have a cause; therefore there is some cause which does not belong to this totality, otherwise one and the same thing would be the cause of itself."[176] For Scotus, the totality of essentially ordered caused things cannot be dependent on something within this totality. Scotus argues that "where there is no first principle, nothing is essentially prior"; and so if we could not demonstrate a first (uncaused) efficient cause, then we would be left with an infinite number of essentially ordered causes existing at the same time, which is impossible.[177] Ockham, however, judges that none of these reasons is sufficient to demonstrate a first efficient cause "in regard to production as specifically distinct from conservation."[178]

Ockham reaches this conclusion because he thinks that if one were to judge from natural reason alone, an infinite multitude of caused things could indeed be caused from within the multitude, just as Scotus admits would be the case with an accidentally ordered (nonsimultaneous) set of effects or causes. One member of the multitude could be caused by another member—for instance, one human by another human, stretching to an infinite number of humans, caused by different members of the multitude—without there needing to be a first efficient cause. Ockham observes that "not every thing which mediately or immediately produces a thing coexists with the thing produced," so that even

Hackett, 1990), ix–li; William J. Courtenay, "The Academic and Intellectual Worlds of Ockham," in *The Cambridge Companion to Ockham*, ed. Paul Vincent Spade (Cambridge: Cambridge University Press, 1999), 17–30; Léon Baudry, *Guillaume d'Occam. Sa vie, ses oeuvres, ses idées sociales et politiques*, vol. 1, *L'homme et les oeuvres* (Paris: Vrin, 1950); Marilyn McCord Adams, *William Ockham*, 2 vols. (Notre Dame: University of Notre Dame Press, 1987); Gedeon Gál, OFM, "William of Ockham Died Impenitent in April 1347," *Franciscan Studies* 42 (1971): 90–95.

176. Ockham, *Philosophical Writings*, 119. For discussion of Ockham's response, see Armand A. Maurer, CSB, *The Philosophy of William of Ockham in the Light of Its Principles* (Toronto: Pontifical Institute of Mediaeval Studies, 1999), 173–79.

177. Ockham, *Philosophical Writings*, 119. For Scotus's viewpoint, see the texts and commentary in William A. Frank and Allan B. Wolter, *Duns Scotus, Metaphysician* (West Lafayette, IN: Purdue University Press, 1995); John Duns Scotus, *A Treatise on God as First Principle*, trans. and ed. Allan B. Wolter, OFM (Chicago: Franciscan Herald Press, 1966). See also Timothy O'Connor, "Scotus on the Existence of a First Efficient Cause," *Philosophy of Religion* 33 (1993): 17–32; James F. Ross and Todd Bates, "Duns Scotus on Natural Theology," in *The Cambridge Companion to Duns Scotus*, ed. Thomas Williams (Cambridge: Cambridge University Press, 2003), 193–237; Rega Wood, "Scotus's Argument for the Existence of God," *Franciscan Studies* 47 (1987): 257–77; and Alexander W. Hall, *Thomas Aquinas and John Duns Scotus: Natural Theology in the High Middle Ages* (London: Continuum, 2007).

178. Ockham, *Philosophical Writings*, 120.

in an essentially ordered series one cannot appeal to the danger of proceeding to infinity.[179] Thus Ockham thinks it is possible for there to be an infinite series of efficient causes regardless of how those causes are related (essentially or accidentally). In sum, "as regards mere production it cannot be proved that one efficient cause is not produced by another, and so *ad infinitum*."[180]

By contrast, Ockham holds that the conservation of all things in being can be the basis of a successful proof of God's existence, since with respect to conservation, one cannot proceed to infinity in an essentially ordered series of causes. From the conservation of all things in being, one can show that there must be a first efficient cause. Ockham explains that "every preservative cause is a productive cause."[181] Unlike in the case of efficient causes, "everything that conserves something else, be it mediately or immediately, exists at the same time with that which is conserved."[182] Since this is so, one cannot proceed to infinity in conserving causes without producing the absurdity of an actual infinity.[183]

But given that every conserving cause is also a productive cause, why has Ockham not thereby also vindicated the proof from efficient causality? In answer, he returns to the thesis (shared by Scotus and Aquinas) that "in essentially ordered causes all causes are required at the same time for the production of the effect."[184] It would seem that there must be a first cause in order for there to be an essentially ordered chain of caused things; otherwise, either there would be an infinity of things actually existing, which is impossible, or else one of the caused things would be the cause of the whole multitude of caused things, which would fall into the absurdity of supposing that something is the cause of itself. To this line of argument, Ockham repeats his fundamental objection: it is possible that "one part is caused by one thing which is part of this multitude, and another by another thing, and so on *ad infinitum*."[185] But this objection, he observes again, does not undermine the proof of God's existence from conservation in being.

In question 1 of *Quodlibet* 1 Ockham asks whether natural reason can prove that there is only *one* God. He contrasts two possible understandings of "God": "some thing more noble and more perfect than anything else besides Him" and "that than which nothing is more noble and more perfect."[186]

179. Ockham, *Philosophical Writings*, 121.
180. Ockham, *Philosophical Writings*, 121.
181. Ockham, *Philosophical Writings*, 123.
182. Ockham, *Philosophical Writings*, 123.
183. For the limitations of this proof even in Ockham, see Adams, *William Ockham*, 2:970.
184. Ockham, *Philosophical Writings*, 123.
185. Ockham, *Philosophical Writings*, 124.
186. Ockham, *Philosophical Writings*, 125. See also the translation of this text in William of Ockham, *Quodlibetal Questions, Volumes 1–2, Quodlibets 1–7*, trans. Alfred J. Freddoso and Francis E. Kelley (New Haven: Yale University Press, 1991), 5–12.

In Ockham's view, the second understanding of "God" can be proved to be true but not the first. There must indeed be some thing "than which nothing is more noble and more perfect." The only alternative would be to proceed to infinity, arriving at the absurd conclusion that there are an infinite number of beings. But to prove that there is some thing "than which nothing is more noble and more perfect" differs from showing that there is only *one* such thing. There may be more than one thing that fits this description. To know that there is only one thing "than which nothing is more noble and more perfect" requires faith.

In the same place, Ockham addresses various arguments put forward by Scotus in favor of the view that natural reason can demonstrate that there is only one God. Scotus proposes that if there were two Gods, each would love itself more than it would love the other, despite the other being infinitely lovable. Ockham replies that "it cannot be demonstrated that each of them is intensively infinite, since this is merely believed."[187] Similarly, against Scotus's view that it would be impossible for an effect to have "two primary and total ends" (i.e., two Gods), Ockham argues that it would in fact be possible for one effect to have two "sufficient" final causes, even though neither of the final causes would be "total."[188] He holds that the existence of only one "total" final cause cannot be demonstrated. In response to Scotus's argument for the impossibility of two necessary beings, Ockham considers that the divine nature could determine itself to be in two Gods rather than one. In such a case, "the concept *necessary being* would be univocally predicated of them—and they would be distinguished by their very selves."[189] The key move in Ockham's responses consists in his denial that God can be proven to be infinite, unbounded by any limitation.[190] For an unbeliever, says Ockham, it would make sense to "claim that infinity *is* incompatible with being and that the opposite cannot be proved."[191]

187. Ockham, *Quodlibetal Questions*, 9.
188. Ockham, *Quodlibetal Questions*, 11.
189. Ockham, *Quodlibetal Questions*, 12.
190. See also question 1 of *Quodlibet* 3, where Ockham argues that since "all things are finite," it follows that "even if one presupposes an efficient causation with respect to all things and an understanding of all things, God's infinity cannot be proved on this basis" (Ockham, *Quodlibetal Questions*, 169). He explains that "the infinity of the cause cannot be proved from a finite effect or from finite effects producible at one and the same time" (Ockham, *Quodlibetal Questions*, 169). He considers, too, that "it is possible for something to be the most eminent in the sense that nothing is better than it, and yet for it to be finite" (Ockham, *Quodlibetal Questions*, 170).
191. Ockham, *Quodlibetal Questions*, 176 (*Quodlibet* 3.1). See also *Quodlibet* 7.11–17, where Ockham examines whether God's infinity can be demonstrated from God's efficient causation, cognition, simplicity, final causality, eminence, or other arguments given by Aristotle.

If one could show that God is in no way composite and is unable to enter into composition with another, would this prove that God is infinite? For Ockham, even this would not be demonstrative. He holds that both an angel and a spiritual soul are in no way composite without thereby being infinite. For Aquinas, an angel is a composite of being and essence, but Ockham rejects this notion of ontological composition. He argues that God is no more or less simple or devoid of composition than any other spiritual substance.[192]

Question 1 of *Quodlibet* 2 takes up whether God can be shown to be the first efficient cause of all things. Ockham holds that God can neither be shown to be the immediate efficient cause of all things nor the efficient cause of any particular thing. Ockham suggests that angels could be sufficient causes for many things, and thus God need not be the immediate cause of everything. The angels, too, might well be uncaused, so far as rational demonstration can tell. As he shows in the first question of *Quodlibet* 1, Ockham thinks it possible that there is more than one necessary being, and he also thinks that not every effect need be reducible to the same first cause. In his view, it is entirely plausible that "the totality of things that are caused is not caused by some one thing, but is instead caused by many things. For one of the things caused is caused primarily by one efficient cause, and another is caused by another, and so on."[193] He emphasizes that he is not saying that things do not have a first efficient cause. A first efficient cause is necessary so as to avoid an infinite regress, but it need not be the same first cause in each case.[194]

In his *Ordinatio* and elsewhere, Ockham accepts Scotus's position that although "we cannot know God in this life in a concept that is simple and proper to Him," nonetheless "we can know God in a common concept that is predicable of Him and others."[195] This concept, as such, applies univocally to God and creatures in the sense that the concept has the same meaning in both cases. Like Scotus, Ockham is well aware that "nothing real is univocal to God and creatures, if we take 'univocal' in its strict meaning; for nothing that

192. See *Quodlibet* 7.13.

193. Ockham, *Quodlibetal Questions*, 96 (*Quodlibet* 2.1).

194. For further discussion of Ockham on the demonstrations of God's existence, see Adams, *William Ockham*, 2:967–79. Graham Oppy similarly opposes Aquinas's second way on the grounds that "there is nothing in the premises that justifies drawing the conclusion that there is *exactly one* first cause" and that "there is nothing in the premises to rule out circles of causes, for example, a situation in which *a* causes *b*, *b* causes *c*, and *c* causes *a*" (Oppy, *Arguing about Gods* [Cambridge: Cambridge University Press, 1999], 99–100).

195. Ockham, *Philosophical Writings*, 102; see also *Quodlibet* 5.14, where Ockham states that "the concept *being* is univocal to God and all other things. This is evident from the fact that everyone concedes that we have some sort of noncomplex cognition of God" (*Quodlibetal Questions*, 449). For discussion see Stephen Dumont, "Henry of Ghent and Duns Scotus," in *Medieval Philosophy*, ed. John Marenbon (London: Routledge, 1998), 291–328.

exists in a creature, whether it be essential or accidental, has perfect similitude with something which really exists in God."[196] When "univocal" is taken in this strict meaning, there can be nothing univocal between God and creatures.

In his *Reportatio*, Ockham comments that "univocal" has various senses. The sense of "univocal" that pertains to God and creatures involves "a concept common to many things which have no likeness, either substantial or accidental."[197] Strictly speaking, God and creatures have absolutely no likeness. Ockham states that "in God and in creatures there is nothing at all, intrinsic or extrinsic, which is of the same kind."[198] God's goodness is not like our goodness. Yet the concept "good," as such, can be affirmed of both God and creatures. Ockham thinks that the particular sense that he gives to univocity accords with what others try to affirm through the doctrine of analogy. When we say that creatures are good and that God is good, Ockham thinks it indisputable that we are using one concept (rather than two), and he makes clear that this concept is neither purely univocal nor purely equivocal.

Since we know God through his created effects, God "is known either in a concept common to Him and others, or in something real which is different from Him."[199] The latter cannot be the case, because if it were true, then we would know a creature, not God. Ockham reasons that "when I know God in this life, I know Him in a concept which is common to Him and to other things, so that the term of the act of knowing is some one thing and not a plurality, and is common to many things."[200] He goes on to remark that it is possible "to abstract from an imperfect creature a concept of wisdom which does not refer more to creatures than to what is not a creature."[201] The concept itself, as such, refers neither to God nor to creatures; it is simply a concept that is predicable not only of material things but also of spiritual things. Ockham recognizes that "the distinction between the wisdom of a creature and the wisdom of God is as great as the distinction between God and a stone."[202] But the concept "wisdom," abstracted from any particular essence, is predicable of both a creature and God.[203]

196. Ockham, *Philosophical Writings*, 106.
197. Ockham, *Philosophical Writings*, 107.
198. Ockham, *Philosophical Writings*, 107.
199. Ockham, *Philosophical Writings*, 110.
200. Ockham, *Philosophical Writings*, 111.
201. Ockham, *Philosophical Writings*, 112.
202. Ockham, *Philosophical Writings*, 112.
203. For further discussion see Alfred J. Freddoso, "Ockham on Faith and Reason," in *Cambridge Companion to Ockham*, 326–49, esp. 341–43. John Lee Longeway describes Ockham as "the founder of European empiricism. Like Locke and Hume, he relied on the logical analysis

Conclusion

Let us recall and briefly evaluate the ways in which the fathers and medievals argued for (and in Ockham's case also against) the demonstrability of the existence of God. Tertullian seeks to show that we can know God from the existence and order of the universe, but he does not do this claim any favors by holding that God, as a substance, must be in some sense material. Gregory of Nazianzus pushes the discussion forward significantly by means of Aristotelian reasoning, as interpreted through a late-Platonic lens. For Gregory, as for Tertullian, the universe's motion and order demonstrate the existence of God. Gregory adds the points that finite things are dependent, that no finite thing can move the whole, and that God is not in the order of moved or moving things but rather is a transcendent mover. Gregory also argues, from the existence of finite perfections, that there must be an infinitely perfect source. By bringing to bear the Greek tradition of philosophical proofs of God's existence, Gregory goes beyond the limitations of Tertullian's Stoic-influenced reasoning, valuable though the latter is.

Augustine, in various comments strewn throughout the *Confessions*, provides a profound sense of our creaturely contingency. Augustine's major contributions to the discussion are Platonic in origin and are found in the Neoplatonists such as Plotinus: namely, our restless desire for being, goodness, and beauty, which can only be quenched by union with transcendent being, goodness, and beauty; the soul's intellectual light as leading us to eternal and unchanging Truth, as we ascend from physical things to intelligible realities; and the fact that we participate in a finite way in existence, so that there must be infinite Being in which we participate.

If Gregory of Nazianzus adds broadly Aristotelian dimensions to Tertullian's Stoic proofs, and Augustine adds Platonic (or Neoplatonic) dimensions, does John of Damascus contribute anything? John repeats the demonstrations of God's existence from the order of the universe and from changeable things. His perspective is fundamentally Aristotelian, like Gregory's. Thus he criticizes the view that God is in some sense material by noting that even a spiritual body would be moveable and would itself require an unmoved cause. He adds the point that the four elements, as contraries, could not hold together in a unity for very long unless they had a transcendent governor, who would also bring the elements into being and preserve them in being.

of language to ground a rejection of Platonic metaphysics" (Longeway, introduction to *Demonstration and Scientific Knowledge in William of Ockham: A Translation of* Summa Logicae *III–II: De Syllogismo Demonstrativo, and Selections from the Prologue to the* Ordinatio, trans. John Lee Longeway [Notre Dame: University of Notre Dame Press, 2007], 1–140, at 1).

John deepens the Aristotelian basis (filtered through late Platonism) of the patristic demonstrations of God's existence.

Anselm's approach is generally more Augustinian or Neoplatonic. He emphasizes that our desire for good things should lead us to recognize the existence of self-subsistent goodness in which all good things participate. Like Augustine, Anselm also attends to the contingency of things: other than God, "whatever exists, exists through something." Anselm's argument that there are degrees of perfection in being and that the chain of ever-greater existing natures cannot go on infinitely accords with Augustine's argument that a living thing is better than a nonliving thing, and a wise living thing better than one that has no intelligence, and so forth to the highest being. Anselm also draws from Augustine his definition of God as "that than which nothing greater can be thought."

The broadly Aristotelian reasoning, inflected with late-Platonic insights, about the existence of God that we find in the Greek-speaking East in Gregory and John of Damascus is continued in the Latin-speaking West by Thomas Aquinas. Aquinas's approach to the existence of God is Aristotelian in the sense that he relies on such principles as ontological composition (essence/being, form/matter), causal interdependency, and above all the act/potency distinction. Like Gregory and John, Aquinas is not solely "Aristotelian" but is influenced by a number of thinkers, such as (in his case) Augustine, Boethius, Pseudo-Dionysius, and John of Damascus himself. He rejects arguments that claim God's self-evidence—not only Anselm's but also those from our desire for the good and from our knowledge of truth. Significantly, Aquinas's demonstrations of God's existence often appeal to the same points that we saw already in Tertullian, namely, that the universe could not have brought itself into being and ordered itself. In the *Summa contra gentiles*, Aquinas devotes a great deal of effort to summarizing and refining demonstrations that originate in Aristotle. These demonstrations hinge on Aristotle's understanding of motion or change, specifically the claim that "everything that is moved is moved by another" and that "with respect to the same motion, nothing is both mover and moved." In an essentially ordered series of causes, it is impossible to proceed to infinity in movers and things moved; there must be a first unmoved mover or else the motion of the intermediate causes could not be accounted for. To the demonstrations of God's existence along these lines, Aquinas adds John of Damascus's demonstration from the fact that "contrary and discordant things" are part of one universal order.

In the *Summa theologiae*, Aquinas offers five demonstrations that sum up the main lines of the patristic witness (especially if we also include his attention to the proofs from desire for the good and knowledge of the truth, which he thinks to be evocative even if they do not strictly work). From the more "Aristotelian" side, as represented by Gregory and John of Damascus, he sets forth the demonstrations from motion and from efficient causality as well as a demonstration from possibility and necessity, which is a broadly Aristotelian version of Augustine's emphasis on creaturely contingency. These demonstrations presume the principle of noncontradiction—something cannot both be and not be in the same way at the same time—and they also presume that being is intelligible as being and can be analyzed in terms of act and potency, so that diverse modes of being are analogously distinguished.[204] His fourth way is from degrees of perfection, and this approach echoes a proof found in Gregory of Nazianzus and is also deeply Augustinian (and Neoplatonic). His fifth way is from the order of the universe, since no nonrational thing could order itself consistently in a teleological fashion. The fifth way takes us back to the basic demonstration that we find in Tertullian and in almost all the fathers, and indeed already in Xenophon.

What then of Ockham? He supposes that the conservation of all things in being shows that a first efficient cause exists, but he does not consider that the demonstration from efficient causality works. For Ockham, it is possible that in a multitude of things, there are enough sources of actualization that one transcendent "first mover" is not needed. In my view, this conclusion rests on failing to appreciate adequately the contingency of all finite things. After all, any accidentally ordered series of finite causes depends on an essentially ordered series in order to exist. Even if the finite causes in an accidentally ordered series are infinite in number (as Aquinas grants), they cannot account for the existence of the series, since the existence of the infinite series would itself be dependent and in need of a cause. With regard to whether natural reason can prove God's unity, the question here is again Aristotelian: Can there be more than one Pure Act? Ockham argues that we can answer in the negative only on the basis of faith, not on the basis of reason. His reasoning, however, relies on his view that all spiritual substances—God, the angels, and spiritual souls—are equally simple. In denying that angels and spiritual

204. For an introduction to the distinction between act and potency, see Feser, *Aquinas*, 9–12. For detailed discussion of the relation of Aquinas's thought to Aristotle's on this point, see John F. Wippel, "Thomas Aquinas and the Axiom That Unreceived Act Is Unlimited," in Wippel, *Metaphysical Themes in Thomas Aquinas II* (Washington, DC: Catholic University of America Press, 2007), 123–51; W. Norris Clarke, SJ, "The Limitation of Act by Potency in St. Thomas: Aristotelianism or Neoplatonism?," in Clarke, *Explorations in Metaphysics: Being—God—Person* (Notre Dame: University of Notre Dame Press, 1994), 65–88. See also Clarke, "Action as the Self-Revelation of Being: A Central Theme in the Thought of St. Thomas," in Clarke, *Explorations in Metaphysics*, 45–64; Steven A. Long, "On the Natural Knowledge of the Real Distinction of Essence and Existence," *Nova et Vetera* 1 (2003): 75–108.

souls, whose being is not their essence, are composite in a way that God is not, Ockham overlooks the unique simplicity of Pure Act. When we demonstrate the existence of pure actuality (a first cause, unmoved mover, source of all things), we demonstrate the existence of something whose being and power are absolutely simple, infinite, unlimited, and unrestricted. In this respect, Ockham would have been aided by a deeper attention to the patristic tradition.

Even Ockham, however, holds that we can demonstrate the existence of God on the basis of the conservation of all things in being.[205] The common thread of this first chapter is thus not completely absent even in Ockham. But since Ockham's demonstration of God's existence from conservation does not include God's unity, the argument from conservation has not yet demonstrated the existence of the true God (who is one). Indeed, with respect to causality, act/potency, and simplicity, Ockham's Aristotelianism lacks some crucial elements that we find in John of Damascus and Aquinas, no doubt in part because Ockham largely excludes Neoplatonic insights. His work therefore foreshadows the broad Reformation and Enlightenment movement away from Aristotelian and Neoplatonic demonstrations of God's existence.

---

205. For a contemporary Thomistic engagement with those who argue that the universe, once in existence, does not need to be conserved in existence by God (and indeed does not need to be caused by God), see Edward Feser, "Existential Inertia and the Five Ways," *American Catholic Philosophical Quarterly* 85 (2011): 237–67. For the position that Feser contests, see especially Bede Rundle, *Why There Is Something Rather Than Nothing* (Oxford: Oxford University Press, 2004). Reading the classical proofs through a Humean lens, Rundle argues that "the notion of beginning to be has no application to the universe, and hence . . . there is in this instance no coming into existence for which we have to find a cause" (ibid., viii). The same view is found in John Stuart Mill, *Three Essays on Religion: Nature, The Utility of Religion, Theism* (Amherst, NY: Prometheus, 1998), 142–43. Mill argues that since the elements of the universe "are not known to us as beginning to exist," it follows that "causation cannot legitimately be extended to the material universe itself, but only to its changeable phenomena" (ibid., 143). For Mill, then, the only possible "first cause" would be "a certain quantum of Force, combined with certain collocations" (ibid., 145). But Aquinas's demonstrations of God's existence are not predicated on the universe having a beginning of existence.

2

Reformation and Enlightenment Views

Due to its strong view of sin's dire consequences, the Protestant Reformation is sometimes assumed to have been on the side of critics of the demonstrability of God's existence. For different reasons, a similar critique of the demonstrability of God's existence is also often associated with the Enlightenment. Of course, as the Reformation historian Diarmaid MacCulloch observes, "much of the Enlightenment was not anti-Christian at all: it was able to alter Christianity and open it to ways of reformulating the questions and answers which made up Christian belief."[1] As MacCulloch remarks, however, during the eighteenth century "Often doubt, scepticism or hatred of the Church . . . moved on to become what we would define as atheism."[2] Is it correct to say, then, that the major thinkers of the Reformation and Enlightenment periods deny that human reason can demonstrate the existence of God?

While some figures from these periods have no room for the demonstrability of God's existence, others strongly insist on human reason's ability to arrive at knowledge of God. Thus, John Calvin argues that our knowledge of God's existence is innate and indelible, although people still fall into idolatry, because the human mind, obscured by sin, is not able to know exactly who or what God is. For Calvin, even those who reject God and are most deeply mired in sin know that God exists. Calvin does not think that there is any

1. Diarmaid MacCulloch, *The Reformation: A History* (New York: Penguin, 2003), 698.
2. Ibid.

need for complex metaphysical proofs of the kind we found in Aquinas, but he fully affirms the fathers' proof from the order of the universe.

Similarly, René Descartes, widely acknowledged as the father of Enlightenment philosophy, affirms that he can demonstrate God's existence with certitude. Beginning with "I think, therefore I am," Descartes reasons that he can conceive of something more perfect than himself, and he can also recognize that he is not the source of this perfection. He has an idea of the infinite, though he is only finite. On this basis Descartes concludes that God must exist.

The Reformation and Enlightenment periods also include creative exponents of the Aristotelian tradition that we saw in Gregory of Nazianzus, John of Damascus, and Aquinas. For instance, the Jesuit theologian Francisco Suárez, while rejecting Aquinas's argument from motion, disagrees with Ockham regarding the argument from efficient causality. Suárez holds that this argument succeeds in demonstrating an unmoved mover, Pure Act. Like Ockham, Suárez is not thereby persuaded of the unity of God, since he supposes that there might be many distinct universes governed by distinct Pure Acts. To demonstrate the unity of God, Suárez argues that singularity must belong intrinsically to the essence of uncreated being.

Nonetheless, the critique of the demonstrations of God's existence can correctly be said to have the sixteenth century for its fundamental starting point, even though Ockham anticipates this critique. Deeply learned in the Stoic and Academic (skeptical) traditions of classical antiquity and negatively impressed by the religious turmoil of his day, Michel de Montaigne holds that human reason cannot arrive at certitude even about animals, much less about God. Since we do not know what laws characterize nature or whether there is one universe or many, and since what we know of existence is ephemeral and constantly changing, we have no real basis for constructing proofs about God's existence. Our ambitions should be chastened by the example of the Stoics, whose proofs from the created order to the Creator never could get beyond pantheism. In Montaigne's view, the effects we see around us are far too faint and weak to show anything about an infinite cause.

Responding to Montaigne, his fellow Frenchman Blaise Pascal grants that the order of the universe does not suffice to demonstrate God's existence. Occasionally, Pascal suggests that some demonstrations of God's existence do indeed work, as for example the demonstration from our finite and contingent existence to an infinite source of existence and from truths to an eternal Truth. But more frequently, Pascal insists that God infinitely exceeds our understanding and that we cannot find God solely through reason. The personal God manifests himself to those who seek to know him in personal ways rather than through impersonal and abstract demonstrations. Pascal also urges us to consider what makes us happy and to notice that nature everywhere shows traces of a fall away from God. In this light, Pascal proposes that since we have to choose to live either as though God exists or as though God does not exist, the former option is the only rational one, given that the potential reward is all on the side of the former option.

The eighteenth-century Scottish philosopher David Hume extends Montaigne's skeptical arguments. His key move is to separate the cause-effect relation into two separate events and to argue that an absolutely necessary relationship between the two events cannot be demonstrated. This gets rid of the principle of causality that is central to many of the classical demonstrations of God's existence. Given that effects may not need causes at all, Hume no longer has to worry about how something could cause itself. Hume also argues that even if one assumes normal causal relations, one can only infer a cause that is exactly proportionate to the effect; anything else is conjecture. Thus we can at best infer a finite, imperfect cause. For Hume, we certainly cannot infer a cause unlike anything that we have ever observed, which is what is done by the demonstrations of God's existence.

The last thinker that I treat in this chapter, Immanuel Kant, considers that God's existence is a postulate of practical reason. Practical reasoning, rooted in the experienced imperatives of the moral law, moves us toward holiness and happiness, which together comprise our highest good. Such movement would be utterly incoherent if God did not exist, since in our short and sinful lives on earth there is no way for us to achieve the holiness and happiness that we seek. When it comes to speculative demonstrations of God's existence, however, Kant argues that every attempt at such a demonstration fails. He argues that the principle of causality applies only within the world of sense, and like Hume, he thinks that we can reason only to a strictly proportionate cause: appealing to an utterly incomprehensible cause is no way to account for a series of dependent causes. Within the sphere of our understanding, we know of nothing for which nonbeing is impossible; we cannot even *conceive* of an "absolutely necessary being." In Kant's view, all the proofs of God's existence depend, like Anselm's *Proslogion*, on an *a priori* concept of a highest being, despite their claim to begin with sense knowledge and to demonstrate God's existence on that basis.

The modern period, therefore, leaves the classical demonstrations of God's existence—advocated in different forms by Calvin and Suárez—seemingly in tatters, even though Pascal's wager (with its appeal to rational pursuit of our highest possible good) and Kant's practical postulate (with its emphasis on our experience of the moral law and our desire for happiness) offer new approaches. The crucial question is whether Montaigne, Hume, and Kant are correct in their epistemology and in their rejection of the principle of causality as an effective path by which to demonstrate the existence of a transcendent, self-subsistent cause of all things.

John Calvin (1509–64)

John Calvin, born in Noyon, France, became a clerk to his local bishop at age twelve. He studied Latin and philosophy in Paris before moving to the University of Orléans and then to the University of Bourges for law studies. His first book, published in 1532, was a commentary on Seneca's *De clementia*. In 1533 he experienced a religious conversion and broke with the Catholic Church. Soon after, due to his association with Nicholas Cop, a Protestant Reformer who was removed from being rector of the Collège Royal in Paris, Calvin went into hiding and eventually fled to Basel. He published the first edition of his massively influential *Institutes of the Christian Religion* in 1536. He became a pastor in Geneva and worked to organize the Reformed Church there, but tension among the reforming parties forced him to return to Basel, and he moved to Strasbourg in 1538. After three years ministering and writing in Strasbourg, he returned to Geneva, where he remained for the rest of his life. He wrote a commentary on almost every book of Scripture and completed the final revision and extensive expansion of the *Institutes* in 1559.[3]

Calvin argues that all humans have some kind of innate knowledge of God's existence. For Calvin, our human misery itself directs us toward God: "Every man, being stung by the consciousness of his own unhappiness, in this way at least obtains some knowledge of God. Thus, our feeling of ignorance, vanity, want, weakness, in short, depravity and corruption, reminds us that in the Lord, and none but He, dwell the true light of wisdom, solid virtue, exuberant goodness."[4] When we come to know our situation, we naturally

3. See Bruce Gordon, *Calvin* (New Haven: Yale University Press, 2009). For Calvin on natural knowledge of God's existence, see especially Paul Helm, *John Calvin's Ideas* (Oxford: Oxford University Press, 2004), chap. 8: "Natural Theology and the *Sensus Divinitas*" (esp. 228, 234). See also T. H. L. Parker, *Calvin's Doctrine of the Knowledge of God*, 2nd ed. (Edinburgh: Oliver & Boyd, 1969); John Beversluis, "Reforming the 'Reformed' Objection to Natural Theology," *Faith and Philosophy* 12 (1995): 189–206. For seventeenth-century Reformed thinkers, see Jeffrey K. Jue, "*Theologia Naturalis*: A Reformed Tradition," in *Revelation and Reason: New Essays in Reformed Apologetics*, ed. K. Scott Oliphint and Lane G. Tipton (Phillipsburg, NJ: P&R, 2007), 168–89.

4. John Calvin, *The Institutes of the Christian Religion* 1.1, trans. Henry Beveridge (Grand Rapids: Eerdmans, 1989), 38. Emil Brunner and Karl Barth debate the value of such texts from Calvin in their exchange from 1934, published as Emil Brunner and Karl Barth, *Natural*

seek for God—even though in our pride we cannot fully know our miserable state until we have known God. The cure for pride is to "raise our thoughts to God, and reflect what kind of Being he is, and how absolute the perfection of that righteousness, and wisdom, and virtue, to which as a standard, we are bound to be conformed."[5] Before the fall, says Calvin, we could have known God by natural reason as our benefactor and father, but the fall placed us at odds with God. We retain a knowledge of God that is distinct from salvific knowledge of Jesus Christ, but unless our knowledge of God leads us to love, trust, and obey God in Christ, it is worthless knowledge.

With this proviso in mind, Calvin argues that God has endowed all humans with a real knowledge of God. Even sinners who reject God know him by natural reason. Their conscience continually condemns and torments them because they know the one whom they are rejecting: "a sense of Deity is indelibly engraven on the human heart."[6] Even idolaters know God to some degree because they still have the instinct to worship. Calvin grants that idolatry obscures this "sense of Deity," but idolatry cannot uproot it. He remarks in this regard, "At length they bewilder themselves in such a maze of error, that the darkness of ignorance obscures, and ultimately extinguishes, those sparks which were designed to show them the glory of God. Still, however, the conviction that there is some Deity continues to exist, like a plant which can never be completely eradicated."[7] In part, Calvin is here responding to

Theology: Comprising 'Nature and Grace' by Professor Dr. Emil Brunner and the Reply 'No!' by Dr. Karl Barth, trans. Peter Fraenkel (Eugene, OR: Wipf and Stock, 2002). Barth considers that had Calvin known Aquinas's work, Calvin would have had to take a much different approach. For Barth, Calvin's approach can be justified to the degree that Calvin relies on biblical revelation rather than on any "independent" basis for knowledge of God. Helm observes, "Perhaps there is an element of wishful thinking in Barth's attitude to Calvin, more a question of what Calvin ought to have believed rather than what he did believe" (Helm, *John Calvin's Ideas*, 210). See also Brunner's *Revelation and Reason: The Christian Doctrine of Faith and Knowledge*, trans. Olive Wyon (Wake Forest, NC: Chanticleer, 1946). Brunner, too, is keen to subordinate reason to revelation. For a response to Barth and Brunner, see G. C. Berkouwer, *General Revelation* (Grand Rapids: Eerdmans, 1955). Berkouwer sides with "the impossibility of a natural theology," while granting that a "non-depraved reason" (were such available to fallen humans) could attain "preliminary but true knowledge of God" and while insisting on "the revelational character of God's working in created reality" (ibid., 73–74, 314). Believers, healed and illumined by faith, can perceive "God's revelation in his works," though here "we are not dealing with an independent source of revelation *in addition to* special revelation, but we are concerned with seeing, recognizing and confessing God in the works of his hands" (ibid., 323).

5. Calvin, *Institutes* 1.1, pp. 38–39.
6. Calvin, *Institutes* 1.3, p. 44.
7. Calvin, *Institutes* 1.4, p. 49. He adds,
Nay, we have still stronger evidence of the proposition for which I now contend—viz. that a sense of Deity is naturally engraven on the human heart, in the fact, that the very reprobate are forced to acknowledge it. When at their ease, they can jest about God, and

arguments that religion was invented by a few men in order to subjugate the ignorant masses. The opposite is the case: the mass of humanity struggles powerfully to extinguish the knowledge of God, but cannot do so no matter how many false gods are devised. Humans devise false gods because they fear the true God and his righteousness.

In addition to considering that all humans have an innate knowledge of God, Calvin also argues for the existence of God based on the order of the universe. He states that God has arranged "so to manifest his perfections in the whole structure of the universe, and daily place himself in our view, that we cannot open our eyes without being compelled to behold him."[8] Although God is incomprehensible to our finite minds, his works make manifest his glory. No one who has seen God's works can be ignorant of God's glorious existence. The universe reveals "the immense weight of glory," so that the visible world serves as an "image" of, or mirror to, the invisible God.[9] In making this point, Calvin twice quotes the Psalms because they often rejoice in God's manifestation of himself through created things. Calvin also quotes and strongly affirms Romans 1:20. The wisdom of God is attested by "proofs which force themselves on the notice of the most illiterate peasant, who cannot open his eyes without beholding them."[10] The study of astronomy or medicine strengthens our appreciation for God's wisdom in ordering the cosmos, but anyone who looks at the stars or the human body will be moved to give glory to God. Calvin approves the view that the human being is a wondrous "microcosm," and he holds (citing Paul's words in Acts 17:27) that "in order to apprehend God, it is unnecessary to go farther than ourselves."[11]

Calvin complains that a number of his contemporaries, like the ancient Epicureans, seek to replace God with a personified "nature" (the world-soul) as the Creator of the universe, notwithstanding the extraordinary evidence provided by natural science. As he says, "Let Epicurus tell what concourse of atoms, cooking meat and drink, can form one portion into refuse and another portion into blood, and make all the members separately perform their office as carefully as if they were so many souls acting with common consent in the superintendence of one body."[12] He then proceeds to a strong defense of the

talk pertly and loquaciously in disparagement of his power; but should despair, from any cause, overtake them, it will stimulate them to seek him, and dictate ejaculatory prayers, proving that they were not entirely ignorant of God, but had perversely suppressed feelings which ought to have been earlier manifested. (ibid.)

8. Calvin, *Institutes* 1.5, p. 51.
9. Calvin, *Institutes* 1.5, p. 51.
10. Calvin, *Institutes* 1.5, p. 51.
11. Calvin, *Institutes* 1.5, p. 52.
12. Calvin, *Institutes* 1.5, p. 53.

spiritual soul, on the basis of which he concludes that there must be an intelligent Creator because human intelligence cannot simply arise from matter. He also points to the immense power of God as manifested by God's sustaining the entire universe in being and by God's governance of the weather and the ocean. He adds that "this method of investigating the divine perfections, by tracing the lineaments of his countenance as shadowed forth in the firmament and on the earth, is common both to those within and to those without the pale of the Church."[13] After bemoaning the fact that few persons pay attention to the divine glory that is so manifest, he concludes by warning once more against mere speculation about God that does not result in obedient love, and by emphasizing that "there is no need of a long and laborious train of argument" to prove God's existence, because the proofs are in fact "so immediately within our reach in every quarter, that we can trace them with the eye, or point to them with the finger."[14] He also cautions against the errors of the pagan philosophers, including pantheism and atheism. Among the pagans, he says, "though all did not give way to gross vice, or rush headlong into open idolatry, there was no pure and authentic religion founded merely on common belief."[15]

I should add a brief note regarding Calvin's *Commentary on Romans*, published in 1539. On Romans 1:19, which in Calvin's translation reads, "Because that which may be known of God is manifest in them; for God has showed it to them," Calvin comments that God wishes us to know "all that appertains to the setting forth of the glory of the Lord," that is to say, "whatever ought to move and excite us to glorify God."[16] Calvin thinks it significant that Paul says that what can be known about God is manifest *in* humans. This means, he suggests, that humans intuitively know what can be known about God. God manifests himself in us so clearly that we cannot fail to know his glory. Calvin states that Paul intends "to indicate a manifestation, by which they [humans] might be so closely pressed, that they could not evade."[17] We cannot avoid possessing sufficient knowledge of God so as to be able to give God glory. For Calvin, this is the same as saying that each person possesses the knowledge of God "engraven on his own heart."[18]

13. Calvin, *Institutes* 1.5, p. 56.
14. Calvin, *Institutes* 1.5, p. 57.
15. Calvin, *Institutes* 1.5, p. 61.
16. John Calvin, *Calvin's Bible Commentaries: Romans*, trans. John King (London: Forgotten Books, 2007 [1847]), 47. Calvin's Latin biblical text for Romans 1:19–20 reads, "Quia quod cognoscitur de Deo manifestum est in ipsis: Deus enim illis manifestavit. Si quidem invisibilia ipsius, ex creatione mundi operibus intellecta, conspiciuntur, aeterna quoque ejus potentia, et divinitas; ut sint inexcusabiles."
17. Calvin, *Romans*, 48.
18. Calvin, *Romans*, 48.

If this is what Paul means by stating that the knowledge of God has been manifested "in them," what does Paul mean when he affirms that the knowledge of God "is manifest" in them? How does it become manifest? Calvin argues that it "is manifest" because the world's beauty clearly reveals its divine author. The manifestation is through external things, but it is also *in* us because we cannot escape the conclusion that the world has a Creator. In Calvin's view, "man was created to be a spectator of this formed world," and "eyes were given him, that he might, by looking on so beautiful a picture, be led up to the Author himself."[19] Simply by opening our eyes and observing the world's beauty, we know that it has a glorious Creator.

Calvin's translation of Romans 1:20 is as follows: "For the invisible things of him from the creation of the world are clearly seen, being understood by the things that are made, even his eternal power and Godhead; so that they are without excuse." The first point that Calvin makes is that God is invisible in himself. We cannot see God with our physical eyes, but nonetheless God's "invisible things" are "clearly seen." How is this so? Calvin observes that God's "majesty shines forth in his works and in his creatures everywhere."[20] There should be no difficulty in discovering the glorious God, since God's majesty is evident through the works and creatures of God. Citing the Letter to the Hebrews, Calvin remarks that when we look into the world as into a mirror, what we see in the mirror is God. The world shows forth many of God's attributes, but Paul mentions two, "eternal power and Godhead." After all, the existence of the world shows that its Creator is powerful and indeed shows that God "must necessarily be without beginning and from himself."[21] If God had a beginning and a cause, God would be among the things of this world. Thus the world reveals not only a Creator, but a Creator with attributes that differentiate him from any creature. Calvin comments that "when we arrive at this point, the divinity becomes known to us."[22] From the things of this world, we can arrive at a knowledge of God that is sufficient for the purpose of giving God glory. The world shows that it must have a Creator, and that this powerful Creator must be self-subsistent.

Paul concludes that "they are without excuse." God has done his part; God has clearly manifested himself so that we cannot use the weakness of the human mind or our dependence on sense-knowledge as an excuse for not glorifying God. Calvin underscores that "the manifestation of God, by which he makes his glory known in his creation, is, with regard to the light itself, sufficiently clear."[23]

19. Calvin, *Romans*, 48.
20. Calvin, *Romans*, 48.
21. Calvin, *Romans*, 48.
22. Calvin, *Romans*, 48.
23. Calvin, *Romans*, 48.

Our sinfulness, however, makes us blind. The lack of sufficiency lies in us, not in God's manifestation. Are we so blind that in fact we do not know that God exists, despite its clarity? Calvin answers no. Our blindness does not hide from us that God exists. Rather, our blindness obscures from us exactly who God is, and so we fall into idolatry. As Calvin puts it, "We conceive that there is a Deity; and then we conclude, that whoever he may be, he ought to be worshipped: but our reason here fails, because it cannot ascertain who or what sort of being God is."[24] We perversely fail to worship God, or rather we worship gods instead of God. Yet we know that some sort of God exists; otherwise the things of this world would be inexplicable, since they make clear that they have a Creator.

Indeed, given the obscuring of our minds, we need faith in order to recognize fully and worship properly the true God. In this regard Calvin cites Hebrews 11:3: "By faith we understand that the world was created by the word of God, so that what is seen was made out of things which do not appear." What Paul ascribes to reason in Romans 1:20, Calvin ascribes to faith in Hebrews 11:3. Calvin explains that faith possesses this role without negating reason's ability to know that God exists: "We are prevented by our blindness, so that we reach not to the end in view; we yet see so far, that we cannot pretend any excuse."[25] Calvin also draws on Acts 14:16–17, where Barnabas and Paul proclaim to the people of Lystra, "In past generations he [God] allowed all the nations to walk in their own ways; yet he did not leave himself without witness, for he did good and gave you from heaven rains and fruitful seasons." Calvin interprets this to mean that God manifested his existence via the good things of this world—God's "witness"—while at the same time God allowed the nations to practice idolatry. Calvin concludes his commentary on Romans 1:19–20 by strongly differentiating between natural knowledge of God through "the things that are made" and saving knowledge of God through faith in Jesus Christ; the former merely leaves us "without excuse."

Michel de Montaigne (1533–92)

Michel de Montaigne, born into a noble family near Bordeaux, received a careful education in Latin philosophy and literature, and his essays reflect the influence of Stoic and Academic philosophy. For thirteen years, he worked

---

24. Calvin, *Romans*, 48. Calvin's reasoning seems broadly similar to Thomas Aquinas's observation, in response to the claim that God's existence is self-evident, that "to know that God exists in a general and confused way is implanted in us by nature. . . . This, however, is not to know absolutely that God exists; just as to know that someone is approaching is not the same as to know that Peter is approaching, even though it is Peter who is approaching" (Aquinas, *Summa theologiae* Ia.2.1, ad 1).

25. Calvin, *Romans*, 48.

as a councilor in Bordeaux's Chambre des Enquêtes. Inheriting his father's estate at age thirty-five, Montaigne devoted himself largely to writing, publishing the first two books of his *Essays* in 1580. In 1581 he became mayor of Bordeaux, a position that he held for four years, although he fled the city during a plague that killed almost half of its inhabitants. During the 1570s and 1580s, a period of religious wars and strife throughout Europe, Montaigne undertook diplomatic and political work for Henry of Navarre, later Henry IV. The final edition of his *Essays* appeared in 1588. On his deathbed, Montaigne requested and received the last rites of the church.[26]

In his essay "Apology for Raimond Sebond"—in length the size of a short book, and among his very first writings—Montaigne critiques Raimond Sebond's natural theology under the guise of defending it. Sebond was a Spanish theologian who published a book titled *Natural Theology, or Book of Things Created* in the early fifteenth century. A theologian named Pierre Brunel gave this book to Montaigne's father, and, at the request of his father (with whom Montaigne was very close), Montaigne translated it into French in 1569. Montaigne notes that at this time, Martin Luther's views were shaking the faith of many French Catholics. He describes the situation of the "common people" in words that aptly apply to himself: "When once certain articles of their religion have been called in question and placed in the scales, they will soon be ready to throw into a like uncertainty all the other articles of their faith, which had no more authority or foundation in their eyes than those which are already shattered."[27]

In his "Apology for Raimond Sebond," Montaigne presents himself as a defender of the faith, fully persuaded by Sebond. But he depicts Sebond as a naïve and deluded rationalist. Montaigne explains, "The author's aim is bold and courageous; for he undertakes, by human and natural reasons, to establish and prove against the atheists all the articles of the Christian religion."[28] The implication is that Sebond thereby goes far beyond earlier theologians, who demonstrated God's existence but not the existence of the Trinity. Tongue in cheek, Montaigne gives this bold undertaking his approval at the outset: "I find him so strong and successful that I do not

26. See Stuart Hampshire, introduction to Michel de Montaigne, *The Complete Works: Essays, Travel Journal, Letters*, trans. Donald M. Frame (New York: Alfred A. Knopf, 2003), xv–xxvi; Sarah Bakewell, *How to Live, or, A Life of Montaigne in One Question and Twenty Attempts at an Answer* (London: Random House, 2010); Donald M. Frame, *Montaigne: A Biography* (London: H. Hamilton, 1965). See also Pierre Manent's *Montaigne: La vie sans loi* (Paris: Flammarion, 2014).
27. Michel de Montaigne, *The Essays of Montaigne*, trans. E. J. Trechmann (New York: Random House, 1946), 369.
28. Montaigne, *Essays of Montaigne*, 370.

think it possible to improve on his arguments; and I believe that no man has equalled him."[29]

After suggesting that Sebond was a follower of the ideas of Thomas Aquinas, Montaigne explains the critique that has been lodged by some thinkers against Sebond's work. The critique is that many Christian beliefs require faith, in which case Sebond could not prove all Christian beliefs by reason. Despite the supposed praise that he has just bestowed on Sebond, Montaigne agrees with the critique. Christian truth, he says, is so beyond human understanding that God's help is needed for us to believe it. If human reasoning alone could demonstrate all Christian beliefs, then the pagan philosophers would have demonstrated them. Montaigne claims to approve of the project of strengthening faith by employing reason on faith's behalf, so long as we recognize that our reason will not "be able to attain to a knowledge so divine and supernatural."[30] Yet Montaigne adds that Sebond is to be commended because unless reason confirms all Christian beliefs, they will collapse. Faith is too shaky a reed upon which to rely.

Montaigne next argues that if faith were the divine gift that it claims to be, the minds and actions of Christians would be gracious and virtuous rather than profoundly weak and dissolute. He suggests that for most if not all of those who call themselves Christians, faith is not real. Those who call themselves Christians are really self-seeking partisans, perfectly willing to burn their opponents at the stake in the name of truth. This is so despite the apparent fact that if we knew God, "we should love him above all other things, for the infinite goodness and beauty that shine in him."[31] Our problem, then, is that we do not know God either by faith or by reason. We are Christians simply because we happen to have been born in a traditionally Christian country and wish to be called Christian out of respect for our ancestors or out of self-seeking considerations with regard to life after death. Sudden fear of death makes "Christians" even out of professing atheists.

In supposed agreement with Sebond's defense of natural theology, Montaigne then professes that the cosmos must have "some marks imprinted on it by the hand of that great architect."[32] Yet he argues that without faith, Sebond's arguments for natural theology fall flat. Neither atheists nor Sebond, he suggests, are truly capable of saying anything about God, because human reason is incapable of arriving at certitude about such a matter, or indeed about anything at all.

29. Montaigne, *Essays of Montaigne*, 370.
30. Montaigne, *Essays of Montaigne*, 371.
31. Montaigne, *Essays of Montaigne*, 374.
32. Montaigne, *Essays of Montaigne*, 376.

Ostensibly in defense of Sebond, Montaigne goes on to advance arguments against the central premises of natural theology—namely, that the order and existence of the cosmos require a Creator, and that we can know this to be the case. With a comedic barb, Montaigne asks rhetorically, "What has induced him [man] to believe that the wonderful motion of the heavenly vault, the eternal light of those torches rolling so proudly over his head, the awe-inspiring agitations of that infinite sea, were established, and endure through so many centuries, for his service and convenience?"[33] The cosmos is far too vast for us to know the slightest portion of it, let alone to know its meaning, and it is quite likely that whatever meaning the cosmos has does not involve us. We are merely another kind of animal, and a lesser kind at that. In fact, we would trade all our philosophical wisdom for health and serenity, which the best philosophy is powerless to increase and often depletes. It is therefore fitting, Montaigne remarks sardonically, that Christianity commends ignorance to us, as an antidote to pride and as befits the obedience of faith. For Montaigne, the most one can say in favor of Christianity is that it is the faith of those who embrace their own ignorance: "So unable are we by our own powers to conceive the sublimity of God, that we least understand those works of our creator that best bear his stamp, and are most his. To meet with a thing that is unbelievable is to the Christian an occasion to believe. It is the more according to reason as it is contrary to human reason."[34]

Not surprisingly, Montaigne proceeds to deny that we can name God from the attributes of creatures. Although we apply to God such feelings as fear, anger, and love, these are feelings whose place in God, if any, we cannot imagine. Likewise, neither wisdom nor intelligence in fact apply to God, because wisdom involves choosing between good and evil (and God could have nothing to do with evil), and intelligence is a discursive search for clarity (and everything must already be clear to God). In the same vein, justice, temperance, and fortitude have to do with human community, bodily pleasures, and earthly dangers, none of which apply to God. Reason thus is unrelated to any knowledge of God that we might have, as is fitting, because such knowledge in Christianity comes solely from faith and obedience to authority. Against the pretensions of reason, we must acknowledge the futility of all the main schools of ancient philosophy. To their credit, the ancient skeptics admit their lack of knowledge, by contrast to the ancient dogmatists—foremost among them Aristotle—who either rely on obscure and unintelligible arguments so as to conceal their ignorance or else focus on posing puzzles without truly seeking to resolve them.

33. Montaigne, *Essays of Montaigne*, 379.
34. Montaigne, *Essays of Montaigne*, 424–25.

Turning explicitly to religion, Montaigne observes that the discussions of God (or gods) that we find in the various religions impiously and anthropomorphically pretend to know what cannot be known, with sheer confusion as the result. Religions make promises about eternal happiness or suffering in the next life that either inventively extend what we experience in this world or else go far beyond what flesh can bear and thus require that we be transformed into something entirely different. By means of examples, Montaigne shows that religions do not hesitate to make up things in this regard. Furthermore, if God or the gods reward what they make possible in our earthly lives, then we do not really deserve either a reward or punishment for what we could not help but do. There is also the despicable practice of propitiating God or the gods by inflicting suffering on innocent victims or by ascetical self-mutilation. The main point is this: God is not "subservient to the vain and feeble conjectures of our understanding."[35]

This principle holds especially with respect to the universe. Even supposing it to be God's creation, we cannot thereby know about God from it, both because God must radically transcend our small capacity to know and because there may be other universes quite unlike ours. We cannot know God on the basis of supposed laws pertaining to nature, since we do not know these laws. This stricture includes notions of "existence" and "motion." What we call our existence is "but a flash in the infinite course of an eternal night."[36] Nor can we assume that God "cannot" do or not do particular things, such as die, because we know nothing of God. All our language about God fails utterly and bears witness merely to our absurd pride: "That his goodness, wisdom, power, are one with his essence: our tongue speaks it, but our intelligence does not comprehend it. And yet our overweening conceit would make the Deity pass through our sieve."[37] We speak of God's providence, too, as if we knew that God cared about every little thing. When we pretend to be honoring God, we are merely glorifying ourselves—just as other animals, if given the chance to make gods, would make them in their image.

With reference to Cicero's *On the Nature of the Gods*, Montaigne shows how the effort to move logically from the created order to a Creator resulted in absurdly attributing the creation of the cosmos to "Nature," pantheistically conceived as a cosmic soul or cosmic animal. To this "Nature," Cicero attributes goodness, love, and justice, because we have these qualities. In Montaigne's view, Circero's example shows that effects give us no real knowledge of

35. Montaigne, *Essays of Montaigne*, 448.
36. Montaigne, *Essays of Montaigne*, 451.
37. Montaigne, *Essays of Montaigne*, 453.

causes, especially when we are talking about God. The thing to do, therefore, is to have no theory whatsoever about God. Whenever we find such a theory, replete with "arguments and proofs," we should assume that it amounts to "nonsense and lies," despite the venerable witnesses who testify to it.[38] Such theories have traction over time because we seek to know the opinion of the supposed experts rather than seeking the truth of the matter. Thus, "The god of scholastic knowledge is Aristotle," and his authority cannot be questioned, although his metaphysical theories are no more likely to be true than are a multitude of other silly theories.[39] In particular, Montaigne dismisses Aristotle's theory of matter and form, along with the notion of first principles that can be known absent divine revelation. As he puts it, "To be convinced of certainty is certain evidence of folly and extreme uncertainty."[40] Montaigne is unpersuaded that we can know anything with certitude, since we cannot even comprehend our own powers of sensation and understanding, and all the philosophers disagree with each other and often make absurd claims. The immortality of the soul here receives an especially withering condemnation as an anxious attempt to claim an afterlife for ourselves.

Toward the end of the essay, Montaigne openly states his opposition to Sebond's natural theology.[41] The controversies among the philosophers, and the inconstancy of our ideas and the sway of our emotions, prove the inability of reason to attain knowledge. Ideas that seem so certain in one age are found in another to be merely superstition. Thus, in the new world Montaigne finds uncivilized humans worshiping the god of rain under the form of a cross, with the implication being that Christians are no less superstitious than worshipers of the god of rain. Further, philosophers cannot agree on what is the highest good that would make us happy or what the laws of conduct should be. Those who argue in favor of natural law consistently fail to agree on its content or to demonstrate that the allegedly immutable laws are accepted by all nations. Only a divine revelation can settle these matters, and yet humans would inevitably disagree on its meaning if it depended on human interpretation. Intelligent humans can be found to advocate any kind of nonsense and to interpret texts in any direction. Nor are our senses trustworthy or consistent. Ultimately, since we are constantly changing and nothing is stable, "nothing certain can be proved of one thing by another, both the judging and the judged being in continual motion and change."[42] Human nature cannot

38. Montaigne, *Essays of Montaigne*, 463–64.
39. Montaigne, *Essays of Montaigne*, 464.
40. Montaigne, *Essays of Montaigne*, 465.
41. See Montaigne, *Essays of Montaigne*, 481.
42. Montaigne, *Essays of Montaigne*, 523.

rise above itself and attain a divine perspective. Montaigne concludes that only God can raise us—but he has already made clear the problems with any discourse about God.

In sum, for Montaigne, we cannot rise from effects to cause because we have no idea what God might or might not have done. Since even with regard to natural things "we can only half infer the causes from the effects," we must throw up our hands with regard to God, since surely God's "condition is too elevated, too remote, too supreme, to suffer itself to be tied and bound by our conclusions."[43] The attributes of God identified by metaphysicians are merely another example of the tendency of each creature to measure "the qualities of all other things by its own qualities."[44] All that man can gain from philosophy, then, "is to have learned to acknowledge his own weakness."[45]

Francisco Suárez (1548–1617)

Francisco Suárez, born into a prominent legal family in Granada, Spain, studied at the University of Granada and the University of Salamanca before entering the Society of Jesus in 1564. Ordained a priest in 1572, he taught philosophy and theology at Segovia, Valladolid, Avila, Rome, Alcala, Salamanca, and Coimbre. Suárez was well versed in the thought of Thomas Aquinas but also often disagreed with him, siding with Scotus and Ockham. His most famous work is his massive *Disputationes metaphysicae*, published in Salamanca in 1597. Suárez taught theology at a time when metaphysical disputation at the highest level was expected of any leading Catholic theologian. His metaphysical logic strongly influenced Descartes, although Descartes did not follow Suárez on the demonstrations of God's existence. Suárez played a major role in the *De Auxiliis* controversy over predestination and premotion, helping to persuade the pope not to take sides in the debate between Jesuit and Dominican theologians.[46]

---

43. Montaigne, *Essays of Montaigne*, 456; cf. 448.

44. Montaigne, *Essays of Montaigne*, 457.

45. Montaigne, *Essays of Montaigne*, 426. Montaigne's admiration for Lucretius, along with Montaigne's own skepticism, make him the main hero of the concluding chapter of Stephen Greenblatt's *The Swerve: How the World Became Modern* (New York: W. W. Norton, 2011), which celebrates modernity's atheistic materialism.

46. See Norman J. Wells, introduction to Francis Suárez, *On the Essence of Finite Being as Such, On the Existence of That Essence and Their Distinction* [Disputation 31 of his *Metaphysical Disputations*], trans. Norman J. Wells (Milwaukee: Marquette University Press, 1983), 3–43; José Pereira, *Suárez: Between Scholasticism and Modernity* (Milwaukee: Marquette University Press, 2007); Joseph H. Fichter, *Man of Spain: Francis Suárez* (New York: Macmillan, 1940). John P. Doyle describes the *Disputationes metaphysicae* as "Suárez's most important

In *Metaphysical Disputation* 29, Suárez offers a lengthy investigation of whether we can demonstrate that God—uncreated being—exists.[47] He first asks whether such a demonstration would be the province of Aristotelian philosophy of nature ("physics"), which deals with the form/matter composite in physical beings and their necessary dependence on other moved movers, or of Aristotelian metaphysics. He mentions the contrasting opinions of Averroes and Avicenna, with the former arguing that the demonstration of God's existence belongs strictly to physics and the latter arguing that it belongs strictly to metaphysics. Taking the position that the demonstration of God's existence is the province of metaphysics, but with the help of physics, Suárez states that "there are just two physical means which we can use to demonstrate separate substance either in general or in the particular case of a first uncreated being."[48] He then proceeds to examine whether the two physical means—from the motion of the heavenly bodies (considered by Aristotle to be everlasting) and from the operations of the human soul, respectively—can suffice for a demonstration of God's existence.

Suárez first denies that "from 'eternal motion' an eternal or immaterial mover" can be demonstrated.[49] He does not think that the perpetual motion of the heavenly bodies shows that Pure Act must be the cause of this motion. It could be, he reasons, that something that has no potency to moving, but nonetheless still has potency of some kind, is the cause of the heavenly bodies' motion. Second, Suárez notes that "in no physical means does it seem that God can be more known than in the contemplation of the rational soul and its operations."[50] If the soul's operations can be known through physics (since the soul is the form of matter), then can the existence of God be demonstrated on this basis? In reply, Suárez argues that to demonstrate God's existence, one would need to proceed not only from the soul's operations

and influential enterprise." See Doyle, introduction to Francisco Suárez, SJ, *The Metaphysical Demonstration of the Existence of God: Metaphysical Disputations 28–29*, trans. and ed. John P. Doyle (South Bend, IN: St. Augustine's Press, 2004), ix–xxiv, at xi. See also Jorge Secada, *Cartesian Metaphysics: The Scholastic Origins of Modern Philosophy* (Cambridge: Cambridge University Press, 2000); Roger Ariew, "Descartes and Leibniz as Readers of Suárez: Theory of Distinctions and Principle of Individuation," in *The Philosophy of Francisco Suárez*, ed. Benjamin Hill and Henrik Lagerlund (Oxford: Oxford University Press, 2012), 38–53.

47. For discussion, see especially Bernie Cantens, "Suárez's Cosmological Argument for the Existence of God," in *Interpreting Suárez: Critical Essays*, ed. Daniel Schwartz (Cambridge: Cambridge University Press, 2012), 89–114. See also William L. Craig, *The Cosmological Argument from Plato to Leibniz* (London: Macmillan, 1980).

48. Suárez, *Metaphysical Demonstration*, 56.

49. Suárez, *Metaphysical Demonstration*, 58.

50. Suárez, *Metaphysical Demonstration*, 64.

but also from "some principle common to other agents and created effects."[51]
Physics is therefore unable to demonstrate God's existence.

Given the insufficiency of physics, Suárez holds that the demonstration of
God's existence cannot follow the lines of the argument from "motion" (from
potency to act). He states that "in place of that physical principle, 'Everything
which is moved, is moved by another,' we must take another metaphysical one
which is far more evident: 'Everything which is made, is made by another,'
whether it is made in the sense of being created, being generated, or in any
other sense."[52] A thing cannot make itself. This avoids the problem of self-
movers, since even if things can move themselves from potency to act, they
certainly cannot make themselves when they do not exist.

Suárez succinctly describes the proof that follows, which depends on the
claim that "all beings in the totality cannot be made" (he accepts a version of
the univocity of being).[53] If all beings were made, then we would either proceed
to infinity in created beings, or reason circularly. Circular reasoning would
suppose that a thing can be produced by that which it itself has produced,
"either immediately or mediately and after many generations"—thereby supposing that the world is in some way cyclic.[54] Suárez rejects circular reasoning
on the grounds that, in fact, one and the same thing cannot produce itself. A
thing that already exists cannot be brought into existence by its own effect.
Yet, Suárez notes that some have imagined that, for instance, a dead father can
be generated by his descendant many generations later. In response to such
hypotheses, Suárez explains that here one falls into the error of proceeding to
infinity. No matter whether the changes in generations are linear or ultimately
circular, there must be "some first ungenerated producer."[55]

Why so? Suárez observes that "if in those circles and changes of generations
we never stop at any first generator," then we would have to suppose that it is
possible "to proceed to infinity in the emanation of one being from another."[56]
He is aware of arguments in favor of such a possibility. For example, in the
case of accidentally ordered causes, where not all the causes need to exist
together (such as grandfather-father-son), Aristotle thought that proceeding
to infinity is possible, since he thought that the world exists from eternity.
Likewise, in the case of essentially ordered causes, where all the causes must
exist together in order to produce the effect, one might simply suppose that an

51. Suárez, *Metaphysical Demonstration*, 65.
52. Suárez, *Metaphysical Demonstration*, 66.
53. Suárez, *Metaphysical Demonstration*, 66.
54. Suárez, *Metaphysical Demonstration*, 67.
55. Suárez, *Metaphysical Demonstration*, 67.
56. Suárez, *Metaphysical Demonstration*, 67–68.

infinite number of causes can work together. If an infinite number of causes can work together to produce an effect, then "that a simultaneous whole, or a whole multitude of causes existing simultaneously, also simultaneously act and exert influence on the same effect is not against the nature of the infinite."[57]

In response to such views, Suárez first notes that one might appeal to arguments that deny that an infinite number of things can actually exist; however many things there are, they must be numerable rather than infinite. But instead of depending on such arguments he thinks it better to follow the path of Aristotle's argument regarding efficient causality, according to which "it is impossible that the whole collection of beings or of efficient causes be dependent in its being and in its operation."[58] One cannot proceed to infinity in a collection of dependent beings (beings that were made by another) because one would then have an infinite collection of beings that would in fact, as a collection, be dependent on another for existence. Nor could one member of the infinite collection be the one on whom the whole collection depends for being, since in such a case that member would cause itself.[59] A collection of dependent beings therefore requires the causality of an independent, uncaused being—a being that transcends the collection of dependent beings.

When speaking of dependent beings, Suárez has in view things that are made and that depend on each other for their coming to be. His argument, then, applies to essentially ordered causes in which "a lower cause depends upon one that is higher, in such a way that the whole being, the power, and the acting of the first be based upon the second."[60] One cannot proceed to infinity in efficient causes of this kind. As Aristotle says, the result of proceeding to infinity would be that "all causes, apart from the last which is immediately joined to the effect, would be middle [causes] and no one would be first—which is impossible."[61] Suárez considers that the same thing holds for action: if all things are dependent in their action (that is to say, cannot cause their own power to act), then the whole collection would itself be likewise dependent and would not be able to act unless there existed Pure Act from which all dependent action has its source.

Returning to the idea of an infinite number of causes working together to produce an effect, Suárez observes that in an essentially ordered series of

---

57. Suárez, *Metaphysical Demonstration*, 69.
58. Suárez, *Metaphysical Demonstration*, 69.
59. Suárez specifies that "to depend efficiently (*efficienter*) is to receive from another one's own being distinct from that which is in the cause" (Suárez, *Metaphysical Demonstration*, 70). He underscores that this differs from the way in which the whole of a composite depends on its form. A form (in the case of living things, the soul) does not make itself.
60. Suárez, *Metaphysical Demonstration*, 71.
61. Suárez, *Metaphysical Demonstration*, 72.

causes, God does not ordain a particular number of intermediate causes between God and the effect. It is not theoretically impossible that this number of intermediate causes might proceed to infinity. Suárez supposes that God could will an infinite number of intermediate causes—for example, an infinite number of angels. He argues that even as enclosed by the extremes (God and the effect), the number of intermediate causes could be infinite. This is so because even between God and the lowest angel, the number of species of angels could be infinite; for no finite creature can ever draw near, ontologically speaking, to the infinite and uncreated God. Suárez considers it highly unlikely that God has in fact so willed, since an infinite number of intermediate causes is not only unnecessary but also goes against what we can perceive. It has to do with possible things rather than with determinate things. But he shows that even an infinite number of intermediate causes, supposing this could exist, would be dependent and finite in being and would therefore require a cause that transcends the set of intermediate causes.

What about accidentally ordered causes—in other words, causes that do not need to be in act simultaneously in order to produce the effect? Here Suárez notes that each human is dependent on others for his or her existence, and each human has been made. Therefore, the whole human race, as a collection, is dependent and has been made. Even if humans were infinite in number, the species as a whole would require a cause that was not a member of the species. Suárez observes that "proceeding in this way, either from one individual to another or from one species to another that has been made, it will be in the end necessary to stop at a thing that is completely not made."[62] The being of humans is obviously received, dependent being. To account for it, in an accidentally ordered series of causes, one needs to posit a cause outside the human species, and ultimately an absolutely independent, uncreated being. Again, this is so even if one thinks, as Aristotle did, that the human species has existed forever and therefore comprises an innumerable multitude. For his part, however, Suárez argues that there cannot have been an infinite number of humans, on the grounds that there must have been "some particular and determinate individual" who first received human nature from a cause outside the human species, and with regard to whom all other humans come later in time.[63] This holds even if the world itself has existed eternally.

Suárez reserves other problems about God for *Metaphysical Disputation* 30, such as whether the uncreated God can have accidents, and whether God is completely immaterial in all possible senses. Thus far in *Metaphysical*

62. Suárez, *Metaphysical Demonstration*, 75.
63. Suárez, *Metaphysical Demonstration*, 76.

Disputation 29, by means of Aristotle's argument from efficient causality, Suárez considers that he has demonstrated that uncreated being exists.

He next turns to Ockham's question about God's unity. Given that uncreated being exists, can its unity be demonstrated? Until the unity of uncreated beings can be demonstrated, Suárez (like Peter d'Ailly) does not think that he can claim to have demonstrated the existence of *God*. It might be, for example, that there are "several uncreated beings which would have no causal order among themselves."[64] In this same section of *Disputation* 29, Suárez also takes up the possibility that God's existence cannot be demonstrated because it is self-evident.

Suárez proceeds to demonstrate the unity of uncreated being, the source or cause of all things. God, of course, cannot be defined; we cannot know what God is within the confines of a finite concept. What then does the word "God" signify? Suárez comes up with the following basic signification: "a certain most noble being which both surpasses all the rest and from which as from a first author all the rest depend."[65] He considers that whatever else "God" means, it must mean that God is necessary being, uncreated, unique, and the source and cause of all other things, which participate in the being of God. To deny that reason can demonstrate the existence of such a being would be to deny what is taught by Paul in Romans 1:19–21, namely, that "knowledge of God can be derived from creatures, in such a way that it makes men inexcusable, if either they do not assent to the existence of God or they neglect to worship him."[66] As Suárez points out, Wisdom 13 teaches the same. Citing Wisdom 13:5 as particularly instructive, he argues that "the beauty of the whole universe and the wonderful connection and order of all things in it do sufficiently declare that there is one first being, by whom all things are governed and from whom they draw their origin."[67] God's existence and unity can be demonstrated from the order of the universe.

In this regard, Suárez first cites various fathers of the church who either demonstrate the existence of God on the basis of the order of the universe or affirm that God's existence can be so demonstrated: John of Damascus, Gregory the Great, John Chrysostom, Dionysius the Areopagite, Augustine, Eusebius of Caesarea, Gregory of Nazianzus, Lactantius, and (Pseudo–)Justin Martyr (in addition to Thomas Aquinas and to Aristotle in books 1 and 12 of his *Metaphysics*). He then raises a number of possible objections to proving the existence of one God from the order of the universe. For example, this

64. Suárez, *Metaphysical Demonstration*, 83.
65. Suárez, *Metaphysical Demonstration*, 85.
66. Suárez, *Metaphysical Demonstration*, 86.
67. Suárez, *Metaphysical Demonstration*, 87.

order might show that there is one governor, but it need not follow that there is one Creator; or the order might show that the governor of the universe is one not by nature but by consensus; or it might be denied that the order of the universe reveals anything about the provenance of spiritual and invisible realities (such as angels); or it might be supposed that there is more than one universe, each of which is created and governed by a distinct uncreated being.

In response, Suárez begins with the objection that the order of the universe manifests a governor but not a Creator. He cites a lengthy passage from Lactantius to show that "the universe can be governed only by him by whose counsel and power it has been created."[68] He then argues that not only each species but also prime matter, the four elements, spiritual souls, and so forth require a cause of being. In cases of propagation and procreation, we see that a species cannot "emanate from itself" or "exist from itself."[69] The intricate order of all these things in relation to each other, an order that manifests wisdom and beauty, shows that their Creator is one and the same as their governor. Suárez goes on to demonstrate that the heavenly bodies, too, belong to this wise and beautiful order and have the same Creator as the rest of the universe. God does not merely arrange things into an ordered universe; rather he creates all things as an ordered universe. The key point that Suárez makes in this section of his exposition is that the heavenly bodies cannot be the creators or governors of the sublunar realm.

Regarding the objection that the order of the universe could be produced by a consensus of first causes or "quasi-partial agents," Suárez explains that this could be possible only if these causes were each too weak to produce the whole universe alone, or if they decided to share in a task that each could have performed alone. If the former, then these causes would be highly imperfect and, in fact, lacking the infinite power that the act of creation requires. Their finite intelligence and will would be weak and changeable, and their providential governance and conservation of the universe would be imperfect and flawed; they would be like pagan gods, always inadequate and in conflict. Likewise, if one were to suppose that these first causes decided to share a task that each could have performed alone, insuperable questions would arise, the foremost being why one would suppose this to be the case. A consensus of first causes could always break down; none could enjoy perfect governance, and the power of each would be limited.

The third objection was that the order of the universe does not tell us about the provenance of spiritual realities such as angels. Could it be that

68. Suárez, *Metaphysical Demonstration*, 89.
69. Suárez, *Metaphysical Demonstration*, 92.

the angels are necessary beings? Suárez notes that simply from the effects that we experience, we cannot demonstrate that angels exist, even though we can conjecture that they do. Instead, reflection on angels' existence must proceed metaphysically. In following this path (which Suárez treats at length in *Metaphysical Disputation 35*) it can be shown not only that angels exist but also that "they have received being from the First Being."[70] Finally, the fourth and last objection was that there might be another universe with a distinct uncreated being as its creator. Suárez grants that "there is no doubt that God could make many worlds."[71] Since angels and potentially other worlds exist, he thinks that the demonstration of God's unity from the order of the world becomes difficult because we cannot know precisely in what the world consists or whether there are multiple worlds.

For this reason, Suárez holds that an *a priori* demonstration is needed at this stage: "after something about God has been demonstrated in an *a posteriori* way, we can from one attribute demonstrate another *a priori*."[72] He has demonstrated, as we have seen, that a necessary and self-sufficient being (God) exists. On this basis, he thinks that he can demonstrate *a priori* that God is one. He rejects some standard arguments for demonstrating God's unity, including Aquinas's contention (in book 1, chapter 42 of the *Summa contra gentiles*) that if there were two or more uncreated beings, they would have to be distinguished by some added component, which would mean that they are composite and therefore cannot exist necessarily. As Suárez says, if this argument were taken as probative, "it would also prove [against Suárez's own view] that there is not one concept of being or of substance which would be common to God and to creatures."[73] He also holds that Aquinas's argument against the existence of two or more uncreated beings cannot account for the distinction of persons in the Trinity.

The *a priori* argument that Suárez settles on for demonstrating God's unity, then, is as follows. He states that "wherever a common character is multipliable in respect to diverse singular natures, granted that it is not necessary that singularity be distinguished in actual reality from the common nature, it is however necessary that it be in some way outside the essence of such a nature."[74] For uncreated being, however, singularity is clearly not

---

70. Suárez, *Metaphysical Demonstration*, 106.
71. Suárez, *Metaphysical Demonstration*, 112.
72. Suárez, *Metaphysical Demonstration*, 113.
73. Suárez, *Metaphysical Demonstration*, 120. See E. Jennifer Ashworth, "Suárez on the Analogy of Being: Some Historical Background," *Vivarium* 33 (1995): 50–75. See also Suárez's *On the Essence of Finite Being as Such*.
74. Suárez, *Metaphysical Demonstration*, 122.

outside its nature, since its nature is its being, and "being belongs only to a singular thing inasmuch as it is singular."[75] Not only its being but also its singularity belong to the nature of uncreated being. Here Suárez agrees with Aquinas: an uncreated and necessary being, possessing being essentially, cannot be *this* singular being unless singularity (like necessity) belongs intrinsically to its essence, because "to be in act entails being singular."[76] Responding to Peter Aureoli's objection that this proves only that there cannot be two uncreated beings that are distinct in number, not that there cannot be two uncreated beings that are distinct in some other way, Suárez explains that an uncreated being "cannot be constituted in such or such an essential character (*ratio*) by something added, even according to concept (*ratio*)."[77] It follows that in no way can an uncreated being be conceived as anything but singular. He goes on to underscore that "a nature which is essentially singular cannot be numerically multiplied"; no diversity of species is possible.[78] He also adds arguments from the perfection of the supreme being and from the causality of the ultimate end.

Recognizing of course that most people do not employ demonstration in order to know God, Suárez goes on to ask from whence comes the widespread—if often confused—knowledge that God exists, given that God's existence is not, strictly speaking, self-evident to us. He answers that belief in God fits with common sense: "For if a man reflects on himself he knows he does not exist from himself, nor does he suffice for himself for his own perfection, nor do all the creatures which he experiences satisfy him."[79] In addition to common sense, there is the fact that human tradition and education have handed down through the generations "a general feeling among all nations that God exists."[80] This tradition, rooted in common sense rather than in demonstrative arguments, is responsible for widespread belief in God, understood as the supreme source of all things.

René Descartes (1596–1650)

Born in the small town of La Haye, France, Réne Descartes spent much of his childhood as a boarding pupil at the Jesuit school of La Flèche in Anjou before earning a degree in law at the University of Poitiers. As a young man,

75. Suárez, *Metaphysical Demonstration*, 122.
76. Suárez, *Metaphysical Demonstration*, 122.
77. Suárez, *Metaphysical Demonstration*, 123.
78. Suárez, *Metaphysical Demonstration*, 125.
79. Suárez, *Metaphysical Demonstration*, 144.
80. Suárez, *Metaphysical Demonstration*, 144.

Descartes served in the army of Prince Maurice of Nassau and traveled widely. After settling in Holland, Descartes published his most important works, including *Discourse on Method* and *Meditations on First Philosophy*, between 1637 and 1641. In 1647 the king of France offered him a pension, and in 1649 he accepted Queen Christina of Sweden's invitation to become her personal tutor. In addition to his more famous philosophical works, he wrote treatises on optics, meteorology, geometry, the human body, and the passions. A lifelong Catholic, his goal was to replace the scholastic philosophy that he had learned at La Flèche with a philosophy that fit modern scientific and mathematical discoveries and that allowed for greater certitude than could be found in the competing schools of scholastic philosophy.[81]

In the fourth discourse of his *Discourse on the Method of Properly Conducting One's Reason and of Seeking the Truth in the Sciences*, Descartes identifies a clear and certain truth: "I think, therefore I am."[82] Were one not to exist, one could not think; it follows that one who thinks exists. Descartes thereby apprehends that he possesses a perfection, since it is better to know than to doubt. In the act of thinking, he can think not only of himself but also of perfections that he does not have. He concludes that to be able to think of something more perfect than himself means that he must have received his own limited perfection from another. As he puts it, "If I had been alone and independent of all other, so as to have had from myself this small portion of perfection that I had by participation in the perfection of God, I could have given myself, by the same reason, all the remainder of perfection that I knew myself to lack, and thus to be myself infinite, eternal, immutable, omniscient, all-powerful."[83] Since he cannot give himself perfection, it follows that the perfections that he can conceive of, but that are superior to him, must have been taught him by God. God therefore must exist.

Descartes adds that certitude about anything other than the existence of God and the soul requires believing in God, because otherwise we cannot be sure that we are not being deceived by our senses or by our mind (or by a demon). He remarks that "if we did not know that all that is in us which

81. Geneviève Rodis-Lewis, "Descartes' Life and the Development of His Philosophy," trans. John Cottingham, in *The Cambridge Companion to Descartes*, ed. John Cottingham (Cambridge: Cambridge University Press, 1992), 21–57; John Cottingham, *Descartes* (Oxford: Blackwell, 1986). See also Roger Ariew, "Descartes and Scholasticism: The Intellectual Background to Descartes' Thought," in *Cambridge Companion to Descartes*, 58–90; as well as Tad M. Schmaltz, *Radical Cartesianism: The French Reception of Descartes* (Cambridge: Cambridge University Press, 2002).

82. René Descartes, *Discourse on Method and the Meditations*, trans. F. E. Sutcliffe (London: Penguin, 1968), 54.

83. Descartes, *Discourse on Method and the Meditations*, 56.

is real and true comes from a perfect and infinite Being, we would have no reason which would assure us that, however clear and distinct our ideas might be, they had the perfection of being true."[84] The proof of God's existence is particularly important, then, because it serves to ground Descartes's knowledge of the world outside his mind.[85]

In his *Meditations*, Descartes follows a similar path to demonstrating the existence of God. Beginning with himself as "a thinking thing," he inquires in the third meditation into whether the idea of God could have originated with himself.[86] He argues that everything that is in himself, he can surely know from himself. But he has a clear and distinct idea of infinite substance, whereas he is merely a finite substance. His idea of infinite substance involves not a negation of the finite but rather an idea of something far more real. The idea of the infinite in his mind therefore precedes that of the idea of the finite. Descartes concludes that the idea of God must have come to him from God. Possessing a true idea of the infinite does not mean understanding the nature of the infinite: Descartes does not expect his finite mind to understand the infinite. Could his knowledge, however, grow until it became infinite, so that he could become God? He answers no, on the grounds that his knowledge, despite being potentially infinite, will never become actually infinite.[87]

Similarly, Descartes asks whether he could exist if there were no God. Without God, from where would his finite existence come (both originally and at this moment of his life)? He reasons that if he could have given himself existence, he would have given himself all the perfections of infinite existence. But as it is, he receives existence from outside himself. Since "there must be at least as much reality in the cause as in its effect," he concludes that a thinking thing like himself must have for its cause another thinking thing, and indeed one that possesses all the perfections that can be conceived. Having received his bodily matter from his parents, then, he has received his being and understanding of all perfections from God. Thus, in his view, "We must necessarily conclude that, from the mere fact that I exist, and that the idea of a sovereignly perfect being, that is to say of God, is in me, the existence of God is very clearly demonstrated."[88]

84. Descartes, *Discourse on Method and the Meditations*, 59.

85. For the split between mind and world in the philosophy of Descartes, see John McDowell, *Meaning, Knowledge, and Reality* (Cambridge, MA: Harvard University Press, 1998).

86. Descartes, *Discourse on Method and the Meditations*, 123.

87. On this proof see Thomas M. Lennon, "Theology and the God of the Philosophers," in *The Cambridge Companion to Early Modern Philosophy*, ed. Donald Rutherford (Cambridge: Cambridge University Press, 2006), 274–98, at 284–85.

88. Descartes, *Discourse on Method and the Meditations*, 129–30.

In his fifth meditation, Descartes begins by reflecting on how the idea of a triangle comes into his mind. He argues that the senses cannot be the fundamental source, because he can imagine a triangle that he has never seen, and "yet it remains true that there is a certain determined nature or form or essence of this figure, immutable and eternal, which I have not invented, and which does not depend in any way on my mind."[89] He can imagine other forms as well, indeed an infinity of other forms, none of which he has possibly seen. Since he knows them "clearly and distinctly," they are true.[90] They do not originate with him, and they are certainly something rather than nothing. On this basis, he formulates an argument for the existence of God. Just as he encounters within himself the idea of a triangle and various truths about triangles, he also finds in himself "the idea of God . . . , that is to say, the idea of a supremely perfect being."[91] And just as the idea of a triangle is inseparable from certain properties that necessarily pertain to the nature of triangles, the idea of God is inseparable from "an actual and eternal existence."[92] Descartes concludes that his idea of God, since it is clear and distinct, must be true (as true as his idea of a triangle); therefore, God must have "actual and eternal existence."

Descartes raises a concern about his conclusion: since existence and essence can be separated in all things, surely they can be separated in God, so that "God may be conceived as not actually existing."[93] In response, he again emphasizes that just as the nature or essence of a triangle cannot be separated from certain mathematical truths about triangles, so also the essence of God is simply inconceivable without existence, since God is by definition "a supremely perfect being."[94] If one were to conceive of God's essence as lacking the perfection of existence, then one would not be conceiving of the supremely perfect being, possessed of all perfections. Yet an idea, however true, may not mean that the content of an idea actually exists in the world, since our thought does not make it necessary that what we conceive actually exists. We can imagine a winged horse, but winged horses do not exist. Is the same the case for God? Descartes thinks not. As he says, "I am not free to conceive a God without existence, that is to say, a supremely perfect being devoid of a supreme perfection, as I am free to imagine a horse with or without wings."[95] If one tries to think of a supremely perfect being that lacks a perfection, one falls into a nonsensical

89. Descartes, *Discourse on Method and the Meditations*, 143.
90. Descartes, *Discourse on Method and the Meditations*, 144.
91. Descartes, *Discourse on Method and the Meditations*, 144.
92. Descartes, *Discourse on Method and the Meditations*, 144.
93. Descartes, *Discourse on Method and the Meditations*, 144.
94. Descartes, *Discourse on Method and the Meditations*, 145.
95. Descartes, *Discourse on Method and the Meditations*, 145.

contradiction. The idea of God imposes by necessity the existence of God. If the idea is true—and it is, because it is clear and distinct—then God exists. Descartes observes in this regard that "only the things I conceive clearly and distinctly have the power to convince me completely."[96] He notes that far from inventing the idea of God according to the whims of his imagination, the idea of God imposes itself on his mind clearly and distinctly, with certain necessary and unavoidable attributes of its own, just as the idea of a triangle does.

If the idea of God is so clear and distinct, however, is it clear to everyone? Descartes notes that some clear and distinct ideas—such as the idea that the square of a triangle's base is equal to the square of its two sides—are difficult to perceive though obvious and incontestable once we have perceived them. The idea of God may be difficult for some (including Descartes himself) to perceive due to the mind's continual bombardment by sense images. But having perceived it, one recognizes that it is the clearest and most manifest of all ideas. Furthermore, the idea of the "supreme and perfect being" is required if one is to have certainty about any other ideas.[97] This is so because if God did not exist, we could suppose that our mind is constituted in such a way as to deceive us. Knowing that God exists, we know that our mind depends on God, who does not deceive. Therefore we can have confidence in the truth of the things that we have perceived "clearly and distinctly" through a process of reasoning, even if we no longer recall the steps of our reasoning.[98]

Although some contemporaries and later scholars have supposed him to be a closet skeptic, Descartes's letters and recorded conversations indicate the importance that these proofs of God's existence held for him.[99] Thus, to Jean de Silhon, a government official and author of *The Two Verities: God and the Immortality of the Soul*, Descartes writes in 1648 that "you will surely admit that you are less certain of the presence of the objects you see than of the truth of the proposition 'I am thinking, therefore I exist.'"[100] One's knowledge that

96. Descartes, *Discourse on Method and the Meditations*, 147.

97. Descartes, *Discourse on Method and the Meditations*, 147.

98. Descartes, *Discourse on Method and the Meditations*, 149. For discussion of Descartes's ontological argument, see Edwin Curley, "Back to the Ontological Argument," in *Early Modern Philosophy: Mind, Matter, and Metaphysics*, ed. Christina Mercer and Eileen O'Neill (Oxford: Oxford University Press, 2005), 46–64; Jean-Luc Marion, "The Essential Incoherence of Descartes's Definition of Divinity," in *Essays on Descartes' Meditations*, ed. Amelie Rorty (Berkeley: University of California Press, 1986), 297–338; Darren Hynes, "Descartes's Ontological Proof: Cause and Divine Perfection," *Analecta Hermeneutica* 2 (2010).

99. For the view that Descartes was secretly a skeptic, see Hiram Caton, *The Origins of Subjectivity: An Essay on Descartes* (New Haven: Yale University Press, 1973).

100. René Descartes, *The Philosophical Writings of Descartes*, vol. 3, *The Correspondence*, trans. John Cottingham, Robert Stoothoff, Dugald Murdoch, and Anthony Kenny (Cambridge: Cambridge University Press, 1991), 331.

one exists comes from a direct intuition, not from discursive reasoning or from the instruction of teachers. It also possesses clarity. On this basis, Descartes goes on to show Silhon that our knowledge of God in this life is not intuitive as it will be in the beatific vision; instead, we must reason about God.

Likewise, in a conversation that same year with the young Dutch scholar Frans Burman, a conversation that Burman reconstructed, Descartes defends his proofs for the existence of God. With regard to the proof offered in the *Discourse on Method*, Descartes tells Burman that even though we explicitly recognize our imperfection before we recognize God's perfection—here Descartes gives the example of our finiteness and God's infiniteness—in fact, "the knowledge of God and his perfection must implicitly always come before the knowledge of ourselves and our imperfections."[101] This is so because in reality, God's perfection exists prior to our imperfection; and since imperfection is defective perfection, no imperfection can exist without reference to an existing perfection. Descartes states, "For in reality the infinite perfection of God is prior to our imperfection, since our imperfection is a defect and negation of the perfection of God. And every defect and negation presupposes that of which it falls short and negates."[102] Here we find resonances with the traditional argument for God's existence from degrees of perfection.

Descartes adds that we cannot of course imagine what God's perfection is like. Even so, we can form an "indefinite conception" of a divine perfection (such as infinite knowledge).[103] Although we can conceive of ourselves growing in knowledge until our knowledge is infinite, we cannot really make ourselves infinitely knowledgeable. The fact that we can conceive this perfection without being able to attain it, Descartes thinks, shows that we are not the source of our existence.

To give one more example, in a 1644 letter to his Jesuit friend Denis Mesland, Descartes observes that we can employ any of God's effects to prove the existence of God. Yet, he argues that all such proofs "are incomplete, if the effects are not evident to us."[104] On this basis, he defends his decision to use his own existence as the effect through which to prove the existence of God, since his own existence is clear to him, whereas he cannot be "equally certain" of the existence of heaven and earth.[105] Likewise, in his view, the impossibility of an infinite regress in an order of causes can only be known if one first discerns

101. Descartes, *Correspondence*, 338.
102. Descartes, *Correspondence*, 338.
103. Descartes, *Correspondence*, 339.
104. Descartes, *Correspondence*, 232.
105. Descartes, *Correspondence*, 232.

within oneself the idea of a first cause and the idea of God. It is only the idea of God that prevents one from positing an infinite number of causes. In this regard, he points out that "in the division of the parts of matter there really is an endless series," which shows that a series can go on forever.[106] This fact is contrary, he suggests, to the view of those who deny an infinite regress without appealing to the presence in the mind of the idea of God.[107]

Blaise Pascal (1623–62)

Blaise Pascal, son of a tax commissioner, was born in Clermont-Ferrand, France, and was educated at home—first in Paris and then in Rouen—under the guidance of his father. In 1640 he published an essay on conic sections, and he went on to invent a calculating machine and to publish significant work on atmospheric pressure, the problem of the vacuum, and mathematics. Beginning in 1646, while experiencing the severe ill health that would afflict him for the rest of his life, he came under the influence of the spirituality of Cornelius Jansenius, whose teachings on grace, predestination, and morality soon became the center of an intense controversy. Five Jansenist propositions were condemned by Pope Innocent X in 1653. On November 23, 1654, Pascal experienced an intense conversion through a personal encounter with God that lasted for about two hours. He wrote down a brief account of this experience that he sewed to the inside of his coat so that it could be kept close to his heart. His *Provincial Letters*, written when the Jansenist controversy was at its height, excoriates the casuistry and moral laxity of the Jesuit order, the main opponent of the Jansenists. From the mid-1650s until his death he prepared notes for a projected apologetic work, which he arranged in bundles under twenty-eight headings. These were preserved by the executors of his estate and published as the *Pensées*.[108]

In the *Pensées*, Pascal invites us to consider what makes us instinctively happy. We are happy when we know that God exists, and we are desolate when we think he does not. As Pascal notes, "*Ecclesiastes* shows that man without God knows nothing and remains inevitably unhappy. To be unhappy

106. Descartes, *Correspondence*, 232.
107. For detailed discussion of Descartes's proofs of God's existence, drawing on a wide variety of Descartes's writings, see Jean-Marie Beyssade, "The Idea of God and the Proofs of His Existence," in *Cambridge Companion to Descartes*, 174–99.
108. See A. J. Krailsheimer, introduction to Blaise Pascal, *Pensées*, trans. A. J. Krailsheimer, rev. ed. (London: Penguin, 1995), ix–xxx; Ben Rogers, "Pascal's Life and Times," in *The Cambridge Companion to Pascal*, ed. Nicholas Hammond (Cambridge: Cambridge University Press, 2003), 4–19; G. S. Fraser, *Pascal: His Life and Works* (London: Harvill, 1952).

is to want to do something but to be unable to do it."[109] Unless we know that God exists, we cannot be happy, because we "can neither know nor not want to know"; we live in a state of unfulfilled and seemingly unfulfillable thirst.[110] Since we nonetheless cannot help but want to be happy, we divert our minds and try to stop thinking about God and death by means of generally pointless but effective "noise and activity."[111] In this regard, gambling serves Pascal as a central example of the effort to divert ourselves. But in addition to gambling, young people are taught that they cannot be happy unless "their health, honour, and wealth, and those of their friends" are assured.[112] This can never be the case, but it provides fodder for diversion, so that they do not need to face the question of "what they are, where they come from, where they are going."[113] If they have to face this question without God, they will be utterly miserable. Pascal concludes soberly, "How hollow and full of filth man's heart is."[114]

Despite human efforts to ignore the central questions, Pascal insists that "all men are in search of happiness. There is no exception to this, whatever different methods are employed."[115] Drawing on classical philosophy, he urges us to know ourselves, to face our unhappiness. It is only in this way that we have a chance of becoming happy by seeking and finding God. Pascal observes, "All very well to shout out to someone who does not know himself to make his own way to God!"[116] If we truly know ourselves we will catch ourselves trying to make finite things our happiness, even when we profess love of God. We must become aware of our corruption. For example, those who seek reputation above all in fact desire "to be the object of men's longing for happiness."[117] As Pascal shows, this desire is a horrible but common distortion. It is rooted, however, in a correct understanding that we cannot be our own source of happiness; we cannot withdraw into ourselves and be autonomously happy (as Montaigne supposes). In this sense, it is good and salutary that "our instinct leads us to believe we must seek our happiness outside ourselves," even though no finite external object can give us happiness.[118]

109. Blaise Pascal, *Pensées and Other Writings*, trans. Honor Levi, ed. Anthony Levi (Oxford: Oxford University Press, 1995), no. 110.

110. Pascal, *Pensées*, no. 110.

111. Pascal, *Pensées*, no. 168.

112. Pascal, *Pensées*, no. 171.

113. Pascal, *Pensées*, no. 171.

114. Pascal, *Pensées*, no. 171.

115. Pascal, *Pensées*, no. 181.

116. Pascal, *Pensées*, no. 174.

117. Pascal, *Pensées*, no. 175.

118. Pascal, *Pensées*, no. 176.

Our inability to give ourselves happiness should instruct us, as Pascal makes clear: "Such a lengthy, continual, and universal test ought to convince us of our powerlessness to achieve good through our own efforts."[119] Nonetheless, as he notes, we generally still do not learn. Yet our very wretchedness—our constant thirsting for something more, something that we cannot give ourselves—is also the sign of our greatness. Humans have greatness because we have a God-shaped void, even if in our wretchedness we seek to fill this void with everything other than God. Pascal asks rhetorically, "What does this greed and helplessness proclaim, except that there was once within us true happiness of which all that now remains is the outline and empty trace?"[120] The key is to seek with all our strength to find the reality that pertains to this "outline and empty trace." Pascal therefore distinguishes sharply between those who do not believe in God but actively seek God, and those who have given up the search: "I make an absolute distinction between those who strive with all their strength to learn about it, and those who live without bothering or thinking about it."[121] The latter have not grasped or are diverting themselves from the true human situation on which all our actions in this world depend. As Pascal describes the situation of such careless individuals: "You do not need a greatly elevated soul to realize that in this life there is no true and firm satisfaction, that all our pleasures are simply vanity, that our afflictions are infinite, and lastly that death, which threatens us at every moment, must in a few years infallibly present us with the appalling necessity of being either annihilated or wretched for all eternity."[122]

The key, then, is to seek to avoid such wretchedness and to make every effort now to know God if he is knowable. For a person who does not believe in God, life is "cloaked in impenetrable darkness" and the most that can be said is that "I see nothing but infinities on all sides, enclosing me like an atom, or a shadow which lasts only for a moment and does not return," since death is a plunge into everlasting nothingness unless God exists.[123] Such a person may decide simply to ignore questions of meaning and to enjoy each moment of life nonetheless, as Montaigne advises. With a great deal of accuracy, Pascal voices the perspective that Montaigne (who is not named here) adopts: "I could perhaps find some enlightenment among my doubts, but I do not want to take the trouble to do so, nor take one step to look for it. And afterwards, sneering at those who are struggling with the task, I will go without forethought

119. Pascal, *Pensées*, no. 181.
120. Pascal, *Pensées*, no. 181.
121. Pascal, *Pensées*, no. 681.
122. Pascal, *Pensées*, no. 681.
123. Pascal, *Pensées*, no. 681.

or fear to face the great venture, and allow myself to be carried tamely to my death, uncertain as to the eternity of my future state."[124] In Pascal's view, such a person cannot be trusted as a friend, because he or she has given up on reason and on life and cannot be trusted in adversity.

What better path does Pascal propose? As we have seen, he argues that our intuitive sense that we have been happy and can be happy is a crucial sign that points toward God. Along these lines, he observes, "Man tries unsuccessfully to fill this void with everything that surrounds him, seeking in absent things the help he cannot find in those that are present, but all are incapable of it. This infinite abyss can be filled only with an infinite, immutable object, that is to say, God himself."[125] Every human attempt to replace God with a lesser good has failed to produce real happiness, despite the vast variety of objects with which humans have tried to replace God. In fact, our idolatrous efforts make us ever more aware that God alone can satisfy us as our true good. Thus Pascal states, "From the time he lost his true good, man can see it everywhere, even in his own destruction, though it is so contrary to God, reason, and nature, all at once."[126] Pascal likes to reiterate that this "true good" is not "within us" any more than it is an external worldly thing.[127] Those who instruct us to find our good by constructing a region of serenely autonomous selfhood (Montaigne) are leading us far more astray than are those who try to divert us with external things.

How then should we seek God? Pascal emphasizes that "we know the truth not only by means of the reason but also by means of the heart."[128] Here he has in view the fact that first principles cannot be demonstrated by reason, since if they could, they would not be first. First principles, he argues, are therefore known "through the heart."[129] This is why skeptics (the "Pyrrhonists" such as Montaigne), for all their efforts, cannot touch the intuitive source of our knowledge of first principles and cannot truly lead anyone to total skepticism. Pascal comments in this regard, "We know that we are not dreaming, however powerless we are to prove it by reason. This powerlessness proves only the weakness of our reason, not the uncertainty of our entire knowledge as they claim."[130] Pascal later expands on his insistence on the centrality of knowing God through the "heart." He states with respect to the actual experience of

124. Pascal, *Pensées*, no. 681.
125. Pascal, *Pensées*, no. 181.
126. Pascal, *Pensées*, no. 181.
127. Pascal, *Pensées*, no. 182.
128. Pascal, *Pensées*, no. 142.
129. Pascal, *Pensées*, no. 142.
130. Pascal, *Pensées*, no. 142.

lived Christianity, "It is the heart that feels God, not reason: that is what faith is. God felt by the heart, not by reason."[131] For Pascal, the "heart" includes the domain of reason, insofar as it has its own reasons for believing: "The heart has its reasons which reason itself does not know: we know that through countless things."[132] As examples, he gives the heart's natural inclination to love universal being and to love oneself.

As we would expect, therefore, Pascal underscores that many of the ways in which we come to know things do not involve rational demonstration. In fact, experience shows that demonstration is one of the weaker ways of coming to know something. In Pascal's view, proofs have a limited value no matter how strong they are. He observes that "the way we are persuaded is not simply by demonstration. . . . Proofs only convince the mind; custom provides the strongest and most firmly held proofs: it inclines the automaton [our instinctive sense], which drags the mind unconsciously with it."[133] Reason alone will not suffice to lead us if custom or our instinctive sense leans in the other direction. Most Christians believe in God by custom or instinctive sense (when combined with the gift of faith) rather than because of any evidence whatsoever given by reason. On these grounds, Pascal urges that we should speak and think frequently about God so as to strengthen our belief or to come to believe. Pascal observes in this regard, "The more we tell ourselves the same thing, the more we bring ourselves to believe it. . . . We must keep silence with ourselves as much as possible, conversing only about God, who we know is the truth. That way we persuade ourselves that he is."[134]

For Pascal, this influence of custom and our willingness to believe what we often repeat do not negate our ability to know truth. In the debate between skeptical "Pyrrhonists" such as Montaigne and "dogmatists" such as Descartes (both of whom he considers to be wrong), Pascal argues that the dogmatists are at least correct that we cannot doubt natural principles such as that we exist.[135] From the knowledge of this basic truth, we can reflect on our existence and become aware of our radical contingency. Indeed, this path of reflection seems to Pascal to constitute something of a proof. As he remarks in a highly condensed fashion, "I am not a necessary being. I am

131. Pascal, *Pensées*, no. 680.
132. Pascal, *Pensées*, no. 680.
133. Pascal, *Pensées*, no. 661.
134. Pascal, *Pensées*, no. 132.
135. See Pascal, *Pensées*, no. 164. See Henry Phillips, "Pascal's Reading and the Inheritance of Montaigne and Descartes," in *Cambridge Companion to Pascal*, 20–39; Pierre Force, "Pascal and Philosophical Method," in *Cambridge Companion to Pascal*, 216–34, at 231–32; B. Croquette, *Pascal et Montaigne. Étude des reminiscences des essays dans l'oeuvre de Pascal* (Geneva: Droz, 1974).

neither eternal nor infinite. But I can certainly see that in nature there is an essential, eternal, and infinite being."[136] Similarly, in an Augustinian vein Pascal suggests that since some things are true, there must be Truth itself as the ground of all truths.[137]

Nonetheless, Pascal considers that the debate about God's existence does not admit of easy resolution. In a memorable passage, he describes the tension that reason experiences when faced with the question of God: "Incomprehensible that God should exist, and incomprehensible that he should not; . . . that the world should be created, that it should not."[138] Faced with this tension, we should turn toward our heart. Pascal considers that only the heart, not reason, can have any experience or feeling of God.[139] The heart's experience can and should be trusted: we will truly become believers precisely by acting as though we were. Pascal sympathizes with the Pyrrhonists to the extent of granting how little humans know and how confused we can be if we depend solely on our reason. Thus he remarks, "Pyrrhonism is the truth. For, after all, men before Jesus Christ did not know where they had got to, nor if they were great and small. And those who said one or the other knew nothing about it, and were guessing, irrationally and at random."[140] By contrast, if we follow the desire and intuition of our heart, we can find our way to God. Adapting Acts 17:23, Pascal states, "The God whom I proclaim is in fact the one whom you already worship without knowing it."[141]

Pascal's best-known argument for God's existence proceeds on the basis of *denying* that we can know by reason whether God exists. Since God is utterly simple, he is infinitely beyond our understanding, with the result that we can only make a wager on whether God does or does not exist.[142] Against Montaigne, Pascal insists that agnosticism is not possible in this regard: we *must* wager either for or against. If we try to remain neutral and refuse to wager, then we de facto have chosen to live as though God did not exist. Pascal then argues that the only reasonable course is to wager for God's existence: "Let us assess the two cases: if you win, you win everything; if you lose, you lose nothing. Wager that he exists then, without hesitating!"[143] Pascal grants

---

136. Pascal, *Pensées*, no. 167.
137. See Pascal, *Pensées*, no. 680.
138. Pascal, *Pensées*, no. 656.
139. See Pascal, *Pensées*, no. 680.
140. Pascal, *Pensées*, no. 570.
141. Pascal, *Pensées*, no. 570.
142. See Pascal, *Pensées*, no. 680.
143. Pascal, *Pensées*, no. 680. For discussion see Nicholas Rescher, *Pascal's Wager* (Notre Dame: University of Notre Dame Press, 1985).

that one might try to elude the logic of the wager by claiming "that it is uncertain if you will win, that it is certain you are taking a risk, and that the infinite distance between the CERTAINTY of what you are risking and the UNCERTAINY of whether you win makes the finite good of what you are certainly risking equal to the uncertainty of the infinite."[144] In other words, why risk something certain (a finite good in this life) for something uncertain (the infinite good of eternal life)?

Pascal responds that the answer will be well known to every gambler. In gambling, we risk a certain finite good for an uncertain finite gain, and this is not unreasonable. Much less is it unreasonable to risk a certain finite good for an uncertain *infinite* gain. After all, there is a 50 percent chance (so far as the skeptic can know, since the skeptic cannot really have any knowledge about it) that the one who gambles for the infinite gain will win. These odds surely make the gamble for an infinite gain worth the finite risk. Pascal concludes, "So our argument is infinitely strong, when the finite is at stake in a game where there are equal chances of winning and losing, and the infinite is to be won."[145]

Here, then, our fallen human inclination toward gambling stands us in good stead. Since the only *rational* wager is to believe, reason itself should compel us to believe in a living God who loves us and wants us to love him and our neighbor. In Pascal's view, the only way that we can reject this proof is if our passions prevent us from following the most reasonable path. Pascal urges his imagined interlocutor, who is unable to believe even despite the compelling rational power of the wager, to "at least realize that your inability to believe, since reason urges you to do so and yet you cannot, arises from your passions. So concentrate not on convincing yourself by increasing the number of proofs of God but on diminishing your passions."[146] The best way to be healed of the passions that prevent us from believing in God is to imitate the example of those who have gone before us in faith, by acting and worshiping as Christians. Furthermore, as Pascal points out, there can be no real harm in doing so, since the result will be that the person will lose only the corrupt "pleasures of high living" and instead "will be faithful, honest, humble, grateful, doing good, a sincere and true friend."[147]

Describing the intense experience of God's presence that he received on November 23, 1654, Pascal suggests that it came to him like "Fire"

144. Pascal, *Pensées*, no. 680.
145. Pascal, *Pensées*, no. 680.
146. Pascal, *Pensées*, no. 680.
147. Pascal, *Pensées*, no. 680.

and filled him with "certainty, joy, certainty, emotion, sight, joy."[148] He identifies the God whom he experienced as the "God of Abraham, God of Isaac, God of Jacob. Not of philosophers and scholars."[149] Along similar lines, he reflects elsewhere on the difference between the impersonal God known to pagan philosophers and the personal, covenantal God known by Jews and Christians. Pascal insists that it is only the personal God who is ultimately worth knowing, since it is only this God who loves, forgives, consoles, and inspires us. He adds that the attempt to find God outside Jesus Christ ends in atheism or deism, both equally deadly. Christians worship the saving God rather than an aloof deist God who is solely "great, powerful, and eternal."[150]

According to Pascal, efforts to come to know God by reflection on the things of this world ultimately fall short because God has not chosen to manifest himself clearly in this way. He explains, "What can be seen there [in the world] indicates neither the complete absence, nor the obvious presence of divinity, but the presence of a God who hides himself. Everything carries this stamp."[151] In hiding himself, God nonetheless shows us enough of himself to let us know that we have lost him and that we are alienated from him. We thereby realize our sinfulness and our need for redemption. Pascal reiterates the point that "nature is such that it points everywhere to a God who has been lost, both within man and elsewhere."[152] If any proofs from created things succeed, then, these proofs will not make everything clear but rather will lead to the hidden God who has been lost due to the consequences of the fall, and whom the heart knows. As Pascal remarks, God wills to be "DEUS ABSCONDITUS [the hidden God (Isa. 45:15)]."[153] To fallen humans, God has given abundant signs of his existence and love, and so if sought, God will be found. Yet God has hidden these signs "in such a way that he will only be perceived by those who seek him whole-heartedly."[154] If we do not give our hearts to God, our minds will not find him, since he is a personal, covenantal, living God.[155]

148. Pascal, *Pensées*, ("The Memorial").
149. Pascal, *Pensées*, ("The Memorial").
150. Pascal, *Pensées*, no. 690.
151. Pascal, *Pensées*, no. 690.
152. Pascal, *Pensées*, no. 708.
153. Pascal, *Pensées*, no. 681.
154. Pascal, *Pensées*, no. 681.
155. For a contemporary Pascalian approach to knowing God, see Rémi Brague, *On the God of Christians: And on One or Two Others* (South Bend, IN: St. Augustine's Press, 2013). For further discussion of Pascal, see Marvin R. O'Connell, *Blaise Pascal: Reasons of the Heart* (Grand Rapids: Eerdmans, 1997); David Wetsel, *Pascal and Disbelief: Catechesis and Conversion in the Pensées* (Washington, DC: Catholic University of America Press, 1994).

David Hume (1711–76)

Born in Edinburgh to a prominent but not wealthy family, David Hume received a classical education and studied at the University of Edinburgh. After a few months as a merchant's assistant, he spent three years at La Flèche in France working on *A Treatise of Human Nature*, published in three volumes in 1739–40. While continuing to write steadily, Hume took positions as aide-de-camp and secretary to a British general, as a law librarian in Edinburgh, as secretary and chargé d'affaires to the British embassy in Paris, and as an undersecretary of state in London. In addition to his numerous philosophical works, Hume wrote a six-volume *History of England, from the Invasion of Julius Caesar to the Revolution in 1688.*[156]

Hume claims at the outset of his *The Natural History of Religion* that "the whole frame of nature bespeaks an intelligent author; and no rational enquirer can, after serious reflection, suspend his belief a moment with regard to the primary principles of genuine Theism and Religion."[157] But both in *The Natural History of Religion* and elsewhere, Hume in fact argues vigorously against this view that we can reason from the "whole frame of nature" to a Creator God.[158]

156. See David Fate Norton, "An Introduction to Hume's Thought," in *The Cambridge Companion to Hume*, ed. David Fate Norton and Jacqueline Taylor, 2nd ed. (Cambridge: Cambridge University Press, 2009), 1–39; A. J. Ayer, *Hume: A Very Short Introduction* (Oxford: Oxford University Press, 2000), 1–20; Ernest Campbell Mossner, *The Life of David Hume*, 2nd ed. (Oxford: Clarendon, 1980). See also David Berman, *A History of Atheism in Britain* (London: Croom Helm, 1988).

157. David Hume, *The Natural History of Religion*, in Hume, *Principal Writings on Religion Including Dialogues concerning Natural Religion and The Natural History of Religion*, ed. J. C. A. Gaskin (Oxford: Oxford University Press, 1993), 134. Hume makes similar comments elsewhere in this work. For example, he states,

> It is remarkable, that the principles of religion have a kind of flux and reflux in the human mind, and that men have a natural tendency to rise from idolatry into theism, and to sink again from theism into idolatry. The vulgar, that is, indeed, all mankind, a few excepted, being ignorant and uninstructed, never elevate their contemplation to the heavens, or penetrate by their disquisitions into the secret structure of vegetable or animal bodies; so far as to discover a supreme mind or original providence, which bestowed order on every part of nature. (ibid., 159; cf. 160)

In his view, history shows that the superstitious elements of religion always win out and misuse reason in the service of superstition:

> A [religious] system becomes more absurd in the end, merely from its being reasonable and philosophical in the beginning. To oppose the torrent of scholastic religion by such feeble maxims as these, that *it is impossible for the same thing to be and not to be*, that *the whole is greater than a part*, that *two and three make five*; is pretending to stop the ocean with a bulrush. Will you set up profane reason against sacred mystery? No punishment is great enough for your impiety. (ibid., 166)

158. See Hume's discussion of ancient skepticism and of the origin of religious impulses in *Natural History of Religion*, 175–77. See also Terence Penelhum, "Hume's Criticisms of Natural Theology," in *In Defense of Natural Theology: A Post-Humean Assessment*, ed. James F. Sennett

In *A Treatise of Human Nature* 1.3.2, Hume inquires into the notion of cause and effect.[159] Since in his view reasoning has to do with determining the relations between objects, he posits that the strength of reasoning depends on the strength of inference about causation. The question here is how to be assured "from the existence or action of one object, that 'twas follow'd or preceded by any other existence or action."[160] To provide an adequate ground for reasoning, we need to be able to ascertain a necessary relationship between the existence or action of the two objects (cause and effect). For example, if when a ball hits a windowpane, the windowpane is shattered, can we conclude with certainty—beyond a mere supposition based on extrapolating from what we have always seen to take place—that the latter event is caused by the former?

In reply Hume remarks that in causation two things seem always to be present: temporal priority of the cause, and contiguity and succession of the cause and effect. First, he notes that cause and effect cannot be cotemporal, since if any cause and effect were cotemporal then all cause-effect relationships would be so, with the result that there could be no succession of time; everything would be coexistent.

On these grounds Hume separates cause and effect in a manner that replaces a two-sided, cotemporal causal relation with two separate, discrete events. These two separate events cannot be reconnected without reasserting the cotemporal causal relation. Not surprisingly, then, Hume proclaims his inability to unite the two separate events: "Having thus discover'd or suppos'd the two relations of *contiguity* and *succession* to be essential to causes and effects, I find I am stopt short, and can proceed no farther in considering any single instance of cause and effect."[161] The commonplace

and Douglas Groothuis (Downers Grove, IL: InterVarsity Press, 2005), 21–41; J. C. A. Gaskin, "Hume on Religion," in *Cambridge Companion to Hume*, 480–513. For Gaskin, "Hume's critique of religion and religious belief is, as a whole, subtle, profound, and damaging to religion in ways that have no philosophical antecedents and few successors" (ibid., 480; cf. 497). With respect to philosophical antecedents, this is an exaggeration, not least given the work of Montaigne. Likewise, Hume's arguments are not nearly as "damaging to religion" as Gaskin supposes. See also Richard H. Popkin, *The History of Scepticism from Savonarola to Bayle* (Oxford: Oxford University Press, 2003). Gaskin notes "Hume's 'abundant prudence' in covering his real opinions with ambiguous irony and even, on occasion, with denials of his own apparent conclusions" ("Hume on Religion," 480; cf. 487–90). Gaskin points out that Hume was too much a skeptic to be an advocate of atheistic certitude, even though Hume strongly rejects the arguments for God's existence. For further discussion see Gaskin's *Hume's Philosophy of Religion*, 2nd ed. (London: Macmillan, 1988).

159. See Martin Bell, "Hume on Causation," in *Cambridge Companion to Hume*, 147–76; Helen Beebee, *Hume on Causation* (London: Routledge, 2006); Abe Roth, "Causation," in *The Blackwell Guide to Hume's* Treatise, ed. S. Traiger (Oxford: Blackwell, 2006), 95–113.

160. David Hume, *A Treatise of Human Nature*, ed. Ernest C. Mossner (New York: Penguin, 1969), 121.

161. Hume, *Treatise of Human Nature*, 124.

idea that the motion of one body causes the motion of another amounts simply to this: "the one body approaches the other; and . . . the motion of it precedes that of the other, but without any sensible interval."[162] Given the terms that Hume has established, we cannot unite the two movements in any more integral manner. This conclusion rids Hume of the kind of causal series that are in view in Aristotelian demonstrations of God's existence from "motion."

Second, Hume observes that two events can possess a relation of contiguity and succession without anyone supposing that one causes the other. It follows that a relation of contiguity and succession does not suffice to establish a necessary cause-effect connection. Indeed, where would such a necessary connection be found? If we take the example of a ball and the windowpane, a necessary cause-effect connection exists neither in the ball hitting the windowpane (the first discrete event) nor in the windowpane breaking (the second discrete event). We see the contact of the ball with the windowpane, and we see that the contact is temporally prior to the breaking of the windowpane. But given that contiguity and succession, however impressive they may be to our senses, can be present without there being a *necessary* cause-effect connection between the two events—the windowpane may have broken for some other reason than being struck by the ball. Any conclusion about the connection of the two events inevitably has the status of conjecture, rooted in what we observe commonly to be the case. This point raises two questions for Hume. First, why do we consider it "necessary" that "everything whose existence has a beginning, shou'd also have a cause?"[163] Second, why do we suppose that particular kinds of causes necessarily have particular kinds of effects?

It may seem indisputable that whatever has a beginning must have been brought into existence by a cause. In challenging this assumption, Hume is aided by his view that certitude in understanding results solely from the discovery of unalterable, necessary relations in the comparison of ideas. These unalterable relations are four in number: resemblance, proportion, degree, and contrariety. There can be no necessity in matters of fact because the motions of bodies could always be otherwise. The only possible place that necessary truth can be found is in unalterable relations of ideas. With regard to whether things that have a beginning must have a cause, therefore, Hume argues that "we can never demonstrate the necessity of a cause to every new existence, or new modification of existence, without shewing at the same time the impossibility there is, that any thing can ever begin to exist without some

162. Hume, *Treatise of Human Nature*, 124.
163. Hume, *Treatise of Human Nature*, 126.

productive principle."[164] The latter point, Hume thinks, cannot be proven. It follows that we are justified in conceiving of something that comes into existence (traditionally speaking, an "effect") without thinking of a "cause."

Yet, if something lacks a cause, does this mean that before it exists, it causes itself to come into being? Hume responds that this question assumes what must in fact be proven—namely, whether a cause is needed. The point is that to say that something can come into existence without a cause is not to say that it is its own cause. Is Hume then claiming that such a thing would have nothing for its cause? No. Hume accepts that nothing, since it is not something, cannot be a cause. Hume is simply excluding all causes. His point is that we cannot prove that when something comes into existence, it must have a cause. If we could prove this, then we would have to grant that something that lacked a cause would either have to cause itself or be caused by nothing. But since we cannot prove that something that comes into existence must have a cause, we do not need to account for causality.

Hume then turns to another objection, which he labels "frivolous."[165] Namely, could it be that the very idea of "effect" cannot really be separated from "cause"? In other words, "effect" seems to be a relative term, requiring "cause." Since he has already separated cause and effect into two events rather than holding them to be coimplicated, Hume does not here take much further trouble over this objection. In his view, the commonplace observation that things have causes has generated the idea that *everything* requires a cause. In response, he argues that we might as well imagine that because we observe that having a wife requires that a man be a husband, it thereby follows that every man is a husband. The point is that when we see beings that have causes, we cannot logically deduce that every being has a cause.

Hume elaborates on his position in section 11 of his later work *An Enquiry concerning Human Understanding*. He frames his discussion as a report of some remarks made by a "friend" of his "who loves skeptical paradoxes," intermixed with some of his own comments.[166] This literary frame is enhanced by his opening salute to the grandeur of philosophy when not weighed down by religious dogmatism and blasphemy laws. His friend replies that religious

164. Hume, *Treatise of Human Nature*, 127. For the view that Hume is correct here, see Todd M. Furman, "In Praise of Hume: What's Right about Hume's Attacks on Natural Theology," in *In Defense of Natural Theology*, 42–57. Furman supposes that the question boils down to the claim that "everything that exists must have a cause or explanation" (ibid., 47), but in fact the issue is first one of potency/actuality (and only then of whether Hume's separation of cause and effect is correct).
165. Hume, *Treatise of Human Nature*, 129.
166. Hume, *An Enquiry concerning Human Understanding* §11, in Hume, *Principal Writings on Religion*, 11.

dogmatism in fact emerges from philosophy and distorts it. When prompted, his friend goes on to defend the example of Epicurus, who taught against the existence of God and divine providence. Although such teaching may seem deleterious for society, in fact the claim to know philosophically that God exists is evidence not of wisdom but of rash presumption. Of course, many philosophers "paint, in the most magnificent colours, the order, beauty, and wise arrangement of the universe; and then ask, if such glorious display of intelligence could proceed from the fortuitous concourse of atoms, or if chance could produce what the greatest genius can never sufficiently admire."[167] Hume's "friend" states that he does not intend to refute this argument in favor of God's existence. He merely wishes to show that it is not demonstrative.

The problem with the argument from the order of the cosmos, says Hume's "friend," is that it relies on rational deduction from effect to cause. The argument from the order of the cosmos claims that the intelligent order that we see in nonintelligent things reveals the ordering presence of an intelligent cause. Hume's "friend" responds that when we infer a cause from an effect—assuming such an inference can be justified—we must infer a cause that is proportionate to the effect, a cause that is sufficient (but no more than this) to produce the effect. To infer a greater cause than is necessary to produce the evident effect would be mere conjecture rather than solid reasoning. This is so because the cause can be known only through the effect, and we must not go further than the effect itself leads us. In addition, once we have inferred the productive cause, we cannot then turn back and claim that this cause must have produced effects other than the ones we can perceive.

What, then, is a cause proportionate to the finite effect that is the cosmos? Put another way, can we infer an infinite cause on the basis of our perception of a finite effect? Given the principle that Hume has stated above, the answer is obviously no. If we claim then to have discovered the existence of God (or gods) on the basis of the order of the cosmos, then this divine cause must be exactly proportionate to the effect and therefore must not only be finite but also no more intelligent, powerful, or good than required to produce the effect. Indeed, since the cause and effect must be exactly proportionate, we can say that the effect will reveal the exact amount of intelligence, power, and goodness that the cause has.[168]

The claims of philosophers who imagine that they have demonstrated the existence of an infinite (and infinitely intelligent, powerful, and good) God

---

167. Hume, *An Enquiry concerning Human Understanding* §11, pp. 13–14.

168. For discussion of the difficulties that arise here, see Paul A. Macdonald Jr., *Knowledge and the Transcendent: An Inquiry into the Mind's Relationship to God* (Washington, DC: Catholic University of America Press, 2009), 7–13.

by reasoning from the finite being and order of the cosmos are therefore
wildly exaggerated. For reasons of their own, they have posited a cause
infinitely greater than needed in order to achieve the effect. The cosmos,
after all, does not show us infinite intelligence and goodness. Rather the
cosmos is full of disorder, foolishness, and sheer absence of intelligence—
even though the cosmos exhibits order and intelligence too. The point is
not that such a great, wonderful God surely does not exist. On the contrary, the sole point is that human reasoning from finite effects can lead
only to a proportionate and finite cause. The cause cannot be inflated
beyond the bounds of what we see in the effects. We owe such inflation of
the divine cause to the inventions of rash philosophers. Even granted that
the orderly cosmos must have a cause, we have no reason to ascribe to the
divine principle "any perfection or any attribute, but what can be found
in the present world."[169]

Where then does religion stand? Insofar as it posits anything different from
what we see around us, it is at best a realm of sheer conjecture. Perhaps the
conjectures are true. But as Hume's "friend" says, "Why take these attributes
for granted, or why ascribe to the cause any qualities but what actually appear in the effect? Why torture your brain to justify the course of nature on
suppositions, which, for aught you know, may be entirely imaginary, and
of which there are to be found no traces in the course of nature?"[170] The
hypothesis of God is a hypothesis invented by human minds rather than
a result of true philosophical reasoning. Thus there can be no blasphemy
on the part of philosophers who, while denying God's existence or providence, certainly do not deny the existence of the cosmos or human suffering
or other such manifest topics to which philosophers may more reasonably
devote themselves. To focus attention on the hypothesis of God is to seek
solace in an invented heavenly future rather than dealing with the problems
of the real world.[171]

169. Hume, *An Enquiry concerning Human Understanding* §11, p. 16.
170. Hume, *An Enquiry concerning Human Understanding* §11, pp. 16–17.
171. See Hume, *An Enquiry concerning Human Understanding* §11, p. 18. See Gaskin's
observation that "Hume is . . . at pains to point out in the *Dialogues* and first *Enquiry* that we
may torture our brains . . . into *reconciling* the suffering of living things with the presupposition that God is perfectly benevolent, but what we cannot do is justify that presupposition by
inference from the given suffering" ("Hume on Religion," 492). In the present book, I do not
address moral rejections of God's existence (rejections grounded on a moral protest about the
existence of evil and suffering). For responses to such moral protests, see David Bentley Hart,
The Doors of the Sea: Where Was God in the Tsunami? (Grand Rapids: Eerdmans, 2005); Brian
Davies, OP, *The Reality of God and the Problem of Evil* (London: Continuum, 2006); and John
F. X. Knasas, *Aquinas and the Cry of Rachel: Thomistic Reflections on the Problem of Evil*
(Washington, DC: Catholic University of America Press, 2013).

Hume's "friend" goes on to answer an objection that Hume puts to him. It may seem that just as we can infer a craftsman from an imperfect and unfinished building, so too we can infer a divine Creator from an imperfect and unfinished cosmos. Surely such a Creator would possess an intelligence superior to what we can find in the imperfect cosmos that the Creator is in the process of perfecting. Hume's "friend" answers that with regard to human art, we can reason from effect to cause and back again, since we know what to expect from human beings. Even assuming that God exists, however, we know only his works. We cannot infer anything about God except through his works. He explains, "As the universe shews wisdom and goodness, we infer wisdom and goodness. As it shews a particular degree of these perfections, we infer a particular degree of them, precisely adapted to the effect which we examine."[172] Human reasoning can go no further than this: given that God does not show himself directly, we can speak of "God" (or of a divine cause) only in exact proportion to the finite, imperfect things that comprise the cosmos. Everything else is mere projection. We have no reason for supposing that God is like us or is more perfect than we are, and indeed we must always keep in mind that God, if he exists, is "remote and incomprehensible" to us and "bears much less analogy to any other being in the universe than the sun to a waxen taper."[173]

In this way Hume, like Montaigne, turns Christian arguments for God's incomprehensibility against Christian philosophy. The result is skepticism about God on the grounds that no philosophy (or religion) can "carry us beyond the usual course of experience."[174] In his own voice rather than that of his "friend," Hume adds a final point that serves as a conclusion: Can a cause really be known when it is known *only* by its effect? Correspondingly, can we truly know something that is absolutely unique and has no parallel with anything that we have ever observed? Hume explains, "It is only when two *species* of objects are found to be constantly conjoined, that we can infer the one from the other."[175] The inference of a cause from an effect is tenuous enough already without adding the element that we have never observed this cause in any other way. If the cause is unlike anything we have ever observed, then it is not likely that our inference from the effect will succeed, especially when the effect (the cosmos) is unique and beyond our full apprehension. Hume states that it seems only reasonable that "both the effect and cause must bear a similarity and resemblance to other effects and causes, which we know, and which we have found, in many instances, to be

172. Hume, *An Enquiry concerning Human Understanding* §11, p. 21.
173. Hume, *An Enquiry concerning Human Understanding* §11, p. 22.
174. Hume, *An Enquiry concerning Human Understanding* §11, p. 22.
175. Hume, *An Enquiry concerning Human Understanding* §11, p. 23.

conjoined with each other."[176] It hardly needs to be said that this is not the case with the cosmos and God.[177]

Immanuel Kant (1724–1804)

Immanuel Kant, born into a middle-class Pietist Lutheran family in Königsberg, Germany, was a student, then a lecturer, and finally a chaired professor at the University of Königsberg. Between his student years and his return to the university as a lecturer, he served for eight years as a household tutor for various East Prussian gentry. As a young scholar, he published three scientific treatises and then turned his attention to metaphysics, logic, anthropology, and ethics. Most of his major works appeared after his fifty-seventh birthday, including the *Critique of Pure Reason*, the *Critique of Practical Reason*, the *Critique of Judgment*, the *Prolegomena to Any Future Metaphysics That Will Be Able to Come Forth as a Science*, and the *Groundwork of the Metaphysics of Morals*.[178]

In the preface to his *Prolegomena to Any Future Metaphysics*, Kant remarks that reading "David Hume was the very thing which many years ago first interrupted my dogmatic slumber and gave my investigations in the field of speculative philosophy quite a new direction."[179] Although Kant seeks

176. Hume, *An Enquiry concerning Human Understanding* §11, p. 24.

177. For further discussion of Hume's views, see Paul Russell, *The Riddle of Hume's Treatise: Skepticism, Naturalism, and Irreligion* (Oxford: Oxford University Press, 2008); Robert J. Fogelin, "Hume's Skepticism," in *Cambridge Companion to Hume*, 209–37.

178. See Paul Guyer, introduction to *The Cambridge Companion to Kant*, ed. Paul Guyer (Cambridge: Cambridge University Press, 1992), 1–25; Roger Scruton, *Kant: A Very Short Introduction*, 2nd ed. (Oxford: Oxford University Press, 2001), 1–14; Paul Guyer, *Kant* (London: Routledge, 2006); Steffen Dietzsch, *Immanuel Kant: Eine Biographie* (Leipzig: Reclam Verlag, 2003).

179. Immanuel Kant, *Prolegomena to Any Future Metaphysics That Will Be Able to Come Forward as a Science*, trans. Paul Carus with revisions by James W. Ellington (Indianapolis: Hackett, 1977), 5. For a succinct discussion, see Frederick C. Beiser, "Kant's Intellectual Development: 1746–1781," in *Cambridge Companion to Kant*, 26–61. The dogmatism to which Kant refers is exemplified in the metaphysics of Christian Wolff (1679–1754) and of Wolff's follower Alexander Gottlieb Baumgarten (1714–62). Baumgarten's textbook on metaphysics was employed by Kant in his classes throughout his career. Beiser notes the similarities between Hume's philosophical skepticism and Kant's 1766 antimetaphysical work *Dreams of a Spirit-Seeker*: "Kant uses the same example as Hume in criticizing the rationalist interpretation of the principle of causality" (Beiser, "Kant's Intellectual Development," 55). But Beiser argues that Kant's "dogmatic slumbers" most probably took place from 1770 to 1772, between the *Dissertation* and his letter to Herz. In using this expression, Kant was probably referring to his confident belief that the *Dissertation* was his final position. A recollection of Hume would have been most fitting after 1772, for it would have helped Kant to formulate in more powerful and precise terms the problem he stated to Herz. If Hume's doubts

to overcome Hume's general skepticism in certain respects, he agrees with Hume's rejection of the validity of the demonstrations of God's existence. After sketching Kant's epistemology with the help of his *Prolegomena to Any Future Metaphysics*, I will survey Kant's arguments against the demonstrations of God's existence in his *Critique of Pure Reason*. I will also examine the reasoning behind his practical postulate that God exists, as found in his *Critique of Practical Reason*.[180]

In the *Prolegomena to Any Future Metaphysics*, Kant begins with Hume's question of how, when we have apprehended one concept (such as "effect"), we can "go beyond it and connect it with another which is not contained in it, in such a manner as if the latter *necessarily* belonged to the former."[181] For Hume, the connection of distinct ideas is rooted ultimately in experience or custom. Must we then be skeptics in the line of Hume? Kant thinks that before answering yes, it is worth striving to see if we can find some "pure synthetic cognitions *a priori*."[182] (A "synthetic" proposition contains its predicate concept in its subject concept, by contrast to an "analytic" proposition.) He begins with mathematics, and the question that first arises is how to conceive of the relation between an object and our mental representation of the object. Can there be a "pure intuition" that provides us with a "synthetic judgment" that is "certain and apodeictic," prior to any "contingent empirical intuition" of the object?[183]

Kant proposes that the answer can be found in considering our intuition of our own subjectivity (the conditions or "form of sensibility"), which "precedes all the actual impressions through which I am affected by objects."[184] He points out that every impression that an object makes on our minds comes

about causality were duly generalized, then they implied that *a priori* concepts could be neither demonstrated *a priori* nor verified in experience. In other words, to use the terminology that Kant evolved at this time, these concepts appeared in judgments that were neither analytic *a priori* nor synthetic *a posteriori* but synthetic *a priori*. The influence of Hume is most visible, then, in Kant's later formulation of the critical problem: "How are synthetic *a priori* judgments possible?" (ibid.; cf. 36)

For the young Kant's relation to Wolff's metaphysics, with attention to the antimetaphysical work of the Pietist philosopher Christian August Crusius (who anticipates Kant's positions in significant ways), see ibid., 27–36. Always somewhat critical of Wolff's metaphysics but nonetheless a defender of metaphysics in his early work, Kant turned fully against metaphysics in the 1760s. See also Paul Guyer, *Knowledge, Reason, and Taste: Kant's Response to Hume* (Princeton: Princeton University Press, 2008).

180. Kant's *Prolegomena* was published after his *Critique of Pure Reason* and *Critique of Practical Reason*.

181. Kant, *Prolegomena*, 22.

182. Kant, *Prolegomena*, 22.

183. Kant, *Prolegomena*, 26.

184. Kant, *Prolegomena*, 27.

through this "form of sensibility": "objects of sense can only be intuited according to this form of sensibility I can know *a priori*."[185] What then gives our representations (concepts) of sense objects certitude as knowledge? Kant argues that we have knowledge of things when we know them as they are in our "form of sensibility."

Contained in our "form of sensibility" are certain "pure intuitions," notably the intuitions of "space" and "time" that ground mathematics. We know space and time not as inhering in things but as *a priori* intuitions, immediate and nonconceptual. Our mental representation of sense objects, then, is inseparable from this "form of sensibility." Although we can recognize that there are objects that truly exist outside us, therefore, "we know nothing of what they may be in themselves, knowing only their appearances, i.e., the representations which they cause in us by affecting our senses."[186] Our certain knowledge is of the appearances of things, which we know through our "form of sensibility." Kant terms his position "*critical* idealism."[187]

In his *Critique of Pure Reason*, Kant approaches the same topic from a somewhat different angle. He observes, "Time and space are . . . two sources of cognition, from which different synthetic cognitions can be drawn *a priori*."[188] As "the pure forms of all sensible intuition," our *a priori* intuitions of time and space ensure the certitude of our knowledge, freeing us from the spectre of skepticism.[189] How so? Kant explains that "these *a priori* sources of cognition determine their own boundaries by that very fact (that they are merely conditions of sensibility), namely that they apply to objects only so far as they are considered as appearances, but do not present things in themselves."[190] Thus, since we know things as they appear to us rather than things in themselves, our knowledge has certitude.

Kant goes on to distinguish between the "phenomenal" (things as they appear to our mind) and the "noumenal" (things in themselves). Kant insists that we only know the "noumenal" phenomenally. Although Kant denies that there

185. Kant, *Prolegomena*, 27.
186. Kant, *Prolegomena*, 33.
187. Kant, *Prolegomena*, 37.
188. Immanuel Kant, *Critique of Pure Reason*, trans. and ed. Paul Guyer and Allen W. Wood (Cambridge: Cambridge University Press, 1998), 183. See Arthur Melnick, *Space, Time, and Thought in Kant* (Dordrecht: D. Reidel, 1989); Lisa Shabel, "The Transcendental Aesthetic," in *The Cambridge Companion to Kant's* Critique of Pure Reason, ed. Paul Guyer (Cambridge: Cambridge University Press, 2010), 93–117. See also Anthony Savile, *Kant's Critique of Pure Reason: An Orientation to the Central Themes* (Oxford: Blackwell, 2005); Eric Watkins, *Kant's Critique of Pure Reason: Background Source Materials* (Cambridge: Cambridge University Press, 2009).
189. Kant, *Critique of Pure Reason*, 183.
190. Kant, *Critique of Pure Reason*, 183.

is any doubt that things in themselves exist, it nonetheless remains a problem for him.[191] For Hume, we assume that effects have causes because this is what our experience accustoms us to infer. For Kant, cause is an *a priori* concept among other *a priori* concepts (or forms of thought), such as substance, existence, possibility, and necessity; these pure concepts are coterminous with the *a priori* intuitions of time and space. By means of these pure concepts, the mind synthetically organizes the sense perceptions that are perceived in space and time. Kant emphasizes that "no objects at all can be represented through pure concepts of the understanding without any conditions of sensibility."[192] According to Kant, philosophers who try to transcend the limits of these principles of understanding inevitably fall into absurd logical antinomies in which the pro and contra are equally valid.[193]

Kant affirms that we can have an idea of "the sum total of all possibility" and an idea of "an All of reality," and in this light he explores our conceptual representations of beings and nonbeing.[194] Just as we can have the concept of the All, so we can have the concept of a determinate thing in itself and the concept of a most real being. He terms the latter concept a "transcendental ideal," and he also calls it "the original being," "the highest being," and the "being of all beings."[195] This transcendental ideal, however, is not something that we posit as really existing; it is simply a concept. It is the basis for our concepts of all other possible things, since "all manifoldness of things is only so many different ways of limiting the concept of the highest reality."[196] When we "hypostatize" or personalize this transcendental ideal, it becomes the

191. For a theological extension of Kant's position, see John Hick, *An Interpretation of Religion: Human Responses to the Transcendent*, 2nd ed. (New Haven: Yale University Press, 2004).

192. See Kant, *Critique of Pure Reason*, 551. See Desmond Hogan, "Kant's Copernican Turn and the Rationalist Tradition," in *Cambridge Companion to Kant's* Critique of Pure Reason, 21–40. For discussion of Kant on causality, see Michael Friedman, "Causal Laws and the Foundations of Natural Science," in *Cambridge Companion to Kant*, 161–99. Friedman attempts to strongly distinguish Kant's position from Hume's. For a differing view—more common in the secondary literature, and to my mind more persuasive—see Paul Guyer, *Kant and the Claims of Knowledge* (Cambridge: Cambridge University Press, 1987).

193. For elaboration see Kant, *Critique of Pure Reason*, 459–550.

194. Kant, *Critique of Pure Reason*, 554–55. See Frederick Rauscher, "The Appendix to the Dialectic and the Canon of Pure Reason: The Positive Role of Reason," in *Cambridge Companion to Kant's* Critique of Pure Reason, 290–309, at 299–300.

195. Kant, *Critique of Pure Reason*, 556–57. For discussion see Michelle Grier, "The Ideal of Pure Reason," in *Cambridge Companion to Kant's* Critique of Pure Reason, 266–89. See also, along these lines, Gordon D. Kaufman's *In Face of Mystery: A Constructive Theology* (Cambridge, MA: Harvard University Press, 1993), which develops his *God the Problem* (Cambridge, MA: Harvard University Press, 1972). For an earlier Kantian reduction of speech about God to symbolism pointing to the unknown ultimate, see Paul Tillich, *Dynamics of Faith* (New York: HarperCollins, 2001).

196. Kant, *Critique of Pure Reason*, 557.

concept of "God"; yet "this use of the transcendental idea would already be overstepping the boundaries of its vocation and its permissibility."[197] Reason has no grounds for claiming that God exists.

Why then do so many people conclude that nothing would exist unless God existed? Kant replies that in order to think about "objects of sense," we must posit or presuppose the sum total of all empirical objects. We therefore tend to hypostatize this sum total: "we think up an individual thing containing in itself all empirical reality," which then serves as the unconditioned, necessary principle for the possibility of all else.[198] We make this leap because of "the inner insufficiency of the contingent," the sense that changing things, which come into existence and go out of existence, "must have a cause" and that ultimately there must be a supreme cause of all things, a cause that is coterminous with the most perfect, highest being.[199]

This leap is made by common people in a prephilosophical way. What happens, then, when philosophy takes up the matter? Kant finds that there are three ways of trying to demonstrate philosophically that God exists. The "physico-theological" proof consists in moving from sense experience (of order and purposiveness, for example) to a transcendent highest cause. The "cosmological" proof rises from the contingency of some being in the world to a necessary transcendent being. Last, the "ontological" proof infers "the existence of a highest cause entirely *a priori* from mere concepts."[200] In Kant's view, none of the three proofs works.

The ontological proof is exemplified for Kant not by Anselm's argument from "that than which nothing greater can be thought" but by the reasoning of Descartes (and Leibniz). Kant gladly admits that "the inference from a given existence in general to some absolutely necessary being seems to be both urgent and correct."[201] But it is questionable whether one can truly frame a concept of an absolutely necessary being. To frame such a concept, one would have to explain why one considers nonbeing to be utterly impossible for something. If nonbeing were in fact impossible for the thing, then the thing would stand "entirely outside the sphere of our understanding."[202] Furthermore, even assuming that one could frame a concept of an absolutely necessary being, this would hardly mean that such a being existed. Kant observes that it is possible to make a necessary (*a priori*) judgment that a triangle has three angles, but it

197. Kant, *Critique of Pure Reason*, 558.
198. Kant, *Critique of Pure Reason*, 559.
199. Kant, *Critique of Pure Reason*, 560.
200. Kant, *Critique of Pure Reason*, 563.
201. Kant, *Critique of Pure Reason*, 564.
202. Kant, *Critique of Pure Reason*, 564.

is not possible to make a necessary judgment that a triangle exists. The same point holds for whether an absolutely necessary being exists. One would have to claim that one has identified a being that simply cannot not exist. But how could one show this? As Kant says, "I cannot form the least concept of a thing that, if all its predicates were cancelled, would leave behind a contradiction."[203] It may be true that there is an absolutely necessary being, but the point is that we literally cannot conceive of a being that simply cannot not be.

Proponents of the ontological proof, however, argue that there is indeed one such case, namely, "the concept of a most real being."[204] Kant therefore delves into what the concept of existence adds to the concept of a thing. He finds that the concept of an existing thing, or even of the most supremely existing thing, does not entail any actual existence of the thing. As he puts it, "Being is obviously not a real predicate, i.e., a concept of something that could add to the concept of a thing."[205] When we say "God is," this does not add the predicate of actual existence to God but instead posits a merely possible concept. The concept of God does not change at all when we posit that God "is."

Kant adds that no matter how complete our concept of the highest being is, we run into the difficulty that our concept of the highest being is not cognizable *a posteriori*. This is so because the highest being, as we conceive it, is not an object of sense. It follows that we make mistakes about our concept of the highest being that we would not make about sensible beings. Kant states, "If the issue were an object of sense, then I could not confuse the existence of the thing with the mere concept of the thing."[206] In our concept of an object of sense, "the object would be thought only as in agreement with the universal conditions of a possible empirical cognition in general, but through its existence it would be thought as contained in the context of the entirety of experience."[207] Our concept of a sensible object contains the possibility of perceiving the object. By contrast, since our concept of the highest being denies that the highest being can be an object of sense, our concept of the highest being contains no possibility of perceiving this object. Therefore we have to ask ourselves what is it that we conceive when we conceive of the highest being—namely, pure existence. Kant determines that if we attempt

203. Kant, *Critique of Pure Reason*, 565.
204. Kant, *Critique of Pure Reason*, 566.
205. Kant, *Critique of Pure Reason*, 567. On Kant's view here (in light of Hume's very similar view), see Barry Miller, *The Fullness of Being: A New Paradigm for Existence* (Notre Dame: University of Notre Dame Press, 2012), 12–13.
206. Kant, *Critique of Pure Reason*, 568.
207. Kant, *Critique of Pure Reason*, 568.

"to think existence through the pure category alone . . . we cannot assign any mark distinguishing it from mere possibility."[208] An object of pure thought (as opposed to an object of sense) is cognized entirely *a priori*, without any reference to sense perception.

This means that although we can have a concept of God (or the highest being), we cannot connect this concept in any way with actual existence. Kant explains that "our consciousness of all existence (whether immediately through perception or through inferences connecting something with perception) belongs entirely and without exception to the unity of experience, and though an existence outside this field cannot be declared impossible, it is a presupposition that we cannot justify through anything."[209] The *a priori* concept of God cannot help us determine whether there actually is a God.

The next section of Kant's *Critique of Pure Reason* addresses the cosmological proof. He argues that the cosmological proof always follows the same basic pattern: "If something exists, then an absolutely necessary being also has to exist. Now I myself, at least, exist; therefore, an absolutely necessary being exists."[210] This proof, Kant suggests, merely pretends to differentiate itself from the ontological proof. It is in fact no more rooted in empirical experience than is the ontological proof. He states that "here one presupposes that the concept of a being of the highest reality completely suffices for the concept of an absolute necessity in existence, i.e., that from the former the latter may be inferred—a proposition the ontological proof asserted, which one thus assumes in the cosmological proof and takes as one's ground."[211] Since Kant has already shown the falsity of the ontological proof, it is clear that the cosmological proof is not going to fare any better. It is only in pure concepts, not in any experience of ours, that a necessary being can be found. One's own existence thus has nothing to do with the proof, but instead the proof again rests on the claim that the concept of the most real being entails the absolute necessity of the existence of the most real being.

Moreover, the cosmological proof makes other important errors. First, it claims to move from a contingent thing to a transcendent cause. For Kant, however, "the principle of causality has no significance at all and no mark of its use except in the world of sense; here, however, it is supposed to serve precisely to get beyond the world of sense."[212] Second, the cosmological proof relies on the denial of the possibility of an infinite regress in a chain of finite causes.

208. Kant, *Critique of Pure Reason*, 568.
209. Kant, *Critique of Pure Reason*, 568.
210. Kant, *Critique of Pure Reason*, 570.
211. Kant, *Critique of Pure Reason*, 571.
212. Kant, *Critique of Pure Reason*, 572.

This appeal to the impossibility of an infinite regress in finite causes cannot be justified either with respect to the realm of experience or with respect "to somewhere beyond it (into which the causal chain cannot be extended at all)."[213] The main point is that we cannot try to explain contingency by appeal to a *transcendent* causality because we cannot move conceptually beyond the realm of our experience. Third, when confronted with a series of conditioned causes, the solution cannot lie in doing away with every condition (and moving to a transcendent, unfathomable cause) because in this case we would also be doing away with the concept of necessity and entering into sheer incomprehensibility rather than a conceptual completion. Fourth, the notion that all reality is united is a logical possibility, but it is not a "transcendental possibility" until the principle of synthesis is located, and this principle can only be found in sensible experience. This point has been shown by the failure of the ontological proof, which can demonstrate the conceptual requirements of the highest reality but cannot show that such a reality exists. Here Kant comments movingly on the inscrutability of the "unconditioned necessity, which we need so indispensably as the ultimate sustainer of all things."[214] The concept of God, as an *a priori* ideal of pure reason, is not inscrutable, but an actual highest being certainly is.

Reflecting further on the ontological and the cosmological proofs, Kant asks what produces "the dialectical but natural illusion that connects the concepts of necessity and highest reality and that realizes and hypostatizes that which can be only an idea."[215] It seems plausible that if something exists, then there must be a necessary being that cannot not be. But one can always conceive of any determinate being as *not* being. Nothing empirically experienced can be conceived as absolutely necessary; within the world we cannot reach an absolutely necessary being that would serve as the supreme ground of all things. Kant considers and rejects the view held by some ancient philosophers that matter itself is such a necessary principle. He grants that we cannot avoid regarding "all combination in the world as if it arose from an all-sufficient necessary cause," but this is simply "a regulative principle of reason" rather than "an assertion of an existence that is necessary in itself."[216] The danger comes when we embrace too readily our natural tendency to hypostatize the concept of a necessary cause. We need the idea of a necessary cause in order to give unity to our concept of nature, but we mistakenly turn this "formal condition of thought" into a concrete, constitutive principle.[217]

213. Kant, *Critique of Pure Reason*, 572.
214. Kant, *Critique of Pure Reason*, 574.
215. Kant, *Critique of Pure Reason*, 575.
216. Kant, *Critique of Pure Reason*, 577.
217. Kant, *Critique of Pure Reason*, 578.

Kant's theory of cognition makes necessary the conclusions that he reaches regarding what he calls the "cosmological" proof. If our reasoning is strictly limited by the "conditions of sensibility," the categories of mind beyond which one cannot go, it follows that inference from effect to cause "has significance only in the world of sense, but . . . outside it does not even have a sense."[218] The same point holds for arguments against an infinite regress of finite causes: Kant's epistemological starting point ensures that one simply cannot think the unthinkability of such an infinite regress. One at best can arrive at sheer incomprehensibility, understood as absolute opaqueness rather than surplus of truth. Kant attacks these elements of the traditional "cosmological" proofs (from contingency and causality), but at the same time he argues that these metaphysical moves are simply a veneer covering over the fact that those who appeal to contingency are merely reprising the "ontological" proof in different outer garments. For Kant, it cannot be taken seriously that the cosmological proofs really start from concrete experience in the world, not least because there is an impassible (cognitive) gulf between finite experience and the infinite cause that the proofs are seeking to demonstrate. So it must be, he thinks, that the cosmological proofs make a show of beginning *a posteriori* but in fact do not actually do so.

Does what Kant calls the "physico-theological" proof fare any better? He begins by making clear that this proof cannot be other than a failure, not least because "if one searches for the unconditioned among conditioned things, then one will seek forever and always in vain, since no law of any empirical synthesis will ever give an example of such a thing, or even the least guidance in looking for it."[219] If one tries to think of a "highest being," it will either be yet another conditioned member of the chain, or else it will be a pure concept that has no relation to the chain. This is so because, as we have seen, "all laws of transition from effects to causes, indeed, all synthesis and extension of our cognition in general, are directed to nothing other than possible experience, and hence merely to objects of the world of sense, and they can have a significance only in regard to them."[220]

That said, Kant is effusive in his praise of the things that led past thinkers to develop physico-theological proofs. He rejoices in the world as "an immeasurable showplace of manifoldness, order, purposiveness, and beauty."[221] Before such vast grandeur, our words, measurements, and judgments are reduced to awed silence and wonder. Indeed, he describes the proof in a manner that calls

218. Kant, *Critique of Pure Reason*, 572.
219. Kant, *Critique of Pure Reason*, 578.
220. Kant, *Critique of Pure Reason*, 578–79.
221. Kant, *Critique of Pure Reason*, 579.

to mind the proofs offered by patristic and medieval thinkers: "Everywhere we see a chain of effects and causes, of ends and means, regularity in coming to be and perishing, and because nothing has entered by itself into the state in which it finds itself, this state always refers further to another thing as its cause," with the result that "the entire whole would have to sink into the abyss of nothingness if one did not assume something subsisting for itself originally and independently outside this infinite contingency, which supports it and at the same time, as the cause of its existence, secures its continuation."[222] He praises this proof as deserving "to be named with respect. It is the oldest, clearest and the most appropriate to common human reason."[223] Kant disavows any intention to undermine this proof, because it is natural to the human mind and "subtle and abstract speculation" will not be able to displace it.[224]

Even so, Kant thinks that this proof requires positing a highest being that possesses "a degree of perfection exceeding everything else that is possible," and doing so through a finite concept.[225] Thus the physico-theological proof inevitably gives way to the futile *a priori* ontological proof. The signs of wise, purposive, artful order in the universe—composed as it is of nonrational things—certainly indicate that there is a sublime cause. Proceeding with the analogy of a craftsman and his craft, however, has profound limits. The physico-theological proof can lead us to a sublime cause, perhaps, but not to a transcendent cause of the kind that God must be. Kant holds that "the proof could at most establish a highest architect of the world, who would always be limited by the suitability of the material on which he works, but not a creator of the world, to whose idea everything is subject."[226] To attempt to say more is to speak about contingency and causality along the lines proposed by the cosmological proof, and Kant has already shown that the cosmological proof only pretends to start from experience rather than from an *a priori* idea. Thus we are back once more to the ontological proof—and to its failure.

Kant agrees with Hume, then, that the best a physico-theological proof can do is to identify a cause proportionate to the finite effect. The physico-theological proof gives "relative representations, through which the observer (of the world) compares the magnitude of the object with himself and his power to grasp it."[227] Since this relation escapes our power of observation, given that we cannot quantify it in any determinate fashion, the physico-theological

222. Kant, *Critique of Pure Reason*, 579.
223. Kant, *Critique of Pure Reason*, 579.
224. Kant, *Critique of Pure Reason*, 580.
225. Kant, *Critique of Pure Reason*, 579.
226. Kant, *Critique of Pure Reason*, 581.
227. Kant, *Critique of Pure Reason*, 582.

proof provides no real knowledge of God, no "determinate concept of the supreme cause of the world."[228] When the empirical path ends in indeterminate concepts about the highest being, the physico-theological proof restarts itself on the basis of the world's contingency. But we have already seen that the "transcendental concepts" used to get from contingency to a determinate concept of "an all-encompassing reality" do not work.[229] In short, when "physico-theologians" find that their path cannot achieve a transcendent concept of God, they undertake a "mighty leap" into the *a priori* "realm of mere possibilities, where on the wings of ideas they hope to approach that which has eluded all their empirical inquiries."[230] They claim to find a determinate concept of God through an empirical path when in fact they are exercising pure reason, albeit in an inappropriate way. They have merely turned back to the ontological proof, which in Kant's view is the only serious proof, albeit an impossible one.

Although Kant does not think that God's existence can be demonstrated, he does consider God's existence to be a postulate of pure practical reason. In his *Critique of Practical Reason*, he holds that God's existence is a speculative or theoretical proposition "attached inseparably to an a priori unconditionally valid *practical* law."[231] The postulates of practical reason are the concepts necessary for practical reason not to be frustrated. Kant's first postulate of practical reason is the immortality of the soul, on the grounds that the will seeks perfect holiness but cannot achieve it in this life. The will's object is "endless progress" toward holiness, but such progress toward full conformity with justice would be impossible and unthinkable if human existence ends at death. Only given the immortality of the soul could the will rationally pursue the highest good (holiness or morality); otherwise it would be a mere mirage, impossible to attain.

Kant then observes that the highest good is not simply holiness but also happiness, the state in which all things are in accord with the person's just will. The practical reason seeks this highest good, but it can only do so rationally if such a happiness is possible. How can the whole of the universe be in accord with a perfectly holy will? The only way is through the existence of an

---

228. Kant, *Critique of Pure Reason*, 582.

229. Kant, *Critique of Pure Reason*, 582.

230. Kant, *Critique of Pure Reason*, 583. For further discussion of Kant's critiques of the ontological, cosmological, and physico-theological proofs, see Allen W. Wood, *Kant's Rational Theology* (Ithaca, NY: Cornell University Press, 1978); Wood, "Rational Theology, Moral Faith, and Religion," in *Cambridge Companion to Kant*, 394–416. See also Karl Ameriks, "The Critique of Metaphysics: Kant and Traditional Ontology," in *Cambridge Companion to Kant*, 249–79.

231. Immanuel Kant, *Critique of Practical Reason*, in Kant, *Practical Philosophy*, trans. and ed. Mary J. Gregor (Cambridge: Cambridge University Press, 1996), 139–271, at 238.

intelligent and good "supreme cause of nature," who ensures the possibility of the highest good, the world's configuration to perfect justice.[232] Practical reason cannot go forward without postulating "the possibility of the *highest derived good* (the best world)."[233] It follows that from the perspective of practical reason, the existence of God is necessary. God's existence is necessary not as the ground of law, but in order for practical reason truly to be what it is, namely, a rational "striving to produce and promote the highest good in the world."[234] Kant finds that only the Christian doctrine of the kingdom of God, "in which nature and morals come into a harmony," provides a concept of the highest good that "satisfies the strictest demand of practical reason."[235]

But does a postulate of pure practical reason add anything to our knowledge? When we postulate God's existence in this way, do we then know that God exists? Kant replies that for pure speculative or theoretical reason, the concept of God remains unthinkable. The concept of God is thinkable only as the practical reason's necessary object. Speculative reason can purify and refine this concept, but only in order to ensure that the concept functions better for practical reason. Kant comments that "for speculative purposes reason has not in the least gained by this."[236] But how can the wall between practical and speculative reason be so sharp, since it would seem that if we cannot think something by speculative reason, we really have no knowledge of it whatsoever?

In reply, Kant explains that "there is indeed a cognition of God but only with practical reference"; the speculative reason knows only "what is required for the possibility of thinking of a moral law."[237] A suprasensible object simply cannot be known by speculative reason, since such an object utterly exceeds the capacities of speculative reason. For Kant, to argue for God's existence "in order to *explain* the arrangements of nature or their changes" is to go beyond what philosophy can achieve, since thereby "one is forced to assume something

---

232. Kant, *Critique of Practical Reason*, 240.
233. Kant, *Critique of Practical Reason*, 240–41.
234. Kant, *Critique of Practical Reason*, 241. Kant goes on to ask,
   But is our cognition really extended in this way by pure practical reason, and is what was *transcendent* for speculative reason *immanent* in practical reason? Certainly, but only *for practical purposes*. For we thereby cognize neither the nature of our souls, nor the intelligible world, nor the supreme being as to what they are in themselves, but have merely unified the concepts of them in the *practical* concept *of the highest good* as the object of our will, and have done so altogether a priori through pure reason but only by means of the moral law and, moreover, only in reference to it, with respect to the object it commands. (ibid., 247)
235. Kant, *Critique of Practical Reason*, 243.
236. Kant, *Critique of Practical Reason*, 249.
237. Kant, *Critique of Practical Reason*, 250.

of which in itself one otherwise has no concept, in order to be able to frame a concept of the possibility of what one sees before one's eyes."[238] Even so, we can know "the concept of the object of a morally determined will (that of the highest good)," and we can know that such an object can be realized only if God exists.[239] In this way, we can know through practical reason, as a postulate without which practical reason could not proceed, that God exists. Kant concludes that "the moral law, by means of the concept of the highest good as the object of a pure practical reason, determines the concept of the original being as the *supreme being*, something that . . . the whole speculative course of reason could not effect."[240]

Yet, the cognitive value of such a "postulate" may still seem suspect. Kant notes that in speculative reasoning, a logical need produces nothing more than a hypothesis. This is so because the existence and movement of things do not depend on whether or not our concepts are logically well-grounded. When we see "order and purposiveness in nature," we may hypothesize the existence of a first cause, but this cannot be more than a hypothesis, because "an inference from an effect to a determined cause, especially to a cause so precise and so completely determined as we have to think in God, is always uncertain and doubtful."[241] Is a practical postulate, too, a mere hypothesis? The answer is no. Kant states that "a need *of pure practical reason* is based on a *duty*, that of making something (the highest good) the object of my will so as to promote it with all my powers; and thus I must suppose its possibility

238. Kant, *Critique of Practical Reason*, 251. Kant adds,
   It is impossible through metaphysics to proceed *by sure inferences* from knowledge of this world to the concept of God and to the proof of his existence, for this reason: that in order to say that this world was possible only through a *God* (as we must think this concept) we would have to cognize this world as the most perfect whole possible and, in order to do so, cognize all possible worlds as well (so as to be able to compare them with this one), and would therefore have to be omniscient. . . . Thus the concept of God always remains, on the path of empirical enquiry (physics), a concept of the perfection of the first being not determined precisely enough to be held adequate to the concept of deity (but with metaphysics in its transcendental part nothing at all is to be accomplished). (ibid., 251–52)
Kant also denies that *a priori* demonstration of God's existence is possible:
   Finally, however, it is absolutely impossible to cognize the existence of this being from mere concepts, because every existential proposition—that is, every proposition that says, of a being of which I frame a concept, that it exists—is a synthetic proposition, that is, one by which I go beyond that concept and say more about it than was thought in the concept, namely, that to this concept *in the understanding* there corresponds an object *outside the understanding*, which it is absolutely impossible to elicit from any inference. (ibid., 251)
239. Kant, *Critique of Practical Reason*, 251.
240. Kant, *Critique of Practical Reason*, 252.
241. Kant, *Critique of Practical Reason*, 254.

and so too the conditions for this, namely, God, freedom, and immortality."[242] But why does "duty" require of us anything more than a hypothesis? By "duty," Kant means the "moral law," which reveals itself in us to be "apodictically certain."[243] We discover in ourselves an inner requirement to follow duty or the moral law. We find that we must "promote the practically possible highest good."[244] But we could not do this unless the highest good were indeed possible. Kant remarks that "it would be practically impossible to strive for the object of a concept that would be, at bottom, empty and without an object."[245]

Unlike a mere hypothesis, therefore, the postulate arises from obedience to "an inflexible command of reason that has its ground *objectively* in the character of things as they must be appraised universally by pure reason."[246] We experience the moral law as an inescapable command. We know that we must obey it. At the same time we know that perfectly obeying the moral law (holiness) and possessing a proportionate happiness are only possible if God exists. Otherwise our quest for holiness and happiness—which together compose the highest good—would be impossible, and following the moral law would not be rational. Thus the practical postulate of God's existence is not based on a mere wish that God should exist. Rather, it is rooted in the very heart of practical reasoning, and it is rightly termed a "pure practical rational belief."[247] For practical reasoning, "the promotion of the highest good, and therefore the supposition of its possibility, is *objectively* necessary."[248] It follows that God must exist, although this remains indemonstrable from the perspective of speculative reason.[249]

---

242. Kant, *Critique of Practical Reason*, 254.
243. Kant, *Critique of Practical Reason*, 254.
244. Kant, *Critique of Practical Reason*, 254.
245. Kant, *Critique of Practical Reason*, 254–55.
246. Kant, *Critique of Practical Reason*, 238.
247. Kant, *Critique of Practical Reason*, 255.
248. Kant, *Critique of Practical Reason*, 257.
249. For critical discussion of Kant's practical postulate, see Gordon E. Michalson Jr., *Kant and the Problem of God* (Oxford: Blackwell, 1999), 20–56, 128–38. Michalson concludes that "the 'back door' God of the *Critique of Practical Reason*—already diminished by virtue of the lean terms of the moral argument and implicated in a new bondage of the [divine] will—is indeed a kind of vanishing point within Kant's scheme. This is why it is perennially difficult to say much about Kant's God, as opposed to the God of metaphysics handbooks" (ibid., 56). Michalson includes a helpful discussion of Kierkegaard's critique of Kant. See also Wood, "Rational Theology, Moral Faith, and Religion," 401–5; Wood, *Kant's Moral Religion* (Ithaca, NY: Cornell University Press, 1970). On the basis of more of Kant's writings than I have surveyed here, Wood holds that "Kant thinks that morality is compatible with a hopeful agnosticism about God's existence" ("Rational Theology, Moral Faith, and Religion," 405), a position consistent with Michalson's thesis. See also Nicholas Wolterstorff's "Is It Possible and Desirable for Theologians to Recover from Kant?," *Modern Theology* 14 (1998): 1–18. For an attempt to complete Kant's philosophy (while critiquing it) by reasserting God as the ground of ethics—in

Conclusion

By not treating the arguments for God's existence in detail, Montaigne suggests that he thinks that his belittling of our power to know anything, let alone to know God, suffices to make his case. He is right to point out that the basic insight that underlies the proofs of God's existence led the Stoics to posit a Creator "God" who is not transcendent but instead inheres as something like the soul of the cosmos. But this does not mean that a deeper reflection on finite being would not be able to discover that such a world-soul would also be finite in being, and therefore that a world-soul could not account for the existence of finite being per se. For Montaigne, as we have seen, to posit an infinite first cause goes beyond the limits of our minds, which cannot even connect effect to cause in many earthly matters. But even granted the limits of our minds, it remains the case that we are simply holding that the existence of finite, ordered things is unintelligible unless there exists an incomprehensible, infinite first cause. Montaigne prefers to rest in the claim that almost nothing (let alone the existence of God) is truly intelligible, but his lengthy discourse, as a communicative act, relies upon the bedrock of intelligibility that he denies.

Hume's position is likewise vulnerable to his own extreme skepticism. Responding to critique of God's existence set forth in Hume's *Dialogues concerning Natural Religion*, Keith Ward puts this problem well:

> Insofar as the attack depends upon Hume's metaphysics and theory of knowl-
> edge, it will lack force, as it would undermine modern science as much as it
> undermines belief in God. Insofar as the attack depends upon Hume's actual
> common-sense beliefs, it will justify belief in God as much as it justifies any
> commonly held belief. Insofar as the attack is upon rational speculation about
> the nature of reality, it will be self-defeating, since Hume himself speculates
> about the nature of reality when he publishes what he calls his "proudest in-
> vention," the theory that all knowledge must rest solely upon an association
> of impressions and ideas.[250]

Hume's notion that we can know only discrete facts but not universal necessities problematizes not only knowledge of God but also knowledge of

a book dedicated to Schubert M. Ogden and with a foreword by David Tracy—see Franklin I. Gamwell, *The Divine Good: Modern Moral Theory and the Necessity of God* (San Francisco: HarperSanFrancisco, 1990).

250. Keith Ward, *God and the Philosophers* (Minneapolis: Fortress, 2009), 64. As Ward asks, furthermore, "If Hume was going to be sceptical about the capacities of human reason, why was he not more sceptical about his own dogmatic Empiricism, about the extraordinary opinion that every item of genuine knowledge must be traced back to the occurrence of specific and discrete impressions?" (ibid., 59).

basic causes and dependencies that we experience all the time. Since Hume eschews inquiry into being, he is only willing to consider how the *idea* of cause relates to the *idea* of effect. He is therefore unable to see how the two are coimplicated in one event. Hume also holds that, even if we do allow ourselves to reason from effect to cause, a finite effect can be attributed only to a finite cause. But once one appreciates finite being, one recognizes that no matter how great the finite being—or no matter how many finite beings compose the vast finite being of the universe (or of many universes)—no finite being can account for its existence solely by reference to another finite being. In Hume's view, of course, we cannot posit anything as a cause that we have not already observed concretely in the world. But Hume's stipulations leave no room for the unique change that must be involved in the gift of being. Since it is not a finite gradation, the "change" from nothing to something must involve infinite causal power. Act is not self-limiting, and so there is no reason that we cannot conceive analogically of unlimited Act (infinite being) even though our concepts are finite.

The central point is that as with Montaigne, Hume's critique of the demonstrations of God's existence obtains its force from the denial that we can truly know the ordinary things around us as substances of various kinds, having real forms of causal interdependency.

Like Hume and Montaigne, Kant is skeptical about our capacity to know natures and causes, but he does think that we are able to construct rational ideas about reality and to act practically with regard to reality in rational ways. For Kant, therefore, God plays a role in theoretical and practical reasoning, but as an idea rather than as a reality that can be known. As we observed, Kant holds that being is not a real predicate but rather is a mere concept.[251] The

---

251. In this regard, W. Norris Clarke, SJ, points out that Kant overlooks
the key role of action as the self-revelation of being in our human knowing. . . . For, on the one hand, Kant must admit action coming from the real world of things-in-themselves into the human knower, since he insists that he is not an idealist, that we do not create by thought the objects of our knowledge. On the other hand, he will not admit that this action is revelatory of anything objective in real things, anything true of them—not even their real existence, since "being" itself represents only the positing by the mind of its own synthesis of the unordered appearances in the sense-manifold and the innate, a priori forms of sense and intellect. But action that is totally non-revelatory of the nature of the agent-source from which it comes is itself unintelligible, cannot be truly action. . . . The root of the trouble lies, I suspect, in Kant's implicit rationalist ideal of knowing the real as knowledge by a detached, uninvolved pure knower of a real being as it is in itself independent of any action upon others, including the knower himself. Of course, such a knowledge is impossible save for a purely creative knower, which we are not. (Clarke, "Is a Natural Theology Still Viable Today?," in Clarke, *Explorations in Metaphysics: Being—God—Person* [Notre Dame: University of Notre Dame Press, 1994], 150–82, at 159)

result of Kant's view is manifest in his misleading description of the "cosmological proof": "If something exists, then an absolutely necessary being also
has to exist. Now I myself, at least, exist; therefore, an absolutely necessary
being exists."[252] In fact, the classical demonstration of God's existence from
contingency does not begin by positing "if something exists," let alone (in
Cartesian fashion) by grounding the demonstration on the fact that "I myself,
at least, exist." Rather, the classical demonstration begins from the motion/
change of things in the world, and affirms a real (rather than solely conceptual)
difference between being and nonbeing, act and potency. Like his critique of
the "cosmological" proof, Kant's critique of the "physico-theological" proof
also relies upon the view that knowledge never arrives at actual beings but is
merely the interplay of concepts derived through the conditions of sensibility.[253]

What about Calvin, Suárez, Descartes, and Pascal? Calvin's argument that
we know intuitively that God exists, so that we do not need complicated
metaphysical demonstrations, manages to avoid the difficulties introduced by
the late-medieval Aristotelianism that we saw in Ockham. Yet, while human
intuitions can be accurate and correct, they can also be erroneous and misleading. If humans have strong intuitions that God must exist, such intuitions
deserve to be followed up by rational arguments—whose demonstrative power
Calvin certainly affirms.

For his part, Descartes seeks to get around the various late-medieval schools
of thought by grounding the demonstrations of God's existence in the recognition of his own existence and in the idea that he could never have arrived at
the notion of absolute perfections had God not given this notion to him, since
he himself does not possess absolute perfections. Descartes also reasons that
our conception of God requires that God exist, since otherwise we literally
could not conceive of a supremely perfect being (and in fact we *can* conceive
of such a being). This approach, which roots the demonstration of God's
existence in our mind's ideas, unfortunately has the drawbacks of Anselm's
approach without possessing its Augustinian strengths. Descartes's view of
his own ideas is also problematically ahistorical: his notions of divine infinity
and perfection are derived in part from his immersion in the previous Christian tradition rather than intuitively coming directly from God.[254]

252. Kant, *Critique of Pure Reason*, 570.
253. For a fully developed version of this view, see Don Cupitt, *Is Nothing Sacred? The Non-
Realist Philosophy of Religion: Selected Essays* (New York: Fordham University Press, 2002).
For a response, see Macdonald, *Knowledge and the Transcendent*, 62–65.
254. For Descartes's argument to God from the concept of an infinitely perfect being, and
for the ways in which later modern philosophers (including Leibniz, Kant, Spinoza, Fichte,
and Schelling) wrestle with this Cartesian approach and its legacy, see Philip Clayton, *The
Problem of God in Modern Thought* (Grand Rapids: Eerdmans, 2000). Unpersuasively in my

For his part, Pascal gets around the late scholastics, Montaigne, and Descartes by largely (though not entirely) accepting that the demonstrations are not probative, while at the same time arguing that such demonstrations fail to reach the heart of the matter anyway. Pascal turns Montaigne's skepticism on its head: the perfect skeptic would have to conclude, as the wager shows, that belief in God is the only rational and reasonable choice. He assumes, however, that the "God" who is the alternative to skepticism is the God of Abraham, Isaac, and Jacob, the God of Jesus Christ.

Does the one broadly Aristotelian position that I treated in this chapter, that of Suárez, offer a more promising path? Not least because of his rejection of the analogy of being, he is unable to appreciate Aristotle's crucial argument from act/potency and motion (or change). Nonetheless, Suárez astutely puts forward the Aristotelian argument that shows that no matter how many contingent beings one posits in an essentially ordered chain of causes, such beings will not be able to account for their own existence without positing a transcendent first cause who is Pure Act. The fact that we cannot know *what* Pure Act is does not (*pace* Montaigne) bear on whether we can know *that* Pure Act is. Suárez imagines that there could perhaps be many universes each governed by a distinct Pure Act, failing to see that such universes are intrinsically (ontologically) linked together simply by their finitude in being. But Suárez's deduction that Pure Act, in order to be *this* singular Pure Act, must be *absolutely* and *essentially* singular strikes me as sound, even if not rising to the level attained by John of Damascus and Aquinas.

It should be clear that the movement away from the broadly Aristotelian and Neoplatonic demonstrations of God's existence during the Reformation and Enlightenment periods did not seriously engage the patristic and medieval arguments for God's existence. Calvin, Montaigne, Descartes, Pascal, Hume, and Kant generally show very little knowledge of the actual content of these earlier arguments. The Greek and Latin traditions, represented especially by John of Damascus and Aquinas, appear to be rejected largely because they are unknown or known in distorted forms.[255] Positively speaking, however, this

view, Clayton proposes that the solution lies in a panentheistic "dialectic between the infinity and the finiteness of God" (ibid., 505).

255. Thus Norris Clarke observes that Kant's
refutation of the so-called "Cosmological Argument" for God is flawed by a serious misreading of the traditional argument as presented by realist metaphysicians like St. Thomas. In the last crucial step of the argument, Kant distorts it to become an attempted deduction of the existence of a Necessary Being (I would prefer to call it a Self-Sufficient Being) from the idea of the *Ens Realissimum* (or infinitely perfect being). St. Thomas would indignantly repudiate such a procedure, all too easily refuted by Kant. The traditional procedure is precisely the opposite. Once the reality of a Self-Sufficient Being has been

forgetfulness provided space for the emergence of some ingenious arguments in favor of God's existence, most notably in Pascal's brilliant notion of the wager, and also perhaps in Kant's practical postulate, defective though it is in its understanding of God.[256]

established from causal arguments, it is then argued that such a being could not be at once self-sufficient and finite, for the latter by nature requires a cause of its being as finite. Therefore the Self-Sufficient Being must be infinite, and so, by an easy step, unique. (Clarke, "Is a Natural Theology Still Viable Today?," 158–59)

Similarly, though from a somewhat different philosophical vantage point, William Desmond observes,

Think of the transcendental anorexia of Kant's notion of existence: existence is not redolent with the fullness of being, or the astonishing fact "that it is at all," or the glorious good of the "to be." Existence reverts to the power of the self to posit, and posit legitimately in accord with the evidences of experience (itself understood in a determinately restricted sense). . . . Kant was the heir of the Wolffian version of the ontological proof in which the concept of God is that of the *ens realissimum*. One thinks also of Descartes in the rationalistic context in which the idea of a *triangle* functions as an analogy to the concept of God. (Desmond, *God and the Between* [Oxford: Blackwell, 2008], 95)

256. See Desmond's comments on Kant's practical postulate, in Desmond, *God and the Between*, 97–102, 146–48.

3

Nineteenth- and Twentieth-Century Responses

In his biographical study of John Henry Newman, *Newman and His Contemporaries*, the historian Edward Short remarks that William Froude, the brother of Newman's close friend Hurrell Froude, "always bristled whenever Newman told him that he would eventually see the unsustainability of doubt. As fond as he was of Newman, William felt no affinity whatever with his friend's Catholic certitude."[1] This division among friends with regard to the reality of God's existence is typical of the nineteenth and twentieth centuries, during which atheism became standard fare among intellectuals. Of the seven thinkers that I treat in this chapter, four defend the demonstrability of God's existence, while three demur.

In a manner that is in some ways reminiscent of Kant's practical postulate, John Henry Newman argues that our experience of conscience provides decisive evidence for the existence of God. Conscience makes evident to us that we have real moral obligation; we feel the presence of a supreme Authority or Judge whose dictates we cannot escape. For Newman, the experience of conscience offers better grounds for demonstrating God's existence than do abstract logical arguments, since after all, our reasoning

1. Edward Short, *Newman and His Contemporaries* (London: T&T Clark International, 2011), 150.

is enacted in history and we rely far more on cumulative probabilities than on syllogistic proof. Newman holds that it is the existence of a *personal* God that matters to us, and we meet this God first in our experience of conscience.

Maurice Blondel and Pierre Rousselot similarly propose that God's existence can be demonstrated by attending to the immanent structures that make up our rational being and action. Against the abstract dryness of the classical demonstrations of God's existence, Blondel argues that in the dynamism of action, we are motivated by contingent goods but recognize that no contingent good will satisfy us: our willing takes us up into a movement greater than ourselves. Underlying all action is the quest for infinite perfection, necessary being. In the face of limitation and contingency, and in the midst of our quest to *be* with more intensity and perfection, we experience the underlying reality of pure action, of the God who joins the relative to the absolute. Thus, Blondel finds that analysis of action allows us to discover (if we so choose) the living God. For his part, Rousselot holds that to know that "this is a being" requires the affirmation that "being exists," and thereby requires the affirmation that there is a synthesis of essence and existence. Our knowledge thus presupposes the existence of God, and our knowing desires the vision of God. In addition, Rousselot argues that love expands our intelligence, both with regard to natural reason and with regard to supernatural faith.

Réginald Garrigou-Lagrange defends the position of Aquinas. His articulation of the principle of causality provides a response to Hume and Kant. Hume's critique of the principle of causality depends on the notion that this principle rests simply on empirical observation of effects following from causes, whereas Garrigou-Lagrange shows that the principle of causality has rather to do with the fact that a contingent thing is not self-existent. It is thus an ontological, not simply an empirical, claim. He also points out that we know things as beings that analogously possess perfections, and he shows that the demonstration of an infinite cause from finite effects relies on the proportionality of effect to cause, not on a proportion between the perfection of the effect and the perfection of the cause. The demonstration of God's existence, he emphasizes, does not claim to arrive at *what* God is, which infinitely exceeds our finite concepts.

For Ludwig Wittgenstein, by contrast, the task of philosophy is largely to encourage us to be silent in the face of the big questions, which he deems to be nonsensical insofar as they cannot be reasoned about. Metaphysical claims, whether pro or contra God's existence, cannot truly be expressed. Against rationalist strictures, Wittgenstein intends thereby to leave room for unspeakable mystical realities. In his later work, Wittgenstein proposes that we know reality only through distinct "languages" or "language games" that instantiate distinct frames of meaning and forms of life. The truth of things can be determined not in itself, but solely with respect to a particular language. There is no way of getting at things in their being; instead we know only the meanings made possible by the language games in which we participate.

Martin Heidegger also critiques the demonstrations of God's existence, on the grounds that reason's urge to encompass everything in concepts overwhelms the sheer disclosure of being. On this view, corrupt philosophy has replaced the historicity of the manifestation of being to human beings with a body of ahistorical metaphysical doctrine. The history of metaphysics ever since the ancient Greeks consists in the disastrous domination of reason and logic over being. For Heidegger, the demonstrations of God's existence, especially as found within the Christian tradition of philosophy, are a prime example of deadly "onto-theology."

Last, Karl Barth emphasizes that only God can unveil God. There can be no knowledge of God apart from God's historical self-revelation in Jesus Christ. The demonstrations of God's existence fail tragically. Yet Barth interprets Anselm as embodying a good use of philosophical reasoning about God, namely, reasoning that begins with faith and therefore presupposes the God revealed in Jesus Christ. On this view, Anselm aims to demonstrate that we cannot conceive of God without God's own self-revelation. Barth emphasizes that "that than which nothing greater can be thought" is not merely an abstract God, but the self-revealing God, the God who manifests himself to us in history by his Word.

The nineteenth and twentieth centuries, therefore, offer a wide range of Christian responses to the skepticism of Montaigne, Hume, and Kant about the possibility of demonstrating God's existence. In different ways, Newman, Blondel, and Rousselot propose that an analysis of our interior experience—whether of conscience, volition, or thought—will enable us to demonstrate the existence of God in a manner that avoids dry and abstract metaphysical reasoning (as Calvin, Descartes, and Pascal also sought to do). Garrigou-Lagrange argues that a better solution is to reinvigorate the broadly Aristotelian paths that were ignored or misunderstood by Montaigne, Hume, and Kant but that flourished in the Greek Fathers and in Thomas Aquinas (as well as in Suárez, though Garrigou-Lagrange does not follow his approach). Wittgenstein, Heidegger, and Barth hold that all efforts to rationally demonstrate the existence of God overlook reason's limitations and falsify both philosophy and theology.

John Henry Newman (1801–90)

The son of a banker whose bank failed when Newman was eighteen, John Henry Newman was born in London and baptized an Anglican. As a teenager he read David Hume, but while in boarding school he converted to Reformed Anglicanism. At the University of Oxford, where he was first an undergraduate and then a fellow of Oriel College, he was influenced first by Richard Whately and then by Hurrell Froude and John Keble. Becoming a high-church Anglican priest, he helped to lead the Oxford Movement before converting to Roman Catholicism in 1845. His seminal *Essay on the Development of Christian Doctrine* marked his conversion to Catholicism, after which he became an Oratorian priest and founder of the Birmingham Oratory. His *Grammar of Assent* was published only a month before the First Vatican Council taught in *Dei Filius* that "God, the source and end of all things, can be known with certainty from the consideration of created things, by the natural power of human reason."[2] He served as founding rector of the Catholic University of Ireland between 1854 and 1858, and in 1879 he was named a cardinal of the Catholic Church by Pope Leo XIII.[3]

In a sermon preached before the University of Oxford on April 13, 1830, Newman probes the topic of "The Influence of Natural and Revealed Religion Respectively." He first notes that by the phrase "natural religion" he does not mean to imply that "any religious system has actually been traced out by unaided Reason."[4] God's grace has always aided human reason in all times and places. By "natural religion" he simply means what pious pagans have been able to discern with regard to God and human morality. He grounds natural knowledge of God and God's will in the faculty of conscience: our experience of conscience reveals to us the existence of a supreme authority and thus of God. As he states, "Conscience implies a relation between the soul and a something exterior, and that, moreover, superior to itself; a relation to an excellence which it does not possess, and to a tribunal over which it has no power."[5] This "Supreme Power" has the authority to claim our obedience and imposes moral obligations on us. As such, conscience effectively grounds

---

2. Vatican I, *Dei Filius* 2, in *Decrees of the Ecumenical Councils*, vol. 2, *Trent to Vatican II*, ed. Norman P. Tanner, SJ (Washington, DC: Georgetown University Press, 1990), 806.

3. See Sheridan Gilley, "Life and Writings," in *The Cambridge Companion to John Henry Newman*, ed. Ian Ker and Terrence Merrigan (Cambridge: Cambridge University Press, 2009), 1–28; Ian Ker, *John Henry Newman: A Biography* (Oxford: Oxford University Press, 1988); Edward Short, *Newman and His Contemporaries* (New York: T&T Clark International, 2011).

4. John Henry Newman, *Fifteen Sermons Preached before the University of Oxford between A.D. 1826 and 1843* (Notre Dame: University of Notre Dame Press, 1997), 17.

5. Newman, *Fifteen Sermons*, 18.

"the belief in a principle exterior to the mind to which it is instinctively drawn, infinitely exalted, perfect, incomprehensible."[6] By obeying the dictates of conscience, then, a pagan could come to know God and to understand God's goodness, power, and wisdom as manifested in the created order.

In Newman's view, pagan philosophy shows both that some knowledge of God "was *attainable*—for what one man may attain is open to another," and that generally such knowledge of God "was not *actually attained*."[7] The best of pagan philosophy exhibits some knowledge of "the infinite power and majesty, the wisdom and goodness, the presence, the moral governance, and, in one sense, the unity of the Deity."[8] But pagan philosophy never truly identified a transcendent Creator God; instead, the best it could do was to imagine an intelligent world-soul. This impersonal world-soul, infinite and eternal, could not merit worship from intelligent beings because each intelligent being forms a part of it.

Describing Paul's speech at the Areopagus of Athens, Newman argues that Paul confirms the "abstract correctness" of some pagan philosophical concepts of God, but that Paul does so in order to introduce the personal, historical character of God by means of the proclamation of Christ Jesus and his resurrection. The Old Testament accentuates God's personal character by ascribing to God human passions and changeability. The purpose of these anthropomorphic ascriptions is made clear by the coming of Jesus, who shows how profoundly personal God is. Newman rejoices that "revelation meets us with simple and distinct *facts* and *actions*, not with painful inductions from existing phenomena, not with generalized laws or metaphysical conjectures, but with *Jesus and the Resurrection*."[9] In Jesus, the divine principle that the pagan philosophers sought manifests himself as a personal redeemer.

After the provision of divine revelation, is there still a purpose for "natural religion"? Newman answers that natural religion has even more value than ever, since in a certain sense "the whole revealed scheme rests on nature for the validity of its evidence."[10] If God did not exist, for example, miracles could hardly be possible. Newman considers that revelation and pagan philosophy both testify to the existence of one God. An appreciation of natural religion also helps us to understand how pagans from all times and places can be among the saved.[11]

6. Newman, *Fifteen Sermons*, 21.
7. Newman, *Fifteen Sermons*, 21.
8. Newman, *Fifteen Sermons*, 22.
9. Newman, *Fifteen Sermons*, 27.
10. Newman, *Fifteen Sermons*, 31.
11. See Francis McGrath, *John Henry Newman: Universal Revelation* (London: Burns & Oates, 1997).

In his *Grammar of Assent*, Newman reflects on first principles, including the principle of causality. As he points out, philosophers inevitably disagree about what the first principles are, producing an "interminable controversy."[12] He holds that the trustworthiness of our conscious powers cannot be a first principle, since we use our conscious powers rather than debate about them. But he accepts that the proposition "there are things existing external to ourselves" is a first principle.[13] He compares this knowledge of external things via our senses to our knowledge of God via our conscience. He argues, however, that some supposed "first principles," such as "there is a right and wrong," are in fact conclusions from experience.

Among these supposed first principles that in fact arise from experience, Newman includes the principle of causality. He thinks that we cannot say that everything must have a cause, because "why in that case stop short at One, who is Himself without cause?"[14] Like Hume, he notes that "when we witness invariable antecedents and consequents, we call the former the cause of the latter," because this is what seems to be the case from our experience.[15] But he does not think that skepticism need follow from this conclusion. He explains, "Starting, then, from experience, I consider a cause to be an effective will; and, by the doctrine of causation, I mean the notion, or first principle, that all things come of effective will."[16] Given that "we have no experience of any cause but Will," we should admit that by his will God can cause something to occur outside the general laws of nature. Yet, regularities in nature, such as "the recurring sensations of hunger and thirst" or the power of gravity, lead us to posit the general lawfulness of the universe as a first principle.[17] Indeed, the general laws of nature constitute for Newman evidence of the existence of God as a governing Mind: "The agency then which has kept up and keeps up the general laws of nature . . . must be Mind, and nothing else, and Mind at least as wide and as enduring in its living action, as the immeasurable ages and spaces of the universe on which that agency has left its traces."[18]

12. John Henry Newman, *An Essay in Aid of a Grammar of Assent* (Westminster, MD: Christian Classics, 1973), 270.

13. Newman, *Grammar of Assent*, 61.

14. Newman, *Grammar of Assent*, 66. Newman does not here acknowledge the point that it is *contingent* beings that must have a cause. See Avery Dulles, SJ, *Newman* (London: Continuum, 2002), 44.

15. Newman, *Grammar of Assent*, 67.

16. Newman, *Grammar of Assent*, 68.

17. Newman, *Grammar of Assent*, 70.

18. Newman, *Grammar of Assent*, 72. See, however, Kevin Mongrain, "The Eyes of Faith: Newman's Critique of Arguments from Design," *Newman Studies Journal* 6 (2009): 68–86.

Newman argues that human reason can know many of the attributes of the one God, so as to make possible a "notional assent" to the truth of God. But in order for us to give a "real assent," grounded not simply in ideas but in personal contact, we must rely on the evidence given by our conscience, our "sense of moral obligation."[19] Conscience, says Newman, is both "a judgment of the reason and a magisterial dictate."[20] When we do or plan to do bad actions, our conscience accuses us; when we do or plan to do good actions, our conscience approves. Because of the conscience's ability to command, constrain, and judge, we experience it as coming not merely from ourselves but from an authority outside ourselves. Thus we feel guilty, despite ourselves, for bad actions that we freely chose to do. As Newman says, the judgment of conscience "implies that there is One to whom we are responsible, before whom we are ashamed, whose claims on us we fear."[21] The authority of conscience leads us to the conclusion that we will indeed face a judgment from a higher authority for what we have done in our lives.

Newman draws a comparison with how animals perceive things. Just as the physical eye of an animal recognizes sensible things by the play of light and shadow on the retina, so also by these shadowy signs conveyed by our conscience, our spiritual eye recognizes the presence of God. The instincts and impressions that guide nonrational animals toward what is good for them are comparable to the instincts and impressions that guide us to God. Even young children experience the imperative voice of conscience. Newman lays stress not only on the experience of guilt over wrongdoing but also on the sense that the moral law confirmed by conscience is a good, just, and beneficent law. Even before learning about God, children can possess a "real apprehension" of God, although the elements of this real apprehension need to be brought to the surface by instruction. Bad actions obscure and weaken this apprehension of God, and good actions strengthen it. Newman concludes that "conscience is a connecting principle between the creature and his Creator; and the firmest hold of theological truths is gained by habits of personal religion."[22]

Probing into the experience of assent, Newman observes that we must distinguish our view of how the logical mind *should* act from how human minds act in practice. Sometimes our assent can withstand our forgetting the

19. Newman, *Grammar of Assent*, 104.
20. Newman, *Grammar of Assent*, 105.
21. Newman, *Grammar of Assent*, 109. See Terrence Merrigan, "Revelation," in *Cambridge Companion to John Henry Newman*, 47–72, at 47–51; Gerard J. Hughes, "Conscience," in *Cambridge Companion to John Henry Newman*, 189–220, at 207–16; Adrian J. Boekraad and Henry Tristram, ed., *The Argument from Conscience to the Existence of God according to J. H. Newman* (Louvain: Nauwelaerts, 1961).
22. Newman, *Grammar of Assent*, 117.

inferences that originally constituted the basis for our assent. Sometimes we retain the inferences but no longer give assent. We may find ourselves asserting things to which we cannot yet give our true assent. We also experience "the influence of moral motives in hindering assent to conclusions which are logically unimpeachable."[23] When confronted with what is in fact a demonstrative argument, we may not be able to hold together all the different steps of the proof and therefore we may withhold assent.

Newman highlights the difference between assent and the inferences that lead to the assent: "Inference is always inference; even if demonstrative, it is still conditional."[24] By contrast, true assent—as opposed to acquiescence or inference—is unconditional. As Newman says, "I may have difficulty in the management of a proof, while I remain unshaken in my adherence to the conclusion."[25] An assent may have shaky grounds or complex circumstances, and we can dissent today from what we assented to yesterday, but a true assent nonetheless is not conditional in the way that an inference is.

Newman recognizes, of course, that focusing on our own mental operations and on possible objections to our position tends to weaken our ability to assent with certitude. As he remarks, "Questioning, when encouraged on any subject-matter, readily becomes a habit, and leads the mind to substitute exercises of inference for assent. . . . Reasons for assenting suggest reasons for not assenting."[26]

With respect to difficult religious matters, Newman readily grants that some philosophical and theological questions are insoluble, such as why an omnipotent and all-loving God permits evil and suffering, or why some have received the privilege of being Christians while others have not. These questions can disturb our peace but should not affect the certitude of our assent, which is not founded on an answer to such unanswerable questions. Likewise, the fact that we have once been mistakenly certain about something does not mean that we need to abandon our certitude about other things. Newman observes that with regard to concrete or historical matters, informal inference involves "the cumulation of probabilities, independent of each other, arising out of the nature and circumstances of the particular case which is under review."[27] Certitude, then, can arise from a set of probabilities.

In Newman's view, God's existence "may be proved and defended by an array of invincible logical arguments," but he points out that "such is not

23. Newman, *Grammar of Assent*, 169.
24. Newman, *Grammar of Assent*, 172.
25. Newman, *Grammar of Assent*, 180.
26. Newman, *Grammar of Assent*, 217.
27. Newman, *Grammar of Assent*, 288.

commonly the method in which those same logical arguments make their way into our minds."[28] Historically embodied reasoning is not pure reason but instead is shaped by various factors specific to the lives of the reasoners. Newman's central point is that the significance of historical context should not lead us to renounce the possibility of certitude—not least because God has created us to reason in this historically embodied way. He compares right judgment in speculative matters (the "illative sense") to how *phronēsis* operates in practical matters.[29]

Toward the end of the *Grammar of Assent*, Newman returns to the topic of natural religion, which comes to us through three channels: our minds, the common testimony of humankind, and human affairs in the world. He accentuates once more the role of conscience, which everyone possesses and which "teaches us, not only that God is, but what He is" (i.e., good).[30] With respect to human affairs in the world, he notes that the first thing that strikes us is God's seeming absence. Among the questions he asks, the following three stand out: "Why does not He, our Maker and Ruler, give us some immediate knowledge of Himself? . . . Why is it possible without absurdity to deny His will, His attributes, His existence? . . . We both see and know each other; why, if we cannot have the sight of Him, have we not at least the knowledge?"[31] He answers these questions by again turning to the testimony of conscience, which convicts us of sin and thereby explains our alienation from the all-holy God.

Newman insists that in demonstrating the existence and attributes of God in a manner that will truly persuade others, it is necessary to do more than simply put together abstract propositions. One must seek real, and not only notional, apprehension of God. Rational arguments, says Newman, "speak to those who understand the speech. To the mere barren intellect they are but the pale ghosts of notions; but the trained imagination sees in them the representations of things."[32] We need to be aware that we have encountered God through our conscience in order to be able truly to apprehend the more abstract arguments in favor of his existence.[33]

---

28. Newman, *Grammar of Assent*, 336.

29. See Dulles, *Newman*, 38–42; Thomas J. Norris, "Faith," in *Cambridge Companion to John Henry Newman*, 73–97, at 88–90; G. Verbeke, "Aristotelian Roots of Newman's Illative Sense," in *Newman and Gladstone: Centennial Essays*, ed. James D. Bastable (Dublin: Veritas, 1978), 177–96.

30. Newman, *Grammar of Assent*, 390.

31. Newman, *Grammar of Assent*, 397.

32. Newman, *Grammar of Assent*, 315. On real versus notional apprehension and assent, see Terrence Merrigan, "Newman on Faith in the Trinity," in *Newman and Faith*, ed. Ian Ker and Terrence Merrigan (Grand Rapids: Eerdmans, 2004), 93–116, at 96–99.

33. For further discussion see John F. Crosby, *The Personalism of John Henry Newman* (Washington, DC: Catholic University of America Press, 2014); Anthony Kenny, "Newman as

Maurice Blondel (1861–1949)

Born into a distinguished middle-class family in Dijon, France, Maurice Blondel studied at the École Normale and became a professor of philosophy in Aix-en-Provence, where he spent the rest of his life. In 1893 he published his *Action: Essay on a Critique of Life and a Science of Practice*, which drew the interest of such figures as William James and Friederich von Hügel. Blondel soon entered into the Modernist controversy that was troubling British and European Catholicism, a controversy whose intensity can be seen in Pope Pius X's encyclical *Pascendi Dominici Gregis* (1907). Against the Modernist biblical scholar Alfred Loisy, Blondel wrote a short but penetrating study, *History and Dogma*. At the same time, he critiqued certain forms of neoscholastic philosophy and theology, both in his periodical *Annales de Philosophie Chrétienne* and in books on such topics as intelligence, mysticism, thought, infinite Being and finite beings, and the question of whether there can be a specifically Catholic philosophy. In 1926, no longer able to see or read, he retired from teaching, but he continued to write via dictation. His influence on the *nouvelle théologie* was profound, especially through Henri de Lubac.[34]

In Blondel's masterwork, *Action*, he begins by evoking our existential situation: "Yes or no, does human life make sense, and does man have a destiny? I act, but without even knowing what action is, without having wished to live, without knowing exactly either who I am or even if I am."[35] As he points out, we are thrown into action, and we have no choice but to make a judgment

a Philosopher of Religion," in *Newman, a Man for Our Time*, ed. David Brown (Harrisburg, PA: Morehouse, 1990), 98–122; Stephen Fields, "Image and Truth in Newman's Moral Argument for God," *Louvain Studies* 24 (1999): 191–210.

34. See Alexander Dru, introduction to Maurice Blondel, *The Letter on Apologetics and History and Dogma*, trans. Alexander Dru and Illtyd Trethowan (Grand Rapids: Eerdmans, 1994), 13–116; Jean Lacroix, *Maurice Blondel: An Introduction to the Man and His Philosophy*, trans. John Guinness (London: Sheed and Ward, 1968); Oliva Blanchette, *Maurice Blondel: A Philosophical Life* (Grand Rapids: Eerdmans, 2010). Blanchette's work is both a biography and an exposition (often polemically charged) of Blondel's philosophical thought. See also Michael A. Conway, "Maurice Blondel and *Ressourcement*," in *Ressourcement: A Movement for Renewal in Twentieth-Century Catholic Theology*, ed. Gabriel Flynn and Paul D. Murray (Oxford: Oxford University Press, 2012), 65–82. Blondel and Pierre Rousselot inspire Henri de Lubac's remark that "nothing can be thought without positing the Absolute in relating it to that Absolute; nothing can be willed without tending towards the Absolute, nor valued unless weighed in terms of the Absolute"; see de Lubac, *The Discovery of God*, trans. Alexander Dru with Mark Sebanc and Cassian Fulsom, OSB (Grand Rapids: Eerdmans, 1996), 36; cf. 62: "Behind the apparent variations, the skeleton of the proof always remains the same. The proof is solid and eternal: as hard as steel. It is something more than one of reason's inventions: it is reason itself" (see also 85–86, 130, 212–14).

35. Maurice Blondel, *Action (1893): Essay on a Critique of Life and a Science of Practice*, trans. Oliva Blanchette (Notre Dame: University of Notre Dame Press, 1984), 3.

about its significance. He notes that the question of action is not one particular question among many: "It is *the* question, the one without which there is none other."[36] To be is to act; to will is to act. There is no consciousness that exists serenely "prior" to action: "we think (it is in the order of things) only after having acted, and in acting, and in order to act."[37] But is it possible to study action without rendering it lifeless? In answer, Blondel proposes "to let the will and action unfold . . . down to the final agreement or to the contradiction between the primitive movement and the end in which it terminates. The difficulty is to introduce nothing external or artificial into this profound drama of life."[38]

In Blondel's analysis, the freedom of the will is never absolute. The will must choose among particular intentions or desires. The object willed, the particular intention or desire that one has chosen, is limited. This "willed will" is not equal to the infinite power of willing (the "willing will"). Through this dialectical tension within the will, Blondel engages the phenomenon of action. The ideal of freedom is equality between the willed will and the willing will, and so the will continually seeks an object more proportionate to its infinite power of willing. With regard to the latter, Blondel observes that "the consciousness of action implies the notion of infinite; and this notion of infinite explains the consciousness of free action."[39] Indeed, for Blondel, "To act is in a way to entrust oneself to the universe," and yet our willing cannot be sated by the universe; thus we act with an orientation toward "an ideal world," "something more real than the real."[40]

What then is the relationship of metaphysics to action and volition? Blondel cautions that "we must not separate thought from the life that sustains its fecundity; nor must we reduce metaphysics to being only a prolongation of the empirical order and a kind of superfluous luxury or an impasse, far removed from the general current of voluntary activity."[41] Our speculative concepts cannot be separated from our practical action, since these concepts arise in our minds as part of our active life and fully belong to this life. In this sense, Blondel ascribes synthetic *a priori* propositions (speculative metaphysics) to action and the internal structure of the will. He states, "Metaphysics has its substance in the acting will. It has truth only under this experimental and dynamic aspect."[42] But just as religion can become a mere means for ethical

36. Blondel, *Action*, 13.
37. Blondel, *Action*, 115.
38. Blondel, *Action*, 115.
39. Blondel, *Action*, 123.
40. Blondel, *Action*, 263, 272, 275.
41. Blondel, *Action*, 277.
42. Blondel, *Action*, 278. For Blondel, human action is a synthetic *a priori* reality (metaphysical): synthetic, because it is the bond between thought and being, and *a priori*, because

progress of the self or society, metaphysics can become a form of pride by which the metaphysician imagines that "through his systems and through his natural religion, he will lay hold of the transcendent Being, conquer and master it in some way . . . as if he were cornering the living truth within a tenuous network of thoughts; as if, through the honor he renders his god in affirming and defining it, he were subordinating it entirely."[43] Blondel makes clear that he has Enlightenment rationalism here in view, since the deluded metaphysician's "superstition is to make believe that he has none and to think he lives by clear ideas and rational practices; he is triumphant in the thought that he has dislodged the old dogmas."[44]

Given that action always reveals its insufficiency to attain what the human heart desires, Blondel finds that in action "it is impossible not to recognize the insufficiency of the whole natural order and not to feel an ulterior need; it is impossible to find within oneself something to satisfy this religious need."[45] We cannot bring our action to completion because we are always seeking an infinite fulfilment (self-sufficiency) that even the greatest finite things cannot satisfy. We also experience ourselves as not belonging to ourselves: we are not the origin of our willing, and we are not free not to will. We find our wills painfully thwarted in areas over which we thought we had control. We cannot avoid sin, make our actions perfect, or erase the bad consequences of past actions. Thus Blondel observes that "before, during, after our acts, there is dependence, constraint, and failure."[46]

Yet, Blondel also finds that these constraints and failures do not put an end to our willing. Rather, even the knowledge of death serves to illumine "the real and actual energy of human willing" and our "implicit certitude of living on."[47] As Blondel says, far from repressing the will, "The contradictions apparently most repugnant to the will, serve only to bring to light its invincible attachment to itself. In what it denies, it affirms itself and builds itself up indestructibly."[48] The will refuses to cease willing because the will does not desire nothingness.

---

it has an immanent structure governed by principles not given in empirical reality. Thus pure reason and practical reason are distinct, but they are not in opposition to each other. Blondel's reconfiguration of Kant's division of the intellect is at the center of his philosophy of action, a philosophy that he sought to situate "between the Aristotelianism that depreciates and subordinates practice to thought and the Kantianism which detaches both orders from each other and exalts the practical order to the detriment of the other [i.e., thought]," as Blondel says in his *Lettres philosophiques* (Paris: Aubier, 1961), 10.

43. Blondel, *Action*, 293.
44. Blondel, *Action*, 293.
45. Blondel, *Action*, 297.
46. Blondel, *Action*, 307.
47. Blondel, *Action*, 310.
48. Blondel, *Action*, 310.

In fact, rather than ceasing to desire what we are not able to attain, we desire it all the more. Our limitations and trials only show us "the indestructibility of all these natural aspirations."[49] Limitations do not show us that our wills are made for limitation. Similarly, the fact that we are not made content by any object of our will shows us that we are inevitably seeking "the one thing necessary," even if we do not know how to name it.[50] If we were not willing "the one thing necessary," then we would either be content or we would give up in the face of our limitations. At the heart of human volition and action, therefore, is a "necessary presence."[51]

With respect to this "necessary presence," mere concepts or definitions cannot suffice. Blondel explains that "it is not that we have to stop at an indefinable sense of the mystery, nor despair of grasping anything of it in thought, nor forbid ourselves from seeking any necessitating proof for it."[52] But he avers that abstract demonstration cannot meet the need that we have for engaging this "necessary presence" as an actual *reality*. He therefore seeks "a proof that results from the total movement of life, a proof that is action in its entirety."[53] Since action is properly seen and experienced as a whole, the components of action can be united into "a demonstrative synthesis" that arrives at an active reality rather than at an abstraction.[54]

In seeking this demonstration of the reality of the "necessary presence," he first asks whether the necessary presence that we think we perceive is in fact "death and nothingness."[55] To affirm the idea of nothingness, we must deny all the elements of action and thought; we must deny precisely "everything that is an immediate object of knowledge and desire."[56] In other words, to think nothingness is inevitably to think its counterpart, because in order to affirm it, we must deny "what we still cannot keep from willing and affirming."[57] Blondel therefore concludes, "Under all these veils is hidden a homage to being; it is nothingness that necessarily confesses it."[58] The concept of "nothingness" exposes the insufficiency and contingency of all things, but it also exposes the necessary presence of being: "Wherever we

49. Blondel, *Action*, 312.
50. Blondel, *Action*, 313.
51. Blondel, *Action*, 314.
52. Blondel, *Action*, 315.
53. Blondel, *Action*, 315.
54. Blondel, *Action*, 316.
55. Blondel, *Action*, 316.
56. Blondel, *Action*, 316.
57. Blondel, *Action*, 316.
58. Blondel, *Action*, 317.

turn, we encounter it; and to flee from it is still a way of running toward it and falling into its hands."[59]

Blondel reflects further on how our action, in which we experience the insufficiency of all phenomena, reveals to us the heteronomy of our willing. With respect to finite objects and domains, the will "can neither give them up nor be satisfied."[60] No finite good can unite and harmonize the willing will and the willed will. Yet we desire finite goods nonetheless. As Blondel observes, "Nothing of what is known, possessed, done, is sufficient unto itself or is annihilated. Impossible to stay with it; impossible to do without it."[61] He argues, then, that action itself contains a proof of the existence of a "necessary being" through the insufficiency and contingency of all finite things. Indeed, were contingency all there is, then "all is nothing and nothing can be. All that we will supposes that it [necessary being] is; all that we are requires it to be."[62] His fundamental point is that "the argument *a contingentia* (from contingency) has a character quite other, a spring more powerful, than has been thought ordinarily. Instead of looking for the necessary outside the contingent, as an ulterior term, it manifests it within the contingent itself, as a reality already present."[63] Thus, whereas the traditional proof mounts through contingent things to posit a necessary, transcendent being as the only possible explanation for the existence of contingent things, Blondel enters into the heart of contingency, as experienced in action (with its simultaneous poverty and surprising fullness), and finds there the necessary being. As he puts it, "The relative necessity of the contingent reveals the absolute necessity of the necessary."[64]

Can we say anything further about this necessary being? Blondel remarks that in our experience the real and the ideal are always striving to catch up with each other, in the "mutual and alternating propulsion of idea and action."[65] In this alternating pattern, the real and ideal must coincide, even though this identity continually escapes us. Since this is so, Blondel reasons that the real must infinitely surpass us: it cannot be from ourselves "that we draw either the light of our thought or the efficaciousness of our action."[66] The proof of God's existence from the analysis of action, then, "gathers all that we have found, without or within ourselves, of intelligibility and intelligence, of

59. Blondel, *Action*, 317.
60. Blondel, *Action*, 317.
61. Blondel, *Action*, 317.
62. Blondel, *Action*, 317.
63. Blondel, *Action*, 318.
64. Blondel, *Action*, 318.
65. Blondel, *Action*, 319.
66. Blondel, *Action*, 319.

movement and force, of truth and thought, in order to manifest its common principle."[67] Since our action and thought can encompass all finite things, the ground of our action and thought—the ground of all finite things—must be "the pure act of perfect thought."[68]

According to Blondel, this version of the "cosmological proof" (via action) cannot be isolated from the "teleological proof" of God's existence. The teleological proof must go beyond simply demonstrating syllogistically the necessity of a wise orderer. Understood through the analysis of action, the teleological proof "shows that the wisdom of things is not in things" and aims to find that which unites wisdom and power, thought and action.[69] This teleological proof leads not to a cause proportionate to its effects, but to a Cause that is the principle of that which exists only relatively in the effects.

Blondel summarizes his teleological proof as follows: Since our thought and action constantly surpass each other, they are imperfect. Yet they could not even be what they are "without the permanent mediation of a perfect thought and a perfect action," since their very imperfection contains the impress of an inaccessible perfection.[70] The key point is that to arrive at this proof, we do not need to abstract finite perfections from things. We need simply to enter into the very center of our thought and action. At this center, we discover that we cannot move from thought to action (or vice versa) without passing through the inaccessible perfection. As Blondel explains, "Thus, the order, the harmony, the wisdom that I discover in myself and in things, is not simply an effect starting from which a reasoning process would force me to go up toward a cause absent from its work."[71] Put another way, we do not need to formulate a deductive syllogism or invoke the principle of causality but rather look within imperfect things (including our thought and action) in order to identify "the presence and the necessary action of a perfect thought and a perfect power."[72]

---

67. Blondel, *Action*, 319.
68. Blondel, *Action*, 319.
69. Blondel, *Action*, 320.
70. Blondel, *Action*, 320.
71. Blondel, *Action*, 320.
72. Blondel, *Action*, 321. As Blondel observes toward the end of his book,

> There is then no object whose reality we can conceive and affirm without having encompassed the total series by an act of thought, without in fact submitting to the exigencies of the alternative which it imposes on us, in short, without passing through the point where shines the light of the Being who illumines every reason and in whose presence every will has to declare itself. We have the idea of an objective reality, we affirm the reality of objects; but to do so, we must implicitly raise the problem of our destiny and subordinate all that we are and all that is for us to an option. We arrive at being and at beings only by way of this alternative: according to the very way we decide on it, it is

Blondel adds that by recognizing this perfect action at the heart of our imperfect action, we gain a better appreciation also for the "ontological proof." Perfect action is not a mere idea but something whose reality we experience in our imperfect action. At the root of our imperfect action lies a perfect identity of being, knowing, and acting. As Blondel says, "We discover within ourselves real perfection and we go on to ideal perfection. We go, so to speak, from ourselves to it, in order to go from it to it."[73] Our idea of perfect action, in other words, is already a reality that we experience in the limitation and dynamism of our action, without being able to grasp perfect action in itself. We discover it as "more interior to us than our own interior."[74] It is the subjective ground of all subjects, and it is perfectly simple. It can hardly be one in any way but by being Trinity, since as personal it cannot be alone. In our action, then, we experience the reality of what our metaphysical expressions can convey only lifelessly. The notion of "pure act," which as an isolated concept in a mere "game of understanding" can only be "vain, false and idolatrous," becomes within the wholeness of the proofs arising from the analysis of action "a practical certitude" that is "true, living and efficacious."[75]

Blondel considers that his achievement consists above all in finding a way to present all the proofs together, in a manner that shows how the proofs "reproduce the movement of life and sustain it."[76] He is quite critical of the traditional presentations of the proofs, which he finds uncompelling because they rely on "what the discursive labor of thought renders lengthy and leaves sterile."[77] The analysis of action breaks through this sterility. Rather than relying on discursive reasoning, we can discover in the immediacy of action that God exists. All the proofs "come from the teachings of action and return to action to teach and vivify it."[78] To learn these proofs and their validity we need only immerse ourselves in actual practice, in life itself. Since action alone "bears on the whole" and engages the full complexity of real life, it is only in action that we discover "the indisputable presence and the binding proof of Being."[79]

It follows that the efforts of the metaphysicians have been rather misplaced, since "dialectical subtleties, no matter how long and ingenious they may be,

inevitable that the meaning of being should change. *The knowledge of being* implies the necessity of the option; *being within knowledge* is not before, but after the freedom of the choice. (ibid., 398–99)

73. Blondel, *Action*, 322.
74. Blondel, *Action*, 322.
75. Blondel, *Action*, 323.
76. Blondel, *Action*, 323.
77. Blondel, *Action*, 323.
78. Blondel, *Action*, 323.
79. Blondel, *Action*, 323.

have no more bearing than a stone thrown at the sun by a child."[80] The proof of God's existence from action is a demonstration, but it is experienced by us with the power of self-evident or intuitive knowledge: "it is in an instant, in a single surge, by an immediate necessity that is made manifest in us *the one* that no reasoning could invent, because no deduction is equal to the plenitude of life in action."[81] In the totality of our action, God is clearly revealed to us, even if we cannot express it conceptually. Moreover, God is revealed in such a way as to make this knowledge, to which we must freely commit ourselves, more than an abstract, lifeless fact—"in a way that makes of him a concrete truth and which will render him efficacious, useful, and accessible to the will."[82]

Blondel hastens to add that this idea of God can nonetheless become an idol. It is true that God is absolute perfection. But we cannot have an adequate apprehension of what absolute perfection means. The result is that "as soon as we think we know God enough, we no longer know him."[83] When God manifests himself to us, he is so awe-inspiring that we naturally fear him. We can choose to turn away, or we can presume proudly on our knowledge. Neither action is acceptable. To those who turn away and remain "willfully blind," Blondel insists that knowledge of God is easily available.[84] Here Blondel again emphasizes that knowledge of God through action is close to self-evident knowledge: "without dialectical complications or long studies, in the twinkling of an eye, for all, at any hour, God is the immediate certitude without which there is no other, the first clarity, the language known without having had to

80. Blondel, *Action*, 323.
81. Blondel, *Action*, 323.
82. Blondel, *Action*, 324. For a cognate emphasis on action or life, see Hans Urs von Balthasar, *The God Question and Modern Man*, trans. Hilda Graef (New York: Seabury, 1967), 69–76; Balthasar, *The Theology of Karl Barth: Exposition and Interpretation*, trans. Edward T. Oakes, SJ (San Francisco: Ignatius, 1992), 322–25. Balthasar argues that

> original sin, from which all actual sin stems, means a negative relationship to the one, indivisible God, who is both Creator as well as bestower of grace. Therefore man can in no case simultaneously stand in a supernaturally negative and in a naturally positive relation to God, as many theologians seem to assume when they think an *odium supernaturale Dei* can be harmonized with an *amor Dei naturalis super omnia*. . . . If the sinful pagan cannot *not* know God by nature, then at least his conscious image of God can in no case be a correct, error-free image, untouched by its rejection of God's supernatural grace. Nonetheless, even this adulteration rests on an original openness to what man *should have* known and what he cannot help still knowing in completing every act of knowledge. And so at the place where for Karl Barth faith stands as the a priori of all knowledge, even the knowledge possessed by the denier of God, there stands, according to Vatican I, these natural-supernatural contacts of the created spirit with the true God, equally Creator and bestower of grace. (ibid., 322; cf. 315 on "the act of obedience that is an essential aspect of reason")

83. Blondel, *Action*, 324.
84. Blondel, *Action*, 325.

learn it."[85] To those who presume on their knowledge, Blondel has stern words. He associates such presumption with a rationalistic metaphysics that has not yet appreciated the path to God via action. Thus he states that "the moment we seem to touch God through a trace of thought, He escapes us, if we do not keep Him, if we do not look for Him, through action. His immobility can be aimed at as a fixed goal only by a perpetual movement. Wherever we stop, He is not; wherever we walk forward, He is."[86] If we think that we can know God through an abstract and uncommitted "speculative examination," we will fail to perceive the living God but instead arrive solely at an idol.[87]

By choosing to manifest his existence to us via the path of action, God shows that our true good lies in cooperative action with him. Blondel speaks of the action of thinking about God as a cooperation with God "in order to achieve the equation of voluntary action in consciousness."[88] He holds that true knowledge of God must therefore involve ongoing action: "it is because action is a synthesis of man with God that it is in perpetual becoming, as if stirred by the inspiration of an infinite growth."[89] When we think of the transcendent God, our action itself becomes transcendent. Indeed, action itself always calls us to a transcendent goal or destiny that gives our acts the character of transcendence. Blondel states, "It is enough that, even masked and disguised, the universal good has secretly solicited the will, for the whole of life to be marked by this indelible impression."[90] We cannot avoid knowing God in this way, since God is always present to us in our action and volition, even when we are trying to deny "the truth of this presence."[91] As Blondel puts it, "Through its inevitable expansion, the human will, even unknown to itself, has divine exigencies. Its wish is to attain and to conquer God; it gropes blindly to reach Him."[92]

In sum, Blondel emphasizes that to know that God exists does not require us to be learned metaphysicians; quite the contrary. In action, everyone discovers God's existence, consciously or unconsciously. Thus even for the professed atheist, the knowledge of God is a constant presence that requires a choice between willing (impossibly) to be god without God or willing to submit to the living God. It is indeed possible to choose idolatry, to refuse to reconcile the willed will and the willing will, by making a particular finite good the

85. Blondel, *Action*, 325.
86. Blondel, *Action*, 325.
87. Blondel, *Action*, 325.
88. Blondel, *Action*, 325.
89. Blondel, *Action*, 325.
90. Blondel, *Action*, 326.
91. Blondel, *Action*, 326.
92. Blondel, *Action*, 330.

ultimate end of action. Such a choice tragically brings about the living death of action due to the resulting inability to see the infinite horizon of the good that the will pursues. Only by choosing God, the "supernatural"—a choice that requires the eyes of faith—can our "natural" action be fully what it is and must be.[93] As Blondel concludes, "Voluntary action is made equal to itself in consciousness only inasmuch as we recognize in it the presence and the cooperation of 'the one thing necessary.'"[94]

Pierre Rousselot (1878–1915)

Born in Nantes, France, Pierre Rousselot entered the Jesuit novitiate at the age of sixteen. In 1908, Rousselot was ordained a Catholic priest and also defended two philosophical dissertations at the Sorbonne, *The Intellectualism of Saint Thomas* and *The Problem of Love in the Middle Ages*—works that both influenced Blondel and were influenced by Blondel. In 1910 Rousselot became a professor of theology at the Institut Catholique in Paris. In the same year, he published *The Eyes of Faith* as two articles in the journal *Recherches de science religieuse*. Trained in the neoscholastic curriculum mandated by Pope Leo XIII, Rousselot sought to give a significant place to connatural knowledge and to the knowledge of God implicit in our judgment that "being exists," without falling into positions that had earlier been judged erroneous by the church (such as those of Georg Hermes and Antonio Rosmini). In 1915, while serving as a sergeant in World War I, Rousselot was killed on the battlefield of Éparges. Known as the father of transcendental Thomism, Rousselot influenced such figures as Joseph Maréchal, Henri de Lubac, and Karl Rahner.[95]

93. See Blondel, *Action*, 357, 380.

94. Blondel, *Action*, 333. For further discussion see James M. Somerville, *Total Commitment: Blondel's L'Action* (Washington, DC: Corpus, 1968); Jean-Luc Marion, "La conversion de la volonté selon *L'Action*," in *Maurice Blondel. Une dramatique de la modernité*, ed. Dominique Folscheid (Paris: Éditions universitaires, 1990), 154–64; Henri Bouillard, *Blondel and Christianity*, trans. James M. Somerville (Washington, DC: Corpus, 1969); James LeGrys, "The Christianization of Modern Philosophy according to Maurice Blondel," *Theological Studies* 54 (1993): 455–84.

95. See John M. McDermott, SJ, *Love and Understanding: The Relation of Will and Intellect in Pierre Rousselot's Christological Vision* (Rome: Gregorian University Press, 1983), 1–7; McDermott, introduction to Pierre Rousselot, SJ, *The Eyes of Faith*, trans. Joseph Donceel, SJ (New York: Fordham University Press, 1990), 1–18; Andrew Tallon, translator's foreword to Pierre Rousselot, *Intelligence: Sense of Being, Faculty of God*, trans. Andrew Tallon (Milwaukee: Marquette University Press, 1999), iii–xxxv. The English title *Intelligence* does not convey the French original, which is *L'Intellectualisme de saint Thomas*. See also F. J. Scott, SJ, "Maurice Blondel and Pierre Rousselot," *The New Scholasticism* 36 (1962): 330–52; Erhard

In his essay "Thomist Metaphysics and the Critique of Knowledge," published in the *Revue néoscholastique de Louvain* in 1910, Rousselot begins by observing that for Aquinas, "not only is the material 'thing' the proper and proportionate object of our earthly intellection, but even the primordial idea of 'concrete being' (for what Thomas named *ens concretum* is precisely what is called 'thing' by the moderns); this primordial idea is found implied and utilized in all the notions we form even of immaterial beings."[96] We can only conceive of immaterial beings analogously on the basis of material things, "by representing them in the image of those material things we conceive here below."[97] Reflecting on the unlimited character of pure form as well as on the act/potency distinction, Rousselot distinguishes God from angels, humans, and other creatures: "God alone is absolutely actual and absolutely simple: God is separated *Esse*."[98] God's essence is existence; in angels, humans, and other creatures, essence limits existence to a particular finite mode.

Rousselot then turns to modes of cognition. We know things in their materiality (representation); angels have direct, unmediated knowledge of things (intuition); and God knows things by their act of existence (vision). Our conceptual knowledge by representation arrives at abstract, universal knowledge, but our knowledge always retains "an internal reference to a subject, or better, to *some* subject."[99] Whereas angels possess intuitive knowledge of things, in our mode of knowing there is always a tension between the universal nature and the concrete thing. By our conceptual representation we affirm the union of the universal nature with the particular thing, but there is always a "remainder." As Rousselot puts it, "Full confidence that reason is made to assimilate things: such is the strength of conceptual knowledge. Inextinguishable persistence of a remainder: such is the essential defect of the concept."[100]

For Rousselot, then, those who argue that we can have an intellectual intuition of being or a pure experience of being are mistaken. Here he particularly has the philosophy of Henri Bergson in view. To have intuitive knowledge—rid of abstraction and penetrating to the very heart of the real—our souls would

Kunz, SJ, *Glaube—Gnade—Geschichte: Die Glaubenstheologie des Pierre Rousselot, SJ* (Frankfurt: Knecht, 1969); Gerald McCool, SJ, *The Neo-Thomists* (Milwaukee: Marquette University Press, 1994), 97–116; J. de Wulf, SJ, *La justification de la foi chez saint Thomas d'Aquin et le P. Rousselot* (Paris: Desclée de Brouwer, 1946).

96. Pierre Rousselot, "Thomist Metaphysics and Critique of Knowledge," in Rousselot, *Essays on Love and Knowledge*, ed. Andrew Tallon and Pol Vandevelde, trans. Andrew Tallon, Pol Vandevelde, and Alan Vincelette (Milwaukee: Marquette University Press, 2008), 149–81, at 150.

97. Rousselot, "Thomist Metaphysics and Critique of Knowledge," 150.

98. Rousselot, "Thomist Metaphysics and Critique of Knowledge," 153.

99. Rousselot, "Thomist Metaphysics and Critique of Knowledge," 159.

100. Rousselot, "Thomist Metaphysics and Critique of Knowledge," 162.

have to know themselves directly, rather than knowing themselves through knowing other things. Such direct, unmediated knowledge of things is not possible for our minds, which operate through sense knowledge. On the same grounds, against Hegelian idealism or rationalism, Rousselot also rejects "the doctrine of those who think there is a conceptual and discursive science adequate to being, that there are reasonings that render being, all the way to its ultimate foundations, clear to intelligence."[101]

Given that humans cannot intuit being, can there be metaphysical knowledge of God? Rousselot thinks that the answer is yes, and that in fact "metaphysics is just as natural and just as justified as life."[102] Every concept of a thing contains the judgment that "this is a being," and thereby every concept presupposes "a viewpoint wherein nature and supposit [an individual instance of nature] coincide, wherein one is seen in the other, without remainder and in full clarity."[103] By affirming conceptually the unity of a nature with a particular thing, our soul—without achieving intuition—exhibits the desire "to express the object in function of the soul itself."[104] Rousselot explains that in every concept, there is present the supposition or presumption "that the soul can *get through* the object, *have it over and done with*, *bring it to light*, and, consequently, bring itself to light."[105] This dynamism toward knowing our own act of intelligence characterizes every act of conceptual representation.

Rousselot points out that the synthesis made by our soul is not simply between the universal nature and the particular thing or subject but also between essence and existence. Here Rousselot refers to our immediate apprehension of existence, "the natural and primitive act by which the spirit all at once conceives being and affirms its existence" by means of the conception "this is a being."[106] In our conception of "this being," the judgment that "being exists" is also present. This judgment ("being exists") unites or synthesizes essence and existence just as the judgment "this is a being" unites or synthesizes nature and subject.

Even when we are thinking of possible things that do not exist, our judgment that the thing does not exist includes, inevitably, the judgment "being exists." And if we can affirm the synthesis of essence and existence in the judgment "being exists," then we have affirmed something that we cannot know intuitively. We have thereby affirmed "implicitly that there is a point of

---

101. Rousselot, "Thomist Metaphysics and Critique of Knowledge," 165.
102. Rousselot, "Thomist Metaphysics and Critique of Knowledge," 168.
103. Rousselot, "Thomist Metaphysics and Critique of Knowledge," 169.
104. Rousselot, "Thomist Metaphysics and Critique of Knowledge," 169.
105. Rousselot, "Thomist Metaphysics and Critique of Knowledge," 169.
106. Rousselot, "Thomist Metaphysics and Critique of Knowledge," 170.

view from which one is seen in the other."[107] The judgment "being exists," which characterizes our intelligence from its first primitive apprehension of being, includes within itself the presumption that essence and existence do indeed form a synthetic unity, even if we cannot intuit this unity.

It follows that our judgment "being exists" must also presume that creative Truth exists, from whose perspective the synthesis of essence and existence is manifest. Rousselot states, "Every act of intellection presupposes not only that reality is intelligible, that reality can be brought to light, but also that reality is somewhere understood, somewhere completely brought to light: therefore it presupposes God."[108] On the basis of a careful analysis of our cognitive acts (which depend on sense apprehension of material things), therefore, we can recognize that our cognition presupposes that God exists. Since we cannot even exercise intelligence without presupposing God's existence, we can conclude that the affirmation that God exists is necessary—unless we wish to descend into irrationality. If we reject God's existence, we reject our own intellectual nature, since the judgment of being is our intellect's first natural reaction to being.

Does this reasoning to God's existence on the basis of an analysis of our cognition of being do away with the classical Thomistic (and patristic) "proofs, which started from *being itself*, and which, through efficient, final, and exemplary causality" demonstrated the existence of God?[109] Rousselot argues that on the contrary, his approach further solidifies and sanctions those proofs. It does so by explaining what otherwise would remain "obscure in what they presuppose in common, which is this twofold judgment: *Being exists*, and *the existent is being* (= reality is intelligible)."[110] These judgments are implicit in the classical proofs, and by bringing their cognitive implications to light via analysis of cognition, Rousselot thinks that he has strengthened the classical proofs. The necessary condition for the judgment "being exists," a judgment that we make at the very outset of rational consciousness, is in fact that God exists. Since our judgment is rooted in *a posteriori* knowledge gained from our senses, this recognition of God's existence as the necessary condition for our knowledge is not a mere *a priori* proof.

107. Rousselot, "Thomist Metaphysics and Critique of Knowledge," 171.
108. Rousselot, "Thomist Metaphysics and Critique of Knowledge," 171. Along these lines, Henri de Lubac comments that "if there were no idea of God whatsoever prior to the reasoning by which we try to provide him with a logical basis in our thought, the critique which we must necessarily make of the general form in which those arguments are set would terminate in the denial of the affirmation of God" (de Lubac, *Discovery of God*, 39; cf. 53–54). See John M. McDermott, SJ, "De Lubac and Rousselot," *Gregorianum* 78 (1997): 735–59.
109. Rousselot, "Thomist Metaphysics and Critique of Knowledge," 172.
110. Rousselot, "Thomist Metaphysics and Critique of Knowledge," 172.

Some of his contemporaries, Rousselot notes, criticize his inquiry into the presuppositions of our judgment that "being exists." In response, he makes clear that he has no intention of trying to demonstrate that being exists; this is something that reason presupposes as a first principle of rationality. Instead, his task consists simply in analyzing our cognitive judgment, "why and how *we affirm* that being exists."[111] In showing that this judgment presupposes the synthesis of essence and existence and thus presupposes God's existence (since only God's essence or nature is existence), he is showing the nature of the soul as a self-transcending dynamism. As he describes this dynamism intrinsic to the soul, "The human is essentially a spirit whose hypostasis does not equal its nature, a spirit incompletely spiritualized; it does not perceive itself yet as a whole spirit, wholly of God and for God; it must attain this through progress and exercise; it must 'gain its soul' by its usage of the sensible world."[112] The analysis of cognition reveals that we desire to fully actualize our spiritual powers by knowing not merely sense particulars but natures, and that we desire to fully actualize our being by knowing God. When the soul awakens and consents to its nature, the soul recognizes that its intellection is an "appetite for the divine."[113] The demonstration of God's existence, then, depends on our natural appetite for direct knowledge of God (i.e., for the vision of God).

In his conclusion to "Thomist Metaphysics and Critique of Knowledge," Rousselot notes that Kantians will think that his critique of knowledge (or of the structure of our cognition), leading as it does to the affirmation that God exists, is built on a metaphysics already determined at the outset. By contrast, Thomistic or scholastic critics will be concerned that his demonstration of God's existence on the basis of his critique of knowledge does not measure up to the Thomistic demonstrations of God's existence. To the Kantians, he responds that no analysis of human cognition can avoid the question of "what we mean by saying: it is," and therefore "the doctrine of the spirit should not only complete, but include and explain the doctrine of being."[114] To Thomistic or scholastic critics, he observes that the classical demonstrations that depend on the distinction between essence and existence show that no viewpoint can be accepted that "claims to explain *being* as such and the whole of being through a particular, definite, determined essence, completely relative to the whole of being."[115] These demonstrations, then, are only strengthened and

111. Rousselot, "Thomist Metaphysics and Critique of Knowledge," 175.
112. Rousselot, "Thomist Metaphysics and Critique of Knowledge," 175.
113. Rousselot, "Thomist Metaphysics and Critique of Knowledge," 177.
114. Rousselot, "Thomist Metaphysics and Critique of Knowledge," 179n46, 180.
115. Rousselot, "Thomist Metaphysics and Critique of Knowledge," 180.

deepened when the structure of cognition shows, too, that God (the absolute synthesis of essence and existence) must exist.[116]

In *The Eyes of Faith*, Rousselot reflects on the relationship of natural intelligence and supernatural intelligence (faith). He observes that "the formal object of natural intelligence is natural being, accommodated to our natural end; the formal object of the knowledge of faith is supernatural being, pertaining to the order of grace, a means to lead us to intuitive vision."[117] For example, when we see the miraculous healing of a sick person, we see "natural being"—a sick person who becomes well—and we also see an event that belongs to the order of grace ("supernatural being"). Grace, then, illuminates something that we also know through natural intelligence: we are enabled to see in a higher way without thereby ceasing to see what a nongraced person would see. We see Jesus Christ the man, but we also see the Son of God; we see the city of Rome, but we also see the Roman Catholic Church. The supernatural "formal object" is not opposed to the natural "formal object" but rather is found "deepening and perfecting it *from within*."[118] Supernatural grace, therefore, is not extrinsic to or opposed to the natural dynamism of intelligence; rather, it elevates natural intelligence. The essence of natural intelligence "consists in its essential aptitude to serve as a means for created spirits to ascend to God, their final end."[119] Supernatural grace elevates natural intelligence so as to lead created spirits "to God, object of the beatific vision."[120]

Rousselot goes on to explain that natural intelligence is moved by being: it encounters being and knows it as true. This movement is extended by faith, which responds to supernatural being. Grace makes the intelligence perceptive with respect to the signs around us that exhibit the truth of the gospel. Saints respond even to something seemingly insignificant, such as a blade of grass, in which they perceive a resplendent manifestation of divine goodness. Rousselot's position here stands between the extremes of voluntarism (faith dependent solely on the will) and rationalism (faith dependent solely on reason). Arguing that faith is both utterly free and utterly reasonable, he observes that the will is operative even in matters of speculative reason, which can take on a different aspect depending on our will. As Rousselot says, speaking of the natural movement of the will, "A love, a passion, an appetite may thoroughly impart its own coloration to the whole world of perceived

116. For discussion, see McDermott, *Love and Understanding*, 134–36.
117. Rousselot, *Eyes of Faith*, 33.
118. Rousselot, *Eyes of Faith*, 34.
119. Rousselot, *Eyes of Faith*, 34.
120. Rousselot, *Eyes of Faith*, 34.

objects, so much so that it powerfully influences, nay, even transforms, our judgments about 'things in themselves.'"[121]

In this sense, we are free even in relation to speculative matters. Our will can move us freely to embrace evidence that, through (natural) love, we see with certitude. The will can freely choose a mode of life that enables us to reasonably embrace new knowledge. With regard to supernatural truth, it can happen that "love arouses the faculty of knowing, and by the same stroke knowledge justifies that love. Without any preceding 'judgment of credibility,' the soul instantaneously believes and can exclaim 'My Lord and my God!'"[122] Such an act is both perfectly free and perfectly reasonable.

In making this case, Rousselot's goal is to show that it is not only supernatural faith that involves a movement of the will. Put another way, the influence of the will on one's assent to a truth is not a mark of irrationality, nor need it weaken the certitude of one's assent. In natural matters of speculative reason, natural love has an impact; so too in supernatural matters of faith, supernatural love has an impact.

Yet, *should* the will affect our judgments of speculative truth in this way? Rousselot observes that intelligence itself involves an appetite, namely, a "natural appetition for the supreme and subsisting Truth."[123] Intelligence is not neutral toward being. Indeed, as ordered to Truth, "reason itself is nothing other than a pure love of Being," which enchants and attracts human intelligence.[124] Human intelligence is a desire, a love, for the Creator of human intelligence. To be reasonable is to be ordered to our ultimate end, First Truth. Our intelligence's ability to attain certitude "comes entirely from the fact that God has inspired it with a natural inclination to the First Truth, that is, to Himself insofar as He is the End of all spiritual beings."[125]

This inclination toward First Truth characterizes our natural intelligence, and it means that intelligence must be conceived "as a connatural inclination and sympathy, as a pure love of God and of being."[126] Intelligence, therefore, is restricted when the will identifies a *finite* good as its highest end. By contrast, intelligence is expanded and increased when the will loves First Truth. Rousselot states that "the loving vision it directs will be a more perfect knowledge along the very lines of intellectuality itself."[127] Does this mean that loving God

---

121. Rousselot, *Eyes of Faith*, 49.
122. Rousselot, *Eyes of Faith*, 50.
123. Rousselot, *Eyes of Faith*, 52.
124. Rousselot, *Eyes of Faith*, 52.
125. Rousselot, *Eyes of Faith*, 54.
126. Rousselot, *Eyes of Faith*, 54.
127. Rousselot, *Eyes of Faith*, 55.

will ensure the correctness of our ideas? Rousselot notes in this regard that saints have been "led into error by some devout inclination."[128] Our ideas about God are not the same thing as our natural inclination toward God as First Truth; the former can be in error.

With respect to supernatural faith (and supernatural love), Rousselot argues that "in the act of faith love needs knowledge as knowledge needs love."[129] The believer can therefore expect to have "sympathetic" or connatural knowledge of the realities of faith, a knowledge in which we experience the attraction of Christian realities and a desire for them as "being good to believe" and as answering our intelligence's "inclination toward the subsisting Truth."[130] In fact, such connatural knowledge is found in natural knowledge as well. Rousselot observes, "Granting that intelligence is the expression of an appetitive tendency is the same as granting that we must not think of the sympathetic tendency in intellectual knowledge as restricted to some particular cases of intellection, but see it as necessarily following from a general law of intelligence as such."[131] This connaturality need not involve a conscious sympathy. Rather, it is rooted in our "most intense desire" to affirm being, our movement or inclination toward First Truth who creates and attracts our minds.[132] As Rousselot remarks, "Genuine sympathetic knowledge is immanent to the very tendency impelling the soul toward or drawing it away from some object, immanent to the very movement of desire or aversion."[133]

The natural inclination toward First Truth, when "healed and transformed," is taken up into the supernatural "affirmation of being contained in the knowledge of faith."[134] In faith's knowledge, we recognize more easily the formative presence of sympathy or connaturality because our supernatural dynamism of love is freely accepted rather than operating at the level of a created given. Thus, for Rousselot, especially in the case of faith's knowledge but also in knowledge per se, we can say that "love gives us eyes, the very fact of loving makes us see."[135]

In his *The Intellectualism of Saint Thomas*, Rousselot warns against conceiving of Aquinas's "intellectualism" in terms of "the primacy of static definitions and discursive [and deductive] reason."[136] Here he separates himself

128. Rousselot, *Eyes of Faith*, 55.
129. Rousselot, *Eyes of Faith*, 56.
130. Rousselot, *Eyes of Faith*, 58–59.
131. Rousselot, *Eyes of Faith*, 59.
132. Rousselot, *Eyes of Faith*, 59.
133. Rousselot, *Eyes of Faith*, 58.
134. Rousselot, *Eyes of Faith*, 59.
135. Rousselot, *Eyes of Faith*, 61.
136. Rousselot, *Intelligence*, 1.

firmly from "dogmatic Scholastics of the nineteenth century" who had "a false perspective because ordinarily they were looking for a theory of rational certitude in what was before anything else an intellectualist metaphysics."[137] Rousselot considers that when at the end of his life Aquinas deemed his writings to be mere straw in comparison to what he had seen, this shows that "Christian life seems to have developed correlatively in Thomas's soul enthusiasm for intelligence and disdain for human reasoning."[138] On this view, by moving from study and writing to full-time contemplation at the end of his life, Aquinas shows both his "intellectual radicalism"—his conviction that reason "is the faculty of the divine" and that its exercise is "the highest and most lovable of human actions"—and his "'mystical' disdain for discursive reasoning" in his desire for the vision of God.[139]

Rousselot thereby seeks to counter those who in his day critiqued medieval scholasticism as dry, abstract, ahistorical, and lifeless. Against such critics, Rousselot emphasizes that for Aquinas, "To know is primarily and principally to seize and embrace within yourself an *other* who is capable of seizing and embracing you: it is to live by the life of another living being. Intelligence is the sense [*sens*] of the divine because it is capable of embracing God in this way."[140] Far from an abstract conceptualism, then, Aquinas's view of the dynamism of human reason has living beings, and the living God, at its core. As Rousselot sums up his account of Aquinas's doctrine of intelligence, "Intelligence is essentially the sense [*sens*] of the real, but it is the sense of the real only because it is the sense of the divine."[141]

Ludwig Wittgenstein (1889–1951)

Ludwig Wittgenstein was born into a wealthy Austrian family in Vienna. Baptized and raised as a Catholic, though counted as Jewish by the Nazis due to his three Jewish grandparents, he lost faith in God as a teenager. He studied mechanical engineering in Berlin before moving to the Victoria University of

---

137. Rousselot, *Intelligence*, 195.
138. Rousselot, *Intelligence*, 183.
139. Rousselot, *Intelligence*, 182–83.
140. Rousselot, *Intelligence*, 7.
141. Rousselot, *Intelligence*, 2. For further discussion of Rousselot, see Aidan Nichols, OP, *From Newman to Congar: The Idea of Doctrinal Development from the Victorians to the Second Vatican Council* (Edinburgh: T&T Clark, 1990), chap. 8: "Henri de Lubac and Pierre Rousselot"; Henri de Lavalette, "Le théoricien de l'amour," *Recherches de science religieuse* 53 (1965): 126–58; Pol Vandevelde, "Between Epistemic Virtue and Metaphysics of Knowledge: The Place of Love in Pierre Rousselot's Epistemology," in Rousselot, *Essays*, 22–50. See also John M. McDermott, SJ, "Sheehan, Rousselot, and Theological Method," *Gregorianum* 69 (1987): 705–17.

Manchester to undertake a doctorate in aeronautics. After reading the works
of Bertrand Russell and Gottlob Frege, he turned his attention to the philosophy of mathematics and logic and attended Russell's lectures at the University
of Cambridge. He served in the Austro-Hungarian army in World War I and
fought on the front lines of the Russian and Italian fronts. On military leave, he
completed the *Tractatus Logico-Philosophicus* in August 1918 before returning to
the front and spending nine months as an Italian prisoner of war. After the war,
he worked with little success as a schoolteacher and as a gardener for Catholic
monasteries; during this period he also designed a modernist house in Vienna
for his sister. In 1929 he received a doctorate in philosophy from Cambridge
University. After lecturing in philosophy at Trinity College (Cambridge) for five
years, he left academic life, traveled to the USSR, and spent a year living in a hut
in Norway. In 1939 he was appointed to a chair in philosophy at Cambridge,
but when World War II broke out, he worked as a dispensary porter at Guy's
Hospital in London and later as a laboratory assistant at the Royal Victoria
Infirmary in Newcastle. He resigned his professorship at Cambridge in 1947.[142]

In his preface to the *Tractatus Logico-Philosophicus*, Wittgenstein states,
"The whole sense of the book might be summed up in the following words:
what can be said at all can be said clearly, and what we cannot talk about we
must pass over in silence."[143] His view is that not much can be said clearly.
The task of philosophy, then, is to help us identify exactly what can and
cannot be said clearly, and thereby to help rid us of the misperceptions that
arise when we attempt to speak about things that in fact we have no basis
for speaking about. Philosophy's negative role is far greater than its positive
role. Wittgenstein makes this point in the preface when, after stating that he
thinks that he has "found, on all essential points, the final solution of the
problems," he adds that he has in this way succeeded in showing "how little
is achieved when these problems are solved."[144] The greatest problems lie
outside the realm or competence of philosophy.[145]

142. See A. C. Grayling, *Wittgenstein: A Very Short Introduction* (Oxford: Oxford University
Press, 2001), 1–15; Ray Monk, *Ludwig Wittgenstein: The Duty of Genius* (London: Jonathan
Cape, 1990). See also Anthony Kenny, "Wittgenstein on the Nature of Philosophy," in *Wittgen-
stein and His Times*, ed. Brian McGuinness (Oxford: Blackwell, 1982), 1–26.

143. Ludwig Wittgenstein, *Tractatus Logico-Philosophicus*, trans. D. F. Pears and B. F. Mc-
Guinness (London: Routledge, 2001), 3. For discussion of the *Tractatus*, see Grayling, *Wittgenstein*, 16–66; Marie McGinn, *Elucidating the* Tractatus: *Wittgenstein's Early Philosophy of Logic
and Language* (Oxford: Oxford University Press, 2006); G. E. M. Anscombe, *An Introduction
to Wittgenstein's Tractatus* (London: Hutchinson & Co., 1971).

144. Wittgenstein, *Tractatus*, 4.

145. For discussion of Wittgenstein's relationship to Christianity and Catholicism, including his negative view of the demonstrations of God's existence (but positive view of Christian
symbolism and intuitions), see especially Fergus Kerr, OP, *"Work on Oneself": Wittgenstein's*

The *Tractatus* is arranged as a series of propositions, each given a number. The first proposition, 1, states, "The world is all that is the case."[146] Wittgenstein goes on to say, "The world is the totality of facts, not of things" (1.1); "the world is determined by the facts, and by their being *all* the facts" (1.11); and "the facts in logical space are the world" (1.13).[147] In 1.21, Wittgenstein states, "Each item can be the case or not the case while everything else remains the same."[148] One can thus conceive of each "fact" discretely. A "fact," he explains, is "the existence of states of affairs" (2), which is a "combination of objects (things)" (2.01). To know a thing or "object" is to know "all its possible occurrences in states of affairs" (2.0123), and thereby to know it as combined with other things, and thus as a "fact."[149] When we know the world, we know facts, not things (1.1). In this sense, "The totality of existing states of affairs is the world" (2.04).[150] When Wittgenstein says of knowing an object that one must "know all its possible occurrences in states of affairs," he means this in the strongest sense: all possibilities must be known. As he says, "A new possibility cannot be discovered later" (2.0123).[151]

Wittgenstein moves in a somewhat more ontological direction in his account of "pictures." A picture, he remarks, "is laid against reality like a measure" (2.1512). A picture, too, is a "fact" (2.141) constituted by a determinate relation of "the representatives of objects" (2.131). A picture represents its subject, and does so more or less accurately, depending on the adequacy of "the correlations of the picture's elements with things" (2.1514). This adequacy depends on something common between the picture and what it depicts: "A picture

Philosophical Psychology (Arlington, VA: The Institute for the Psychological Sciences Press, 2008), 34–59; Kerr, *Theology after Wittgenstein*, 2nd ed. (London: SPCK, 1997). Kerr remarks that "Wittgenstein's lifelong objection to natural theology was that it purports to exhibit as the conclusion of an argument something that should have been manifest from the outset—if only we could see the world without demanding a certain kind of explanation" ("*Work on Oneself*," 49; cf. *Theology after Wittgenstein*, 192, 194). See also the essays in *Wittgenstein and Philosophy of Religion*, ed. Robert L. Arrington and Mark Addis (New York: Routledge, 2001); as well as Russell Nieli, *Wittgenstein: From Mysticism to Ordinary Language; A Study of Viennese Positivism and the Thought of Ludwig Wittgenstein* (Albany, NY: State University of New York Press, 1987). Nieli argues, "The metaphysical-theological language in the German speaking world of Wittgenstein's time had become so corrupted and debased by ideological disputes between rival religious, philosophical, and political factions, that men of spiritual sensitivity . . . could only turn away from it as a medium of expression and counsel their fellow men to a path of silence" (*Wittgenstein*, 131).

146. Wittgenstein, *Tractatus*, 5.
147. Wittgenstein, *Tractatus*, 5.
148. Wittgenstein, *Tractatus*, 5.
149. Wittgenstein, *Tractatus*, 6.
150. Wittgenstein, *Tractatus*, 9.
151. Wittgenstein, *Tractatus*, 9.

can depict any reality whose form it has" (2.171). Furthermore, a picture depicts something else, but what makes it able to do this is not depicted in the picture. Wittgenstein states, "A picture cannot, however, depict its pictorial form: it displays it" (2.172).[152] He holds that "logical pictures can depict the world" (2.19) and that "a picture depicts reality by representing a possibility of existence and non-existence of states of affairs" (2.201).[153] Logical pictures of facts are thoughts (3), and no logical pictures can be said to be true *a priori* (2.225; cf. 3.04 and 3.05).[154]

Turning to the status of propositions, Wittgenstein argues that a proposition is a logical picture of a state of affairs (4.03). Most important, he considers that "most of the propositions and questions to be found in philosophical works are not false but nonsensical. Consequently we cannot give any answer to questions of this kind, but can only point out that they are nonsensical" (4.003).[155] Obviously, among these nonsensical questions would be the question of whether God exists. Given what he has said above about facts, the world, and logical pictures (thoughts), there is no possibility for our language to speak in any way about the transcendent. Wittgenstein comments that "the deepest problems are in fact *not* problems at all" (4.003), to which he adds that "what we cannot speak about we must pass over in silence" (7).[156]

Wittgenstein makes clear that there may be realities—including "God"— that exist despite the fact that reason cannot say anything intelligible about them. Given his notion of what "world" means, Wittgenstein can be expected to say, as he does, "God does not reveal himself *in* the world" (6.432). He can likewise be expected to say that philosophers can only speak about things that "have nothing to do with philosophy," such as propositions about natural science, and to urge that whenever a philosopher wants "to say something metaphysical," other philosophers should "demonstrate to him that he had failed to give a meaning to certain signs in his propositions" (6.53). His purpose in showing metaphysical statements to be nonsensical is to enable his reader to "climb up beyond" Wittgenstein's propositions—as he says, the reader "must, so to speak, throw away the ladder after he has climbed up it" (6.54). Only by transcending the propositions of the *Tractatus*—transcending them not by negating them, but in a mystical sense—can the reader "see the world aright" (6.54). It is only once there are "no questions left" (no intelligible

152. The quotations in this paragraph come from Wittgenstein, *Tractatus*, 10–11.
153. Wittgenstein, *Tractatus*, 11. For difficulties with these claims, see Grayling, *Wittgenstein*, 64.
154. Wittgenstein, *Tractatus*, 12.
155. Wittgenstein, *Tractatus*, 22–23.
156. Wittgenstein, *Tractatus*, 23, 89.

questions) that the "answer" can be seen, an answer that consists precisely in the transcending of the questions. In this sense, Wittgenstein states, "The solution of the problem of life is seen in the vanishing of the problem" (6.521). Once the questions have been shown to be unintelligible, and the problem of life not able to be posed by reason, then a mystical solution can make itself felt. He observes, "There are, indeed, things that cannot be put into words. They *make themselves manifest*. They are what is mystical" (6.522).[157]

Toward the end of the *Tractatus*, Wittgenstein attempts to leap directly to the question—admittedly an unaskable question in his view—of why something exists rather than nothing. Attempting to push past the supremacy of "facts" (in his sense of the term), he states, "It is not *how* things are in the world that is mystical, but *that* it [the world] exists" (6.44). The sheer existence of the world is a radical mystery, but it is not a question that can "be put into words" because no answer to this question could be put into words (6.5). In this sense the "*riddle*" of existence simply "does not exist" (6.5). The problem with skepticism of the Humean sort is that "it tries to raise doubts where no questions can be asked. For doubt can exist only where a question exists, a question only where an answer exists, and an answer only where something *can be said*" (6.51).[158]

When Wittgenstein states that "reality is compared with propositions" (4.05) and that "a proposition can be true or false only in virtue of being a picture of reality" (4.06; cf. 4.1), he arguably is drawing close to philosophical realism.[159] Yet he later states, in a Humean vein, that "it is an hypothesis that the sun will rise tomorrow: and this means that we do not *know* whether it will rise" (6.36311); and that "there is no compulsion making one thing happen because another has happened. The only necessity that exists is *logical* necessity" (6.37).[160] In order to emphasize that the "laws of nature" are not inviolable and cannot explain everything (6.371 and 6.372), Wittgenstein weakens the cause-effect relation. As he says, "Just as the only necessity that

157. The quotations in this paragraph come from Wittgenstein, *Tractatus*, 88–89. Grayling observes that "both in the *Tractatus* and in several letters he emphasizes the point that they are what the *Tractatus* is, in the end, really about—even though this is shown by the *Tractatus*'s being (almost) silent about them" (*Wittgenstein*, 55). See also Wittgenstein's *Lectures and Conversations on Aesthetics, Psychology, and Religious Belief*, ed. Cyril Barrett (Berkeley: University of California Press, 1966), esp. 53–54.

158. The quotations in this paragraph come from Wittgenstein, *Tractatus*, 88.

159. Wittgenstein, *Tractatus*, 27.

160. Grayling notes that Wittgenstein's philosophical influences for the *Tractatus* were Bertrand Russell (and through him, Gottlob Frege, G. W. Leibniz, and David Hume) and Arthur Schopenhauer (and through him, Immanuel Kant). As Grayling points out, Wittgenstein "did not study the classic philosophers carefully (most of them he did not study at all) and he actively discouraged his students from doing so" (*Wittgenstein*, 15; cf. 66).

exists is *logical* necessity, so too the only impossibility that exists is *logical* impossibility" (6.375). On this view, the law of noncontradiction has logical rather than a metaphysical content: "The statement that a point in the visual field has two different colours at the same time is a contradiction" (6.41; cf. 4.461).[161]

Within the "world," therefore, there is no inbuilt meaning. Wittgenstein holds that if there is any meaning in things, this meaning is found only outside the philosophically knowable realm. He remarks, "If there is any value that does have value, it must lie outside the whole sphere of what happens and is the case. For all that happens and is the case is accidental. What makes it non-accidental cannot lie *within* the world, since if it did it would itself be accidental" (6.41).[162] Likewise, no philosophical or propositional ethics is possible—ethics can only be known in the way that aesthetics can be known. Questions about death and afterlife also have to be rethought. Death, Wittgenstein argues, is not a moment of life, and eternity can be experienced simply by living in the present (6.4311). For its part, the notion of an immortal soul answers no question that could be intelligible inside space and time: "Or is some riddle solved by my surviving for ever? Is not this eternal life itself as much of a riddle as our present life?" (6.4312). He proposes, "The solution of the riddle of life in space and time lies *outside* space and time" (6.4312).[163] This is so, however, in the sense that the question—the riddle—cannot truly be posed within space and time, because metaphysical questions are barred.

In Wittgenstein's *Philosophical Investigations*, he moves in a quite different, but even less metaphysical, direction from that of the *Tractatus*.[164] Reflecting on the different contexts that affect the meaning of words, he observes, "When children play at trains their game is connected with their knowledge of trains. It would nevertheless be possible for the children of a tribe unacquainted with trains to learn this game from others, and to play it without knowing that it was copied from anything. One might say that the game did not make the same *sense* to them as to us."[165] He notes that there are a wide variety of languages or domains within languages, in the sense that, for example, the symbolism of chemistry and the mathematical notation of calculus are

161. The quotations in this paragraph come from Wittgenstein, *Tractatus*, 84–86.
162. Wittgenstein, *Tractatus*, 86.
163. Wittgenstein, *Tractatus*, 87.
164. For discussion of the *Philosophical Investigations*, see Grayling, *Wittgenstein*, 75–125; Marie McGinn, *The Routledge Guidebook to Wittgenstein's* Philosophical Investigations, 2nd ed. (London: Routledge, 2013); R. J. Fogelin, *Taking Wittgenstein at His Word: A Textual Study* (Princeton: Princeton University Press, 2009).
165. Wittgenstein, *Philosophical Investigations*, ed. G. E. M. Anscombe and R. Rhees, trans. G. E. M. Anscombe, 3rd ed. (Oxford: Blackwell, 2001), 82.

their own languages. We can invent languages that have to do strictly with highly specialized domains. Wittgenstein remarks in this vein, "It is easy to imagine a language consisting only of orders and reports in battle.—Or a language consisting only of questions and expressions for answering yes or no. And innumerable others."[166] With each such language, a new way of understanding the world and being in the world appears; words have a new and precise meaning in each language. Most important, each such language provides a new "life-form" for those who operate within the framework of meaning established by the language.[167]

Truth and falsity, then, are specific to particular language games. A "proposition" is deemed true or false only within the standards of truth contained in a particular language. For example, in the game of chess, one can say truly that one can only check the king; but this truth applies only to the game of chess. Languages are no different. Wittgenstein remarks that "what a proposition is is in one sense determined by the rules of sentence formation (in English for example), and in another sense by the use of the sign in the language-game."[168] Thus, to say "I am afraid" has a quite different meaning in the language game that is a theatrical play as opposed to other contexts. We often employ "the same expression in different games," but the meaning depends on the particular language game.[169] Even such things as "$2 \times 2 = 4$" have their meaning and certitude not in relation to being per se but within the language game of mathematics. Wittgenstein explains, "We remain unconscious of the prodigious diversity of all the everyday language-games because the clothing of our language makes everything alike. Something new (spontaneous, 'specific') is always a language-game."[170] Unlike the Wittgenstein of the *Tractatus*, who occasionally leaves some room (whether intentionally or not) for our access to being, the Wittgenstein of the *Philosophical Investigations* makes clear that there is no deeper level of truth "below" that of language. Languages or narratives are the closest we can get to the real, to what is.[171]

166. Wittgenstein, *Philosophical Investigations*, 7.
167. Wittgenstein, *Philosophical Investigations*, 7.
168. Wittgenstein, *Philosophical Investigations*, 45.
169. Wittgenstein, *Philosophical Investigations*, 161.
170. Wittgenstein, *Philosophical Investigations*, 191.
171. See Grayling's observation: "Most Wittgensteinians deny that the later philosophy constitutes a form of 'anti-realism,' but at the same time it appears that Wittgenstein himself thinks that the most one can say on the question of an independently existing reality is that the language-games in which we deal with things like, say, chairs, tables, and the rest, *presuppose* a commitment on our part to there being such a reality" (*Wittgenstein*, 116). D. Z. Phillips argues that God's reality only manifests itself in the language and practices of believers: God's reality cannot be truly thought in any other way. See Phillips, *Religion without Explanation* (Oxford: Blackwell, 1976); Phillips, *Wittgenstein and Religion* (New York: St. Martin's, 1993).

Réginald Garrigou-Lagrange (1877–1964)

Réginald Garrigou-Lagrange, whose father was a civil servant, was born in Auch, southwestern France. He intended to study medicine at the University of Bordeaux but instead, after experiencing a conversion to deeper faith, entered the Dominican novitiate in 1897. He studied first under Ambroise Gardeil at Le Saulchoir and then at the Sorbonne. After a brief period teaching the history of philosophy, specializing in the early modern period, he began teaching dogmatic theology. His first book, *The Common Sense: The Philosophy of Being and the Dogmatic Formulations*—a critique of the modernist view that we can know neither God nor Christian dogma with certitude—appeared in 1909. Numerous publications followed, including *God, His Existence and His Nature: A Thomist Solution of Agnostic Antinomies* (1914) and *On Revelation as Proposed by the Catholic Church* (1918), the latter of which defends the credibility of the gospel and of the Catholic Church primarily on public grounds rather than on grounds internal to the believing subject. In this period, motivated by his antimodernist concerns and by the severe anticlericalism of the liberal Third Republic, he supported the monarchist *Action française* (condemned in 1926 by Pope Pius XI), and during World War II he supported the Vichy puppet government of France. In the 1940s, he argued that the *nouvelle théologie* risked a return to the modernist denial that Catholic dogma possesses enduring cognitive content. He taught at the Angelicum in Rome from 1909 to 1959.[172]

When Garrigou-Lagrange addresses the question of the existence of God in his commentary on the *Prima Pars* of the *Summa theologiae*, he begins by considering *a priori* demonstrations of God's existence, such as Anselm's argument in the *Proslogion*.[173] In Garrigou-Lagrange's view, no matter how evident it is that a definition entails existence, it is still just a definition, just

---

See also George Lindbeck, *The Nature of Doctrine: Religion and Theology in a Postliberal Age* (Philadelphia: Westminster, 1984). For a critique of such approaches, see Francesca Aran Murphy, *God Is Not a Story: Realism Revisited* (Oxford: Oxford University Press, 2007); Paul A. Macdonald Jr., *Knowledge and the Transcendent: An Inquiry into the Mind's Relationship to God* (Washington, DC: Catholic University of America Press, 2009). See also Andrew Moore's argument for a "Christocentric realism" in *Realism and Christian Faith: God, Grammar, and Meaning* (Cambridge: Cambridge University Press, 2003), with his criticisms of Phillips and Lindbeck in chaps. 4–5. Moore's position requires realism to "begin from an ontological commitment to the triune God" (ibid., 19).

172. See Aidan Nichols, OP, *Reason with Piety: Garrigou-Lagrange in the Service of Catholic Thought* (Naples, FL: Sapientia, 2008); Richard Peddicord, OP, *The Sacred Monster of Thomism: An Introduction to the Life and Legacy of Reginald Garrigou-Lagrange*, OP (South Bend, IN: St. Augustine's Press, 2005).

173. See Réginald Garrigou-Lagrange, OP, *The One God: A Commentary on the First Part of St. Thomas' Theological Summa*, trans. Bede Rose, OSB (St. Louis: B. Herder, 1943), 98. For

an idea. It cannot enable us to know the existence of God in reality. He also addresses the argument for God's existence from our knowledge of truth and our desire for the good. This argument holds that "it is at once evident that truth exists, especially primal Truth; and it is likewise evident that good exists, especially the supreme Good."[174] Garrigou-Lagrange answers that in fact we know only that truth in general exists, just as we desire the good but are often confused about what constitutes the good. Because of this obscurity and confusion, our understanding of truth and our attraction to good are not sufficient for self-evident knowledge of God.

Garrigou-Lagrange places this discussion within a broader philosophical context: "St. Anselm's argument would be valid and fundamentally true if absolute realism were true, that is, if the formal universal had objective existence, as Plato, the Platonists, the ontologists, and Spinoza thought."[175] It is the theories of the nineteenth-century "ontologists," theories repudiated by Vatican I's *Dei Filius*, that most concern Garrigou-Lagrange here. He argues that logically speaking, their "absolute realism" entails that "being in general would be identical with the divine being"; in other words, the transcendence of God would be denied.[176] For the "ontologists" God is inevitably equated with the light of the human intellect. Garrigou-Lagrange states, "These extreme realists say that what first comes to our mind is the divine being," and he warns that "in this case being in general is identified with the divine being, as Parmenides maintained among the ancient philosophers and Spinoza among the moderns."[177] What is at stake is the transcendence of God. Along the same lines, Garrigou-Lagrange emphasizes that we do not "know positively what God is," and so God's existence cannot be cognitively self-evident for us.[178] What Anselm's argument does make clear, however, is that if God exists, he is self-existent. God's existence, in other words, is not like any existence that we know.

Garrigou-Lagrange treats in detail modern philosophical views that, while differing significantly from Anselm's intent, nonetheless share the view that we can move from a concept that requires divine existence to divine existence itself. He summarizes Descartes's proof: "Whatever is contained in the clear and distinct idea of anything, the same is true; but real existence is contained

more extensive discussion see Garrigou-Lagrange's *God: His Existence and His Nature*, trans. Bede Rose, OSB (St. Louis: B. Herder, 1955).

174. Garrigou-Lagrange, *One God*, 99.
175. Garrigou-Lagrange, *One God*, 99.
176. Garrigou-Lagrange, *One God*, 99.
177. Garrigou-Lagrange, *One God*, 100.
178. Garrigou-Lagrange, *One God*, 100.

in the clear and distinct idea of God; therefore God exists."[179] In response to Descartes, Garrigou-Lagrange reiterates the distinction between the "order of essences known by abstraction" and the "order of real and actual existence," and he emphasizes that our idea of God is not only abstract but also analogical, derived from creatures.[180] He engages Leibniz's argument for God's existence in a similar fashion. Leibniz holds that for Descartes's position to be true, we must show that God exists outside the mind, which Leibniz shows by arguing that if the idea of God is possible—and it is—then it follows that God exists because his essence implies existence. Garrigou-Lagrange replies that "we do not know God's essence," and so therefore "we cannot know a priori whether He is capable of existing."[181]

Instead, we must rise from finite being to its infinite cause, known not univocally but analogically. Garrigou-Lagrange grants that Aquinas's five ways, all of which reason from effect to cause, depend on first principles that cannot themselves be demonstrated, namely, "the notion of being," "the principle of contradiction or of identity," and "the principle of causality."[182] But if these first principles are not valid, then rationality itself—and not merely the demonstrations of God's existence—is a delusion, since denying these first principles requires denying reason's ability to know ordinary reality. Even to deny these first principles, one must at least implicitly appeal to them; they are knowable not through demonstration but through understanding the meaning of the terms, and the terms cannot but go together. In this regard, Garrigou-Lagrange shows that Hegel's challenge to the principle of noncontradiction leads to absurdity.

Against Hume and Kant, then, Garrigou-Lagrange insists that we can have truly intellectual knowledge of reality in and through sense experiences, a knowledge that attains to the ontological and causal dimension of things. We can know something of the existence, unity, truth, and goodness of things, as well as of their essential natures and properties. In so doing, we come to know that ordinary realities are contingent, exhibit ontological dependence on one another (principle of causality), and follow the principle of noncontradiction and identity (a thing cannot be and not be in the same way at the same time). Although these first principles (causality and noncontradiction) are nondemonstrable because they come prior to demonstrative reasoning, they are unavoidable in practice. Every human being makes use of the principle of

179. Garrigou-Lagrange, *One God*, 102.
180. Garrigou-Lagrange, *One God*, 102.
181. Garrigou-Lagrange, *One God*, 103. See Markus Enders, "Swinburne's Reconstruction of Leibniz's Cosmological Argument," *Analecta Hermeneutica* 2 (2010).
182. Garrigou-Lagrange, *One God*, 106.

noncontradiction and identity, and every human action and legal system pre-supposes the principle of causality. For Garrigou-Lagrange, skeptics about our most basic knowledge of being and causality undermine their own skepticism by making use of universal truth claims both in order to argue theoretically and to act practically.

From this perspective, Garrigou-Lagrange turns to the five ways by which Aquinas demonstrates the existence of God. As a preface to this section, he notes that Kant rejects the fundamental move that Aquinas makes, since for Kant the principle of causality is a useful law of our mind but cannot be shown to be a law of real being. In the medieval period, Garrigou-Lagrange points out, the nominalist Nicholas of Ultricuria likewise denied "the real validity of the principle of causality."[183] The Kantian or fideist position can in Garrigou-Lagrange's view be refuted both by common experience and by Romans 1:20 as interpreted dogmatically by Vatican I. Garrigou-Lagrange adds that Kant's practical postulate is not of sufficient demonstrative power to meet the requirements of Vatican I.

Garrigou-Lagrange observes that Vatican I's definition does not require "that reason can demonstrate creation out of nothing, but that it can demonstrate the existence of God, the first Cause, and that the divine attributes of infinity, eternity, supreme wisdom, providence, and sanctity are included in this notion."[184] For Vatican I, the point is to uphold the possibility of the demonstration of God's existence rather than to identify a particular path according to which God's existence has been demonstrated. Citing Wisdom 13:1, Garrigou-Lagrange emphasizes that this possibility must be one that people can and do achieve—even though God's own *revelation* that God exists remains "morally necessary" given all that we must know in order to attain the end (sharing in the divine life) for which God created us.[185]

There are two kinds of demonstration, *a priori* (from the cause) and *a posteriori* (from the effect). Garrigou-Lagrange notes that only the latter is

183. Garrigou-Lagrange, *One God*, 109.
184. Garrigou-Lagrange, *One God*, 110.
185. Garrigou-Lagrange, *One God*, 111. With Karl Barth's concerns in view, Eugene Rogers rightly remarks with respect to Vatican I, "So far from seeking to promote an Enlightenment anthropocentrism, Leo sought instead to break it—just by praising those aspects of the human being that depended 'by nature' on something independent of and over against it. In positing natural knowledge he sought to dispossess it; in praising it he sought to put it in its place" (Rogers, *Thomas Aquinas and Karl Barth: Sacred Doctrine and the Natural Knowledge of God* [Notre Dame: University of Notre Dame Press, 1995], 211). For this work of putting natural knowledge of God in its rightful place, as the gift of the God who made us rational and as a preparation for faith, see especially Thomas Joseph White, OP, *Wisdom in the Face of Modernity: A Study in Thomistic Natural Theology* (Ave Maria, FL: Sapientia, 2009), 282–90.

possible with respect to God, and it can only show *that* God is rather than *what* God is. An *a posteriori* demonstration depends on the principle of causality, understood not merely as something justified empirically through observation of phenomena (as Hume supposes), let alone solely as a category of our mind (Kant), but ontologically, "because a contingent being is not its own reason for existence."[186] The ontological grounding of the principle of causality requires a realist epistemology: the object of the human intellect is the being of sensible things. Since our mind's object is being, we recognize intuitively that the principle of noncontradiction—a thing cannot be and not be in the same way at the same time—is fundamentally an ontological claim having to do with the being of things rather than a logical or conceptual claim.

Garrigou-Lagrange goes on to explain why "one cannot deny the principle of causality without denying the principle of contradiction [i.e., noncontradiction]."[187] The two principles are inextricably linked because a contingent being, which by definition can either exist or not exist, is not self-existent and therefore *must* depend on something for being. If a contingent being in fact depended on nothing for its being (against the principle of causality), then this would contradict its very definition as contingent (against the principle of noncontradiction). "To be caused" belongs to contingent beings as such, rather than merely to all the contingent things we have observed. Put simply, "that which is not self-existent is dependent upon another for its existence."[188]

Garrigou-Lagrange next examines the meaning of a thing's "proper cause." A proper cause must be necessarily and immediately required for the effect. In the case of particular effects, one will look for a particular cause; thus Socrates is the proper cause of his son. In the case of the most universal effect, one will look for the most universal cause; thus only God can cause being.

---

186. Garrigou-Lagrange, *One God*, 113. Jacques Maritain argues that all humans have an intuition of God's existence in the act of knowing beings. He states, "In perceiving Being Reason knows God—the self-subsisting Act of being—in an enigmatic but inescapable manner" (Maritain, "A New Approach to God," in his *The Range of Reason* [New York: Charles Scribner's Sons, 1952], 86–102, at 87). He goes on to explain, "These three intellective leaps—to actual existence as asserting itself independently from me; from this sheer objective existence to my own threatened existence; and from my existence spoiled with nothingness to absolute existence—are achieved within that same and unique intuition, which philosophers would explain as the intuitive perception of the essentially analogical content of the first concept, the concept of Being" (ibid., 88). I doubt that our knowing of beings gives us an enigmatic intuition of God's existence, but much depends on how "enigmatic" Maritain supposes this intuition to be. Certainly the demonstration of God's existence is present and available to anyone who reflects carefully on the existence of finite beings.

187. Garrigou-Lagrange, *One God*, 113.
188. Garrigou-Lagrange, *One God*, 115.

Socrates causes the beginning of the effect, but only God causes the being of the effect. In this sense, as Aquinas observes, "From every effect the existence of its proper cause can be demonstrated."[189] The effects that must ground a demonstration of God's existence can only be the most universal effects, since only they will lead to God as their proper cause.

Before reviewing each of the five ways, Garrigou-Lagrange shows how they lead to the proper cause of a universal effect—all motions, all caused causality, all contingent being, all things that can have greater or lesser being (or truth or goodness), and all ordered things. Garrigou-Lagrange also notes that Aquinas is talking about essentially ordered causes, not accidentally ordered ones. Since Aquinas considers that it is theoretically possible that the universe is eternal, an infinite series of accidentally ordered causes is quite possible, whereas proceeding to infinity in essentially ordered causes is impossible. For Aquinas, "it is not impossible for a man to be generated by man to infinity."[190] The impossibility of infinite regress arises only when, in terms of essentially ordered causes, we ask from whence an infinite chain of human causes would receive its being and motion. He concludes that "in the proofs for God's existence, we must not proceed according to a series of past causes, but we must get away from this series and rise above it to an actually existing higher cause."[191]

Garrigou-Lagrange reiterates that the principle of causality does not have to do simply with empirical observation. Instead, it has to do with being, because "efficient causality is the production or realization of actual being."[192] Nor does the principle of causality express a mere mental or logical relation; rather, it attains intellectively to extramental being. Garrigou-Lagrange points out that even Kantians "hold that they are really the authors of their books; hence they admit that causality expresses a reality, and not only what is merely subjective."[193] The same holds for a man who commits murder: he is not "the cause of death only in the manner in which we conceive of it."[194] If we deny that the intellect knows intelligible being, then all that we can know is mental being, concepts. If all we know are our concepts, then we truly do not know anything at all, let alone know that God exists.

Garrigou-Lagrange presses the point that we do indeed know things as beings, and as beings that analogically possess perfections. We know "a good

189. Aquinas, *Summa theologiae* Ia.2.2.
190. Aquinas, *Summa theologiae* Ia.46.2.7; quoted in Garrigou-Lagrange, *One God*, 120.
191. Garrigou-Lagrange, *One God*, 123.
192. Garrigou-Lagrange, *One God*, 125.
193. Garrigou-Lagrange, *One God*, 126.
194. Garrigou-Lagrange, *One God*, 126.

stone, a good fruit, a good horse," and so forth.[195] Since the perfection of goodness is predicated analogically and does not imply any limitation of being,
there is no reason that it cannot be applied analogically to God. Does it limit
God, however, to call him a "cause"? No, so long as we do so analogically,
just as causality is analogically predicated of diverse creatures. God cannot
be the material or formal cause of a creature, but he can be the efficient and
final cause without incurring any limitation of being. God's efficient and final
causality of creatures, however, must be understood analogically, since the
"uncreated mode of the divine causality will not be for us positively knowable
in this life."[196] Again, we do not know what God is. In demonstrating God's
existence, we use as a "definition" of God not a concept of God's essence
but instead simply a "nominal definition of God" drawn from his effects; for
example, the term "prime mover" names God with respect to the effect of
motion that he produces.[197]

However, a problem seems to arise here, one recognized by many of the
modern philosophers surveyed above. Garrigou-Lagrange puts it as follows:
"A cause can be demonstrated only by an effect that is proportionate to it; but
God's effects are finite, and hence they are not proportionate to Him, since
He is infinite."[198] Aquinas's answer is that the demonstration here pertains
solely to "that God is" not to "what God is." Garrigou-Lagrange adds that
an *a posteriori* demonstration requires only a certain kind of proportion, and
here the proportion of causality (effect to cause) suffices despite the infinite
difference between the perfection of the cause and the perfection of the effect.

Each of Aquinas's five ways is based on a specific universal condition of
created things: "the fact of corporeal or spiritual motion, of causality, of contingency, of composition and imperfection, and of ordination in the passive
sense."[199] In Garrigou-Lagrange's view, the five ways depend on the principle
of causality and, within this principle, on the fact that we cannot proceed
to infinity in essentially ordered causes, since without a first cause there can
be no intermediate causes in an essentially ordered causal series. Garrigou-
Lagrange mentions here that Suárez undermines the demonstrative power of
the five ways by denying the universality of the principle of causality. Suárez
denies that "whatever is set in motion, is set in motion by another," and this
especially undermines the first, second, and fifth ways. Suárez also denies the
real distinction between essence and existence, which especially undermines

195. Garrigou-Lagrange, *One God*, 127.
196. Garrigou-Lagrange, *One God*, 128.
197. Garrigou-Lagrange, *One God*, 129.
198. Garrigou-Lagrange, *One God*, 129.
199. Garrigou-Lagrange, *One God*, 135.

the third and fourth ways. In both regards, Garrigou-Lagrange argues that Suárez was mistaken.

Garrigou-Lagrange also observes that none of the five ways depends strictly on sensible or physical things; rather, the five ways can take as their starting point any creature, including the human soul or an angel. He finds, too, that Aquinas arranged the five ways in an intentional order. Aquinas starts with what we easily know (motion, efficient causality) and moves to deeper principles (perfection, order). According to Garrigou-Lagrange, other ways of demonstrating God's existence, such as that based on moral obligation or that based on eternal Truth, can be reduced to one or another of the five ways. Garrigou-Lagrange also thinks that there is also a general, commonsense demonstration of God's existence that proceeds from the principle that the more perfect does not come from the less perfect.

In summarizing the first way, from motion, Garrigou-Lagrange observes that Aquinas has in view diverse kinds of movement or change, both physical and spiritual. The key principles are that "whatever is in motion, is put in motion by another" and that we cannot proceed to infinity in an essentially ordered series of movers. The first way arrives at an unmoved mover, who is Pure Act, self-subsisting Being. The second way, from efficient causality, likewise depends on the two principles of the first way, and arrives at an uncaused, transcendent cause. The third way begins with contingent things—which can be or not be—and emphasizes that "they have not in themselves the reason of their existence."[200] They therefore depend for existence on an absolutely necessary being, without which nothing contingent could be. The fourth way starts from the degrees of perfections manifest in things. It shows that perfections are predicated analogously and that imperfect things are united by sharing in one perfection. They could not be united unless their unity was caused by something that fully possesses the perfection. Garrigou-Lagrange thus accentuates the causal element in the fourth way. The fifth way, from order in the world, argues that chance cannot explain teleological order in nonrational things, an order that is equally manifest on a small scale and on a large scale. As Garrigou-Lagrange puts it, "To be directed presupposes a directing cause."[201] He notes Kant's objection that this argument can merely demonstrate some finite intelligence. To this objection, he replies that the demonstration of a finite, governing intelligence would itself require that there be a higher, infinite governing intelligence. The fifth way, Garrigou-Lagrange points out, is the foundation of Wisdom 13:1 and Psalm 19:1.

200. Garrigou-Lagrange, *One God*, 144.
201. Garrigou-Lagrange, *One God*, 151.

What has been found through the five ways? Has the living God, the God who makes covenant, been demonstrated to exist? Garrigou-Lagrange argues that all the five ways lead to "He who is" (Exod. 3:14). The five ways demonstrate the existence of a God who is self-subsisting existence, perfect wisdom and goodness, the transcendent creator and governor of the universe. This God receives more concrete testimony in Scripture, but it is the same God. Further, the rejection of these demonstrations requires the rejection of the principles of causality and noncontradiction, and thus the rejection of rationality itself.

What about the problem of evil, which Aquinas acknowledges to be a common and strong objection to the view that God exists? Garrigou-Lagrange holds that this objection, stated forcefully by John Stuart Mill, can be answered by observing that God draws good out of evil so as to bring about a greater good—as, for instance, Adam and Eve's sin, which led to the incarnation of the divine Son.[202]

Martin Heidegger (1889–1976)

Martin Heidegger was born into an impoverished Catholic family in Messkirch, Germany, where his father was sexton and cellarman of the local church. In high school, while preparing for the priesthood, he became interested in philosophy by reading Franz Brentano's *On the Various Meanings of Being according to Aristotle*. After a short period in the Jesuit novitiate, he prepared for the diocesan priesthood at the University of Freiburg, but a spiritual crisis in 1911 ended his interest in the priesthood. Two years later he completed his dissertation, a study of the act of judgment (influenced by the work of Edmund Husserl), followed by a habilitation thesis titled *Duns Scotus's Theory*

---

202. For an attack on neo-Thomism in general and Garrigou-Lagrange in particular, arguing that the Second Vatican Council rejected Garrigou-Lagrange's approach to God, see M.-D. Chenu, OP, "Vérité évangélique et métaphysique wolfienne à Vatican II," *Revue des sciences philosophiques et théologiques* 57 (1973): 632–40. The notion that Garrigou-Lagrange's metaphysics derived more from Christian Wolff, an eighteenth-century German Protestant (indebted to Suárez) whose views were critiqued by Kant, than from Aquinas, found some purchase in preconciliar French Catholic polemics but can be dismissed today. For a helpful account of the complementary strengths and weaknesses of the theological approaches of Garrigou-Lagrange and Chenu, see Thomas Joseph White, OP, "The Precarity of Wisdom: Modern Dominican Theology, Perspectivalism, and the Tasks of Reconstruction," in *Ressourcement Thomism: Sacred Doctrine, the Sacraments, and the Moral Life*, ed. Reinhard Hütter and Matthew Levering (Washington, DC: Catholic University of America Press, 2010), 92–123. See also the treatment of Garrigou-Lagrange's theology in Adam G. Cooper, *Naturally Human, Supernaturally God: Deification in Pre-Conciliar Catholicism* (Minneapolis: Fortress, 2014), chap. 5.

of Categories and Meaning.[203] During World War I, he served in the postal and meteorological services. Around this time he broke definitively with the Catholic Church. After working as a lecturer at the University of Freiburg and an assistant to Husserl, he became a professor at Marburg in 1923, where he entered into a long-standing adulterous relationship with Hannah Arendt. He succeeded Husserl as professor of philosophy at the University of Freiburg shortly after publishing his masterwork, *Being and Time* (1927). Elected rector of the university in 1933, he joined the Nazi party. In 1934, he resigned from his position as rector and halted his political activities, though without renouncing his party membership. After World War II, he continued to publish extensively on such topics as humanism, technology, the nature of philosophy, and art.[204]

In *Being and Time*, Heidegger argues that the fruitful inquiry of the early Greeks into "being" was quickly domesticated in a manner that trivialized the inquiry. Ontology—along with a proper understanding of λόγος (disclosure and perception)—has been concealed and covered up since the death of Aristotle. Heidegger conceives of his task as recovering the Greeks' original insights and developing them much further. Thinkers have pretended to understand "being" and have thereby avoided grappling with its meaning in the powerful way that the early Greeks did.

What is "being," then, and how do we seek an answer to this question? Heidegger remarks that the "being" that "determines beings as beings" is not itself yet another being.[205] In seeking to understand being itself, therefore, we must contemplate beings and seek the disclosure of being; this disclosure, if it occurs, will occur in and through beings because "being is always the being of a being."[206] We are beings who inquire into being; the meaning of being must

203. One of Heidegger's principal sources, *De modis significandi sive Grammatica speculativa*, was long attributed to Scotus, but Martin Grabmann discovered that it was written by Thomas of Erfurt.

204. See Michael Inwood, *Heidegger: A Very Short Introduction* (Oxford: Oxford University Press, 1997); Patricia Altenbernd Johnson, *On Heidegger* (Belmont, CA: Thomson Learning, 2000); Hugo Ott, *Martin Heidegger: A Political Life*, trans. Allan Blunden (New York: Basic Books, 1994); Rüdiger Safranski, *Martin Heidegger: Between Good and Evil*, trans. Ewald Osers (Cambridge, MA: Harvard University Press, 1998). See also the diverse views about the relation of Heidegger's philosophy to theology offered by S. J. McGrath, *The Early Heidegger and Medieval Philosophy: Phenomenology for the Godforsaken* (Washington, DC: Catholic University of America Press, 2006); David Walsh, *The Modern Philosophical Revolution: The Luminosity of Existence* (Cambridge: Cambridge University Press, 2008), 232–90; and Lawrence Paul Hemming, *Heidegger's Atheism: The Refusal of a Theological Voice* (Notre Dame: University of Notre Dame Press, 2002).

205. Martin Heidegger, *Being and Time*, trans. Joan Stambaugh, rev. Dennis J. Schmidt (Albany, NY: State University of New York Press, 2010), 5.

206. Heidegger, *Being and Time*, 8.

thus include an exposition of the inquirer, the *human* being who inquires into being. We humans cannot truly understand ourselves or other things without understanding ourselves as *Dasein*—that is, as beings interested in our own being, an interest that defines our being: "It is proper to this being [*Dasein*, the *human* being] that it be disclosed to itself with and through its being."[207] In this context, Heidegger critically describes theology as a misguided quest "for a more original interpretation of human being's being toward God, prescribed by the meaning of faith itself and remaining within it."[208]

Heidegger goes on to describe being a self as a being-in-the-world that is a relational being-with: the "I" is always caught up in and with "those among whom one also is," so that one does not first know one's "I" individually, and only then in relation to other beings.[209] He also examines how anxiety discloses the being of *Dasein* as care, which seeks freedom for authentic self-actualization in the world and which fears various forms of nonbeing. Always reaching out ahead of itself, *Dasein* thus has a "*constant unfinished quality*."[210] Along these lines Heidegger explores "being-toward-death" or "being-toward-the-end": *Dasein*, in order to know its being rightly, must be aware "of its ownmost, nonrelational, and insuperable potentiality-of-being."[211] Death, then, already belongs in a certain sense to the kind of being that we are. Anticipation of our death "discloses to existence that its extreme possibility lies in giving itself up, and thus it shatters all one's clinging to whatever existence one has reached. In anticipation, *Dasein* guards itself against falling back behind itself, or behind the potentiality-for-being that it has understood."[212] Anticipation and embrace of our own possibility, rather than closure or clinging to states of being, are the key to authentic being-toward-death.

Heidegger also investigates what conscience is. He defines conscience as "the call of care from the uncanniness of being-in-the-world that summons Dasein to its ownmost potentiality-for-being-guilty."[213] Thus, he does not define conscience in terms of a bad or good conscience, or in terms of its function of warning us against evildoing. Instead, he argues that conscience

---

207. Heidegger, *Being and Time*, 11.

208. Heidegger, *Being and Time*, 9. He adds, "Theology is slowly beginning to understand again Luther's insight that its system of dogma rests on a 'foundation' that does not stem from a questioning in which faith is primary and whose conceptual apparatus is not only insufficient for the range of problems in theology but rather covers them up and distorts them" (ibid.).

209. Heidegger, *Being and Time*, 115.

210. Heidegger, *Being and Time*, 227.

211. Heidegger, *Being and Time*, 246.

212. Heidegger, *Being and Time*, 253.

213. Heidegger, *Being and Time*, 277.

awakens us to the possibility of authenticity by summoning *Dasein* "to its factical potentiality-of-being-a-self."[214]

Examining temporality and historicity, Heidegger recognizes that "history belongs to the being of Dasein" and that the "world *is* only in the mode of *existing* Dasein, which, as being-in-the-world, is *factical*."[215] The key here is to underscore the historicity of being as we experience it, as opposed to an *ahistorical* (and thereby reifying and onto-theological) metaphysical treatise. He emphasizes the importance of authenticity in anticipating death, in handing oneself over freely for death. Indeed, he observes, "*Authentic being-toward-death, that is, the finitude of temporality, is the concealed ground of the historicity of Dasein*."[216] This is the real meaning and content of history. From history he moves to historiography and its relation to the disclosure of *Dasein*, here drawing on Nietzsche and responding to Wilhelm Dilthey. In order not to fall into onto-theology, historiography must have its roots in the anticipation of future possibility. In dialogue with Hegel, he then reflects on the nature of time as a simultaneous passing away and coming into being: the future is again the key element.

Being and Time ends here. As an unfinished work, the book does not fulfill Heidegger's ambition to critique the history of philosophizing about being. Heidegger's original outline, found in chapter 2 of his introduction to *Being and Time*, plans for "a phenomenological destruction of the history of ontology along the guideline of the problem of temporality."[217] He aims to move beyond the obscuring of the question of being that turned it into a body of doctrine rather than a real question rooted in the temporality/historicity of *Dasein*. He makes clear that he is the first philosopher in over two millennia truly to grapple with the central philosophical question.

This brief tour of *Being and Time* prepares us to understand Heidegger's view of the demonstrations of God's existence. In his *Introduction to Metaphysics*, originally delivered as course lectures in 1935 and published in 1953, Heidegger addresses a number of the topics of what he had planned to be the second part of *Being and Time*. He states, "Being-human, according to its historical, history-opening essence, is *logos*, the gathering and apprehending of the Being of beings: the happening of what is most uncanny, in which, through doing violence, the overwhelming comes to appearance and is brought to stand."[218] In this happening, the question of Being is raised in such a way

214. Heidegger, *Being and Time*, 282.

215. Heidegger, *Being and Time*, 362.

216. Heidegger, *Being and Time*, 367.

217. Heidegger, *Being and Time*, 37.

218. Martin Heidegger, *Introduction to Metaphysics*, trans. Gregory Fried and Richard Polt (New Haven: Yale University Press, 2000), 182.

that no concealment or obscuring is possible. To make of *logos* a mere faculty of reason is a fundamental error. Rather, the rational human being is such because of the uncanny, overwhelming, violent reality—known from within "the urgency of historical Dasein"—that "Being-human is grounded in the opening up of the Being of beings."[219] When reason and logical thinking come to dominate Being, then this uncanniness and violence is not recognized and Being is lost from view. When we arrive at the medieval distinction between existence and essence, we no longer have Being but simply the idea of Being. In this situation, "The visage offered by the thing, and no longer the thing itself, now becomes what is decisive."[220]

For Heidegger, Parmenides should be credited with the decisive, though quickly forgotten, insight about Being. This insight is that Parmenides "precisely does not say that Being should be conceived on the basis of apprehending—that is, as something merely apprehended—but that apprehending is for the sake of Being."[221] The opposite position from that of Parmenides is to conceive of Being intellectually, as an idea that we have apprehended. As a mere idea, Being becomes an essence or whatness, and beings themselves become mere defective imitations. A sterile rationalism takes over: "Logos, in the sense of saying and asserting, now becomes the domain and place where decisions are made about truth—that is, originally, about the unconcealment of beings and thus about the Being of beings."[222] No longer in the service of unconcealment, *logos* becomes a force of concealment. The result is to turn ontology into the study of the categories of Being.

For Heidegger, then, "The old disputed question of whether the principle of contradiction has an 'ontological' or a 'logical' meaning in Aristotle is wrongly posed, because for Aristotle there is neither 'ontology' nor 'logic.'"[223] In Aristotle, according to Heidegger, Being rather than the idea of Being is central. Aristotle's work seeks to open up space for the inbreaking of Being (truth as unconcealment), rather than to develop a system of logic about Being (truth as correctness about ideas). The loss of Aristotle's true perspective infected medieval and modern philosophy, and indeed has infected all philosophy influenced by Christianity—although Heidegger emphasizes that

219. Heidegger, *Introduction to Metaphysics*, 187, 188.
220. Heidegger, *Introduction to Metaphysics*, 195.
221. Heidegger, *Introduction to Metaphysics*, 195.
222. Heidegger, *Introduction to Metaphysics*, 198–99. As Heidegger goes on to say, "The dominant views now obstruct our own view of beings. Beings are deprived of the possibility of turning themselves *toward* apprehension, appearing on their own right. The view granted by beings, which usually turns itself toward us, is distorted into a view on beings. The dominance of views thus distorts beings and twists them" (ibid., 205).
223. Heidegger, *Introduction to Metaphysics*, 200.

this loss was due to the greatness of the insight, which in any case could only be preserved by being retrieved "more originally in its originality."[224]

Heidegger laments that "Christianity reinterprets the Being of beings as Being-created."[225] Things become even worse, however, once the Christian doctrine of creation is excluded by philosophers, for then human reason becomes absolute. The result is that "the Being of beings must become thinkable in the pure thinking of mathematics."[226] Being then is reduced to serving technological reason. Heidegger concludes, "Ever since idea and category have assumed their dominance, philosophy fruitlessly toils to explain the relation between assertion (thinking) and Being by all possible and impossible means—fruitlessly, because the question of Being has not been brought back to its adequate ground and basis, in order to be unfolded from there."[227] For Heidegger, the quest for Being is always a questioning.

At the beginning of his *Introduction to Metaphysics*, Heidegger remarks that he has in view the person who takes the "originary leap" by asking, "Why are there beings at all instead of nothing?"[228] Rather than seeking a logical demonstration, such a person embraces the question of Being and leaves it as a question, a challenge that continually overwhelms and exceeds reason and logic. Heidegger considers that this stance of questioning is sadly undercut by Christianity. The person "for whom the Bible is divine revelation and truth" does not ask the question of Being because he or she imagines that the answer is already known, namely, God the uncreated Creator. Such a person "cannot authentically question without giving himself up as a believer."[229] The fundamental philosophical question or existential stance is, according to Heidegger, mere "foolishness" from the perspective of Christian faith. Thus, in his view, "a 'Christian philosopher' is a round square and a misunderstanding."[230]

224. Heidegger, *Introduction to Metaphysics*, 204.
225. Heidegger, *Introduction to Metaphysics*, 207.
226. Heidegger, *Introduction to Metaphysics*, 207. Heidegger observes that
    as soon as this thinking achieves dominance in the modern age, as self-sufficient reason, the real development of the division between Being and the ought is made ready. This process is completed in Kant. For Kant, beings are nature—in other words, whatever can be determined and is determined in mathematical-physical thinking. The categorical imperative, which is determined both by and as reason, is opposed to nature. (ibid., 212)
227. Heidegger, *Introduction to Metaphysics*, 203–4. He later adds, "The thinking that is guided by *logos* as assertion provides and maintains the perspective in which Being is viewed. Hence if Being itself is to be opened up and grounded in *its* originary distinction from beings, then an originary perspective needs to be opened up" (ibid., 219). This perspective requires moving from "being and thinking" to "being and time."
228. Heidegger, *Introduction to Metaphysics*, 7.
229. Heidegger, *Introduction to Metaphysics*, 8.
230. Heidegger, *Introduction to Metaphysics*, 8.

In his revised seminar lecture from 1957, "The Onto-theo-logical Constitution of Metaphysics," Heidegger begins with Hegel. For Hegel, it is the Idea
that is Being, Life, and Truth. Heidegger explains that for Hegel, "Being is
the absolute self-thinking of thinking," but always in the context of the history of thinking, understood as "the Idea's self-externalization."[231] Heidegger
distinguishes his own historical perspective on Being from that of Hegel by
noting that he looks not to Idea, but to "Being with respect to its difference
from beings."[232] He argues that such a perspective on Being, with its focus on
difference as such, is a new perspective, one that has been veiled in the history
of metaphysical thought. Taking this path involves a "step back out of metaphysics into its essential nature."[233]

Reflecting on the history of metaphysics in the West, Heidegger observes
that metaphysics as ontology and theology has fallen on hard times because
of a new "experience of a thinking which has discerned in onto-theo-logy
the still *unthought* unity of the essential nature of metaphysics."[234] Here he
defines philosophy as "the free and spontaneous self-involvement with beings
as such."[235] He emphasizes that Being must have primacy: Being, not thinking,
is "the ground that grounds."[236] By contrast, he considers that for ontology and
theology—for "metaphysics"—thinking possesses primacy. In these "Logics,"
thought comes to "provide the ground of beings as such and account for them
within the whole" and to "account for Being as the ground of beings."[237] When
this happens, Logic takes over Being. Hence, for Heidegger, "metaphysics"
in the West merits the name "onto-theo-logic."[238] In metaphysics as ontology
and theology, we find "the Being of *beings*" and "the beings *of Being*," but
the difference between the two (Being and beings) has remained veiled to our
thinking; indeed, the "between" itself surpasses our thought.

231. Martin Heidegger, "The Onto-theo-logical Constitution of Metaphysics," in his *Identity
and Difference*, trans. Joan Stambaugh (Chicago: University of Chicago Press, 1969), 42–74, at
43–44. Heidegger has in view especially Hegel's *Science of Logic*, trans. A. V. Miller (Amherst,
NY: Humanity Books, 1998), but see also Hegel's *Lectures on the Proofs of the Existence of God*,
ed. and trans. Peter C. Hodgson (Oxford: Oxford University Press, 2007). In Hegel's view, Kant's
criticism of the arguments for God's existence "failed to recognize their deeper foundation and so
was unable to do justice to their true content" (*Lectures on the Proofs of the Existence of God*,
163). This deeper foundation is the opening up of finite spirit to infinite spirit. For discussion
of Hegel see William Desmond, *Hegel's God: A Counterfeit Double?* (London: Ashgate, 2003).
232. Heidegger, "Onto-theo-logical Constitution of Metaphysics," 47.
233. Heidegger, "Onto-theo-logical Constitution of Metaphysics," 51.
234. Heidegger, "Onto-theo-logical Constitution of Metaphysics," 55.
235. Heidegger, "Onto-theo-logical Constitution of Metaphysics," 56.
236. Heidegger, "Onto-theo-logical Constitution of Metaphysics," 58.
237. Heidegger, "Onto-theo-logical Constitution of Metaphysics," 59.
238. Heidegger, "Onto-theo-logical Constitution of Metaphysics," 60.

Heidegger, then, directs our attention to this difference, this "between." He does so in order to help us see that "the Being of beings means Being which is beings," the Being that "becomes present in the manner of a transition to beings."[239] As opposed to logically representing "the Being of beings" as the "*causa sui*" ("God"), Heidegger's breakthrough consists in finding "the Being of beings" in the "unconcealing overwhelming" manifested in the manner of "arrival" of beings, an "arrival that keeps itself concealed in unconcealedness."[240] What does this rather obscure language mean? Heidegger holds that in the difference, the "between," "the overwhelming and the arrival are held toward one another, are borne away from and toward each other."[241] It is in the "between" (between Being and beings, "as the differentiation of overwhelming arrival") that we find the "*unconcealing keeping in concealment.*"[242] The tension of overwhelming and arrival, held together in the "between," enables us to think "Being" precisely as Being *gives itself* in beings. Heidegger states, "Being shows itself in the unconcealing overwhelming as that which allows whatever arrives to lie before us, as the grounding in the manifold ways in which beings are brought before us."[243]

At this stage, Heidegger returns to the "onto-theological constitution of metaphysics."[244] The basic point is that metaphysics apprehends the "difference" as perduring, and thus not *as difference*. Metaphysics "is determined by what differs in the difference."[245] Hence metaphysics arrives at being in general (onto-logic) and at the highest being (theo-logic). The solution to this situation is to return to the difference, to the "between" in which "Being grounds beings, and beings, as what *is* most of all, account for Being."[246] By attending to the "between," Heidegger tries to avoid separating (reifying) "Being" and "beings" in a way that neglects how Being gives itself in beings in the tension of "overwhelming" and "arrival." The separation of Being and beings leads to identifying "Being" as the ground, "the cause as *causa sui*."[247] For Heidegger, such a "God" must be rejected, since it is based on a failure of philosophy. In fact, properly religious wonder and awe are only found in the

239. Heidegger, "Onto-theo-logical Constitution of Metaphysics," 64.
240. Heidegger, "Onto-theo-logical Constitution of Metaphysics," 64–65.
241. Heidegger, "Onto-theo-logical Constitution of Metaphysics," 65.
242. Heidegger, "Onto-theo-logical Constitution of Metaphysics," 65.
243. Heidegger, "Onto-theo-logical Constitution of Metaphysics," 68.
244. Heidegger, "Onto-theo-logical Constitution of Metaphysics," 71.
245. Heidegger, "Onto-theo-logical Constitution of Metaphysics," 70.
246. Heidegger, "Onto-theo-logical Constitution of Metaphysics," 69.
247. Heidegger, "Onto-theo-logical Constitution of Metaphysics," 72.

"god-less thinking" that apprehends the tension of the "between," in which Being and beings are each ground and grounded.[248]

In Heidegger's view, once one clears away metaphysics, with its notion of God as cause and as the highest/necessary being, then different and new possibilities appear for thinking about God, or the gods, or the holy. These are possibilities for which humanity must wait and cannot force to appear.[249] In short, Heidegger urges that we move "back out of metaphysics into the active essence of metaphysics, back out of oblivion of the difference as such into the destiny of the withdrawing concealment of perdurance."[250]

248. Heidegger, "Onto-theo-logical Constitution of Metaphysics," 72.

249. For discussion of Heidegger's elimination of "any conception of some transcendent being as cause and origin of everything" (Heidegger, "Onto-theo-logical Constitution of Metaphysics," 64), see Fergus Kerr, OP, *Immortal Longings: Versions of Transcending Humanity* (Notre Dame: University of Notre Dame Press, 1997), 46–67. For the argument that Heidegger's views are intrinsically nihilistic, and for a defense of "metaphysics" ("thinking that orients itself by beings" [Heidegger, "Onto-theo-logical Constitution of Metaphysics," xxii]), see Stanley Rosen, *The Question of Being: A Reversal of Heidegger* (New Haven: Yale University Press, 1993). By contrast, Julian Young points out that in Heidegger's later writings, Heidegger does make use of the language of "origin" when discussing God and the world, and Heidegger's account of "transcendence" can be positive at times: see Young, *Heidegger's Later Philosophy* (Cambridge: Cambridge University Press, 2001). See also two essays, from 1929 and 1946 respectively, that express Heidegger's view of transcendence and of waiting for the manifestation of God/the gods: "On the Essence of Ground" (trans. William McNeill) and "Letter on 'Humanism'" (trans. Frank A. Capuzzi) in Heidegger, *Pathmarks*, ed. William McNeill (Cambridge: Cambridge University Press, 1998), 97–135 and 239–76. For the "mystical" or "religious" Heidegger, see also John D. Caputo, "Heidegger and Theology," in *The Cambridge Companion to Heidegger*, ed. Charles B. Guignon, 2nd ed. (Cambridge: Cambridge University Press, 2006), 270–88.

250. Heidegger, "Onto-theo-logical Constitution of Metaphysics," 72. He notes in conclusion, however, that he remains uncertain whether the languages of the West, shaped by the metaphysics of "onto-theo-logic," can sustain this overcoming of metaphysics. With regard to Christianity, Heidegger's fundamental critique is that the history of theology or Christian thought takes place within the wider and more determinative narrative of the covering up or withdrawal of being and the thinking of being in the history of metaphysics. To the extent that Christianity participates in "metaphysics," it has lost its meaning and vitality for thinking about being (or anything else) today. See also Merold Westphal, *Overcoming Onto-theology: Toward a Postmodern Christian Faith* (New York: Fordham University Press, 2001); Westphal, "The Importance of Overcoming Metaphysics for the Life of Faith," *Modern Theology* 23 (2007): 253–78; Jean-Luc Marion, *God without Being: Hors-Texte*, trans. Thomas A. Carlson (Chicago: University of Chicago Press, 1991); John D. Caputo, "How to Avoid Speaking of God: The Violence of Natural Theology," in *Prospects for Natural Theology*, ed. Eugene Thomas Long (Washington, DC: Catholic University of America Press, 1992), 128–50. From a related perspective, see Kevin W. Hector, *Theology without Metaphysics: God, Language, and the Spirit of Recognition* (Cambridge: Cambridge University Press, 2011). For a contemporary metaphysics in response especially to Hegel and Heidegger, and in dialogue with Aquinas, see William Desmond, *The Intimate Strangeness of Being: Metaphysics after Dialectic* (Washington, DC: Catholic University of America Press, 2012); Desmond, *God and the Between* (Oxford: Blackwell, 2008). See also the intensive discussion of Heidegger offered by William J. Richardson, SJ, *Heidegger: Through Phenomenology to Thought*, 3rd ed. (The Hague: Martinus Nijhoff, 1974).

Karl Barth (1886–1968)

Born in Basel, Switzerland, Karl Barth studied at the University of Bern, where his father taught theology. Barth also studied at the University of Berlin, where the lectures of Adolf von Harnack impressed him, and at the Universities of Tübingen and Marburg. He then spent ten years as a pastor in Safenwil, Switzerland, where he came to reject theological liberalism and published a major theological commentary on Romans. In 1921 he became professor of Reformed theology at the University of Göttingen; four years later he moved to the University of Münster, and five years after that to the University of Bonn. He published the first volume of his massive *Church Dogmatics* in 1932. During this same period he lectured and published on a wide variety of subjects, including classic Reformed texts, various books of the New Testament, ethics, the theology of Friedrich Schleiermacher, the analogy of being, natural theology, and Anselm's *Proslogion*. Due to his leadership in the Confessing Church and his role in drafting the Barmen Declaration against the Nazis, Barth was dismissed from Bonn in 1935. He returned to Switzerland, where he taught at the University of Basel for the rest of his career.[251]

In the first volume of the *Church Dogmatics*, Barth warns against "judging the utterance of the Church about God in accordance with alien principles rather than its own principle."[252] For Barth, "There never has actually been a *philosophia christiana*, for if it was *philosophia* it was not *christiana*, and if it was *christiana* it was not *philosophia*."[253] Christ is the criterion by which Christians must criticize and correct all talk about God. Barth remarks, "Talk about God has true content when it conforms to the being of the Church, i.e., when it conforms to Jesus Christ."[254] Furthermore, our knowledge about God is an act of obedience to Jesus Christ rather than a secure possession of our own. We must recognize that "only in God and not for us is the true basis of Christian utterance identical with its true content."[255] Rather than resting content in any formulation of truth about God, we must always listen

---

251. See John Webster, "Introducing Barth," in *The Cambridge Companion to Karl Barth*, ed. John Webster (Cambridge: Cambridge University Press, 2000), 1–16; Eberhard Busch, *Karl Barth: His Life from Letters and Autobiographical Texts* (Philadelphia: Fortress, 1976).

252. Karl Barth, *Church Dogmatics* I/1, trans. G. W. Bromiley, ed. G. W. Bromiley and T. F. Torrance, 2nd ed. (Edinburgh: T&T Clark, 1975), 6. For discussion see Keith Johnson, *Karl Barth and the Analogia Entis* (London: T&T Clark, 2010); K. Diller, "Karl Barth and the Relationship between Philosophy and Theology," *Heythrop Journal* 51 (2010): 1035–52; George Hunsinger, *How to Read Karl Barth: The Shape of His Theology* (Oxford: Oxford University Press, 1991); Christoph Schwöbel, "Theology," in *Cambridge Companion to Karl Barth*, 17–36.

253. Barth, *Church Dogmatics* I/1, 6.

254. Barth, *Church Dogmatics* I/1, 12.

255. Barth, *Church Dogmatics* I/1, 16.

anew to Jesus Christ so as to allow him to challenge and correct what we presume to know.

Barth goes on to rule out the view that knowledge of God can be obtained indirectly from the created world outside of Christ. This is so because our corrupted minds on their own cannot rise even to indirect knowledge of God, and also because only God can unveil God. When we know God, this knowledge can only be God's sheer gift. Barth observes, "It is the *Deus revelatus* who is the *Deus absconditus*, the God to whom there is no path nor bridge, concerning whom we could not say nor have to say a single word if He did not on His own initiative meet us as the *Deus revelatus*."[256] God's self-revealing is always free, because God never ceases to be mystery. If we could know God outside of God's always free unveiling, we would be in control of God. Barth rejects "independent, arbitrary, so-called natural knowledge of God" in favor of "the knowledge of God by His revelation in faith."[257]

For Barth, then, the content of faith cannot be abstracted from its form, namely, "its impartation in the person of the Revealer Jesus of Nazareth."[258] Christ does not give a name ("Father") to what "all serious philosophy has called the first cause or supreme good, the *esse a se* or *ens perfectissimum*, the universum, the ground and abyss of meaning, the unconditioned, the limit, the critical negation or origin."[259] Rather, since the Revealer and the content of revelation (the knowledge of God) cannot be disjoined, it follows that "this entity, the supposed philosophical equivalent of the Creator God, has nothing whatever to do with Jesus' message about God the Father."[260] Every philosophical idea about God, even the best ones (such as Plato's "genuinely pure" idea of God), is an idol.[261] Only Jesus makes the true God known. Put another way, "What God reveals in Jesus and how he reveals it, namely in Jesus, must not be separated from one another according to the New Testament."[262]

Barth strengthens this point in part one of the second volume of his *Church Dogmatics*, published in 1940. Here he observes that "one would think that there was nothing simpler and more obvious" than the fact that we can find God's "knowability only in the readiness of God Himself, which is to be understood as His free good-pleasure."[263] We cannot know God on our own

256. Barth, *Church Dogmatics* I/1, 321.
257. Barth, *Church Dogmatics* I/1, 440.
258. Barth, *Church Dogmatics* I/1, 390.
259. Barth, *Church Dogmatics* I/1, 391.
260. Barth, *Church Dogmatics* I/1, 391.
261. Barth, *Church Dogmatics* I/1, 391.
262. Barth, *Church Dogmatics* I/1, 399.
263. Karl Barth, *Church Dogmatics* II/1, trans. T. H. L. Parker, W. B. Johnston, Harold Knight, and J. L. M. Haire, ed. G. W. Bromiley and T. F. Torrance (Edinburgh: T&T Clark, 1957), 85.

terms or from our own resources. By contrast, Barth states that Vatican I's *Dei Filius* approves of the effort of human reason to know "God" in the abstract, separate from the knowing of God insofar as God is Creator and Lord, the God of Abraham and Isaac and Jacob, and Father, Son, and Holy Spirit. Such an approach looks "away and above what God is among us and for us" and seeks to apprehend the being or existence of God.[264] It also involves the analogy of being, in which God and humans are both comprehended under the term "being."

Barth here pauses briefly to address the Catholic philosopher Gottlieb Söhngen's insistence in 1934, in response to Barth, that Catholic doctrine has always located the analogy of being under the analogy of faith. While observing that it would be good if Söhngen were right, Barth points out that Söhngen's position cannot be found in other modern Catholic thinkers, let alone in the teaching of the Catholic magisterium. Barth concludes that his charge of an unwarranted abstraction from divine revelation holds. In teaching that God can be known by reasoning from the world, Catholic theology has committed itself to an abstract "God" that is in fact a false god, a creation of the human mind rather than the God who actively and truly saves us in Jesus Christ. In Barth's view, we must decisively reject this "construct which obviously derives from an attempt to unite Yahweh with Baal, the triune God of Holy Scripture with the concept of being of Aristotelian and Stoic philosophy."[265]

Indeed, any alleged rational demonstration of God's existence actually says nothing whatsoever about the real God. As Barth puts it, "The assertion that reason can know God from created things applies to the second and heathenish component of this concept of God, so that when we view the construct on this side we do not recognise God in it at all."[266] Natural theology involves nothing less than "a mortal attack on the Christian doctrine of God," and precisely for this reason is utterly irrelevant to the truth about God.[267]

Barth's *Anselm: Fides Quarens Intellectum; Anselm's Proof of the Existence of God in the Context of His Theological Scheme*, originally published in 1931, also deserves mention here.[268] Barth considers Anselm to be supportive of his own view that God's revelation in Jesus Christ is the source of all our knowledge of God. Beginning in faith, Anselm takes joy in seeking

264. Barth, *Church Dogmatics* II/1, 81.
265. Barth, *Church Dogmatics* II/1, 84.
266. Barth, *Church Dogmatics* II/1, 84.
267. Barth, *Church Dogmatics* II/1, 85.
268. G. R. Evans reads Anselm in a similar way as does Barth: see her *Anselm and Talking about God* (Oxford: Oxford University Press, 1978).

understanding. Anselm's "proof" for the existence of God is thus first and foremost an expression of faith. As Barth says, "Anselm wants 'proof' and 'joy' because he wants *intelligere* and he wants *intelligere* because he believes. Any reversal of this order of compulsion is excluded by Anselm's conception of faith."[269] Anselm, then, is not undertaking the proof as a kind of preamble to faith or "an intellectual storming of the gates of heaven"; rather, precisely his *faith* presses him to seek understanding.[270]

Since humans are in the image and likeness of God (Gen. 1:26), faith in God's Word completes our likeness to God and thereby establishes our knowledge of God. In seeking understanding, faith seeks a deeper participation in God. Thus, understanding properly operates within faith. Anselm recognizes, too, that God alone can have an adequate idea of God. Barth observes in this regard that "every one of the categories known to us by which we attempt to conceive him is, in the last analysis, not really one of his categories at all. God shatters every syllogism."[271] God cannot be expressed, but true statements can nonetheless be made about him—even though these statements will have the relative certainty of theology rather than the absolute certitude of faith. Without right faith, says Barth, right knowledge (and right love) are impossible. To know God, we need faith and the pure heart that comes with obedient faith; only in this way can we obtain the real encounter with God that Anselm seeks.

Examining the meaning of "*ratio*" and "*necessitas*" in the *Proslogion*, Barth argues that Anselm holds that any understanding of God is rooted in faith, even if it involves rational arguments. Anselm has in view "the rationality of the object of faith."[272] Barth rules out the notion that Anselm allows for or seeks "an independent knowledge [of God] alongside that of faith, able to draw from its own sources."[273] Far from beginning with philosophical reason and general human experience, Anselm begins the *Proslogion* with faith and prayer.

Barth grants that when Anselm treats of the being of God in the *Monologion* and the second part of the *Proslogion*, Anselm comes close to "*a priori* theology," or at least is not precise enough in his method.[274] However, he denies that Anselm, in the *Monologion*, is undertaking a "cosmological proof" of God's existence along the lines of Aquinas's five ways. The existence of God

---

269. Karl Barth, *Anselm: Fides Quaerens Intellectum; Anselm's Proof of the Existence of God in the Context of His Theological Scheme* (Eugene, OR: Pickwick, 2009), 16–17.
270. Barth, *Anselm*, 26.
271. Barth, *Anselm*, 29.
272. Barth, *Anselm*, 52.
273. Barth, *Anselm*, 53.
274. Barth, *Anselm*, 56.

(as well as the doctrine of *creatio ex nihilo* and the doctrine of the creative Word) is already presupposed in the *Monologion* on the grounds of faith. In this regard, Barth takes pains to distance Anselm, "so far as the contents of his 'proofs' are concerned," from his "inevitable philosophical ancestry (Augustine, Plotinus, Plato)."[275] For Anselm, proofs flow from theology, in the sense of faith seeking maximal understanding.

Barth considers that Anselm writes for his fellow Christians and Benedictines rather than to persuade nonbelievers, even though Anselm is well aware of nonbelievers and seeks to demonstrate, from within faith, the rationality of faith. Anselm recognizes that there is no possibility of leading nonbelievers to any knowledge of God unless and until they receive the gift of faith. At the same time, however, Barth also recognizes that Anselm considers that he and nonbelievers, together, can search for the rationality of faith. Both the nonbeliever and Anselm want to understand the content of faith, and so in this sense Anselm can "engage in a discussion with him [the unbeliever] without either accepting the unbeliever's criterion, such as universal human reason, or stipulating that the unbeliever in order to become competent to discuss must first be converted into a believer."[276]

Since Anselm never brackets faith, is it possible for nonbelievers (lacking the light of faith) to understand his proofs? What benefit can nonbelievers gain from Anselm's proofs, since no proofs can suffice to give us faith? Barth answers that perhaps Anselm thinks that "the doubt, denial and derision of the unbeliever are not really to be taken so seriously as the unbeliever himself would take them."[277] On this view, the purpose of Anselm's theological proof is to proclaim the gospel, and Anselm trusts in God that the proclamation will be fruitful.

In naming God "something beyond which nothing greater can be conceived," Anselm does not say that God has been or could be conceived by a finite mind.[278] The name does not itself provide the content for the idea of God; the "givenness" of God's name must come from another source. Barth holds that "to reach a knowledge of God the revelation of this same God from some other source is clearly assumed" by Anselm's proof.[279] Thus Anselm responds to his critic Gaunilo by pointing out that no Christian could dispute that the name "something beyond which nothing greater can be conceived" applies

---

275. Barth, *Anselm*, 57.
276. Barth, *Anselm*, 67.
277. Barth, *Anselm*, 70.
278. Barth gives a German paraphrase of the Latin: "Etwas über dem ein Grösseres nicht gedacht werden kann."
279. Barth, *Anselm*, 75.

to God. The point is that "Anselm did not regard this designation for God as a non-essential theologoumenon and certainly not as a constituent part of a universal human awareness of God, but as an article of faith."[280] *Faith* cannot conceive of anything greater than the self-revealing God.

In Barth's view, Gaunilo mistakenly thinks that Anselm is bracketing faith rather than reasoning in faith. Having made this error, Gaunilo criticizes Anselm's proof as though it were solely the product of reason. Gaunilo therefore argues that Anselm has not shown that "something beyond which nothing greater can be conceived" actually exists. But Barth responds that Anselm receives from revelation the truth that the God who is named in this way exists. For Gaunilo, says Barth, Anselm's proof reduces to a claim to have proven the greatest being in the chain of beings.[281] In fact, however, Anselm has developed a proof that demonstrates both God's absolute incomprehensibility and our absolute inability to conceive of God without revelation. It is a valid proof of the God known in faith, precisely because of "its austere character as a rule for thinking about God."[282]

Barth is aware that in evaluating Anselm's proof positively, "the appearance must be avoided that it is a case of elevating existence in thought analytically to actual existence."[283] He explains again that the proof presupposes God's existence in order to show "the impossibility of conceiving the non-existence of God."[284] God's existence is not like the existence of other things. God is Truth, and only God exists as he does. There is no Truth unless God exists. As Barth states, "God does not exist only in thought but over against thought. Just because he exists not only 'inwardly' but also 'outwardly' (*in intellectu et in re*), he (from the human standpoint) 'truly' exists, exists from the side of truth and therefore really exists."[285] God's existence provides the ground for the concept of existence, which God transcends.

Thus, Anselm is not seeking to discover "a universal minimum knowledge of God."[286] Rather, he is working from within faith to understand the God whose incomprehensible existence and Truth radically transcend and ground ours. The "fool" who denies God's existence should hear Anselm's words and

---

280. Barth, *Anselm*, 76–77; cf. 122.
281. This is indeed the way we often find Anselm's proof described, as for example in Simon Blackburn's claim that "Anselm defines God as a being 'than which nothing greater can be conceived'" (Blackburn, *Think: A Compelling Introduction to Philosophy* [Oxford: Oxford University Press, 1999], 154).
282. Barth, *Anselm*, 87.
283. Barth, *Anselm*, 93.
284. Barth, *Anselm*, 94.
285. Barth, *Anselm*, 101.
286. Barth, *Anselm*, 106.

realize that God truly is "the One who manifests himself in the command not to imagine a greater than he."[287] If the fool denies this God, the fool at least has had to confront the gospel proclamation in the form of the meaning of God's revealed name. This name henceforth possesses a recognizable meaning even for the fool.

When Anselm goes on to show that a God who exists only in our knowledge would be lesser than a God who existed in reality, and therefore that if the true God exists in our knowledge then he must also exist in reality, Barth summarizes the import of Anselm's conclusion as follows: "God exists in the knowledge of the hearer when the Name of God is preached, understood and heard. But he cannot exist merely in the knowledge of the hearer because a God who exists merely thus stands in impossible contradiction to his own Name as it is revealed and believed, because, in other words, he would be called God but would not be God."[288] This emphasis on revelation, preaching, and belief—none of which Anselm mentions at this stage of the proof—fits with Barth's consistent rendering of the proof. Barth emphasizes, too, that Anselm's proof has only shown a negative: the true God cannot solely exist in the human mind. The positive statement about God's existence depends on its rootedness in a revealed article of faith, namely, that God is "something beyond which nothing greater can be conceived."

For Barth, Gaunilo's fundamental mistake is that he "is obviously in search of a proof of God from some sort of experience, a proof which would have nothing to do with Anselm's *intellectus fidei* and which would be excluded by Anselm's very concept of God."[289] The proof sought by Gaunilo is the sort of proof with which the thirteenth century (especially Aquinas) was enamored, as Barth mentions more than once.[290] Repeatedly, Barth takes Anselm's frame-

---

287. Barth, *Anselm*, 107.
288. Barth, *Anselm*, 128.
289. Barth, *Anselm*, 131.
290. In Barth's "No! Answer to Emil Brunner," Barth states,

> No one who has even to a small extent studied St. Thomas or the formulations of the Vatican Decree, or who has discussed these matters with a Roman Catholic theologian of any erudition, will be able to say that according to Roman Catholic doctrine there is an "unrefracted *theologia naturalis*" with which sin "has as it were nothing to do," a system of natural theology, a self-sufficient rational system, detachable from the *theologia revelata* and capable of serving it for a solid foundation. How can Brunner make this out to be Roman Catholic doctrine: "The *theologia naturalis* is derivable from reason alone," by which nature, i.e., the divine order of creation, is entirely and adequately comprehensible and accessible? (Barth, "No! Answer to Emil Brunner," in Emil Brunner and Karl Barth, *Natural Theology: Comprising 'Nature and Grace' by Professor Dr. Emil Brunner and the Reply 'No!' by Dr. Karl Barth*, trans. Peter Fraenkel [Eugene, OR: Wipf and Stock, 2002], 95)

Barth goes on to say that in Catholic theology

work—faith, prayer, and belief—to mean that Anselm could not possibly have thought himself able to prove that God exists. In light of faith's testimony to God's existence, Anselm must mean only to prove that the kind of existence that God has cannot be like that of any creature. All other things can be conceived of as not existing, but God's existence is such that the rules of the "general concept of existence" do not apply to him.[291] Barth presents Gaunilo as imputing to Anselm a Cartesian position. On this view, from the necessity of his own existence, Anselm develops an account of necessary ideas culminating in the necessary idea that God exists. Summarizing Anselm's response to this charge, Barth presents Anselm as a proto-Barth, demonstrating that God's revealed existence is utterly unlike creaturely existence. What Anselm is doing, in short, is not proving God's existence but rather reflecting in faith on the "thought-content of this Name," that is to say, on what is requisite to "be the legitimate bearer of this [revealed] name."[292]

Regarding Anselm's point that knowing God is the key to ceasing to be a "fool," Barth explains: "God himself compels this knowledge. Whoever knows him himself cannot think, 'God does not exist.' No one has been able to do it who knew him."[293] For Barth, what Anselm means to say is that "God is he who, revealing himself as Creator, is called *quo maius cogitari nequit* and therefore who immediately confronts us with his Name as the one who forbids us to conceive a greater than him."[294] This self-revealing God and the "compulsion" of our encounter with him (moving beyond all idolatry) are for Barth the heart of Anselm's "proof of faith by faith."[295]

Two other passages from Barth's writings can be taken as representative of his general viewpoint. In *The Word of God and the Word of Man* (1924), Barth states, "There is no way from us to God—not even a 'via negativa'—not even a 'via dialectica' nor 'paradoxa.' The god who stood at the end of some human way . . . would not be God."[296] In "No! Answer to Emil Brunner" (1934)

a true knowledge of God derived from reason and nature is *de facto* never attained without prevenient and preparatory grace. . . . According to the Roman Catholic, reason, if left entirely without grace, is incurably sick and incapable of any serious theological activity. Only when it has been illumined, or at least provisionally shone on by faith, does reason serve to produce those statements concerning God, man and the world, which, according to Roman Catholic doctrine, are not only articles of revelation but have to be considered as truths of reason. (ibid., 96)

291. Barth, *Anselm*, 134.
292. Barth, *Anselm*, 148, 149.
293. Barth, *Anselm*, 167.
294. Barth, *Anselm*, 169.
295. Barth, *Anselm*, 170.
296. Karl Barth, *The Word of God and the Word of Man*, trans. Douglas Horton (London: Hodder & Stoughton, 1928), 177.

Barth observes, "Freedom to know the true God is a miracle, a freedom of God, not one of our freedoms. . . . How can man ever in any sense know 'of himself' what has to be known here?"[297] To suppose that human reason, by itself, could demonstrate God's existence is to fall into idolatry.[298]

Conclusion

Newman is certainly right that we rely more on what he calls the "illative sense," through which we arrive at certitude on the basis of cumulative probabilities built up in the course of our experiences, than we do on syllogistic or logical demonstration. Furthermore, he is right that what we seek is "real apprehension" and not merely "notional apprehension," valuable though the latter may be. We want experiential knowledge of God rather than simply demonstrative knowledge that God—Pure Act, the eternal and transcendent source of all things—exists. The mystical intuitions and language-specific meaning promoted by Wittgenstein have their value in the way that they emphasize the centrality of such experience.

In this regard, Blondel's and Rousselot's approaches to the demonstrations of God's existence are deeply attractive. Blondel argues that at the very core of our experience, our action, we recognize that we cannot be satisfied by contingent things and that we are seeking infinite perfection. Even when our will is frustrated and we realize that we cannot attain what we are seeking in finite goods, we continue to will. In this situation, it becomes clear that what we are seeking is "the one thing necessary," and that this "necessary presence," pure actuality, is at the very core of our volition. For his part, Rousselot argues that in the very structure of our cognition, we find a presumption of the synthesis of essence and existence. For our knowledge that "this is a being," we must affirm that "being exists," a judgment that expresses the synthesis of essence and existence. Since we cannot have intuitive knowledge of this synthesis, it functions as a presupposition of our knowing. As such, our acts

297. Barth, "No!," 117.
298. For further discussion, from diverse perspectives, see Henri Bouillard, *The Knowledge of God*, trans. Samuel D. Femiano (New York: Herder and Herder, 1968); Eugene F. Rogers Jr., *Thomas Aquinas and Karl Barth: Sacred Doctrine and the Natural Knowledge of God* (Notre Dame: University of Notre Dame Press, 1995); Keith L. Johnson, "Natural Revelation in Creation and Covenant," in *Thomas Aquinas and Karl Barth: An Unofficial Catholic-Protestant Dialogue*, ed. Bruce L. McCormack and Thomas Joseph White, OP (Grand Rapids: Eerdmans, 2013), 129–56; Matthew Rose, "Karl Barth's Failure," *First Things* no. 244 (June/July 2014): 39–44; Kenneth Oakes, *Karl Barth on Theology and Philosophy* (Oxford: Oxford University Press, 2012). Rogers is indebted to Victor Preller's *Divine Science and the Science of God: A Reformulation of Thomas Aquinas* (Princeton: Princeton University Press, 1967).

of understanding presuppose that the synthesis of essence and existence—God himself—exists. Rousselot also reminds us that the movement by which we seek truth is related intimately to our loves. We possess a "sympathetic" or connatural knowledge that is rooted in our created inclination toward being.[299] Our intelligence is never "neutral" toward being. Since God is infinite being and the source of all finite being, we are constantly in a condition of being drawn toward God. Thus if we identify a finite good as our ultimate Good, our reason itself becomes constricted. Indeed, both on the natural and supernatural levels, intelligence expands and becomes fully itself when we love. Love gives us eyes for seeing the truth about God.

These two phenomenological descriptions of our interior life as always oriented implicitly toward a transcendent horizon are largely accurate and inspiring, and their use can serve as signs or indirect evidences of the existence of God. The fact that we are able to will an infinite good that does not pass away and to think of eternal necessary existence is indeed a sign that we are derived from God and made for God. But as demonstrations that God exists, these efforts to engage and overcome Kantian idealism do not succeed.[300] Blondel and Rousselot affirm that that toward which the human being is directed (God) in intellect and will must exist, but God's existence need not follow from the fact that the idea of God is inescapable.[301] Like Newman's

299. On this important point see also Kevin E. O'Reilly, *Aesthetic Perception: A Thomistic Perspective* (Dublin: Four Courts, 2007), esp. 63–65; Jacques Maritain, "On Knowledge through Connaturality," in his *Range of Reason*, 22–29. Maritain observes, however, that
> knowledge through connaturality has nothing to do with metaphysics itself: metaphysics proceeds purely by way of conceptual and rational knowledge. Like all rational knowledge it presupposes sense experience; and insofar as it is metaphysics, it implies the intellectual intuition of being *qua* being. But neither in this intellectual intuition nor in sense-perception is there the smallest element of knowledge through inclination. . . . If one confuses the planes and orders of things, if poetic knowledge or mystical experience or moral feeling claim to become philosophical knowledge, or if a philosophy which despairs of reason tries to capture those kinds of knowledge through connaturality, and to use them as an instrument—everyone loses his head, knowledge through inclination and metaphysics are simultaneously spoiled. (ibid., 29)

300. For the contrary view, see W. Norris Clarke, SJ, *The Philosophical Approach to God: A New Thomistic Perspective*, 2nd ed. (New York: Fordham University Press, 2007). See also Germain Grisez, *Beyond the New Theism* (Notre Dame: University of Notre Dame Press, 1975); Adriaan T. Peperzak, *Thinking: From Solitude to Dialogue and Contemplation* (New York: Fordham University Press, 2006), 160–61. Peperzak, however, grants that "so many people do not seem to desire union with God at all" (*Thinking*, 163; cf. xii–xiii). For background see Aidan Nichols, OP, *The Conversation of Faith and Reason: Modern Catholic Thought from Hermes to Benedict XVI* (Chicago: Hillenbrand, 2011).

301. It is not possible to respond to Kantian skepticism by appealing to the structure of human operations and their teleology, since Kant presupposes from the beginning that such structure and teleology are not real but constructions of the intellect. More basic philosophical

appeal to conscience, Blondel's and Rousselot's approaches serve as probable arguments that on their own are insufficient, but that nonetheless repay attention due to the depth of their phenomenological insight into our experience.[302]

Avoiding any hint of *a priori* argumentation may help to address the concerns of Heidegger and Barth. In very different ways, they suggest that metaphysical demonstrations (were such to be possible, which they deny) encapsulate, domesticate, and distort the self-revealing reality that the demonstrations purport to show. For Heidegger, the demonstrations of God's existence inevitably envision "Being" as a logical concept, an onto-theology. David Hart rightly credits Heidegger with recognizing "that the particular pathology of modernity lies—to some very large degree—in the loss of a certain kind of wonder or perplexity, a certain sense of the abiding strangeness of being within the very ordinariness of being."[303] But for Heidegger, as Hart goes on to say, "being is so entirely pure of determination as to be convertible with nothing."[304] The result is that Heidegger's position ultimately reduces to a nihilism that cannot distinguish meaningfully between peaceful and violent manifestations of being.[305] Hart notes that Heidegger "ever more absolutely identifies the event of being not only with the 'presencing' and 'whiling' of beings but also with their annihilation."[306]

Heidegger is also wrong to suppose that the demonstrations of God's existence enclose God in a logical concept ("Being"). Although demonstrative reasoning shows us *that* God is, we cannot know *what* God is. We cannot know what it means for God to "be," since infinite existence cannot be compared with finite existence, other than to rule out certain things that would limit

questions have to be confronted first, especially whether our intellect has real knowledge of realities and their existence and causes. See Étienne Gilson, *Thomist Realism and the Critique of Knowledge*, trans. M. A. Wauck (San Francisco: Ignatius, 1986).

302. For a defense of the demonstration of God's existence from the imperative command of conscience (granting that this imperative command can be blunted), see Crosby, *Personalism of John Henry Newman*, 200–211. Crosby admits that the imperative command does not show whether God is one: "The 'higher authority' experience in conscience is veiled; whether there is one or multiple centers of authority cannot be easily discerned. Newman takes for granted that this higher authority is centered in the one God of Christian monotheism" (ibid., 211). See Ronald A. Knox, *In Soft Garments: A Collection of Oxford Conferences*, 2nd ed. (New York: Sheed & Ward, 1953), 16–18, 21–22. Knox accepts Newman's argument from conscience but recognizes that the content of the human conscience seems highly variable across cultures and time periods.

303. David Bentley Hart, "The Offering of Names: Metaphysics, Nihilism, and Analogy," in *Reason and the Reasons of Faith*, ed. Paul J. Griffiths and Reinhard Hütter (New York: T&T Clark, 2005), 255–91, at 258.

304. Ibid., 260.

305. See ibid., 261.

306. Ibid., 260.

God's existence. We can know that God is Pure Act, good, wise, eternal, and so forth. But because God is infinite, such names apply to God only analogically, in a manner that exceeds our comprehension as infinitely greater than the perfections that we know on the basis of our experience of finite being. The knowledge about God that the demonstrations obtain is strictly limited. But the demonstrations make clear that God has created our minds to "seek God, in the hope that they might feel after him and find him" (Acts 17:27). They also distinguish God from creaturely existence and ensure that the God we worship is not conceived as a mere creature.

While the demonstrations have real value, they do not and cannot substitute for the self-manifestation of God. The gift of knowing God is indeed utterly a gift. This is so not only because reason itself is a gift, but even more importantly because the demonstrations do not meet our deepest need for knowledge of God. We want to know God personally, intimately, experientially; we want to know God as our Creator and Redeemer, and we want to know him in an everlasting relationship. The demonstrations cannot achieve this relationship for us, or even come close to doing so. They cannot substitute for the manifestation of the transcendent God of Abraham, Isaac, and Jacob, the God who in his holiness and power is a "devouring fire" (Deut. 9:3) and who in his love is "merciful and gracious, slow to anger, and abounding in steadfast love and faithfulness" (Exod. 34:6). We are embodied and historical creatures, and so God meets us in history, in communities built up by his revelatory presence.[307]

Thus the oppositions that Barth and Heidegger draw are unnecessary. When properly understood, the demonstrations of God's existence do not lead us to a domesticated idea or exhaustive concept of what God is. Rather, the demonstrations of God's existence open us even more fully to the transcendent God who freely creates us and comes to us. The demonstrations certainly do not undermine the historicity of our encounter with this God, since it

---

307. This emphasis on history is applied to "natural theology" itself in Ephraim Radner's *The World in the Shadow of God: An Introduction to Christian Natural Theology* (Eugene, OR: Cascade, 2010). For Radner, the "natural history of religion" stands as a kind of "natural theology": "What do we grasp of God's outline, as it were, as Christians speak and act, and use words and gestures in such and such a way?" (ibid., 24; cf. 30). Radner notes that in the modern period, "'Natural theology' came to have for its practitioners a greater stature, in terms of truth, than doctrinally oriented theologies set forth within the Church's seminaries" (ibid., 7). In reaction to this unfortunate development, as Radner observes, "the last century has seen a growing unanimity among traditional Christians, classically enunciated by Karl Barth, that 'natural theology' in its modern sense—and perhaps in all senses—is both useless and probably even corrupting of the Church's understanding of God" (ibid.). This, however, is also an unfortunate development. As an example of natural theology, he offers a set of poems that describe the world.

is only the historical encounter that fulfills us. Furthermore, this historical encounter cannot be accomplished merely by demonstrating that God exists. The demonstrations explode our concepts by underscoring the awe-inspiring transcendence of God. Barth's interpretation of Anselm is a distortion of what Anselm actually is doing, but Barth is not wrong to think that Anselm begins with faith. Yet beginning with faith does not exclude a demonstration that in itself (though in the service of faith) begins with reason. As Denys Turner remarks in response to Barth, the fact that God is the creative source of human reason means that we need not construe "the relation between a standpoint of natural theology and a standpoint of faith as being mutually exclusive, whether construed 'objectively' as alternative sources of truth about God, or 'subjectively' as regards the acts of response respectively of reason to creation and of faith to the divine election."[308] To know by reason that God is Pure Act, eternal, good, infinite, perfect, and so on, is not to arrive at an idol. On the contrary, our ability to arrive at such knowledge by rational demonstration informs our desire to know the living God in a fully personal manner, which is possible only through his self-revelation.

But do not the demonstrations of God's existence trace back to the Greek philosophers, who worshiped gods and believed many things about God that are in opposition to divine revelation? Again, the limitations of the demonstrations are crucial to observe. One can demonstrate that Pure Act exists without thereby developing an adequately full knowledge of God, let alone worshiping God properly. There is no need to tie ourselves up in interpretative knots for the purpose of undermining the clear meaning of Paul's statement that God's "invisible nature, namely his eternal power and deity, has been clearly perceived in the things that have been made" (Rom. 1:20). The demonstrations that God exists do not threaten to overwhelm the free gift of God's revelation. On the contrary, they support that revelation by showing that God wants to be known and has created us to know him, to such a degree that even our turning away from him cannot fully blind us to his existence.

Hume and Kant rejected reason's ability to know being, and I have already addressed their viewpoints above. In the present chapter, it is Wittgenstein who raises this issue most forcefully. For Wittgenstein, most clearly in his *Philosophical Investigations* but also in the strictures against metaphysical inquiries that we find in the *Tractatus*, it is impossible to get beyond the level of our concepts or language. "Being" is thus a predicate or a conceptual property of a thing, and we cannot strictly say that a thing *exists* if by this we

---

308. Denys Turner, *Faith, Reason and the Existence of God* (Cambridge: Cambridge University Press, 2004), 12–13.

mean to speak about a thing's act-of-being. From this perspective, too, analogous modes of being are impossible to conceive: one simply has the concept
"being," which must make do for all existing things. The demonstrations of
God's existence are thereby cut off before they can begin, since without real
knowledge of being (act/potency, analogous modes of being) there can be
no sense to the principle of causality or the principle of noncontradiction.

David Hart, treating these views as found in Gottlob Frege, points out
in this regard that "a reasonable person, uncorrupted by analytic modes of
discourse, might wonder whether something can be said about what concrete
existence actually *is*."[309] It may do for philosophers to proceed as though all
we know is our conceptual grammar, but can we really hold that the difference
between being and nonbeing is fundamentally a logical or grammatical one
rather than an ontological one? Can we really think of the being of a rock,
for example, as only a conceptual predicate or property and not as *actual*
(contingent) being? Surely not. We recognize that the being of a thing is its
act-of-being, its power to be, and we can distinguish actuality from potency.

Hart observes, "Actual being—not the proposition that some concept has
at least one instance somewhere, but rather the real actuality of some particular thing among other particular things—is that thing's effective power
to act and to be acted upon."[310] Wittgenstein's account of language games,

---

309. David Bentley Hart, *The Experience of God: Being, Consciousness, Bliss* (New Haven:
Yale University Press, 2013), 127. See also Barry Miller's response to analytic philosophy's
critique of the notion of being: Miller, *The Fullness of Being: A New Paradigm for Existence*
(Notre Dame: University of Notre Dame Press, 2012). As Miller says,

> According to a fairly standard view, there are various reasons that preclude existence from
> being a real property of concrete individuals. One such reason is that "exists" cannot
> be predicated of individuals, and another is that first-level properties are parasitic on
> individuals for their actuality, which is something that existence could never be. A third is
> that, unlike all other real properties, existence would not add anything to an individual.
> Moreover, even if, per impossible, existence were to survive all three counter-indications,
> it would be nothing but the most vacuous of properties. These claims, however, are
> testimony to what happens when wrong questions are asked, when false assumptions
> are made, and when the possibility of a new paradigm for existence is not so much as
> entertained. In other words, they testify to the substantial flaws underlying the familiar
> claim "Existence is not a predicate" and the Frege-Russell-Quine view not only of "exists"
> as exclusively a second-level predicate but of existence as no more than a Cambridge
> property of individuals. (ibid., ix; cf. chap. 7 for a summary of Miller's position)

For the view to which Hart and Miller are responding, see for example Bertrand Russell,
Logic and Knowledge, ed. R. C. Marsh (London: Allen and Unwin, 1955); Gottlob Frege, "Dialog
mit Pünjer über Existenz," in *Gottlob Frege: Posthumous Writings*, ed. P. Long and R. White
(Oxford: Blackwell, 1979), 53–67; C. J. F. Williams, *What Is Existence?* (Oxford: Oxford University Press, 1981). See also Hermann Weidemann, "The Logic of Being in Thomas Aquinas,"
in *The Logic of Being*, ed. S. Knuuttila and J. Hintikka (Dordrecht: Reidel, 1985), 181–200.

310. Hart, *Experience of God*, 131.

like Kant's account of the categories of our understanding, suggests that we cannot arrive at a "thing's effective power to act and to be acted upon," but we know experientially that we can do so. Thus, Hart speaks of "that universal and primordial human experience of simple wonder at the being of things."[311] The demonstrations of God's existence depend on the mind's ability to "wonder at the being of things," and thus to know actual being rather than simply "being" as a conceptual predicate.

This openness to actual being is emphasized by Garrigou-Lagrange. In light of the challenges posed by modern thinkers such as Descartes, Hume, and Kant, Garrigou-Lagrange insists on our ability to reason from finite existence to infinite existence, Pure Act. Given the accordance of Aquinas's reasoning with that of the Greek fathers, the convergence on this point between Garrigou-Lagrange as a Catholic theologian and Hart as an Eastern Orthodox theologian is not surprising.[312] In this regard at least, Vatican I's *Dei Filius* expresses the consensus of the Eastern and Western Christian traditions.

---

311. Ibid., 129.

312. For Hart's critique of premotion and predestination as understood by Garrigou-Lagrange, however, see Hart, "Impassibility as Transcendence: On the Infinite Innocence of God," in *Divine Impassibility and the Mystery of Human Suffering*, ed. James F. Keating and Thomas Joseph White, OP (Grand Rapids: Eerdmans, 2009), 299–323.

Conclusion

In contemporary culture, discourse about God has become deeply impoverished. Speaking of his fellow professional philosophers, William Desmond observes, "The most important question, the most fascinating question, the most enigmatic question, makes us squirm—squirm though we wear the unmoved mask of agnostic indifference."[1] Most philosophers today do not wish to raise the "most important question"—the question of God. For example, Marietta McCarty's bestselling *How Philosophy Can Save Your Life: Ten Ideas That Matter Most* is silent about the idea of God. Instead, the "ten ideas that matter most" turn out to be simplicity, communication, perspective, flexibility, empathy, individuality, belonging, serenity, possibility, and joy.[2] Of course, these ten ideas cannot ultimately save anyone's life, and we can hardly retain "serenity" and "joy" in the face of the eternal annihilation that we would face if there were no God. The American writer and activist Grace Paley commented in an interview near the end of her life, "The moment I take my last breath everything will end. Bye-bye—in fact, farewell."[3]

1. William Desmond, *God and the Between* (Oxford: Blackwell, 2008), 17.
2. See Marietta McCarty, *How Philosophy Can Save Your Life: Ten Ideas That Matter Most* (New York: Penguin, 2009). McCarty grants that there are eternal truths, though so far as I know she does not mention God. She states that "eternal ideas *do* exist untouched by time. These pure concepts are true for all time and in all places, concepts such as Love, Truth, and . . . Flexibility. . . . While the physical world shifts to and fro, non-tangible ideas remain the same—Joy, Friendship, Equality—and as philosophers we must reevaluate our understanding of them through reflection and dynamic conversations" (ibid., 105).
3. Antonio Monda, *Do You Believe? Conversations on God and Religion*, trans. Ann Goldstein (New York: Random House, 2007), 127. Most of the interviews with famous cultural figures that Monda records in his book (with some exceptions, such as the interview with Elie Wiesel) are discouraging, not least with respect to the level of ignorance about "God."

Paley assumed that she would be annihilated, utterly swallowed up into the everlasting passage of time. This worldview is commonplace today in what Carlos Eire, in *A Very Brief History of Eternity*, terms with subtle irony the professional "thinking class."[4]

Given this situation, some philosophers have taken to trying to explain how a human life that leads to everlasting annihilation is nonetheless endurable. In his bestselling *The Atheist's Guide to Reality: Enjoying Life without Illusions*, Alex Rosenberg accepts that logical rigor compels atheists such as himself to conclude that "death is the end of our existence" and that "individual human life is meaningless, without a purpose, and without ultimate human value"—as is the entirety of human history.[5] He still thinks that we can make it through the day, often quite contentedly.

If Rosenberg is right in his premises, at a basic level it does not matter how we live; all human actions converge on the not-so-distant horizon line of life's fundamental meaninglessness, and today "let us crown ourselves with rosebuds before they wither," and "let our might be our law of right, for what is weak proves itself to be useless" (Wis. 2:8, 11).

A similar positing of the fundamental purposelessness of our existence appears in the work of Rosenberg's fellow atheist and Duke University colleague Owen Flanagan. Flanagan urges us to find meaning by pursuing lives of self-sacrificial love even though we know that, inevitably and without the slightest doubt, we will soon be annihilated forever.[6] Death is seemingly not

4. Carlos M. N. Eire, *A Very Brief History of Eternity* (Princeton: Princeton University Press, 2009), 224.

5. Alex Rosenberg, *The Atheist's Guide to Reality: Enjoying Life without Illusions* (New York: W. W. Norton, 2011), 19, 314. See also Andrew Melnyk's *A Physicalist Manifesto: Thoroughly Modern Materialism* (Cambridge: Cambridge University Press, 2003); and Edward O. Wilson, *The Meaning of Human Existence* (New York: W. W. Norton, 2014). See Edward Feser's response to eliminative materialism in his *The Last Superstition: A Refutation of the New Atheism* (South Bend, IN: St. Augustine's Press, 2008), 166–267; as well as David Bentley Hart's superb chapter on consciousness in his *The Experience of God: Being, Consciousness, Bliss* (New Haven: Yale University Press, 2013).

6. See Owen Flanagan, *The Really Hard Problem: Meaning in a Material World* (Cambridge, MA: MIT Press, 2007). See also his *Consciousness Reconsidered* (Cambridge, MA: MIT Press, 1992) and *Self-Expressions: Mind, Morals, and the Meaning of Life* (Oxford: Oxford University Press, 1996). Regarding the question of whether life has a "meaning" without God, Julian Baggini's *Atheism: A Very Short Introduction* offers an Epicurean response not likely to include self-sacrificial love: "What most people want is companionship, a job they enjoy, and sufficient money for a good quality of life. Given all those things, life seems meaningful enough, since that overall package is a good in itself" (Baggini, *Atheism: A Very Short Introduction* [Oxford: Oxford University Press, 2003], 65). For the point that there can be no good and evil (no objective moral standards) without God—a point accepted by Alex Rosenberg but not explicitly by Baggini, who advocates for moral consequentialism—see David Baggett and Jerry L. Walls, *Good God: The Theistic Foundations of Morality* (Oxford: Oxford University Press, 2011).

a problem for Flanagan, since he considers it to be merely a return to nonexistence. But once we have existed and have known and loved others (and have in turn been known and loved), our death does not just involve a mere return to nonexistence; it is also an everlasting destruction of the personal communion that we once enjoyed, a destruction that renders all of our relationships null and void forever.[7] The net result then is the same as that which we outlined above: Rosenberg's and Flanagan's premises render human existence absurd and indeed horrific on the most fundamental level. Rosenberg and Flanagan have arrived at their positions by assuming that Hume, Kant, and modern science have once and for all ruled out even the question of God's existence.[8]

By comparison with Rosenberg and Flanagan, many popular scientists today are still interested in the classical demonstrations of God's existence, if only out of eagerness to expose these demonstrations as fraudulent. In a "Contrarian Theological Afterword" to his highly entertaining *The Whole Shebang: A State-of-the-Universe(s) Report*, for example, Timothy Ferris describes the "cosmological proof" as claiming "that any hierarchy of existence requires some overarching state of existence, that of an extant God."[9] Instead of a transcendent source of all finite being, which is what the cosmological proof actually entails, Ferris imagines the "cosmological proof" as demonstrating a hierarchy of beings, with God as merely the supreme being on the scale. He complains, "The cosmological proof has enjoyed a long reign, due in part to the sentiments of thinkers who regard the origin of the universe as a problem inaccessible to science."[10] He supposes that the question is what produced the material universe, whereas in fact the real question is how to account for finite, contingent existence. Even if we discovered that the universe was produced by another universe, this problem—the inability of contingent being to account for its own existence— would remain in full force.[11]

7. See S. L. Frank, *The Meaning of Life*, trans. Boris Jakim (Grand Rapids: Eerdmans, 2010), esp. chap. 4. For the origins of nihilism, see Desmond, *God and the Between*, 21.

8. See, however, Rosenberg and Tom L. Beauchamp, *Hume and the Problem of Causation* (Oxford: Oxford University Press, 1981).

9. Timothy Ferris, *The Whole Shebang: A State-of-the-Universe(s) Report* (New York: Simon & Schuster, 1997), 306.

10. Ibid.

11. William Lane Craig's *The Kalam Cosmological Argument* (New York: Macmillan, 1979) takes as its starting point the fact that the universe began to exist (the Big Bang). Without rejecting the "Kalam Cosmological Argument," I find Aquinas's first and second ways to be markedly superior because they do not rely on the claim that the universe cannot have always existed. For support of the "Kalam Cosmological Argument," see Garrett J. DeWeese and Joshua Rasmussen, "Hume and the *Kalam* Cosmological Argument," in *In Defense of Natural*

Without grasping the real question of being, therefore, Ferris asks, "Why, for instance, must we think of existence as a slippery slope, such that divine intervention is constantly required to prevent things from sliding down into the despond of nonexistence? And is causation really so deep a precept of nature as to render God requisite?"[12] Certainly, with respect to the real question of being, being is not "a slippery slope" that one can "slide down." The real problem is how contingent actuality could possibly be. For Ferris, the "cosmological proof" simply "pastes the tag of 'existing' on things, then asserts that the existence of any being requires the existence of an ultimate being."[13] But this assumes that "being" is a mere concept, a mere predicate that one "pastes" onto things. Ferris concludes that "we would clearly be better off if we left God out of cosmology altogether"—not recognizing that his real opponents are glad to do so, since cosmology properly deals only with intraworldly causes.[14] He takes one last jab at the cosmological proof: "Feeble indeed is a machine that requires the constant intervention of its designer to keep it running."[15] If only he knew that the proponents of the demonstrations of God's existence entirely reject this Deistic god.

Richard Dawkins is perhaps the most well-known scientific critic of the demonstrations of God's existence, but he is notorious for his failure to grasp them. Dawkins summarizes Aquinas's first way as being based on the logic that "something had to make the first move, and that something we call God."[16] He summarizes the third way as positing that "there must have been a time when no physical things existed. But, since physical things exist now, there must have been something non-physical to bring them into existence, and that something we call God."[17] He summarizes the fifth way as saying that "things in the world, especially living things, look as though they have been designed."[18]

How could Dawkins have arrived at such distortions? To be the first mover is not simply "to make the first move." The third way is about ontological possibility and necessity, not about the need for something nonphysical to

Theology: A Post-Humean Assessment, ed. James F. Sennett and Douglas Groothuis (Downers Grove, IL: InterVarsity, 2005), 123–49. Mistakenly, Craig argues for God's temporality once God has created: see William Lane Craig, "Timelessness and Omnitemporality," in *God and Time: Four Views*, ed. Gregory E. Ganssle (Downers Grove, IL: InterVarsity Press, 2001), 129–60.

12. Ferris, *Whole Shebang*, 306.
13. Ibid., 308.
14. Ibid., 310.
15. Ibid., 311.
16. Richard Dawkins, *The God Delusion* (New York: Houghton Mifflin, 2006), 77.
17. Ibid.
18. Ibid., 79.

explain physical things. The fifth way is about teleological order, not about mechanistic design. Regarding Aquinas's rejection of infinite regress in the first and second ways, Dawkins suggests that one could end the regress more neatly by hypothesizing "a 'big bang singularity,' or some other physical concept as yet unknown. Calling it God is at best unhelpful and at worst perniciously misleading."[19] The view that one can end the regress by adding yet another finite cause or motion—such as "a 'big bang singularity'"—shows that Dawkins has failed to understand Aquinas's argument. Dawkins appears to think that Aquinas is arguing simply to a Deistic "God" who stands within the order of finite beings.[20] Rather, the real crux of Thomas's argumentation is how to account for motion/change in beings in which there is an evident admixture of potency and act, for which reason they cannot account for their own actuality. This is why, for Thomas, essentially ordered causal chains come to rest not just in a first mover but in a first mover who is "put in motion by no other," that is to say Pure Act.[21]

Stephen Hawking and Leonard Mlodinow begin their *The Grand Design* with the claim that "philosophy is dead."[22] Their understanding of the philosophical demonstrations of God's existence, however, is next to nothing. Remarking that Aquinas "employed Aristotle's ideas about the

19. Ibid., 78.
20. For the same view, presented as an analysis of the "cosmological argument" but in fact a grave distortion of Aquinas's first and second ways, see Baggini, *Atheism*, 94–95. Baggini supposes that the argument's own principles should lead us to posit a cause for God, and he notes that the argument (even were one to imagine that it worked) only arrives at the greatest being among beings. For criticism of Dawkins on this issue and other ones, see Hart, *Experience of God*, 20–23; Alister McGrath, *Dawkins' God: Genes, Memes, and the Meaning of Life* (Oxford: Blackwell, 2005); Thomas Crean, OP, *A Catholic Responds to Professor Dawkins* (Oxford: Family Publications, 2007); Ian S. Markham, *Against Atheism: Why Dawkins, Hitchens, and Harris Are Fundamentally Wrong* (Oxford: Wiley-Blackwell, 2010); Keith Ward, *Why There Almost Certainly Is a God: Doubting Dawkins* (Oxford: Lion Hudson, 2008); Terry Eagleton, *Reason, Faith, and Revolution: Reflections on the God Debate* (New Haven: Yale University Press, 2009). See also the critique of "fundamentalist atheists" (268) offered by Conor Cunningham, *Darwin's Pious Idea: Why the Ultra-Darwinists and Creationists Both Get It Wrong* (Grand Rapids: Eerdmans, 2010), as well as Aidan Nichols, OP, "The New Atheism and Christian Cosmology," in *The Beauty of God's House: Essays in Honor of Stratford Caldecott*, ed. Francesca Aran Murphy (Eugene, OR: Cascade, 2014), 205–19, and James Le Fanu, *Why Us? How Science Rediscovered the Mystery of Ourselves* (New York: Pantheon, 2009). As Ward comments, "Although they are not by any means the only arguments for God's existence, Thomas Aquinas' 'Five Ways in which one can prove that there is a God' are perhaps the best known. Dawkins claims that they are easily exposed as vacuous, and he does so in just three pages. This would be a very impressive achievement, except that he does not in fact deal with Aquinas' Five Ways at all" (*Why There Almost Certainly Is a God*, 102).
21. Aquinas, *Summa theologiae* Ia.2.3.
22. Stephen Hawking and Leonard Mlodinow, *The Grand Design* (New York: Random House, 2010), 5.

order in nature to argue for the existence of God" (although Aquinas credits the fifth way to John of Damascus), they compare Aquinas's argument to that of an unnamed eighteenth-century Christian theologian who absurdly claimed "that rabbits have white tails in order that it be easy for us to shoot them."[23] They then imagine themselves to be resolving matters when they reach the conclusion that "because there is a law like gravity, the universe can and will create itself from nothing. . . . Spontaneous creation is the reason there is something rather than nothing, why the universe exists, why we exist. It is not necessary to invoke God to light the blue touch paper and set the universe going."[24] But not only would the law of gravity by itself be something rather than nothing, but also the notion that the demonstrations of God's existence hinge on the need for something "to light the blue touch paper and set the universe going" fails to comprehend anything about the real demonstrations and what they show. It envisions "God" as simply one supreme being among beings rather than the source of all finite actuality; it envisions God's creative and ongoing gift of being as simply the starting of a cosmic motor.

Not only in popular science but also in contemporary humanities God is too often imagined as something like the Great Pumpkin, beyond rational discourse. For example, in her *Cultivating Humanity: A Classical Defense of Reform in Liberal Education*, Martha Nussbaum appreciatively discusses the University of Notre Dame's efforts to construct "a distinctively religious campus that is also a place of genuine inquiry and debate."[25] But her discussion of how to renew the "cultivation of humanity" in modern universities—how to nourish students' "ability to think critically, to examine themselves, and to respect the humanity and diversity of others"—all too predictably never mentions the need for university professors and students to discuss the topic of God's existence.[26] Surely, however, the question of whether there is a God will be integral to answering what "humanity" is and what human cultivation and critical thinking involves.

As Brad Kallenberg points out, Wittgenstein provides a reason for doubting that the demonstrations of God's existence can make sense within a secular framework. Kallenberg summarizes Wittgenstein's concern: "How do I know

23. Ibid., 163.

24. Ibid., 180. The same misunderstanding is found in Baggini, *Atheism*, 95: "God is invoked to explain what we cannot currently explain. . . . In this case God has retreated to behind the blue-touch paper that started the universe going. Such a God is fast running out of places for believers to hide him." This is fortunate because such a God is not the God in which Christians believe.

25. Martha C. Nussbaum, *Cultivating Humanity: A Classical Defense of Reform in Liberal Education* (Cambridge, MA: Harvard University Press, 1997), 278.

26. Ibid., 300.

that two people mean the same when each says he believes in God? *Practice* gives the words their sense."[27] In other words, when we hear someone express belief in "God," we do not know what kind of "God" (or "god") is at issue. For Kallenberg, it is a mistake to suppose that "arguments about God's existence require no special attending behaviors to get their point."[28] Such "special attending behaviors" include "the practice of prayer or praise."[29]

I agree that whether or not we pray may make a difference in how we respond intellectually to the demonstrations of God's existence. But the reasoning of the various demonstrations—like that of the various critiques of these demonstrations—is open to being assessed by Christian and non-Christian, theist and nontheist. They do not depend for their logic on faith or prayer. Appreciatively summarizing Aquinas's view, which I share, John Haldane states that "even those who do not already have an idea of God are in a position to determine that God exists simply by reflecting on the natural order"—even if such rational reflection is profoundly aided by grace and thus by prayer.[30]

Given the importance of reasoning about God, the notion that "God" means solely what individuals experience it to mean—a notion that is widespread in popular spirituality today—must be rejected. Deepak Chopra claims that "'God' is an empty term except as it finds expression through the revelations of all the saints, prophets, and mystics of history."[31] If Chopra had argued

27. Ludwig Wittgenstein, *Culture and Value*, ed. G. H. von Wright and Heikki Nyman, trans. Peter Winch (Oxford: Blackwell, 1980), 85e, cited in Brad J. Kallenberg, "Praying for Understanding: Reading Anselm through Wittgenstein," *Modern Theology* 20 (2004): 527–46, at 528.

28. Kallenberg, "Praying for Understanding," 527.

29. Ibid., 543.

30. J. J. Haldane, "Atheism and Theism," in J. J. C. Smart and J. J. Haldane, *Atheism and Theism* (Oxford: Blackwell, 1996), 84–167, at 141. With regard to the significance of grace even for human reasoning, Thomas Joseph White, OP, remarks that

> Aquinas himself, who is not pessimistic about the human capacity to arrive at knowledge of God, notes the effects on the intellect in its concrete historical exercise by the draw of disordered passions, the cupidity of the heart, ignorance and laziness, the difficulty of the subject matter, and the weight of received opinions that are erroneous. . . . To claim that we have natural capacities for philosophical knowledge of God, then, implies that these capacities exist as properties intrinsic to the soul, even in its state of fallenness without grace. This does not mean, however, that we can employ them properly in our fallen state without the agency of the grace of Christ, or even flawlessly with such grace. (White, "'Through Him All Things Were Made' [John 1:3]: The Analogy of the Word Incarnate according to St. Thomas Aquinas and Its Ontological Presuppositions," in *The Analogy of Being: Invention of the Antichrist or the Wisdom of God?*, ed. Thomas Joseph White, OP [Grand Rapids: Eerdmans, 2011], 246–79, at 276–77)

31. Deepak Chopra, *God: A Story of Revelation* (New York: HarperCollins, 2012), 1. Indebted to Hindu tradition, Chopra identifies four paths to God: devotion, understanding,

simply that we need to pay attention to the saints, prophets, and mystics rather than solely to philosophers (or to theologians for that matter), then his point would be well taken. Pascal and Newman likewise make clear that demonstrative reasoning is secondary for real human connection to God. But to say that "'God' is an empty term" except as experienced in divine revelations is mistaken, since "God" has a meaning available to reason rather than solely being available to private religious experience.

Not surprisingly, the seeming refutation of the demonstrations has caused serious problems for Christianity in the West. As Fergus Kerr has pointed out, "A main reason for the decline of church-going in Western Europe . . . is that people take it for granted that no such proofs are available."[32] For such people, belief in God is utterly irrational, a by-product of the naive simplicity of previous evolutionary stages. Roger Scruton comments that a growing number of people in the West imagine that belief in God is "a sign of emotional and intellectual immaturity."[33]

service, meditation. In his view, the particular religions have collapsed under the weight of historical particularity. The four paths, however, remain just as open as ever, and "each of us must undertake the inner journey of our own choosing" (ibid.). It is the fourth path that most fascinates Chopra and serves him as a proof of God's existence:

> We are conscious beings who want to know where our awareness came from. Only consciousness can understand consciousness; hence the long tradition of the inner journey. The saints and sages of the past were Einsteins of consciousness, explorers into the nature of reality. They were testing the soul hypothesis, and if these explorers came back with the same findings, century after century, culture after culture, why not give their findings credence? (ibid., 276)

Chopra argues that our consciousness is a movement within the divine consciousness, although his language is somewhat ambiguous here (and arguably still allows for divine transcendence): "We are essentially divine, because God is just another name for the origin and source of consciousness. . . . If God's mind is an infinite version of our mind, all our thoughts are movements within the divine mind" (ibid., 277). For a better version of this approach to God from the experience of consciousness, see Hart's *Experience of God*, chaps. 4–5.

32. Fergus Kerr, OP, *Theology after Wittgenstein*, 2nd ed. (London: SPCK, 1997), 191–92. In Kerr's view, "a belief in the existence of God that is arrived at independently of any moral or affective considerations, including pre-reflective responses to the world, though it may engage philosophers' attention, is unlikely to have much to do with the realities of religion" (ibid., 192). Much depends on what he means here by "the realities of religion."

33. Roger Scruton, *The Face of God* (London: Continuum, 2012), 1. See, for instance, A. C. Grayling's statement that "when a religion is adopted in later years the impulse for it is almost wholly emotional rather than rational; proselytising of teenagers and adults typically targets loneliness, confusion, failure, grief, anxiety and depression as opportunities for conversion. The psychological support given by the fellowship thus offered is attributed by the convert to his newly formed relationship with that religion's deity" (Grayling, *The God Argument: The Case against Religion and for Humanism* [London: Bloomsbury, 2013], 68). By contrast, Scruton defines the "religious person" as

> one who experiences the deep need to give thanks. . . . His need to give thanks is not circumstantial but metaphysical. It is rooted in the experience of being itself, in his way

Julian Baggini's work exemplifies this position. For Baggini, "Belief in the supernatural is belief in what there is a lack of strong evidence to believe in."[34] He proposes that the acceptance of little or no evidence for a belief is what primarily differentiates believers in God from atheists. In his view, therefore, believers in God are such because they accept beliefs "that lack or are contrary to evidence, experience, or logic": "religious belief postulates the existence of entities which we have no good evidence to believe exist."[35] Baggini points to two biblical stories about faith: Abraham's near sacrifice of Isaac (Gen. 22) and doubting Thomas (John 20). The assumption here is that these biblical stories, shorn from their context, display believers' commitment to irrationality in their relationship with God.[36] Baggini imagines that he has shown that "it is disingenuous for believers to put forward arguments to support their beliefs."[37]

> of understanding what it is to be. Being, for the religious person, is a gift, not a fact. It is through understanding this that we overcome our metaphysical loneliness, and understanding may require privation and suffering, through which we discard the dross of our own distractions. Hence the world, and the objects contained in it, come before the religious consciousness as the signs of another perspective—the perspective that has "given these things to me" (*Face of God*, 171)

See also Scruton's *The Soul of the World* (Princeton: Princeton University Press, 2014), chap. 8.

34. Baggini, *Atheism*, 32.

35. Ibid., 32–33; cf. 76–77. For the same view, see Richard Dawkins, *The Selfish Gene*, 2nd ed. (Oxford: Oxford University Press, 1989), 330: "What, after all, is faith? It is a state of mind that leads people to believe something—it doesn't matter what—in the total absence of supporting evidence." A. C. Grayling likewise argues that

> *having faith*—holding beliefs and accepting doctrines either without evidence or in the face of countervailing evidence, which most religious people actually regard as a virtue—directly controverts canons of intellectual integrity. "Faith" is not a respectable or admirable thing; having been so long paraded as a virtue and worthy of respect, the truth is otherwise: its critics have no compunction in saying that it is irresponsible, lazy and too often dangerous. (*God Argument*, 69)

For Grayling, Christian Scripture obviously counts as no evidence, but this strikes me as a belief that itself lacks evidence. Like Dawkins's, Baggini's understanding of Christianity appears to be quite limited. For example, not appreciating that in order to be united to God we need to love, Baggini presents the Christian God as a petty tyrant who demands worship and threatens us with hell. Baggini agrees that "we should be good" (*Atheism*, 35), but this seems to him to be a requirement that can be rather easily accomplished. He imagines that for religious believers who see "this world as a kind of preparation for the next," "life isn't really valuable in itself at all" (ibid.). For responses to this kind of argument, see David Bentley Hart's *Atheist Delusions: The Christian Revolution and Its Fashionable Enemies* (New Haven: Yale University Press, 2009). See also McGrath, *Dawkins' God*, 88–118.

36. On the meaning of Abraham's near sacrifice of Isaac and of Jesus's wounds, see Scruton, *Soul of the World*, 181–82.

37. Baggini, *Atheism*, 98–99. In his view, "The atheist may begin with the basic laws of logic, such as the principle that a thing cannot both be and not be at the same time. But the believer often begins with a conviction that God exists that is even stronger than the logician's belief in

On the contrary, the knowledge that God exists is still available to all who are willing to consider what Scruton calls "the topic of contingent being" and the puzzle of "being *qua* being."[38] And as David Hart emphasizes, the true irrationality is on the side of unbelief, since it turns existence and consciousness into a surd: "it makes sense to believe in both reason and God, and it may make a kind of nonsensical sense to believe in neither, but it is ultimately contradictory to believe in one but not the other."[39] Thus, rigorously thinking through the logical consequences of his atheism, Alex Rosenberg admits that "the 'thoughts' in the brain can't be about anything at all, either things inside or outside the brain. The brain doesn't store information that way. Rather, it stores information about the world in vast sets of input/output circuits that respond appropriately to one another and to their environment."[40] Of course, Rosenberg is convinced that he knows quite a good deal about reality—even though his "thoughts" are no more than neural circuitry. He remarks, for example, "There is no reason to doubt atheism. What we know about physical and biological science makes the existence of God less probable than the existence of Santa Claus. And the parts of physics that rule out God are not themselves open to much doubt. There is no chance that they will be revised by anything yet to be discovered."[41]

This is sheer nonsense, since there is no "physical and biological science" that could ever even possibly "rule out God." God is the infinite source of physical and biological things, but God is neither embodied nor detectable in any way by the empirical methods of scientific inquiry. Rosenberg's remark that "parts of physics . . . rule out God" shows how widespread metaphysical

their first principles. This belief trumps all reason" (ibid., 106–7). Actually, the metaphysics of certain demonstrations of God's existence begins with "the principle that a thing cannot both be and not be at the same time."

38. Scruton, *Face of God*, 166–67. Scruton criticizes the efforts of some strands of analytic philosophy to deny that being is intelligible as being. He goes on to say, "Being presents us with unified individuals, and therefore with plenitude; it presents us with truth, and therefore with knowledge; and it presents us with goodness, and therefore with the end or purpose of the world. These are *a priori* features of being, and ways in which being *makes itself known to us*" (ibid., 168).

39. Hart, *Experience of God*, 19.

40. Rosenberg, *Atheist's Guide to Reality*, 195. For the argument that strict materialism rules out the possibility of knowing "truth," since our knowing is nothing more than a neural phenomenon, see Victor Reppert, *C. S. Lewis's Dangerous Idea: A Philosophical Defense of Lewis's Argument from Reason* (Downers Grove, IL: InterVarsity, 2003). See also Michael C. Rea's thesis that philosophical naturalism is able to ground neither realism (the view that objects exist independently of our minds) nor materialism: Rea, *World without Design: The Ontological Consequences of Naturalism* (Oxford: Oxford University Press, 2002).

41. Rosenberg, *Atheist's Guide to Reality*, 275.

ignorance has become, so that such a claim could even be uttered by a philosophy professor at a major university. The seeds for this crop of ignorance were planted long ago. As John Courtney Murray noted in 1964, "The fixed philosophical attitude today is to say that a natural theology is impossible, that it is impossible for human reason, beginning only with the data of experience, to construct a valid doctrine of God."[42] And there is nothing particularly new in this philosophical attitude; modern sophistry has its ancient predecessors. The biblical book of the Wisdom of Solomon describes the sad quandary experienced by persons who believed that "we were born by mere chance, and hereafter we shall be as though we had never been; because the breath in our nostrils is smoke, and reason is a spark kindled by the beating of our hearts. When it is extinguished, the body will turn to ashes, and the spirit will dissolve like empty air" (Wis. 2:2–3).[43] Reflecting on modern skepticism, Murray complains that despite its claim to be more rational than belief in God, skepticism "calls an arbitrary halt to the movement of the mind."[44] This it certainly does, not least by refusing to confront seriously the puzzle of "being *qua* being."

42. John Courtney Murray, SJ, *The Problem of God: Yesterday and Today* (New Haven: Yale University Press, 1964), 74. He adds that the darling of the academy in the 1950s and 1960s, Karl Marx, despite his fierce commitment to atheism, never took seriously the task of defending it intellectually or understanding the arguments against it. Murray observes,

> Here and there he [Marx] argues in the vein of the Academy—against the notion of creation, for instance. He only succeeds in making it clear to his reader that he did not even understand the state of the question. For instance, he confuses the problem of the duration of the world with the problem of its contingency. For the greater part, however, he is content simply to accept the proposition, which he took immediately from Feuerbach, that religion is fantasy, that God is the creation of man's own imagination. (ibid., 106)

43. Or as Edward O. Wilson puts it:

> We were created not by a supernatural intelligence but by chance and necessity as one species out of millions of species in Earth's biosphere. Hope and wish for otherwise as we will, there is no evidence of an external grace shining down on us, no demonstrable destiny or purpose assigned us, no second life vouchsafed us for the end of the present one. We are, it seems, completely alone. And that in my opinion is a very good thing. It means we are completely free. (Wilson, *Meaning of Human Existence*, 173)

Amazingly, Wilson thinks that the result of knowing that there is no God will be a new freedom to pursue the unity of the human race, in care for each other and for the earth. In his view, the crucial thing is, although human activities now threaten to destroy the earth's ecosystem, "Human beings are not wicked by nature. We have enough intelligence, goodwill, generosity, and enterprise to turn Earth into a paradise both for ourselves and for the biosphere that gave us birth. We can plausibly accomplish that goal, at least be well on the way, by the end of the present century" (ibid., 176). Humans have been plagued by bad governance, "tribal organized religions," and "tribal conflict," but once the idea of God and other blind faiths is gotten out of the way, things can develop well. Ultimately, of course, everything is meaningless; the entirety of human history will be but a blip on the cosmic screen.

44. Murray, *Problem of God*, 96.

As a Christian believer, Murray adds a further observation: "How odd of God it would have been had he made man reasonable so that, by being reasonable, man would become godless."[45] How odd indeed, and as Murray recognizes, God did no such thing.

45. Ibid., 76. Murray takes up Wisdom 13 and its portrayal of the Hellenistic philosophers who studied the things of nature but could not find their Creator; as Murray notes, these "ancient scientists" are "ancestors of a long lineage today grown vast in number" (ibid., 83). See also Gustave Weigel, SJ, *The Modern God: Faith in a Secular Culture* (New York: Macmillan, 1963), 32–33. After describing the dominant naturalistic worldview with its rejection of any God or life after death, Weigel observes, "In the academy and on the stoa this vision of life and divinity is taught. Its prophets believe in it, and they proclaim it as the good news of salvation. The journals of thought accept it and give it first rights in their pages. Any other theology is given tolerance but not approval" (ibid., 33).

Select Bibliography

Introduction

Aristotle. *Metaphysics*. Translated by Hippocrates G. Apostle. Grinnell, IA: The Peripatetic Press, 1979.

———. *Nicomachean Ethics*. Translated by H. Rackham. Cambridge, MA: Harvard University Press, 1934.

———. *Physics*. Translated and edited by Glen Coughlin. South Bend, IN: St. Augustine's Press, 2005.

Barr, James. *Biblical Faith and Natural Theology*. Oxford: Oxford University Press, 1993.

Brague, Rémi. *On the God of Christians: (And on One or Two Others)*. Translated by Paul Seaton. South Bend, IN: St. Augustine's Press, 2013.

Buckley, Michael J., SJ. *At the Origins of Modern Atheism*. New Haven: Yale University Press, 1987.

Cicero. *De natura deorum, Academica*. Translated by H. Rackham. Cambridge, MA: Harvard University Press, 1951.

Desmond, William. *God and the Between*. Oxford: Blackwell, 2008.

Dillon, John. *The Heirs of Plato: A Study of the Old Academy (347–274 BC)*. Oxford: Oxford University Press, 2003.

Fergusson, David. *Faith and Its Critics: A Conversation*. Oxford: Oxford University Press, 2009.

Feser, Edward. *Aquinas*. Oxford: Oneworld, 2009.

Gerson, L. P. *Aristotle and Other Platonists*. Ithaca, NY: Cornell University Press, 2005.

————. *God and Greek Philosophy: Studies in the Early History of Natural Theology*. London: Routledge, 1994.

Hart, David Bentley. *The Experience of God: Being, Consciousness, Bliss*. New Haven: Yale University Press, 2013.

Hauerwas, Stanley. *With the Grain of the Universe: The Church's Witness and Natural Theology*. Grand Rapids: Brazos, 2001.

Kenney, John Peter. *Mystical Monotheism: A Study in Ancient Platonic Theology*. Hanover, NH: Brown University Press, 1991.

Kerr, Fergus, OP. *After Aquinas: Versions of Thomism*. Oxford: Blackwell, 2002.

MacIntyre, Alasdair. *God, Philosophy, Universities: A Selective History of the Catholic Philosophical Tradition*. Lanham, MD: Rowman & Littlefield, 2009.

Maritain, Jacques. *An Essay on Christian Philosophy*. Translated by Edward H. Flannery. New York: Philosophical Library, 1955.

Markham, Ian. *Truth and the Reality of God: An Essay in Natural Theology*. Edinburgh: T&T Clark, 1998.

Mascall, E. L. *The Openness of Being: Natural Theology Today*. London: Darton, Longman & Todd, 1971.

McPherran, Mark L. *The Religion of Socrates*. University Park, PA: Pennsylvania State University Press, 1996.

Nichols, Aidan, OP. *A Grammar of Consent: The Existence of God in Christian Tradition*. Edinburgh: T&T Clark, 1991.

Pannenberg, Wolfhart. *Metaphysics and the Idea of God*. Translated by Philip Clayton. Grand Rapids: Eerdmans, 1990.

Pelikan, Jaroslav. *Christianity and Classical Culture: The Metamorphosis of Natural Theology in the Christian Encounter with Hellenism*. New Haven: Yale University Press, 1993.

Philo of Alexandria. *The Works of Philo: Complete and Unabridged*. Rev. ed. Translated by C. D. Yonge. Peabody, MA: Hendrickson, 1993.

Plato. *Euthyphro, Apology, Crito, Phaedo, Phaedrus*. Translated by Harold North Fowler. Cambridge, MA: Harvard University Press, 1960.

————. *Republic*. Translated by Paul Shorey. In *The Collected Dialogues of Plato*, edited by Edith Hamilton and Huntington Cairns, 576–844. Princeton: Princeton University Press, 1961.

————. *Timaeus, Critias, Cleitophon, Menexenus, Epistles*. Translated by R. G. Bury. Cambridge, MA: Harvard University Press, 1961.

Plotinus. *The Enneads*. Translated by Stephen MacKenna. Burdett, NY: Larson, 1992.

Rowe, William L. *Philosophy of Religion: An Introduction*. 4th ed. Belmont, CA: Wadsworth, 2007.

Scruton, Roger. *The Face of God*. London: Continuum, 2012.

Sedley, David. *Creationism and Its Critics in Antiquity*. Berkeley: University of California Press, 2007.

Sokolowski, Robert. *The God of Faith and Reason: Foundations of Christian Theology*. 2nd ed. Washington, DC: Catholic University of America Press, 1995.

Tanner, Norman P., SJ, ed. *Decrees of the Ecumenical Councils*. Vol. 2, *Trent to Vatican II*. Washington, DC: Georgetown University Press, 1990.

Van Riel, Gerd. *Plato's Gods*. London: Ashgate, 2013.

Wright, N. T. *The Letter to the Romans: Introduction, Commentary, and Reflections*. In *The New Interpreter's Bible*. Vol. 10, *Acts, Romans, 1 Corinthians*, 395–770. Nashville: Abingdon, 2002.

———. *Paul and the Faithfulness of God*. Minneapolis: Fortress, 2013.

Xenophon. *Memorabilia*. Translated by E. C. Marchant. In *Memorabilia, Oeconomicus, Symposium, Apology*. Cambridge, MA: Harvard University Press, 1923.

Chapter 1: Patristic and Medieval Arguments for God's Existence

Athanasius. *On the Incarnation*. Translated and edited by a Religious of CSMV. Crestwood, NY: St. Vladimir's Seminary Press, 1993.

Williams, A. N. *The Divine Sense: The Intellect in Patristic Theology*. Cambridge: Cambridge University Press, 2007.

Tertullian

Osborn, Eric. *Tertullian: First Theologian of the West*. Cambridge: Cambridge University Press, 1997.

Rankin, David. *Tertullian and the Church*. Cambridge: Cambridge University Press, 1995.

Tertullian. *Ad Nationes*. In *Latin Christianity: Its Founder, Tertullian*. Ante-Nicene Fathers 3, edited by Alexander Roberts and James Donaldson, rev. A. Cleveland Coxe. Peabody, MA: Hendrickson, 1994.

————. *Against Marcion.* In *Latin Christianity: Its Founder, Tertullian. Ante-Nicene Fathers* 3, edited by Alexander Roberts and James Donaldson, rev. A. Cleveland Coxe. Peabody, MA: Hendrickson, 1994.

————. *Against Praxeas.* In *Latin Christianity: Its Founder, Tertullian. Ante-Nicene Fathers* 3, edited by Alexander Roberts and James Donaldson, rev. A. Cleveland Coxe. Peabody, MA: Hendrickson, 1994.

————. *Apology.* Translated by S. Thelwall. In *Latin Christianity: Its Founder, Tertullian. Ante-Nicene Fathers* 3, edited by Alexander Roberts and James Donaldson, rev. A. Cleveland Coxe. Peabody, MA: Hendrickson, 1994.

————. *The Prescription against Heretics.* In *Latin Christianity: Its Founder, Tertullian. Ante-Nicene Fathers* 3, edited by Alexander Roberts and James Donaldson, rev. A. Cleveland Coxe. Peabody, MA: Hendrickson, 1994.

————. *The Soul's Testimony.* In *Latin Christianity: Its Founder, Tertullian. Ante-Nicene Fathers* 3, edited by Alexander Roberts and James Donaldson, rev. A. Cleveland Coxe. Peabody, MA: Hendrickson, 1994.

Tertullian, Origen, and Cyprian. *On the Lord's Prayer.* Translated by Alistair Stewart-Sykes. Crestwood, NY: St. Vladimir's Seminary Press, 2004.

Gregory of Nazianzus

Beeley, Christopher A. *Gregory of Nazianzus on the Trinity and the Knowledge of God: In Your Light We Shall See Light.* Oxford: Oxford University Press, 2008.

Gregory of Nazianzus. *On God and Christ: The Five Theological Orations and Two Letters to Cledonius.* Translated by Frederick Williams and Lionel Wickham. Crestwood, NY: St. Vladimir's Seminary Press, 2002.

————. *On God and Man: The Theological Poetry of St. Gregory Nazianzus.* Translated by Peter Gilbert. Crestwood, NY: St. Vladimir's Seminary Press, 2001.

McGuckin, John A. *Saint Gregory of Nazianzus: An Intellectual Biography.* Crestwood, NY: St. Vladimir's Seminary Press, 2001.

Norris, Frederick. *Faith Gives Fullness to Reasoning: The Five Theological Orations of Gregory Nazianzen.* Leiden: Brill, 1997.

Augustine

Augustine. *City of God.* Translated by Henry Bettenson. New York: Penguin, 1984.

———. *Confessions*. Translated by Henry Chadwick. Oxford: Oxford University Press, 1991.

———. *The First Catechetical Instruction*. Translated by Joseph P. Christopher. Westminster, MD: Newman, 1946.

———. *Lectures or Tractates on the Gospel according to St. John*. Translated by John Gibb and James Innes. In *Augustine: Homilies on the Gospel of John, Homilies on the First Epistle of John, Soliloquies*, edited by Philip Schaff. Peabody, MA: Hendrickson, 1995.

———. *On Christian Doctrine*. Translated by D. W. Robertson Jr. New York: Macmillan, 1958.

Brown, Peter. *Augustine of Hippo: A Biography*. 2nd ed. Berkeley: University of California Press, 2000.

Lancel, Serge. *Saint Augustine*. Translated by Antonia Nevill. London: SCM, 2002.

Levering, Matthew. *The Theology of Augustine: An Introductory Guide to His Most Important Works*. Grand Rapids: Baker Academic, 2013.

Paffenroth, Kim, and Robert P. Kennedy, eds. *A Reader's Companion to Augustine's Confessions*. Louisville: Westminster John Knox, 2003.

Rist, John M. *Augustine: Ancient Thought Baptized*. Cambridge: Cambridge University Press, 1994.

John of Damascus

Boethius. *The Consolation of Philosophy*. Translated by S. J. Tester. In Boethius, *The Theological Tractates and The Consolation of Philosophy*. Cambridge, MA: Harvard University Press, 1973.

John of Damascus. *Writings*. Translated by Frederick H. Chase. Washington, DC: Catholic University of America Press, 1958.

Louth, Andrew. *St. John Damascene: Tradition and Originality in Byzantine Theology*. Oxford: Oxford University Press, 2002.

Anselm of Canterbury

Anselm. *Monologion and Proslogion, with the Replies of Gaunilo and Anselm*. Translated by Thomas Williams. Indianapolis: Hackett, 1995.

Davies, G. R. *The Cambridge Companion to Anselm*. Edited by Brian Davies and Brian Leftow. Cambridge: Cambridge University Press, 2004.

Southern, R. W. *Saint Anselm: A Portrait in a Landscape*. Cambridge: Cambridge University Press, 1990.

Thomas Aquinas

Chenu, M.-D., OP. *Toward Understanding St. Thomas*. Translated by A.-M. Landry, OP, and D. Hughes, OP. Chicago: Henry Regnery, 1964.

Kretzmann, Norman. *The Metaphysics of Theism: Aquinas's Natural Theology in* Summa contra gentiles *I*. Oxford: Clarendon, 1997.

Rocca, Gregory. *Speaking the Incomprehensible God: Thomas Aquinas on the Interplay of Positive and Negative Theology*. Washington, DC: Catholic University of America Press, 2004.

Te Velde, Rudi A. *Aquinas on God: The "Divine Science" of the* Summa Theologiae. London: Ashgate, 2006.

Thomas Aquinas. *Commentary on the Gospel of John: Chapters 13–21*. Translated by Fabian Larcher, OP, and James A. Weisheipl, OP. Edited by Daniel A. Keating and Matthew Levering. Washington, DC: Catholic University of America Press, 2010.

———. *On Being and Essence*. Translated by Armand Maurer. 2nd rev. ed. Toronto: Pontifical Institute of Mediaeval Studies, 1968.

———. *Summa contra gentiles, Book One: God*. Translated by Anton C. Pegis, FRSC. Notre Dame: University of Notre Dame Press, 1975.

———. *Summa contra gentiles, Book Three: Providence, Part I*. Translated by Vernon J. Bourke. Notre Dame: University of Notre Dame Press, 1975.

———. *Summa theologiae*. 5 vols. Translated by the Fathers of the English Dominican Province. Westminster, MD: Christian Classics, 1981.

Torrell, Jean-Pierre, OP. *Saint Thomas Aquinas*. Vol. 1, *The Person and His Work*. Translated by Robert Royal. Washington, DC: Catholic University of America Press, 1996.

Turner, Denys. *Thomas Aquinas: A Portrait*. New Haven: Yale University Press, 2013.

White, Thomas Joseph, OP, ed. *The Analogy of Being: Invention of the Antichrist or the Wisdom of God?* Grand Rapids: Eerdmans, 2011.

Wippel, John F. *The Metaphysical Thought of Thomas Aquinas: From Finite Being to Uncreated Being*. Washington, DC: Catholic University of America Press, 2000.

William of Ockham

Adams, Marilyn McCord. *William Ockham*. 2 vols. Notre Dame: University of Notre Dame Press, 1987.

Frank, William A., and Allan B. Wolter. *Duns Scotus, Metaphysician.* West Lafayette, IN: Purdue University Press, 1995.

Hall, Alexander W. *Thomas Aquinas and John Duns Scotus: Natural Theology in the High Middle Ages.* London: Continuum, 2007.

Marenbon, John, ed. *Medieval Philosophy.* London: Routledge, 1998.

Maurer, Armand A., CSB. *The Philosophy of William of Ockham in the Light of Its Principles.* Toronto: Pontifical Institute of Mediaeval Studies, 1999.

Scotus, John Duns. *A Treatise on God as First Principle.* Translated and edited by Allan B. Wolter, OFM. Chicago: Franciscan Herald Press, 1966.

Spade, Paul Vincent, ed. *The Cambridge Companion to Ockham.* Cambridge: Cambridge University Press, 1999.

William of Ockham. *Philosophical Writings: A Selection.* Translated by Philotheus Boehner, OFM. Revised by Stephen F. Brown. Indianapolis: Hackett, 1990.

———. *Quodlibetal Questions.* Translated by Alfred J. Freddoso and Francis E. Kelley. New Haven: Yale University Press, 1991.

Williams, Thomas, ed. *The Cambridge Companion to Duns Scotus.* Cambridge: Cambridge University Press, 2003.

Conclusion to Chapter 1

Clarke, W. Norris. *Explorations in Metaphysics: Being—God—Person.* Notre Dame: University of Notre Dame Press, 1994.

Mill, John Stuart. *Three Essays on Religion: Nature, The Utility of Religion, Theism.* Amherst, NY: Prometheus, 1998.

Wippel, John F. *Metaphysical Themes in Thomas Aquinas II.* Washington, DC: Catholic University of America Press, 2007.

Chapter 2: Reformation and Enlightenment Views

MacCulloch, Diarmaid. *The Reformation: A History.* New York: Penguin, 2003.

John Calvin

Berkouwer, G. C. *General Revelation.* Grand Rapids: Eerdmans, 1955.

Calvin, John. *Calvin's Bible Commentaries: Romans.* Translated by John King. London: Forgotten Books, 2007 (1847).

————. *The Institutes of the Christian Religion.* Translated by Henry Beveridge. Grand Rapids: Eerdmans, 1989.

Gordon, Bruce. *Calvin.* New Haven: Yale University Press, 2009.

Helm, Paul. *John Calvin's Ideas.* Oxford: Oxford University Press, 2004.

Parker, T. H. L. *Calvin's Doctrine of the Knowledge of God.* 2nd ed. Edinburgh: Oliver & Boyd, 1969.

Michel de Montaigne

Bakewell, Sarah. *How to Live, or, A Life of Montaigne in One Question and Twenty Attempts at an Answer.* London: Random House, 2010.

Frame, Donald M. *Montaigne: A Biography.* London: H. Hamilton, 1965.

Montaigne, Michel de. *The Complete Works: Essays, Travel Journal, Letters.* Translated by Donald M. Frame. New York: Alfred A. Knopf, 2003.

————. *The Essays of Montaigne.* Translated by E. J. Trechmann. New York: Random House, 1946.

Francisco Suárez

Craig, William L. *The Cosmological Argument from Plato to Leibniz.* London: Macmillan, 1980.

Fichter, Joseph H. *Man of Spain: Francis Suárez.* New York: Macmillan, 1940.

Hill, Benjamin, and Henrik Lagerlund, eds. *The Philosophy of Francisco Suárez.* Oxford: Oxford University Press, 2012.

Pereira, José. *Suárez: Between Scholasticism and Modernity.* Milwaukee: Marquette University Press, 2007.

Schwartz, Daniel, ed. *Interpreting Suárez: Critical Essays.* Cambridge: Cambridge University Press, 2012.

Secada, Jorge. *Cartesian Metaphysics: The Scholastic Origins of Modern Philosophy.* Cambridge: Cambridge University Press, 2000.

Suárez, Francisco, SJ. *The Metaphysical Demonstration of the Existence of God: Metaphysical Disputations 28–29.* Translated and edited by John P. Doyle. South Bend, IN: St. Augustine's Press, 2004.

————. *On the Essence of Finite Being as Such, On the Existence of That Essence and Their Distinction* [Disputation 31 of his *Metaphysical Disputations*]. Translated by Norman J. Wells. Milwaukee: Marquette University Press, 1983.

René Descartes

Caton, Hiram. *The Origins of Subjectivity: An Essay on Descartes*. New Haven: Yale University Press, 1973.

Cottingham, John, ed. *The Cambridge Companion to Descartes*. Cambridge: Cambridge University Press, 1992.

———. *Descartes*. Oxford: Blackwell, 1986.

Descartes, René. *Discourse on Method and the Meditations*. Translated by F. E. Sutcliffe. London: Penguin, 1968.

———. *The Philosophical Writings of Descartes*. Vol. 3, *The Correspondence*. Translated by John Cottingham, Robert Stoothoff, Dugald Murdoch, and Anthony Kenny. Cambridge: Cambridge University Press, 1991.

McDowell, John. *Meaning, Knowledge, and Reality*. Cambridge, MA: Harvard University Press, 1998.

Mercer, Christina, and Eileen O'Neill. *Early Modern Philosophy: Mind, Matter, and Metaphysics*. Oxford: Oxford University Press, 2005.

Rorty, Amelie, ed. *Essays on Descartes' Meditations*. Berkeley: University of California Press, 1986.

Rutherford, Donald, ed. *The Cambridge Companion to Early Modern Philosophy*. Cambridge: Cambridge University Press, 2006.

Schmaltz, Tad M. *Radical Cartesianism: The French Reception of Descartes*. Cambridge: Cambridge University Press, 2002.

Blaise Pascal

Fraser, G. S. *Pascal: His Life and Works*. London: Harvill, 1952.

Hammond, Nicholas, ed. *The Cambridge Companion to Pascal*. Cambridge: Cambridge University Press, 2003.

O'Connell, Marvin R. *Blaise Pascal: Reasons of the Heart*. Grand Rapids: Eerdmans, 1997.

Pascal, Blaise. *Pensées*. Rev. ed. Translated by A. J. Krailsheimer. London: Penguin, 1995.

———. *Pensées and Other Writings*. Translated by Honor Levi. Edited by Anthony Levi. Oxford: Oxford University Press, 1995.

Rescher, Nicholas. *Pascal's Wager*. Notre Dame: University of Notre Dame Press, 1985.

Wetsel, David. *Pascal and Disbelief: Catechesis and Conversion in the Pensées*. Washington, DC: Catholic University of America Press, 1994.

David Hume

Ayer, A. J. *Hume: A Very Short Introduction*. Oxford: Oxford University Press, 2000.

Beebee, Helen. *Hume on Causation*. London: Routledge, 2006.

Gaskin, J. C. A. *Hume's Philosophy of Religion*. 2nd ed. London: Macmillan, 1988.

Hume, David. *Principal Writings on Religion Including Dialogues concerning Natural Religion and The Natural History of Religion*. Edited by J. C. A. Gaskin. Oxford: Oxford University Press, 1993.

———. *A Treatise of Human Nature*. Edited by Ernest C. Mossner. New York: Penguin, 1969.

Mossner, Ernest Campbell. *The Life of David Hume*. 2nd ed. Oxford: Clarendon, 1980.

Norton, David Fate, and Jacqueline Taylor, eds. *The Cambridge Companion to Hume*. 2nd ed. Cambridge: Cambridge University Press, 2009.

Popkin, Richard H. *The History of Scepticism from Savonarola to Bayle*. Oxford: Oxford University Press, 2003.

Russell, Paul. *The Riddle of Hume's Treatise: Skepticism, Naturalism, and Irreligion*. Oxford: Oxford University Press, 2008.

Sennett, James F., and Douglas Groothuis, eds. *In Defense of Natural Theology: A Post-Humean Assessment*. Downers Grove, IL: InterVarsity, 2005.

Immanuel Kant

Guyer, Paul, ed. *The Cambridge Companion to Kant*. Cambridge: Cambridge University Press, 1992.

———. *Kant*. London: Routledge, 2006.

———. *Kant and the Claims of Knowledge*. Cambridge: Cambridge University Press, 1987.

———. *Knowledge, Reason, and Taste: Kant's Response to Hume*. Princeton: Princeton University Press, 2008.

Kant, Immanuel. *Critique of Practical Reason*. In Immanuel Kant, *Practical Philosophy*, translated and edited by Mary J. Gregor, 139–271. Cambridge: Cambridge University Press, 1996.

———. *Critique of Pure Reason*. Translated and edited by Paul Guyer and Allen W. Wood. Cambridge: Cambridge University Press, 1998.

————. *Prolegomena to Any Future Metaphysics That Will Be Able to Come Forward as a Science*. Translated by Paul Carus with revisions by James W. Ellington. Indianapolis: Hackett, 1977.

Melnick, Arthur. *Space, Time, and Thought in Kant*. Dordrecht: D. Reidel, 1989.

Michalson, Gordon E., Jr. *Kant and the Problem of God*. Oxford: Blackwell, 1999.

Savile, Anthony. *Kant's Critique of Pure Reason: An Orientation to the Central Themes*. Oxford: Blackwell, 2005.

Scruton, Roger. *Kant: A Very Short Introduction*. 2nd ed. Oxford: Oxford University Press, 2001.

Watkins, Eric. *Kant's Critique of Pure Reason: Background Source Materials*. Cambridge: Cambridge University Press, 2009.

Wood, Allen W. *Kant's Rational Theology*. Ithaca, NY: Cornell University Press, 1978.

Conclusion to Chapter 2

Clayton, Philip. *The Problem of God in Modern Thought*. Grand Rapids: Eerdmans, 2000.

Cupitt, Don. *Is Nothing Sacred? The Non-Realist Philosophy of Religion: Selected Essays*. New York: Fordham University Press, 2002.

Ward, Keith. *God and the Philosophers*. Minneapolis: Fortress, 2009.

Chapter 3: Nineteenth- and Twentieth-Century Responses

Short, Edward. *Newman and His Contemporaries*. London: T&T Clark, 2011.

John Henry Newman

Bastable, James D., ed. *Newman and Gladstone: Centennial Essays*. Dublin: Veritas, 1978.

Boekraad, Adrian J., and Henry Tristram, eds. *The Argument from Conscience to the Existence of God according to J. H. Newman*. Louvain: Nauwelaerts, 1961.

Brown, David, ed. *Newman: A Man for Our Time*. Harrisburg, PA: Morehouse, 1990.

Crosby, John F. *The Personalism of John Henry Newman*. Washington, DC: Catholic University of America Press, 2014.

Ker, Ian. *John Henry Newman: A Biography*. Oxford: Oxford University Press, 1988.

Ker, Ian, and Terrence Merrigan, eds. *The Cambridge Companion to John Henry Newman*. Cambridge: Cambridge University Press, 2009.

McGrath, Francis. *John Henry Newman: Universal Revelation*. London: Burns & Oates, 1997.

Newman, John Henry. *An Essay in Aid of a Grammar of Assent*. Westminster, MD: Christian Classics, 1973.

———. *Fifteen Sermons Preached before the University of Oxford between A.D. 1826 and 1843*. Notre Dame: University of Notre Dame Press, 1997.

Maurice Blondel

Balthasar, Hans Urs von. *The God Question and Modern Man*. Translated by Hilda Graef. New York: Seabury, 1967.

———. *The Theology of Karl Barth: Exposition and Interpretation*. Translated by Edward T. Oakes, SJ. San Francisco: Ignatius, 1992.

Blanchette, Oliva. *Maurice Blondel: A Philosophical Life*. Grand Rapids: Eerdmans, 2010.

Blondel, Maurice. *Action (1893): Essay on a Critique of Life and a Science of Practice*. Translated by Oliva Blanchette. Notre Dame: University of Notre Dame Press, 1984.

———. *The Letter on Apologetics and History and Dogma*. Translated by Alexander Dru and Illtyd Trethowan. Grand Rapids: Eerdmans, 1994.

Bouillard, Henri. *Blondel and Christianity*. Translated by James M. Somerville. Washington, DC: Corpus, 1969.

Flynn, Gabriel, and Paul D. Murray, eds. *Ressourcement: A Movement for Renewal in Twentieth-Century Catholic Theology*. Oxford: Oxford University Press, 2012.

Lacroix, Jean. *Maurice Blondel: An Introduction to the Man and His Philosophy*. Translated by John Guinness. London: Sheed and Ward, 1968.

Lubac, Henri, de, SJ. *The Discovery of God*. Translated by Alexander Dru with Mark Sebanc and Cassian Fulsom, OSB. Grand Rapids: Eerdmans, 1996.

Somerville, James M. *Total Commitment: Blondel's L'Action*. Washington, DC: Corpus, 1968.

Pierre Rousselot

McCool, Gerald, SJ. *The Neo-Thomists*. Milwaukee: Marquette University Press, 1994.

McDermott, John M., SJ. *Love and Understanding: The Relation of Will and Intellect in Pierre Rousselot's Christological Vision*. Rome: Gregorian University Press, 1983.

Nichols, Aidan, OP. *From Newman to Congar: The Idea of Doctrinal Development from the Victorians to the Second Vatican Council*. Edinburgh: T&T Clark, 1990.

Rousselot, Pierre, SJ. *Essays on Love and Knowledge*. Edited by Andrew Tallon and Pol Vandevelde. Translated by Andrew Tallon, Pol Vandevelde, and Alan Vincelette. Milwaukee: Marquette University Press, 2008.

———. *The Eyes of Faith*. Translated by Joseph Donceel, SJ. New York: Fordham University Press, 1990.

———. *Intelligence: Sense of Being, Faculty of God*. Translated by Andrew Tallon. Milwaukee: Marquette University Press, 1999.

Ludwig Wittgenstein

Anscombe, G. E. M. *An Introduction to Wittgenstein's* Tractatus. London: Hutchinson, 1971.

Arrington, Robert L., and Mark Addis, eds. *Wittgenstein and Philosophy of Religion*. New York: Routledge, 2001.

Fogelin, R. J. *Taking Wittgenstein at His Word: A Textual Study*. Princeton: Princeton University Press, 2009.

Grayling, A. C. *Wittgenstein: A Very Short Introduction*. Oxford: Oxford University Press, 2001.

Kerr, Fergus, OP. *Theology after Wittgenstein*. 2nd ed. London: SPCK, 1997.

———. *"Work on Oneself": Wittgenstein's Philosophical Psychology*. Arlington, VA: The Institute for the Psychological Sciences Press, 2008.

Lindbeck, George. *The Nature of Doctrine: Religion and Theology in a Postliberal Age*. Philadelphia: Westminster, 1984.

McGinn, Marie. *Elucidating the* Tractatus: *Wittgenstein's Early Philosophy of Logic and Language*. Oxford: Oxford University Press, 2006.

———. *The Routledge Guidebook to Wittgenstein's* Philosophical Investigations. 2nd ed. London: Routledge, 2013.

McGuinness, Brian, ed. *Wittgenstein and His Times*. Oxford: Blackwell, 1982.

Monk, Ray. *Ludwig Wittgenstein: The Duty of Genius*. London: Jonathan Cape, 1990.

Moore, Andrew. *Realism and Christian Faith: God, Grammar, and Meaning*. Cambridge: Cambridge University Press, 2003.

Nieli, Russell. *Wittgenstein: From Mysticism to Ordinary Language. A Study of Viennese Positivism and the Thought of Ludwig Wittgenstein*. Albany, NY: State University of New York Press, 1987.

Phillips, D. Z. *Religion without Explanation*. Oxford: Blackwell, 1976.

———. *Wittgenstein and Religion*. New York: St. Martin's, 1993.

Wittgenstein, Ludwig. *Philosophical Investigations*. 3rd ed. Translated by G. E. M. Anscombe. Edited by G. E. M. Anscombe and R. Rhees. Oxford: Blackwell, 2001.

———. *Tractatus Logico-Philosophicus*. Translated by D. F. Pears and B. F. McGuinness. London: Routledge, 2001.

Réginald Garrigou-Lagrange

Cooper, Adam G. *Naturally Human, Supernaturally God: Deification in Pre-Conciliar Catholicism*. Minneapolis: Fortress, 2014.

Garrigou-Lagrange, Réginald, OP. *God: His Existence and His Nature*. Translated by Bede Rose, OSB. St. Louis: B. Herder, 1955.

———. *The One God: A Commentary on the First Part of St. Thomas' Theological Summa*. Translated by Bede Rose, OSB. St. Louis: B. Herder, 1943.

Maritain, Jacques. *The Range of Reason*. New York: Charles Scribner's Sons, 1952.

Nichols, Aidan, OP. *Reason with Piety: Garrigou-Lagrange in the Service of Catholic Thought*. Naples, FL: Sapientia, 2008.

Peddicord, Richard, OP. *The Sacred Monster of Thomism: An Introduction to the Life and Legacy of Reginald Garrigou-Lagrange, OP*. South Bend, IN: St. Augustine's Press, 2005.

Martin Heidegger

Desmond, William. *God and the Between*. Oxford: Blackwell, 2008.

———. *Hegel's God: A Counterfeit Double?* London: Ashgate, 2003.

———. *The Intimate Strangeness of Being: Metaphysics after Dialectic*. Washington, DC: Catholic University of America Press, 2012.

Hector, Kevin W. *Theology without Metaphysics: God, Language and the Spirit of Recognition*. Cambridge: Cambridge University Press, 2011.

Hegel, G. W. F. *Lectures on the Proofs of the Existence of God*. Edited and translated by Peter C. Hodgson. Oxford: Oxford University Press, 2007.

———. *Science of Logic*. Translated by A. V. Miller. Amherst, NY: Humanity, 1998.

Heidegger, Martin. *Being and Time*. Translated by Joan Stambaugh. Revised by Dennis J. Schmidt. Albany, NY: State University of New York Press, 2010.

———. *Identity and Difference*. Translated by Joan Stambaugh. Chicago: University of Chicago Press, 1969.

———. *Introduction to Metaphysics*. Translated by Gregory Fried and Richard Polt. New Haven: Yale University Press, 2000.

———. *Pathmarks*. Edited by William McNeill. Cambridge: Cambridge University Press, 1998.

Hemming, Lawrence Paul. *Heidegger's Atheism: The Refusal of a Theological Voice*. Notre Dame: University of Notre Dame Press, 2002.

Inwood, Michael. *Heidegger: A Very Short Introduction*. Oxford: Oxford University Press, 1997.

Johnson, Patricia Altenbernd. *On Heidegger*. Belmont, CA: Thomson Learning, 2000.

Kerr, Fergus, OP. *Immortal Longings: Versions of Transcending Humanity*. Notre Dame: University of Notre Dame Press, 1997.

McGrath, S. J. *The Early Heidegger and Medieval Philosophy: Phenomenology for the Godforsaken*. Washington, DC: Catholic University of America Press, 2006.

Ott, Hugo. *Martin Heidegger: A Political Life*. Translated by Allan Blunden. New York: Basic Books, 1994.

Richardson, William J., SJ. *Heidegger: Through Phenomenology to Thought*. 3rd ed. The Hague: Martinus Nijhoff, 1974.

Rosen, Stanley. *The Question of Being: A Reversal of Heidegger*. New Haven: Yale University Press, 1993.

Safranski, Rüdiger. *Martin Heidegger: Between Good and Evil*. Translated by Ewald Osers. Cambridge, MA: Harvard University Press, 1998.

Walsh, David. *The Modern Philosophical Revolution: The Luminosity of Existence*. Cambridge: Cambridge University Press, 2008.

Westphal, Merold. *Overcoming Onto-theology: Toward a Postmodern Christian Faith*. New York: Fordham University Press, 2001.

Young, Julian. *Heidegger's Later Philosophy*. Cambridge: Cambridge University Press, 2001.

Karl Barth

Barth, Karl. *Anselm: Fides Quarens Intellectum; Anselm's Proof of the Existence of God in the Context of His Theological Scheme*. Eugene, OR: Pickwick, 2009.

———. *Church Dogmatics* I/1. 2nd ed. Translated by G. W. Bromiley. Edited by G. W. Bromiley and T. F. Torrance. Edinburgh: T&T Clark, 1975.

———. *Church Dogmatics* II/1. Translated by T. H. L. Parker, W. B. Johnston, Harold Knight, and J. L. M. Haire. Edited by G. W. Bromiley and T. F. Torrance. Edinburgh: T&T Clark, 1957.

———. *The Word of God and the Word of Man*. Translated by Douglas Horton. London: Hodder & Stoughton, 1928.

Bouillard, Henri. *The Knowledge of God*. Translated by Samuel D. Femiano. New York: Herder and Herder, 1968.

Brunner, Emil, and Karl Barth. *Natural Theology: Comprising "Nature and Grace" by Professor Dr. Emil Brunner and the Reply "No!" by Dr. Karl Barth*. Translated by Peter Fraenkel. Eugene, OR: Wipf and Stock, 2002.

Busch, Eberhard. *Karl Barth: His Life from Letters and Autobiographical Texts*. Philadelphia: Fortress, 1976.

Hunsinger, George. *How to Read Karl Barth: The Shape of His Theology*. Oxford: Oxford University Press, 1991.

Johnson, Keith. *Karl Barth and the Analogia Entis*. London: T&T Clark, 2010.

McCormack, Bruce L., and Thomas Joseph White, OP, eds. *Thomas Aquinas and Karl Barth: An Unofficial Catholic-Protestant Dialogue*. Grand Rapids: Eerdmans, 2013.

Oakes, Kenneth. *Karl Barth on Theology and Philosophy*. Oxford: Oxford University Press, 2012.

Rogers, Eugene F., Jr. *Thomas Aquinas and Karl Barth: Sacred Doctrine and the Natural Knowledge of God*. Notre Dame: University of Notre Dame Press, 1995.

Webster, John, ed. *The Cambridge Companion to Karl Barth*. Cambridge: Cambridge University Press, 2000.

Conclusion to Chapter 3

Clarke, W. Norris, SJ. *The Philosophical Approach to God: A New Thomistic Perspective*. 2nd ed. New York: Fordham University Press, 2007.

Gilson, Étienne. *Thomist Realism and the Critique of Knowledge*. Translated by M. A. Wauck. San Francisco: Ignatius, 1986.

Grisez, Germain. *Beyond the New Theism*. Notre Dame: University of Notre Dame Press, 1975.

Knox, Ronald A. *In Soft Garments: A Collection of Oxford Conferences*. 2nd ed. New York: Sheed & Ward, 1953.

Miller, Barry. *The Fullness of Being: A New Paradigm for Existence*. Notre Dame: University of Notre Dame Press, 2012.

Nichols, Aidan, OP. *The Conversation of Faith and Reason: Modern Catholic Thought from Hermes to Benedict XVI*. Chicago: Hillenbrand, 2011.

Peperzak, Adriaan T. *Thinking: From Solitude to Dialogue and Contemplation*. New York: Fordham University Press, 2006.

Conclusion

Baggett, David, and Jerry L. Walls. *Good God: The Theistic Foundations of Morality*. Oxford: Oxford University Press, 2011.

Chopra, Deepak. *God: A Story of Revelation*. New York: HarperCollins, 2012.

Cunningham, Conor. *Darwin's Pious Idea: Why the Ultra-Darwinists and Creationists Both Get It Wrong*. Grand Rapids: Eerdmans, 2010.

Dawkins, Richard. *The Selfish Gene*. 2nd ed. Oxford: Oxford University Press, 1989.

Eagleton, Terry. *Reason, Faith, and Revolution: Reflections on the God Debate*. New Haven: Yale University Press, 2009.

Eire, Carlos M. N. *A Very Brief History of Eternity*. Princeton: Princeton University Press, 2009.

Flanagan, Owen. *The Really Hard Problem: Meaning in a Material World*. Cambridge, MA: MIT Press, 2007.

Hart, David Bentley. *Atheist Delusions: The Christian Revolution and Its Fashionable Enemies*. New Haven: Yale University Press, 2009.

Le Fanu, James. *Why Us? How Science Rediscovered the Mystery of Ourselves*. New York: Pantheon, 2009.

McCarty, Marietta. *How Philosophy Can Save Your Life: Ten Ideas That Matter Most*. New York: Penguin, 2009.

McGrath, Alister. *Dawkins' God: Genes, Memes, and the Meaning of Life*. Oxford: Blackwell, 2005.

Monda, Antonio. *Do You Believe? Conversations on God and Religion*. Translated by Ann Goldstein. New York: Random House, 2007.

Murray, John Courtney, SJ. *The Problem of God: Yesterday and Today*. New Haven: Yale University Press, 1964.

Nussbaum, Martha C. *Cultivating Humanity: A Classical Defense of Reform in Liberal Education*. Cambridge, MA: Harvard University Press, 1997.

Weigel, Gustave, SJ. *The Modern God: Faith in a Secular Culture*. New York: Macmillan, 1963.

Recent Books Appreciative of Proofs of God's Existence

Braine, David. *The Reality of Time and the Existence of God: The Project of Proving God's Existence*. Oxford: Oxford University Press, 1988.

Crean, Thomas, OP. *A Catholic Responds to Professor Dawkins*. Oxford: Family Publications, 2007.

Emonet, Pierre-Marie, OP. *God Seen in the Mirror of the World: An Introduction to the Philosophy of God*. Translated by Robert R. Barr. New York: Crossroad, 2000.

Evans, C. Stephen. *Natural Signs and Knowledge of God: A New Look at Theistic Arguments*. Oxford: Oxford University Press, 2010.

———. *Why Believe? Reason and Mystery as Pointers to God*. Grand Rapids: Eerdmans, 1996.

Feser, Edward. *The Last Superstition: A Refutation of the New Atheism*. South Bend, IN: St. Augustine's Press, 2008.

Markham, Ian S. *Against Atheism: Why Dawkins, Hitchens, and Harris Are Fundamentally Wrong*. Oxford: Wiley-Blackwell, 2010.

Martin, Christopher. *Thomas Aquinas: God and Explanations*. Edinburgh: Edinburgh University Press, 1997.

Miller, Barry. *From Existence to God: A Contemporary Philosophical Argument*. London: Routledge, 1992.

———. *A Most Unlikely God: A Philosophical Enquiry*. Notre Dame: University of Notre Dame Press, 1996.

Moreland, Anna Bonta. *Known by Nature: Thomas Aquinas on Natural Knowledge of God*. New York: Crossroad, 2010.

Murphy, Francesca Aran. *God Is Not a Story: Realism Revisited*. Oxford: Oxford University Press, 2007.

Rea, Michael C. *World without Design: The Ontological Consequences of Naturalism*. Oxford: Oxford University Press, 2002.

Reppert, Victor. *C. S. Lewis's Dangerous Idea: A Philosophical Defense of Lewis's Argument from Reason*. Downers Grove, IL: InterVarsity, 2003.

Sennett, James F., and Douglas Groothuis, eds. *In Defense of Natural Theology: A Post-Humean Assessment*. Downers Grove, IL: InterVarsity, 2005.

Smart, J. J. C., and John Haldane. *Atheism and Theism*. Oxford: Blackwell, 1996.

Spitzer, Robert J., SJ. *New Proofs for the Existence of God: Contributions of Contemporary Physics and Philosophy*. Grand Rapids: Eerdmans, 2010.

Swinburne, Richard. *The Existence of God*. 2nd ed. Oxford: Oxford University Press, 2004.

Turner, Denys. *Faith, Reason and the Existence of God*. Cambridge: Cambridge University Press, 2004.

Wahlberg, Mats. *Reshaping Natural Theology: Seeing Nature as Creation*. New York: Palgrave Macmillan, 2012.

Ward, Keith. *Why There Almost Certainly Is a God: Doubting Dawkins*. Oxford: Lion Hudson, 2008.

White, Thomas Joseph, OP. *Wisdom in the Face of Modernity: A Study in Thomistic Natural Theology*. Ave Maria, FL: Sapientia, 2009.

Recent Books against the Proofs of God's Existence

Baggini, Julian. *Atheism: A Very Short Introduction*. Oxford: Oxford University Press, 2003.

Blackburn, Simon. *Think: A Compelling Introduction to Philosophy*. Oxford: Oxford University Press, 1999.

Dawkins, Richard. *The God Delusion*. New York: Houghton Mifflin, 2006.

Ferris, Timothy. *The Whole Shebang: A State-of-the-Universe(s) Report*. New York: Simon & Schuster, 1997.

Grayling, A. C. *The God Argument: The Case against Religion and for Humanism*. London: Bloomsbury, 2013.

Hawking, Stephen, and Leonard Mlodinow. *The Grand Design*. New York: Random House, 2010.

Melnyk, Andrew. *A Physicalist Manifesto: Thoroughly Modern Materialism*. Cambridge: Cambridge University Press, 2003.

Oppy, Graham. *Arguing about Gods*. Cambridge: Cambridge University Press, 1999.

———. *Ontological Arguments and Belief in God*. Cambridge: Cambridge University Press, 1995.

Rosenberg, Alex. *The Atheist's Guide to Reality: Enjoying Life without Illusions*. New York: W. W. Norton, 2011.

Rundle, Bede. *Why There Is Something Rather Than Nothing*. Oxford: Oxford University Press, 2004.

Wilson, Edward O. *The Meaning of Human Existence*. New York: W. W. Norton, 2014.

Subject Index

239

Name Index

243